Entrepreneurial Mana und Standortentwicklung – Perspektiven für Unternehmen und Destinationen

Edited by
E. Kreilkamp, Lüneburg, Deutschland
Ch. Laesser, St. Gallen, Schweiz
H. Pechlaner, Eichstätt-Ingolstadt, Deutschland
K. Wöber, Wien, Österreich

The publications in this series are committed to the entrepreneurial management orientation of business ventures and sites. In this context, regions, destinations, and places are on the one hand considered as competitive units, on the other hand they constitute the spatial context to allow for modelling the business ventures' competitive capacities.

Edited by

Prof. Dr. Edgar Kreilkamp
Leuphana Universität Lüneburg

Prof. Dr. Christian Laesser
Universität St. Gallen

Prof. Dr. Harald Pechlaner
Katholische Universität
Eichstätt-Ingolstadt

Prof. Dr. Karl Wöber
MODUL University Vienna

Benedict C. Doepfer

Co-Innovation Competence

A Strategic Approach to Entrepreneurship in Regional Innovation Structures

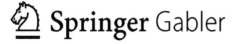

Springer Gabler

Benedict C. Doepfer
Nürnberg, Germany

Dissertation Katholische Universität Eichstätt-Ingolstadt, 2012

ISBN 978-3-658-00254-1   ISBN 978-3-658-00255-8 (eBook)
DOI 10.1007/978-3-658-00255-8

The Deutsche Nationalbibliothek lists this publication in the Deutsche Nationalbibliografie;
detailed bibliographic data are available in the Internet at http://dnb.d-nb.de.

Library of Congress Control Number: 2012952926

Springer Gabler
© Springer Fachmedien Wiesbaden 2013

Printed on acid-free paper

Springer Gabler is a brand of Springer DE.
Springer DE is part of Springer Science+Business Media.
www.springer-gabler.de

Foreword

The relevance of regional proximity as an influential factor on corporate competitiveness and specifically innovation performance in many studies has been a matter of analysis in economic, geographic and management literature. An active configuration of the entrepreneurial scope of action within the regional context in form of a co-innovation competence which is understood as a specific development process of corporate resources and capabilities to implement interorganizational value creation, however, has been a minor field of research. The cooperative generation of innovation may primarily be based on economic motives but the establishment of networks and their exploitation are based on the intensity and quality of interactions and respectively the emergence of social capital among network actors. These aspects need to be considered as pivotal for the effectiveness of interorganizational interaction to perform innovation.

The dissertation of Benedict Doepfer contributes to this discussion by attempting an approach of a new research framework which includes the factors of a co-innovation competence and their effects on the parameters of a regional economic climate. The identification of determining factors of networking as a strategy to create and shape the entrepreneurial scope of action within the regional context provides the guiding idea of this work. Here he emphasizes the necessity of a vital regional innovation climate supporting the generation and commercial exploitation of knowledge. Specifically young knowledge-intensive entrepreneurial firms rely on their regional context and regional networks to detect and pursue entrepreneurial opportunities. In a highly specialized competitive landscape open innovation may be performed more effectively under these conditions. Based on the liabilities of young entrepreneurial firms, however, the relevance of regional innovation promotors is emphasized as a critical component of a successful innovation strategy.

Based on a mixed-methods empirical approach he proves that co-innovation in fact is a critical aspect for young entrepreneurial firms: On the one hand networking is perceived as an opportunity to transform ideas into market innovations, on the other hand, it is seen as an inefficient condition leading knowledge drainage which is based on the high intensity of learning in networks. Social structures and the corresponding establishment of social capital are mentioned as necessary precondition to build a reputation and in consequence to increase competitiveness.

Benedict Doepfer elaborates a new perspective of interactive and cooperative value creation based on networking specificy at the example of young knowledge-intensive entrepreneurial firms and therefore provides a valuable contribution to entrepreneurship research as well as the field of regional development. Specifically the introduced concept

of co-innovation competence which relates to a dynamic perspective of corporate resources and capabilities as a source of innovation performance closes a critical gap in the
recent academic discussion. The findings offer several links for further research as well as a
set of practical implications for entrepreneurs and innovation promotors. I can therefore
recommend this book to academic colleagues and likewise to managers and entrepreneurs.

Professor Dr. Harald Pechlaner

Preface

Inter-organizational value creation based on the accessibility of complementary assets has become an imperative in the field of technological innovation. The popularity of the concepts 'open innovation' and 'innovation networks' emphasizes this trend within a specialized economy. However, certain barriers remain to engage in co-innovation projects specifically if high innovation risk is at stake. Thus, a certain co-innovation competence may be required to effectively explore and exploit the entrepreneurial opportunities arising from the corporate environment.

In this work a networked approach to value creation processes of young knowledge-intensive entrepreneurial firms is critically analyzed by assessing precise strategies and tactics for these firms to exploit their surrounding regional economic structures. In this context, the concept of co-innovation competence is introduced and empirically analyzed. Thus, this work, on the one hand, contributes to entrepreneurship research by inter-relating regional characteristics and corporate competences to performance and, on the other hand, offers practical implications for entrepreneurs as well as entrepreneurship and innovation promotors with regard to the establishment of inter-organizational knowledge exchange and co-innovation.

This work is based on a doctoral research project at the Center for Entrepreneurship of the Catholic University of Eichstätt-Ingolstadt, Germany. During the time at the Center I had the chance to be involved in an industrial research project empirically analyzing the knowledge networks and the value creation competence of the Ingolstadt region. This work greatly took advantage from the project by offering an insight into the 'real' challenges that dynamic regions and the corporations within them have to face, either to maintain or in case of young entrepreneurial firms to establish their competitiveness. In this regard, I particularly like to thank my academic advisor Professor Dr. Harald Pechlaner who, on the one hand, was a supporting mentor on an academic and professional level as well as, on the other hand, a transformational leader contributing intensively to my personal development on various stages within this time. Furthermore, I am greatly thankful for the co-supervision of my dissertation by Professor Dr. Michael Kutschker. His profound knowledge of strategic management and mutual critical discussions have positively influenced the quality of this work. In addition great thanks belongs to my colleagues and friends from the academic world who have been extremely valuable sparring partners as well as coaches certainly influencing my academic development. In particular, I would like to mention Professor Dr. Marc-Michael Bergfeld, Munich Business School, acting as expert and specifically as relational promotor opening the doors of the international academic world by e.g. arranging a research visit to the Manchester Institute of Innovation Research at Manchester Business School.

The empirical investigation of this work would not have been possible without the entrepreneurs of young knowledge-intensive firms who participated in the survey as well as in the interviews providing the data for analysis. Furthermore, the set of promotors of innovation of Ingolstadt region needs to be mentioned as valuable discussion partners for reflecting my ideas of co-innovation competence. In particular I would like to thank Norbert Forster, managing director of the business incubator of Ingolstadt (EGZ), who has been a helpful partner in establishing contacts to entrepreneurial firms as well as to the actors of the regional informal network of promotors.

This work is dedicated to my most important network of promotors, my family. The deepest gratitude belongs to my lovely wife Dr. Anna-Katharina Doepfer, who created an environment which allowed me to drift off into the depth of the academic world and to keep the problems of daily life in the back seat. Furthermore, I greatly thank my parents Reinhild Otterbein-Doepfer and Dr. Bernhard Doepfer for always supporting and implicitly guiding my curriculum vitae as well as providing a safety net for all the paths I have taken within this time. Additionally I would like to thank my parents-in-law Dr. Karin and Dr. Carsten Timm and my grandmother Ruth Otterbein for taking strong positions in my promotor network.

In memoriam of my grandfather Dr. Heinrich Otterbein.

Benedict C. Doepfer

Table of Contents

List of Figures

List of Tables

List of Abbreviations

B2B	Business to business
GEM	Global Entrepreneurship Monitor
NIH	Not invented here
NIS	National innovation systems
I&C	Information and communication
IC	Intellectual capital
IP	Intellectual property
IT	Information technology
KIBS	Knowledge-intensive business services
OEM	Original equipment manufacturer
R&D	Research and development
RIS	Regional innovation system
RFID	Radio frequency identification
RQ	Research question
SME	Small- and medium-sized enterprise
TCE	Transaction cost economics

"To borrow Abraham Lincoln's words, enterprises must be designed by the people, for the people, of the people, and we might add, co-creating value with the people."[1]

1. Introduction

1.1 Relevance of the Investigation

"Paradoxically, the enduring competitive advantages in a global economy lie increasingly in local things - knowledge, relationships, and motivation that distant rivals cannot match [...] innovation and competitive success in so many fields are geographically concentrated."[2]

A structural economic change has emerged from the effects of global competition leading to a demand shift toward individualized, requirement-specific products and services. Furthermore, a shortening of product life cycles has arisen due to increased customer requirements for continuous improvement and innovation.[3] To compensate for the increasing cost structures due to the shift described the achievement of synergy effects within the production process may be seen as a vital component to optimizing the variety of the product portfolio or, more precisely, as a requirement for future competitiveness. Vertical disintegration and the outsourcing of the previously internally provided value creation processes have been pegged as creators of a field of entrepreneurial opportunities for the establishment of new knowledge-intensive service providers and suppliers.[4] In the current competitive landscape, therefore, the specialization and the external sourcing of knowledge and technology has become a central aspect of strategic management decisions.[5] This refers to the accessibility of knowledge and complementary assets as essential component to engage in new innovation projects.[6] Within the research and development

---

1 Ramaswamy/Goullart 2010, p. 245.
2 Porter 1998a, p. 77-78.
3 The historical development of the Apple iPhone serves as empirical example for this recent development. The smartphone was introduced to the market in June 29th 2007 while the fifth generation of the product was released in October 14th 2011. Within this time several innovations were introduced in the device to meet customer requirements for mobile multimedia as well as internet usage. Despite the development of these technological features, the invention of the App Store needs to be mentioned. Here, every customer has the chance to individualize the product to her or his specific needs which can be considered as a main reason for the success of the product. This can be seen in the number of approximately 37 million phones sold only in the period of October to December of 2011 (Apple Inc. 2012).
4 See Doellgast/Greer 2007; Chen 2005; O'Farrell/Moffat/Hitchens 1993.
5 See e.g. Porter/Stern 2001, p. 28; van de Vrande/Vanhaverbeke/Duysters 2009, p. 62.
6 See Teece 1986, p.289.

(R&D) and the innovation management literature the concept of 'open innovation' "a paradigm that assumes that firms can and should use external ideas as well as internal ideas, internal and external paths to market, as the firms look to advance their technology,"[7] has brought a new understanding of innovation performance to an inter-organizational perspective that has taken a ubiquitous position in the latest R&D and innovation research.[8]

Various modes of inter-corporate transactions are known and have been analyzed in the strategic management literature.[9] The aspect of cooperation for innovation can be identified as an output focused approach to inter-organizational cooperation. Due to the mentioned effects of shorter product life cycles and competitive intensity resulting from disintegration as well as increasing complexity of R&D projects, corporations perceive a more intense economic risk in innovation and new product development projects.[10] The dynamics of technology markets evolve into continuously changing market conditions due to creative destruction.[11] This attribute is understood as the core element of entrepreneurship and refers to a process in which individuals pursue opportunities to create market innovations.[12] In this understanding of entrepreneurship the term is predominantly directly linked to innovation.[13] It postulates a given set of capabilities of the entrepreneur to pursue entrepreneurial opportunities and to establish sustainable corporate development.[14] In this case "we should be aware that in future the concept of an all-round qualification will become obsolete. We most certainly will have to apply the principles of division of labor to this problem."[15] Utilizing external resources within such entrepreneurial processes in the sense of relationship- and network-based entrepreneurship has found attention in recent entrepreneurship literature.[16] Based on these findings, entrepreneurial networks mainly strive to reduce the pressure on small- and medium-sized firms (SMEs) relying upon the network structure as a framework for building network contacts, contributing to and profiting from the network.[17] Network efficiency in this context is decisive for en-

---

7   Chesbrough 2003a, p. xxvi.
8   See e.g. Gassmann 2006; Enkel/Gassmann/Chesbrough 2009; Gassmann/Enkel/Chesbrough 2010.
9   See e.g. Mizruchi/Schwartz 1992; Cropper et al. 2008; Zentes/Swoboda/Morschett 2005; Pisano/
      Verganti 2008.
10   See Gassmann 2006, p. 224.
11   See Schumpeter 1996, pp. 81-86.
12   See Stevenson/Jarillo 1990; Krackhardt 1995, pp. 53-55; Pechlaner/Doepfer 2010, pp. 84-85.
13   See Drucker 2002; Bessant/Tidd 2011.
14   See Man/Lau/Chan 2002, p. 132.
15   Faltin 2001, p. 127.
16   See Harryson 2006; 2008. These findings are based on research discussing network theory (e.g. Birley
      1985; Witt 2004; O'Donnell et al. 2001) and social capital theory in the context of entrepreneurship
      (Liao/Welsch 2003; Yli-Renko/Autio/Sapienza 2001).
17   See Witt 2004, p. 394-395.

abling access to critical ressources and for reducing the likelihood of corporate failure,[18] while also balancing the investment into social capital according to organizational goals.[19]

Nonetheless, entrepreneurs face especially in knowledge-intensive industries strong opposition to openly sharing ideas and cooperating in innovation projects with corporate and institutional partners due to potential knowledge and technology drainage.[20] "Openness and free exchange of information, however, make companies more vulnerable to risks of information leakage."[21] Among entrepreneurs of knowledge-intensive firms this perception is magnified due to the relevance of specific knowledge as a critical component for future competitiveness.[22] Entrepreneurs therefore tend to protect their knowledge and to follow a rather closed process of entrepreneurial pursuit. Consequently, even though research can be identified as elaborating a profound understanding of networked entrepreneurship, the identification of the precise conditions for open entrepreneurial behavior in the sense of an open innovation construct toward a competence-based approach remain scarce.

As stated above, recent economic development may positively influence the relevance of regional economies to promote innovation performance. Regional proximity among the institutional actors has been identified as a decisive factor in reducing innovation barriers and allows for the establishment of the inter-organizational knowledge flows.[23] Under such conditions, regional innovation systems arise from the vitalization of regional knowledge bases,[24] and offer an entrepreneurial climate for the elaboration of new ideas and the performance of innovation.[25] Consequently, from an integrative perspective of networked entrepreneurship and entrepreneurial climate, the establishment and effects of regional entrepreneurial networks remain to be researched as central components to strategically approaching entrepreneurship within regional structures.

An empirical study in the automotive region of Ingolstadt, Germany, forms the basis for the problem statement.[26] Figure 1 illustrates the economic network of organizations allo-

---

18   See Baum/Calabrese/Silverman 2000, p. 267.
19   See Krackhardt/Hanson 1993, p. 110.
20   See Gans/Stern 2003; Keupp/Gassmann 2009, p. 338.
21   Hoecht/Trott 1999, p. 258.
22   See Smith/Lohrke 2008, p. 316.
23   See Glaeser et al. 1992; Jacobs 1969; Storper/Veneables 2004; Eriksson 2011.
24   See Asheim/Coenen 2005.
25   See Goetz/Freshwater 2001, pp. 64-65. The concept of entrepreneurial climate has been researched empirically by Sternberg (e.g. 2009), who elaborated a list of regional characteristics influencing the general requirements for entrepreneurial performance (also see Brixy et al. 2011, p. 22). Further research referring to the concept as entrepreneurial milieu has also been done (e.g. Löfsten/Lindelöf 2003). The most cited example of such a vital regional entrepreneurial climate is the Silicon Valley, California, USA, which Lee et al. (2000) call 'a habitat for innovation and entrepreneurship.'
26   For a geographical presentation of the Ingolstadt region, see Appendix 1.

cated in the automotive industry within the Ingolstadt region. The figure draws on a network analysis conducted in an empirical research project.[27] Each dot in the figure represents a corporation or a research institute of various sizes depending on the number of connections within the network. Clearly, one corporation can be identified as the core player, the car manufacturer AUDI AG, causing a rather centered network structure. Furthermore, the 26 colored dots refer to young knowledge-intensive entrepreneurial corporations founded after 2005. These appear on the left hand as either isolated actors or operating only in direct relations with the big player, or linked to a regional network of corporations and research institutes on the right-hand side. The figure, therefore, exemplifies the idea that entrepreneurs share only limited relations to local organizations and remain predominantly in dual transaction relationships. The reason may lie, on the one hand, in a lack of trust and suspicion of opportunistic behavior,[28] or, on the other hand, in a lack of reciprocal willingness to build social relations to neighboring organizations apprehending networking inefficiencies.[29]

The development of entrepreneurial networks, consequently, seems to require certain competences by the entrepreneur to identify and build relations to potential collaborative partners as well as exploit these relations for collaborative innovation. Furthermore, the regional structure may be a critical component influencing the ability and willingness of entrepreneurs to engage in inter-organizational collaboration. The regional economic structure, understood as a multi-level innovation system, is framed by a linking level of promotors that act as intermediaries and information and technology brokers. They enable regional corporations to innovate by transferring knowledge and establishing social capital among the regional actors. Therefore, the interplay of entrepreneurs with such regional innovation promotors may be considered as decisive for the ability of the entrepreneur to strategically exploit regional innovation structures and to achieve entrepreneurial performance.

---

27   See Thierstein et al. 2011. For a detailed look at the research project also see
      www.wertschoepfungplus.de.
28   See Nooteboom 2000a, p. 919; Hoecht/Trott 1999, p. 266.
29   See Woolcock/Narayan 2000, p. 231.

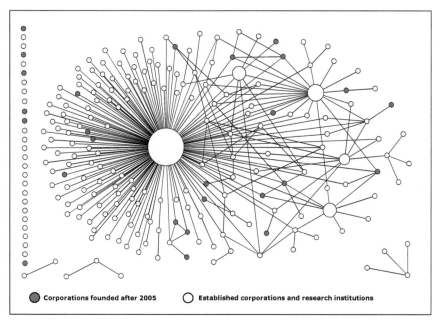

Corporations founded after 2005   ◯ Established corporations and research institutions

Figure 1: Automotive economic network of the Ingolstadt region
Source: Based on Thierstein et al. 2011, p. 102.

1.2 Contribution of the Investigation

The organizational and institutional embeddedness of geographical networks might be crucial in explaining the differences in effectiveness of Open Innovation in different regions or nations… Open innovation has to be connected to regional economics in the future."[30]

The primary goal of this investigation is to elaborate this matter in the form of a theoretically grounded composition of co-innovation competence toward a strategic approach to entrepreneurship in regional innovation structures. This work analyzes the entrepreneurship and entrepreneurial behavior of young knowledge-intensive firms in the context of the open innovation paradigm applied to regional structure economics. Research in the field of knowledge-intensive business services (KIBS) has emphasized the ubiquitous evolvement of inter-firm networks based on the co-operation of manufacturing firms with

---

30   Vanhaverbeke 2006, p. 216.

specialized service firms to realize an inter-organizational flow of knowledge.[31] These are seen as carriers of advanced knowledge and can be characterized by "the ability to receive information from outside of the company and to transform this information together with firm-specific knowledge into useful services for their customers."[32] However, in the litera-ture there is an on-going discussion regarding the precise definition of KIBS, whether it contains the perspective that KIBS offer "products and services to other organizations so that these conform to the institutionalized expectations of their environments."[33] In this work knowledge-intensive firms will be applied as an umbrella term, emphasizing the knowledge-intensive character of the firms analyzed located within the economic sector of corporate services.

Following a multidisciplinary approach drawing on strategic management and economic geography research, a strategic approach to entrepreneurship in regional innovation struc-tures is elaborated.[34] In this context, the concept of open innovation is applied to a discus-sion of regional structure economics emphasizing the exploration and exploitation of local knowledge for the pursuit of entrepreneurial opportunities. Because an intensive flow of knowledge among the actors is postulated within the open innovation literature[35] as well as in discussions of regional innovation structures,[36] an analysis of an integrated perspec-tive allows for the identification of the enabling factors and constraints. By drawing on the problem statement elaborated above, the hindering aspects to establishing social capital among regional actors in the sense of an entrepreneurial network become clear. Also at-tributes need to be identified that cause the development of a vital regional entrepreneur-ial climate and the establishment of inter-organizational innovation among regional actors.

This work contributes to the field of entrepreneurship in a twofold manner. On the one hand, a competence-based approach will be elaborated within a strategic entrepreneur-ship perspective in order to set the stage for formulating a strategic approach regarding collaborative and networked innovation within a regional context. This aspect relates to the identified research gap identified by Liao/Welch (2001), who recommend an analysis of the "strategies, and tactics nascent entrepreneurs utilize to transfer structural capital into cognitive capital, and in turn create relational capital."[37] On the other hand, from the

---

31   See Gallouj 2002; Andersson/Hellerstedt 2009; Bunker Whittington/Owen-Smith/Powell 2009.
32   Hipp 1999, p. 94.
33   See Alvesson 1993, p. 1004.
34   Choi/Pak (2006, p. 351) define multidisciplinarity as follows: "Multidisciplinarity draws on knowledge from different disciplines but stays within their boundaries." This indicates that concepts of economic geography appropriate to this investigation are reflected and transferred to a strategic management thought pattern.
35   See Chesbrough 2003a, p. XXV; Elmquist/Fredberg/Ollila 2009, p. 327; Christensen/Olesen/Kjaer 2005, p. 1534; Sawhney/Prandelli 2000, p. 25.
36   See e.g. Etzkowitz/Klofsten 2000; Cooke 2005; Sternberg 2009.
37   Liao/Welch 2001, p. 167.

perspective of entrepreneurship and regional development, the suggestion by Da-
vidsson/Honig (2003) that "the facilitation and support of business networks and associations may provide the most consistent and effective support for emerging businesses,"[38]
the influential components regarding the interaction process of entrepreneurs with regional innovation promotors as decisive character of the regional entrepreneurial climate
is elaborated.

1.3 Course of Investigation

This work follows a linear cognitive process according to a basic understanding of empirical
research of a Popperanian sequence in order to achieve a progressive cognizance.[39] Based
on a literature review, the current state of the scientific discussion is elaborated, offering a
field for the deduction of constitutive research questions for empirical investigation. The
presentation and interpretation of the empirical results allows an inductive approach to
elaborate research as well as empirical implications. Figure 2 provides a graphical overview
of the course of investigation according to the following procedure:

Chapter 2 presents the state of discussion regarding the critical components of this
work by introducing core concepts and essential definitions, serving as a basis for further
analysis. A review of the literature in the fields of entrepreneurship and innovation research, open innovation, and regional innovation structures forms a sound foundation for
understanding the critical components of entrepreneurship in regional innovation structures. The regional environment of an entrepreneurial firm is held to be crucial for its ability to detect and pursue entrepreneurial opportunities resulting from regional knowledge
spillovers. Understanding the regional innovation structure as a network of actors from
various organizations and institutions striving for inter-organizational innovation, one can
identify the determinants for operating within corresponding settings. To exploit the external environment of the entrepreneurial firm by absorbing external knowledge the establishment of social relations to various partners externally as well as the development of
co-innovation competence internally is emphasized. Chapter 3 offers the theoretical basis
of this work by presenting the evolution of entrepreneurial networks based on social capital theory before elaborating a competence-based approach to co-innovation.

---

38   Davidsson/Honig 2003, p. 325.
39   See Popper 2005.

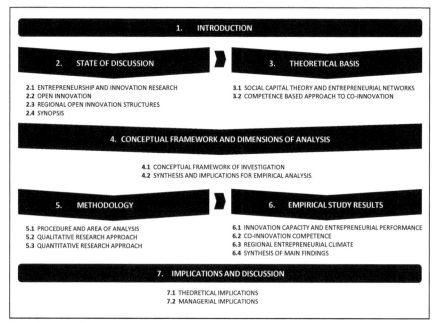

Figure 2: Course of investigation

By drawing on the present state of discussion and the theoretical basis, Chapter 4 presents the conceptual framework of this investigation. This framework refers to previous studies linking organizational factors as internal dimensions and environmental factors as external dimensions to entrepreneurial performance.[40] Based on a discussion of the terms and concepts introduced an approach to a co-innovation strategy is elaborated before the main research questions for empirical analysis are deduced. The latter refer to the interplay of co-innovation competence of the entrepreneurial firm and the entrepreneurial climate of the regional structure and its dependencies on entrepreneurial performance. Chapter 5 presents the methodology as applied to the elaborated research questions. With reference to the concept of triangulation, based on the multi-disciplinary literature review conducted, a quantitative and qualitative analysis is applied in a combined manner.[41] A regional setting has to be identified for investigation in order to elaborate a strategic approach to entrepreneurship in regional innovation structures. Previous studies indicate that the re-

---

40   See e.g. Lumpkin/Dess 1996; Lerner/Haber 2000; Eriksson 2011.
41   See Todd 1979.

gion of Ingolstadt, Germany, offers a dynamic economic setting that enables open innovation and knowledge exploration and exploitation among local actors as well as the necessary structure for analysis.[42]

To determine the interplay of co-innovation competence and regional entrepreneurial climate, on the one hand entrepreneurs of young knowledge-intensive firms[43] and, on the other hand, regional innovation promotors are identified as objects of analysis within the economic structure of Ingolstadt region. Innovation promotors may be understood as institutional representatives who contribute to the regional innovation capacity by encouraging regional corporations to innovate. These may be located in institutions such as technology brokers, government agencies, industrial associations and research institutes.[44] 15 such actors have been identified as displaying a regional network of promotors in the Ingolstadt region. In open-question interviews the selected actors discussed their perception of the regional entrepreneurial climate, their personal contribution to entrepreneurship and technology transfer promotion in the region as well as their vision for future directions.

To gain insight into the entrepreneurial perspective, 249 knowledge-intensive firms in the sector of corporate services, founded by an entrepreneur or entrepreneurial team after 2005 were identified in the region of Ingolstadt.[45] 33 corporations were randomly selected from the database for interviews to present their perception of the regional entrepreneurial climate and their attitude toward achieving innovation in cooperation with regional actors. Furthermore, to gain quantifiable data as a supporting component to the information received from the interviews, the 249 identified entrepreneurial firms were sent a survey, 43 of which participated by returning complete valuable information. In this connection, Chapter 6 presents the results. Here, qualitative data serve as the dominant factor drawing on a semantical network analysis, whereas survey-based statistical results are presented to strengthen the qualitative results identified. Chapter 7 concludes this

---

42 See Pechlaner/Bachinger 2010, pp. 1747-1748; Prognos 2010a; 2010b; Thierstein et al. 2011; Doepfer et al. 2012.

43 This work draws on the categorization of the entrepreneurial firm as applied to the Global Entrepreneurship Monitor (see Kelley/Bosma/Amorós 2011, p. 13). Here, a total early-stage of entrepreneurial activity is introduced differentiating the 'nascent entrepreneur' from the owner-manager of a new business. While nascent entrepreneurs can be "individuals trying to start an independent business" (Delmar/Davidsson 2000, p. 2) the definition of 'new business entrepreneurs' varies in the literature in its characterizing components over time. This work applies the term young entrepreneurial firm as an umbrella term for newly established operating entities still in an early stage of their corporate life cycle (also see Bouwen/Steyaert 1990; Kroll/Walters 2007).

44 See Fichter 2009, p. 361; Lynn/Mohan/Abram 1996.

45 The number of corporations identified is based on data provided by the regional Chamber of Commerce as well as additional research to verify the selection criteria. At the time of investigation a founding year later than 2005 indicates a corporate history of maximum six years as a timetable suitable for the selected term of a young entrepreneurial firm.

work by offering, on the one hand, the theoretical implications of the results, on the other hand, as well as the managerial implications differentiating between entrepreneurs of knowledge-intensive firms and regional promotors of innovation.

"Entrepreneurs create jobs. They drive and shape innovation, speeding up structural changes in the economy [...] Entrepreneurship is thus a catalyst for economic growth and national competitiveness."[46]

2. State of the Discussion

2.1 Entrepreneurship and Innovation Research

2.1.1 Strategic Entrepreneurship and the Entrepreneurial Firm

"The historical evolution of ideas about the entrepreneur is a wide-ranging subject."[47] A variety of approaches toward to a defining and conceptualizing entrepreneurship from a broad array of cross-disciplinary perspectives can be identified in the literature.[48] There is a wide perception that entrepreneurship is as a process of discovery, evaluation, and exploitation[49] in which individuals pursue opportunities to create market innovations[50] and therefore cause creative destruction on current market conditions.[51] Due to their superior efficiency such entrepreneurs set new market standards by founding new firms or organizational entities and crowding out established corporations reluctant to change their routines.[52] Within this understanding of entrepreneurship the term is, consequently, predominantly directly linked to innovation[53] and defines the function of the entrepreneur as "to reform or revolutionize the pattern of production by exploiting an invention [...] for producing a new commodity."[54] Entrepreneurship can also be defined as "acts of organizational creation, renewal, or innovation that occur within or outside an existing organization."[55] This perspective refers to a Schumpeterian point of view of entrepreneurship, which emphasizes the importance of innovation in context of new venture creation. A successful entrepreneur creates profits based on an innovation premium realized by specific capabilities. The will to act and the resources under control shape the values and attitudes

---

46   Kelley/Bosma/Amorós 2011, p. 12.
47   Ricketts 2006, p. 33.
48   See for a detailed overview: Ireland/Webb 2007b, pp. 897-914.
49   See Shane/Venkataraman 2000, p. 218.
50   See Stevenson/Jarillo 1990 p. 23; Krackhardt 1995, pp. 53-55; Pechlaner/Doepfer 2010, pp. 84-85.
51   See Schumpeter 1996, pp. 81-87.
52   See Brouwer 2002, p. 90.
53   See Drucker 2002; Bessant/Tidd 2011.
54   Schumpeter 1996, p. 132.
55   Sharma/Chrisman 1999, p. 17.

of the entrepreneur.[56] This perception does not fit the concept of the 'economic man' balancing marginal costs and benefits. Rather, entrepreneurial behavior is understood as a non-rational striving for the improvement of individual social status regardless of the time and effort spent.[57] This intrinsic motivation is seen as a source of economic development and as the initiator of business cycles.[58] "Entrepreneurship depends on the decisions that people make about how to undertake that process."[59]

In contrast to this resource-based perspective of entrepreneurship, which neglects the demand side and market conditions as an active and influential part in the innovation process[60] researchers have emphasized an analysis of prevailing market conditions as the source of entrepreneurial opportunities. Entrepreneurial behavior, consequently, may also draw on the capability of the entrepreneur to identify imbalances of demand and supply and on individual skills from specific expertise.[61] Consequently, the question arises "whether opportunities make entrepreneurs or whether entrepreneurs create opportunities."[62] This approach reflects a reduction of risk, based on an analytical procedure to minimize uncertainty of economic success within market entry. Risk-taking considered inherent in entrepreneurship within the pursuit of innovative entrepreneurial opportunities[63] and is considered a typical characteristic of a successful entrepreneur.[64] In this context risk can be thought of as "the investment of resources in which the decision maker knows the probability distribution of all possible outcomes from entrepreneurial action, but does not know which outcome will occur."[65]

Based on the dimensions of entrepreneurial behavior presented, innovativeness and risk taking, the concept of entrepreneurial orientation allows extending these attributes to approach the complex phenomenon.[66] The decisive impetus for engaging in innovative and risky ventures is the independent spirit to act autonomously. "Autonomy refers to the independent action of an individual or a team in bringing forth an idea or a vision and carrying it through to completion."[67] Furthermore, in order to profit from the discovery of market opportunities a proactive behavior is considered as decisive to realizing a first-mover premium. Pro-activeness meets a market-based perspective toward entrepreneur-

56   See Littunen 2000, p. 295.
57   See Brouwer 2002, pp. 90-91.
58   See Schumpeter 1978.
59   Shane/Locke/Collins 2003, p. 258.
60   See Metcalfe 2006, p. 76.
61   See Kirzner 1973, pp. 30, 68.
62   Saravasvathy 2004, p. 308.
63   See Miller 2007, p. 57.
64   See Littunen 2000, p. 295.
65   Shepherd/McMullen/Jennings 2007, p. 77.
66   See Lumpkin/Dess 1996, pp. 140-149.
67   Lumpkin/Dess 1996, p 140.

ship and emphasizes the potential of exploiting emerging markets by anticipating and pursuing opportunities. The final component of entrepreneurial orientation is the relevance of competitive aggressiveness, which is elaborated by drawing on corporate strategy. Since young ventures are apparently more likely to fail compared to established businesses, aggressive market behavior is seen as critical to the survival of the venture.[68] Consequently, instead of reacting toward changing market conditions entrepreneurs need to act proactively "taking the initiative in an effort to shape the environment to one's own advantage."[69] This dimension of entrepreneurial orientation shows a strong linkage to strategic management and includes organizational factors and environmental aspects into an entrepreneurial thought pattern, leading toward an integrated perspective of entrepreneurship and strategy.

2.1.1.1 Strategic Entrepreneurship

"An entrepreneurial opportunity consists of a set of ideas, beliefs and actions that enable the creation of future goods and services in the absence of current markets for them."[70]

Among researchers a long-run discussion has been taking place whether a combination of entrepreneurship and strategic management can be applied to an organizational setting.[71] Based on the origins of strategy with reference to an organization of forces and ressources within a military context,[72] strategy can be understood as a set of decision making rules for guidance or organizational behavior.[73] "The essence of strategy is choosing to perform activities differently than rivals do."[74] Based on the analysis of market conditions to identify attractive market positions[75] and the possession of valuable, rare, imperfectly imitable, and non-substitutable resources specific to the firm, strategic approaches have been elaborated to achieve competitive advantage.[76] Later research in the field emphasizes the relevance of firm-specific knowledge and the development of dynamic capabilities drawing on systematic learning routines in interaction with external stakeholders such as competi-

---

68 Porter (2004) emphasizes the relevance of aggressive market behavior to achieve competitive advantage with reference to a cost-leadership position and pricing strategy (pp. 19; 508), pursuit of learning (p. 87), patenting (p. 440), and investments for growth (p. 467).
69 Chen/Hambrick 1995, p. 457.
70 Saravasvathy et al. 2003, p. 142.
71 See e.g. Gronhaug, K./Reve, T. 1988; Ireland 2007.
72 See Kotler/Singh 1981; von Oetinger 2001.
73 See Ansoff 1984, p. 31.
74 Porter 1996, p. 64.
75 See Porter 1998b; Porter 2004.
76 See Barney, 1991, pp. 106-112; Grant 1991.

tors and customers.[77] Strategic management, consequently, follows a perspective of a systematic and effective advantage-seeking behavior.[78] The transferability to less established and less hierarchical organizations, characterized by flexibility, intrinsic motivation and an opportunity-seeking behavior, requires specific consideration. Therefore, the application of strategic management aspects has been discussed as striving for the elaboration of a strategic entrepreneurship concept.

The concept of strategic entrepreneurship can be understood as a combination of entrepreneurship and strategic management unifying the opportunity-based behavior of entrepreneurship with the strategic advantage-seeking behavior to create entrepreneurial performance and wealth.[79] With reference to the elaborations of Ireland/Hitt/Sirmon (2003) a theoretical framework of strategic entrepreneurship is presented describing the core components (entrepreneurial mindset, entrepreneurial culture and leadership, strategic resource management, and the application of creativity and innovation development) and their interplay toward competitive advantage and wealth creation (see Figure 3).

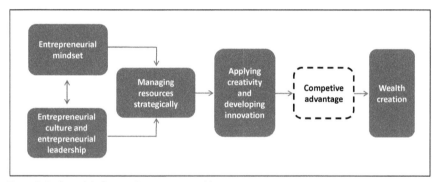

Figure 3: Path model of strategic entrepreneurship
Source: Ireland/Hitt/Sirmon 2003, p. 967.

* Entrepreneurial mindset: Capturing the benefits of uncertainty by taking risks to exploit new opportunities clears the way to outperform competitors.[80] An entrepreneurial mindset draws on this attitude and can be defined as "a growth-oriented perspective through which individuals promote flexibility, creativity, continuous innovation, and re-

---

77   See Grant 1996a, p. 113; Teece/Pisano/Shuen 1997; Teece 2009.
78   See Ireland/Hitt/Sirmon 2003, p. 966.
79   See Hitt et al. 2001, p. 481; Ireland/Hitt/Sirmon 2003, p. 963.
80   See Miles et al. 2000, p. 101; Shepherd/McMullen/Jennings 2007, p. 77.

newal."[81] The recognition of entrepreneurial opportunities represents an initiator for the entrepreneurial process and may be seen as the decisive competence of the entrepreneur.[82] Caused by an asymmetric share of information within dynamic market conditions, entrepreneurial opportunities might result from changes in legislation or technology leading toward a fluctuation of the relative value of resources currently controlled.[83] Furthermore, the ability of the entrepreneur to be alert toward an increasing demand of a certain product or service or in general the identification of market imbalances in the form of "flashes of superior insights" must be considered.[84] To exploit the opportunities arising from these circumstances an entrepreneurial mindset systematically approaches the time required and the relevant wealth-creating goals in order to pursue the opportunity in the form of an entrepreneurial framework.[85] Consequently, apart from opportunity recognition competencies, strategic and organizing competencies are considered relevant components within the entrepreneurial mindset.[86]

- Entrepreneurial culture and entrepreneurial leadership: Based on a combined organizational approach toward opportunity- and advantage-seeking behavior "an effective entrepreneurial culture is one in which new ideas and creativity are expected, risk-taking is encouraged, failure is tolerated, learning is promoted, product, process and administrative innovations are championed, and continuous change is viewed as a conveyor of opportunities."[87] Organizations of such culture are attractive to people with entrepreneurial mindsets acting either as intrapreneurs[88] or entrepreneurial leaders. According to Covin/Slevin (2002) an entrepreneurial leadership can be characterized by six imperatives: (1) The enrichment of human capital by developing individual entrepreneurial capabilities such as creativity and strategic resource management. (2) An open flow of information among organizational members regarding radical innovation projects. (3) The communication of values resulting from opportunities identified. (4) The question-

---

81 Ireland/Hitt/Sirmon 2003, p. 968.
82 See Man/Lau/Chan 2002, 132.
83 See Shane/Venkataraman 2000, p. 220.
84 See Alvarez/Barney 2002, p. 89. Faltin (2010) emphasizes in his approach to entrepreneurship 'flashes of superior insight' as decisive component of entrepreneurial success. Based on the case study of Teekampagne, he discusses the hypothesis that good ideas are more relevant than capital to start a successful venture. Teekampagne directly imports Darjeeling tea from the plant in Nepal to Germany, cutting out various stages of the import process offering a high-quality product at lowest market price (www.teekampagne.de/en).
85 See Ireland/Hitt/Sirmon 2003, p. 969.
86 See Man/Lau/Chan 2002, 132.
87 Ireland/Hitt/Sirmon 2003, p. 970.
88 See Pinchot 1985; Pinchot/Pellman 1999.

ing of the dominant logic[89] by evaluating resource allocation decisions. (5) The questioning of the corporate vision to identify the perspective of the firm toward opportunities. (6) Being strategically entrepreneurial and developing a corporate culture of opportunity- and advantage-seeking behavior.

- Strategic resource management: This draws on the elaborations of the resource-based view of the firm defining resources as tangible and intangible assets such as capabilities and knowledge controlled by a corporation enabling the firm to implement strategies to improve performance.[90] These resources are of strategic relevance to the firm if they are valuable, rare, imperfectly imitable, and non-substitutable.[91] Ireland/Hitt/Sirmon (2003, pp. 973-977) elaborate on financial capital, human capital, and social capital as the critical portfolio of tangible and intangible resource requiring a strategic management due to its dynamic character within a strategic entrepreneurship perspective. This approach contains three dimensions to managing resources strategically: (1) Portfolio structuring refers to a continuous evaluation whether resources create synergies in combination with other resources of the corporation's portfolio. (2) A bundling of resources aims at creating specific capabilities required to implement corporate strategies. This may serve, on the one hand, to maintain competitive advantages or, on the other hand, (3) to create a leverage of capabilities across business units exploiting opportunities to achieve competitive advantage.[92]

- Application of creativity and innovation development: This refers to the concept of creative destruction, where innovations continuously crowd-out obsolete goods, services and processes initiating corporate growth and wealth creation.[93] Creativity, consequently, can be understood as the basis for innovation and defined as "an approach to work that leads to the generation of novel and appropriate ideas, processes, or solutions."[94] Depending on the individual perspective of knowledge base and competences the intensity of innovation impact may differ. Furthermore, organizational structure plays a decisive role in the capability of people to be creative.[95] Therefore, one has to differentiate between sustaining innovations that incrementally improve current products or services and radical innovations that require restructuring and organizational change due to a higher innovation impact.[96] Using strategic entrepreneurship effective-

---

89   For a detailed discussion of the concept of 'dominant logic', see Prahalad/Bettis 1986; Bettis/Prahalad 1995.
90   See Barney 1991, p. 101.
91   See Barney 1991, pp. 106-112.
92   See Ireland/Hitt/Sirmon 2003, p. 979.
93   See Schumpeter 1996, pp. 81-87.
94   Perry-Smith/Shally 2003, p. 90.
95   See Amabile 1998.
96   For a more detailed discussion of the dimensions of innovation see Chapter 2.1.2.1.

ly "leads to a comprehensive and integrated commitment to both sustaining and dis-ruptive innovations as drivers of wealth creation."[97]

The interplay of the aspects introduced toward to gain competitive advantage and wealth creation requires a continuous balance of opportunity- and advantage-seeking behavior. It can be anticipated that "successful organizations as ones in which strategic entrepreneur-ship will be used to deal with the organizational tension that surfaces as firms try to simul-taneously emphasize today what they already do well (relative to competitors) while ex-ploring for opportunities to build the foundation for their future success. Thus, we believe that superior firm performance will be a function of the degree to which firms learn how to combine the best of strategic management and entrepreneurship past the source of today's and tomorrow's competitive advantages."[98]

2.1.1.2 The Entrepreneurial Firm

Based on the elaborated understanding of entrepreneurship as a process of discovery, evaluation, and exploitation of opportunities to create market innovations,[99] an entrepre-neurial firm is understood as a corporation "that engages in product-market innovations, undertakes somewhat risky ventures, and is first to come up with 'proactive' innovations, beating competitors to the punch."[100] The entrepreneurial firm is characterized by an en-trepreneurial orientation or posture emphasizing the pursuit of opportunities, in the light of the risk involved to achieve innovation, which requires an anchoring of a specific thought pattern within management practices as well as corporate strategy. This pattern is embodied in the entrepreneur or the employees of a decision-making authority such as top management. "An entrepreneurial strategic posture is characterized by frequent and extensive technological and product innovation, an aggressive competitive orientation, and a strong risk-taking propensity by top management."[101] This perspective allows under-standing entrepreneurship as a management approach. It is based on the pursuit of oppor-tunities combining, on the one hand, management practices such as planning, organization and control and, on the other hand, the implementation of entrepreneurial behavior ap-plicable to new ventures as well as established organizations.[102]

---

97   See Ireland/Hitt/Sirmon 2003, p. 983.
98   Ireland/Webb 2007a, p. 59.
99   See Shane/Venkataraman 2000, p. 218; Stevenson/Jarillo 1990 p. 23; Krackhardt 1995, pp. 53-55.
100 Miller 1983, p. 771.
101 Covin/Slevin 1989, p. 79.
102 See Drucker 2002, p. 131; Stevenson/Jarillo 1990, p. 23.

New ventures, especially in technological fields, may demand high specific technological knowledge but lack the required management skills to follow a sustainable development of the organization. Established corporations, instead, face the pressure of continuous improvement and innovation performance to sustain market share and competitiveness, and therefore require continual stimulation of entrepreneurial spirit. Drawing on the works of Sharma/Chrisman (1999, p. 11) and Brown/Davidsson/Wilkund (2001, p. 953), which describe a firm-level perspective of entrepreneurship in the form of a corporate entrepreneurship paradigm as an area of research which "is still in its infancy," several contributions can be identified that systemize and ground the construct. "Corporate entrepreneurship refers to the process whereby the firms engage in diversification through internal development. Such diversification requires new resources combinations to extend the firm's activities in the areas unrelated, or marginally related, to its current domain of competence and corresponding opportunity set."[103] The field of corporate entrepreneurship, consequently, offers a unified perspective of entrepreneurial behavior and management practices conceptualized as opportunity-based firm behavior, respectively, entrepreneurial management.[104]

The construct of entrepreneurial management, which has raised attention in the academic discussion following the contribution by Stevenson/Jarillo (1990), considers the concept of entrepreneurship as something radically different than corporate management. While corporate management is understood as an administrative process aligned for the most efficient use of resources controlled, "entrepreneurial management may be seen as a 'mode of management' different from traditional management, with different requirements of control and rewards systems,"[105] set on pursuing and exploiting opportunities regardless of the resources currently controlled.[106] Although the concept was published as 'a paradigm of entrepreneurship' in the Strategic Management Journal, only few articles can be identified that directly refer to the terminology.[107] Based on the works by Stevenson,[108] Brown/Davidsson/Wilkund (2001) operationalize the entrepreneurial management construct and create a continuum for differentiating an entrepreneurially focused organization from an administratively focused organization (see Table 1). Within this continuum an entrepreneurial firm refers to the character of a promotor striving for the pursuit of

---

103 Burgelman 1983, p. 1349. For an overview of definitions of corporate entrepreneurship see Sharma/Chrisman (1999, p. 14).
104 See Brown/Davidsson/Wiklund 2001, p. 953; Stevenson/Jarillo 1990, p. 21.
105 Stevenson/Jarillo 1990, p. 25.
106 See Stevenson/Jarillo 1990, p. 23; Brown/Davidsson/Wilkund 2001, p. 955.
107 See e.g. Steier/Chrisman/Chua 2004; Rae 2007; Freiling 2009. For a systematic literarute review on 'entrepreneurial management,' see Pechlaner/Doepfer (2010, pp. 83-85).
108 See Stevenson 1983; Stevenson/Gumpert 1985; Stevenson/Jarillo 1986; Stevenson/Jarillo 1990.

opportunities, whereas an administrative firm is characterized by a trustee aiming at an efficient use of resources. This comparison is based on the following eight dimensions:

Entrepreneurial focus		Conceptual dimensions		Administrative Focus
Driven by perception of opportunity	←	Strategic orientation	→	Driven by controlled resources
Revolutionary with short duration	←	Commitment to opportunity	→	Evolutionary
Multi stage at minimal exposure	←	Commitment of resources	→	Single state with complete commitment
Episodic	←	Control of resources	→	Ownership
Flat, multiple informal networks	←	Management structure	→	Hierarchy
Based on value creation	←	Reward philosophy	→	Based on responsibility and seniority
Rapid growth	←	Growth orientation	→	Safe, slow, steady
Promotion of search for opportunity	←	Entrepreneurial culture	→	Opportunity search based on resources controlled

Table 1: Continuum of entrepreneurial management
Source: Based on Brown/Davidsson/Wilkund 2001, p. 955.

- Commitment to opportunity and strategic orientation: A promotor focuses on the emergence of opportunities and is willing to act ad hoc accordingly to pursue the opportunity regardless of the prevailing conditions. A trustee, in comparison, primarily analyzes the situation to evaluate potential risks. The opportunity, consequently, is assessed within the framework of resources controlled and is seen as attractive if an opportunity for increasing efficiency can be identified.[109] Strategic orientation in this case is based on efficiency-seeking behavior, whereas the promotor derives strategy directly from emerging opportunities leading to a reconfiguration of processes defined.[110]

- Commitment of resources and control of resources: While a trustee aims for a long-term bonding to resources, preferably in terms of ownership, and a complete control of these as a basis for entrepreneurial behavior,[111] a promotor follows the idea of making "a little bit more with a little bit less."[112] The entrepreneurial behavior of the promotor aims at the pursuit of opportunities regardless of the resources controlled. Consequently, value creation is maximized by exploiting opportunities, whereas a bonding to the necessary resources is minimized. In multi-stage testing the extent of resources necessary is determined preserving the flexibility to react quickly to changing conditions.[113]

---

109 See Paladino 2007, p. 549.
110 See Brown/Davidsson/Wilkund 2001, p. 956.
111 See Covin/Slevin 1991, p. 15.
112 See Stevenson 1983, p. 11.
113 See Brown/Davidsson/Wilkund 2001, p. 956; Stevenson 1983, p. 10.

An entrepreneurially focused firm proposes a minimum bondage to tangible resources; the establishment of intangible resources such as knowledge, capabilities, and competencies is strived for.

- Management structure and reward philosophy: A promotor strives for the establishment of a flat structure with multiple informal networks. This creates a working atmosphere in which all members can act freely to pursue the exploitation of opportunities. Consequently, firms with an entrepreneurial focus align payment directly to value creation performance. A trustee, instead, prefers a clear hierarchical structure and precisely defined areas of responsibility aligned for an efficient use of ressources controlled. Therefore, payment is linked to hierarchical levels and the corresponding responsibility of existing resources.[114]

- Growth orientation and entrepreneurial culture: Corporations with an entrepreneurial focus aim at realizing high growth rates.[115] Achieving this goal requires an intense specificity of an entrepreneurial culture characterized by the pursuit of opportunities and the inter-connected willingness to take risks.[116] The active practice of such a culture stimulates the development of new ideas as well as the promotion of creativity and the testing of new possibilities. Enabling a collective exchange of ideas and creating a creative climate characterize a culture of this kind.[117] In comparison, a corporation with an administrative focus tends to avoid volatility and shows more risk-averse behavior and thus targeting steady and continuous growth rates and causing a sustainable impact on corporate development.[118] A working atmosphere is created in which a pursuit of opportunities is only supported only within the framework of feasibility and resources controlled.[119]

Thus, the entrepreneurial firm may be characterized by an entrepreneurial focus promoting the pursuit of opportunities, even though most corporations are unlikely to be entrepreneurial over the entire spectrum.[120] Taken together, the concept of an entrepreneurial firm refers to the thought pattern of Stevenson's elaborations which emphasize a opportunity-based firm behavior expressed by a strategic and organizational design of the facilitating members' of the organization to take entrepreneurial action and therefore to pursue and exploit opportunities to achieve corporate performance.

---

114 See Brown/Davidsson/Wilkund 2001, p. 956.
115 See Stevenson/Jarillo 1986, p. 10.
116 See Stevenson/Jarillo 1990, p. 25.
117 See Tidd/Bessant 2009, pp. 130, 433; Trott 2008, p. 76.
118 See Bessant/Tidd 2011, p. 323.
119 See Brown/Davidsson/Wilkund 2001, p. 956.
120 See Brown/Davidsson/Wilkund 2001, p. 965.

2.1.2 Toward an Understanding of Innovation

2.1.2.1 Defining Innovation

"It is a serious mistake to treat innovation as if it were a well-defined, homogeneous thing that could be identified as entering the economy at a precise date."[121]

Based on the concept of creative destruction which refers to the introduction of a new commodity to the market substituting prevailing operations and products and leading to a restructuring of market conditions;[122] an innovation can be understood as a new process or product introduced to a market setting.[123] Defining the precise meaning of innovation is challenging due to the variety of perspectives toward the dimensions of innovation in terms of newness and outcome.[124] As Table 2 illustrates scholars have long attempted to define innovation. While early works emphasize newness, as such, as decisive character of innovation further contributions can be identified highlighting the outcome of an innovation in the form of a new product meeting customers' needs.[125] The relevance of perspective toward the unit of adoption within the diffusion of innovation is emphasized by Rogers (1983; 2003). An innovation, consequently, can be differentiated regarding the individual perspective leading to an understanding of the subjectivity of newness. "An innovation is the adoption of a change which is new to an organization and to the relevant environment."[126] From a subjective perspective the individual perception of newness may determine the intensity of innovativeness. With regard to the resource-based perspective of a firm, this implies that, due to subjectivity, a corporation might be innovative by applying new models such as technologies or processes to its current operations regardless of market standards or competitive behavior. From a market-based perspective this entails that a global market innovation can be considered objectively new, whereas national or regional market innovations can be a matter of subjectivity with reference to the market entry of non-national or non-regional corporations providing a new commodity to the corresponding market.[127] Bringing the matter down to the individual: "if the idea seems new to the individual, it is an innovation."[128]

---

121 Kline/Rosenberg 1986, p. 283.
122 See Schumpeter 1996, p. 81-87.
123 See Utterback 1996, p. xvii.
124 For an overview of dimensions of innovation, see e.g. Doepfer 2008, pp. 19-20.
125 See Moore/Tushman 1982, p. 132.
126 Knight 1967, p. 478.
127 See Johne 1999, p. 7.
128 Rogers 2003, p. 12.

Definition of Innovation	Character	Author
"An innovation is any thought, behaviour or thing that is new because it is qualitatively different from existing forms."	Newness	Barnett 1953, p. 7
"We consider as an innovation any idea, practice, or material artefact perceived to be new by the relevant unit of adoption. The adopting unit can vary from a single individual to a business firm, a city, or a state legislature."	Newness	Zaltman/Duncan/Holbe 1973, p. 10
"Most generally, innovation can be seen as the synthesis of a market need with the means to achieve and produce a product to meet that need."	Outcome	Moore/Tushman 1982, p. 132
"Innovation is an idea, practice or object that is perceived as new by an individual or other unit of adoption. It matters little, so far as human behaviour is concerned, whether or not an idea is objectively new. [...] The perceived units of the idea for the individual determines his or her reaction to it. If the idea seems new to the individual, it is an innovation."	Newness	Rogers 1983, p. 11
"Innovation is a process whereby new ideas are out into practice."	Newness/ Outcome	Rickards 1985, p. 10
"Innovation = invention + exploitation. The invention process covers all efforts aimed at creating new ideas and getting them to work. The exploitation process includes all stages of commercial development, application, and transfer, including the focussing of ideas or inventions towards specific objectives, evaluating those objectives, downstream transfer of research and/or development results, and the eventual broadbased utilization, dissemination, and diffusion of the technology-based outcomes."	Newness/ Outcome	Roberts 1987, p. 3
"Innovation is defined as adoption of an internally generated or purchased device, system, policy, program, process, product or service that is new to the adopting organization."	Newness/ Outcome	Damanpour 1991, p. 556

Table 2: Defining innovation

Despite the controversy regarding the subjectivity of the perception of newness, the out-come of innovation as an object of innovation offers a second dimension of analysis. "Innovation should be seen in the Schumpeterian sense as any change (however incremental) to products, processes or organizational forms, and is to be understood in terms of systems."[129] As stated, innovation may result in a variety of forms reaching beyond a product perspective as in Moore/Tushman (1982, p. 132), which considers process innovations[130] as well as services innovations[131] and organizational, structural or systemic innovations.[132] Aligned with the perspective of innovation as an outcome of a process (from idea generation to organizational adoption[133] and market diffusion[134]) two characteristics of innova-

---

129 Bunell/Coe 2001, p. 570. Also see Cooke/Uranga/Etxebarria 1998, p. 1564.
130 See Utterback 1996, p. 167.
131 See Scheuing/Johnson 1989; Sundbo 1997; Gallouj/Weinstein 1997; Hipp/Hariolf 2005.
132 See Damanpour 1991, p. 556; Bunell/Coe 2001, p. 570; Bergfeld 2009, p. 10.
133 See Rickards 1985, p. 10; Zaltman/Duncan/Holbe 1973, p. 10. The idea generation phase is also refered to as the invention process, emphasizing the relevance of idea implementation rather than the genera-tion (Roberts 1987, p. 3).
134 See Utterback 1996.

tion intensity can be identified representing a third dimension of analysis. As indicated, innovations may be of radical or incremental nature: Incremental innovations refer to an extension or modification of existing models; radical innovations, on the other hand, are also termed 'discontinuous' or breakthrough innovations arising "from tabula rasa to commercial success."[135] Consequently, incremental innovations can be seen as triggers of continuous improvement, increasing the efficiency of the resources used and the systems applied. Radical innovations, on the other hand, aim for higher effectiveness based on revolutionary changes creating a substantial benefit for the customer and the development of new competencies for the corporation.

2.1.2.2 Innovation Competence

To determine the innovation competence of a corporation, main formative components need to be identified. According to Bergfeld (2009, p. 13-16) innovation competence is based on the combination and configuration of innovation capabilities and innovation resources. The present technological base of a corporation represents the resource-based component of innovation competence. This is based primarily on explicit knowledge representing technology in a codified manner as in patents and specific operating skills. These skills are embodied in human resources in the form of detailed capabilities to employ technological knowledge as in the utilization of industrial machinery. Capabilities in this work are defined as a "repeatable pattern of action in the use of assets to create, produce, and/or offer products to the market"[136] and in this context can be understood as rather explicit and therefore 'lower-order capabilities.' Also with reference to these essentials, a functionality profile representing the range of services as well as performance levels offered need to be mentioned and the technological recipes to characterize innovation resources.[137] Technological recipes are defined as "the particular choice and combination of technologies, design practices, configurations of subsystems, etc., which actually deliver the performance... in brief, the 'signature' of the specific skills and knowledge deployed."[138]

The described attributes of innovation resources illustrate the strong connection of these components to implicit forms of knowledge. The technological recipes may be formalized and considered as tacit resources, whereas especially in dynamic conditions the

---

135 Brazeal/Herbert 1999, p. 38. As an empirical example for a radical innovation the authors present the case of 3M's Post-It Notes. The results of a failed adhesive development within their core industrial market, the technology was applied to the market of office supplies creating a breakthrough innovation.
136 See Sanchez/Heene/Thomas 1996, p. 7.
137 See Coombs 1996, pp. 351-352.
138 See Coombs 1996, p. 352.

configuration of assets to achieve corporate performance may require implicit knowledge and capabilities. Therefore, these explicit technologies require a combined application with innovation capabilities to initiate new technology life cycles,[139] and to enable continuous innovation performance.

Contrary to the described characteristics of innovation resources, innovation capabilities relate to rather implicit and tacit elements. These capabilities are dedicated to corporate management and leadership in order to coordinate and configure the prevailing innovation resources and corporate assets to achieve corporate performance. They can therefore be described as 'higher-order capabilities.'[140] "To be strategic, a capability must be honed to a user need (so that there are customers), unique (so that the products/services can be priced without too much regard for the competition), and difficult to replicate (so that profits will not be competed away)."[141] Innovation capabilities, consequently, are based on specific tacit knowledge and market expertise as well as innovation skills. On the one hand, tacit knowledge is described by its embeddedness within the human mind and is connected to an action or involvement within a specific context, which makes it difficult to formalize.[142] The relevance of implicit knowledge as a decisive component of innovation competence emphasizes the social dimension of the construct requiring inter-personal communication for knowledge transfer.[143] On the other hand, innovation skills relate to corporate values and the managerial system promoting innovation performance.[144] A decisive skill in this context is creativity, which can be understood as "the ability to flexibly produce work that is novel (i.e., original and unexpected), high in quality, and useful."[145] Due to market dynamics innovation capabilities require a dynamic component to be capable of reacting to market changes and integrating state-of-the-art external knowledge into corporate processes as well as organically generating future innovation projects. "The term 'dynamic' refers to the capacity to renew competences so as to achieve congruence with the changing business environment."[146]

This understanding of innovation competence in the form of a combined perspective of innovation resources and innovation capabilities emphasizes the relevance of integrating market knowledge and external sources into the innovation process leading to an interactive approach of co-innovation competence. This work aims to contribute to this consider-

---

139   See Bergfeld 2009, p. 14.
140   See Collis 1994, p. 144; Grant 1996, pp. 377-378.
141   Teece/Pisano 1994, p. 539.
142   See Nonaka 1994, p. 16.
143   See Foray 2006, pp. 81-82.
144   See Bergfeld 2009, p. 13.
145   Sternberg/Pretz/Kaufman 2003, p. 158.
146   Teece/Pisano/Shuen 1997, p. 515. For a grounding discussion of the competence-based view of the firm, see Chapter 3.2.1.

ation. To enable a sound discussion, in the following sections a review of corresponding literature will be elaborated, starting off with an overview of the open innovation concept as a basis for understanding inter-organizational value creation, respectively, co-innovation.[147]

2.2 Open Innovation

2.2.2 The Evolution and Conceptual Framework of Open Innovation

2.2.2.1 The Evolution of Open Innovation

Various modes of inter-corporate transactions are known and have been analyzed within strategic management literature.[148] The aspect of co-operation for innovation can be identified as an output-focused approach to inter-organizational co-operation. Whereas in the past corporations focused on building internal R&D capacities and protecting them from outside the boundaries of the firm, corporations have turned away from this perspective and opened up their innovation processes to integrate external sources of innovation within various stages of their innovation process.[149] Triggered by the increasing competitive intensity on global markets, corporations face the challenge of shortened innovation cycles, limited resources and a demand for complex innovations, all of which require a more interactive approach to innovation.[150] Consequently a shift can be identified emerging from a closed innovation perspective which is based on a controlled process from internal idea exploration to commercialization,[151] to an open interactive innovation process.[152] The open innovation paradigm illustrates this shift of perspectives on corporate innovation from an internal process to an inter-organizational collaborate activity and can be described as „the use of purposive inflows and outflows of knowledge to accelerate internal innovation, and expand the markets for external use of innovation, respectively."[153]

When researching the concept form an evolutionary perspective in strategic management literature one discovers that researchers have been well aware of open inter-

---

147 See Chapter 3.2.2.
148 See e.g. Mizruchi/Schwartz 1992; Zentes/Swoboda/Morschett 2005; Pisano/Verganti 2008.
149 See Gassmann 2006, p. 223.
150 See Franke 2002, p. 1; Gassmann/Enkel 2006, p. 137; Enkel 2009, p. 178; Quinn 2000, p. 13.
151 See Chesbrough 2003a p. 21.; Herzog 2008, p. 19.
152 See Chesbrough 2003a; 2003b; Almirall/Casadesus-Masanell 2010.
153 Chesbrough 2003a, p. 18. The introduction of the terminalogy was based on an analysis of leading US technology corporations such as Xerox, IBM and Intel who have successfully performed open innovation.

organizational innovation processes before the concept of open innovation was published by Chesbrough in 2003, emphasizing the potentials of external knowledge sources.[154] Therefore, the opportunity to source knowledge and technology to identify innovation potentials outside the boundaries of the firm cannot be considered a new phenomenon. The main terminologies elaborated above can be summarized by referring to the concepts of absorptive capacity, outsourcing innovation, innovation networks and co-creation of innovation.[155]

- Absorptive capacity: The term refers to the potentials of exploring and integrating knowledge located outside of corporate boundaries to improve innovation performance and can be defined as "the ability of a firm to recognize the value of new, external information, assimilate it, and apply it to commercial ends."[156] The concept refers to previous research stating that innovation performance relies on the accessibility of complementary assets.[157] Consequently, corporations lacking technological knowledge need to have the capability to identify potential knowledge sources, absorb relevant knowledge, and achieve internal transformation and diffusion due to its application knowledge.[158] Therefore, the ability to recognize and evaluate, assimilate, and commercialize external knowledge has received further attention and became part of the discussion on inter-organizational learning[159] leading to an analysis of sources of inter-organizational competitive advantage as described within the relational view.[160]

Within this context the term 'open company development strategy' was introduced to refer a strategic approach to a transaction-based innovation development focusing on the synergetic combination of individual skills, technologies and competences toward an extended R&D.[161] Similarly from an organizational perspective the integration of resources from outside the firm into the value creation process was described as an 'open system model' of the organization in 1996.[162] Furthermore, the 'open-market innovation' construct was established to refer to contract-based transactions among corpora-

---

154 See e.g. Nelson/Winter 1982; Teece 1986.
155 See also Harryson 2006, pp. 354-360. Harryson 2008 pp. 291-293.
156 Cohen/Levintal 1990, p. 128. For a more detailed discussion of the concept see Chapter 3.2.2.1.
157 See Teece 1986, p.289; Harryson 2006, p. 354.
158 See Lichtenthaler 2006, p. 68; Zahra/George 2002, p. 192.
159 See Lane/Lubatkin 1998, pp. 464-466.
160 See Dyer/Singh 1998. The authors identify four components for the establishment of inter-organization competitive advantage: (1) relation-specific assets, (2) knowledge-sharing routines, (3) complementary assets, (4) effective governance.
161 See Nyström 1990; Pisano 1990; 1991.
162 See Sanchez/Heene 1996 p. 41; 1997 p. 24.

tions such as licensing and joint ventures emphasizing the exchange of knowledge and ideas.[163]

- Outsourcing innovation: Outsourcing relates to the co-operation of economically independent entities and is based on a contractual agreement clarifying reciprocal expectations of the collaboration partners.[164] The outsourcing discussion is guided by a desire to achieve a competitive advantage and to increase corporate performance through efficiency-seeking via cost reduction and increasing effectiveness through competence leveraging.[165] Consequently, the perspective of outsourcing was lead by the strategic decision of 'making' and thus keeping the processes and competences in-house or 'buying' them by sourcing competences and know-how from product and service markets.[166] In cases of strict core competence focus[167] transaction cost theory provides a suitable theoretical framework to analyze outsourcing decision-making based on efficiency criteria.[168] As a systematic literature review shows, outsourcing innovation in this context prior to the concept of open innovation has been a small field of investigation and was primarily limited to the external acquisition of readymade technology.[169] Consequently, outsourcing innovation is not executed in co-operative arrangements but only result from corporate value creation traded between firms. Within this perspective the service provider is the delivering party that executes innovation with reference to late-stage technology integration from external providers within the idea of open innovation.

A collaboration for innovation among institutional actors may arise from a transaction based outsourcing perspective and evolve into a competence-based approach unleashing innovation potential beyond routine R&D activities,[170] "proper outsourcing of entire business processes can speed and amplify major innovative changes."[171] The establishment of organizational processes for an innovation sourcing strategy streamlines the discussion about a more interactive outsourcing for innovation approach.[172] This trend is displayed in outsourcing literature emphasizing the relevance of partnership and rela-

163 See Rigby/Zook 2002, p. 82.
164 See Hollekamp, p. 27.
165 See Quinn 1999; Bengtsson/Haartman/Dabhilkar 2009, 35; Espino-Rodríguez/Padrón-Robaina 2006, p. 52; Quélin/Duhamel 2003, p. 654.
166 See Picot/Hardt 1998, p. 625; Osterloh/Frost 2006, p. 194.
167 See Prahalad/Hamel 1990.
168 See Williamson 1985; 1987; 1999, p. 1098.
169 See for publications up to 2003 concerning outsourcing and innovation: MacPherson 1997; Cant/Jeynes. 1998; Howells 1999; Quinn 2000; Jones 2000; McDermott/Handfield 2000; Howells 2000; Love/Roper 2001; Quinn 2002; Linder/Jarvenpaa/Davenport 2003.
170 See Gooroochurn/Hanley 2007; Weeks/Feeny 2008; Doepfer 2008.
171 Quinn 2000, p. 17.
172 See Linder/Jarvenpaa/Davenport: 2003, p. 46.

tionship building within outsourcing alliances and external collaboration.[173] Consequently, over time, the topic of outsourcing has emerged from being a mere cost perspective to an innovation driven approach of inter-organizational collaboration. Therefore, the literature on outsourcing for innovation has contributed to the discussion of open innovation by elaborating the strategic parameters for integrating external factors on different stages of the innovation process.

- Innovation networks: Building networks to increase corporate performance is a well-known strategy, especially in the context of R&D collaboration.[174] In 1991 Freeman predicted "networking between autonomous firms will grow still more important and will become the normal way of conducting product and process development."[175] Linking this statement to innovation potentials of networks, an increase in patenting, product improvement and new product development, an increase in time-to-market velocity and access to new markets can be identified.[176] Frequently, innovation is caused by a combination of knowledge elements and innovation networks offer an enhancing infrastructure to enable such a combination of knowledge and therefore create a climate of innovation.[177] The concept of innovation networks therefore can be defined as an economic mechanism of innovation activity among independent corporations and institutions based on complex reciprocal and relatively stable social ties in which economic advantages are generated cooperatively and expressed in innovative products and processes.[178]

Networked innovation, with reference to innovation as an output of collaboration, represents the unification of geographically and functionally distributed knowledge sources depending on the organizational capability to share, transfer, and absorb knowledge.[179] This emphasizes, on the one hand, the capacity of the individual network participant to profit from the network and ,on the other hand, the relevance of the network attributes as a source of innovation.[180] Derived from the perspective that the possession of proprietary individual know-how (based on internal knowledge, experience, and skills) represents a competitive advantage,[181] the network requires establish-

---

173 See Mahnke/Özcan 2006; Weeks/Davis 2007; Baloh/Jha/Awazu 2008; Ciappini/Corso/Perego 2008; Sen/MacPherson 2009; Bergfeld/Doepfer 2009; Wallenburg 2009.
174 See e.g. Powel/Koput/Smith-Doerr 1996; Hellström/Malmquist 2000; Ozcan/Eisenhardt 2009.
175 Freeman 1991 p. 499.
176 See Powell et al. 1996; Gemünden et al. 1996; Almeida/Kogut 1999; Baum et al. 2000; Jones 2000, p. 341.
177 See Pittaway et al. 2004.
178 See Duschek 2002, p. 44.
179 See Millar/Demaid/Quintas 1997, p. 399.
180 See Beckman/Haunschild 2002, p. 117.
181 See von Hippel 1987, p. 291.

ing a diverse set of know-how keepers. In the context of the network quality aspect the relevance of know-who was discussed. Know-who is understood as "the ability to acquire, transform and apply that know-how through personal relationships."[182] The relevance of social ties to knowledge keepers returns the discussion of networked innovation to the early concept of outsourcing innovation which has been merging over time. In this context, trust as a critical factor of success among innovation partners has become a decisive component in corporate strategy and therefore represents an important aspect in inter-organizational innovation analysis.[183]

- Co-creation of innovation: A profound body of literature analyzes the role of customers as a source of knowledge within the innovation process.[184] Customer integration into new product or service development processes in the form of lead users was introduced in 1988 by von Hippel emphasizing the potential of reducing market risk in the diffusion of innovations.[185] Even though customer integration into corporate processes is understood among practitioners as a cornerstone to the open innovation construct, co-creation of values with customers was introduced earlier in the field of services management focusing on the aspect of co-creation of experiences.[186] Here it is argued that "informed, networked, empowered, and active consumers are increasingly co-creating value with the firm. The interaction between the firm and the consumer is becoming the locus of value creation and value extraction."[187] Based on this thought researchers claim the identification of innovative ways to co-create value with customers as a decisive aspect in strategic management to create a unique competitive advantage.[188] Concepts such as 'mass customization' derived from this discussion emphasizing the role of the customer as co-designer of mass products[189] have laid the path for elaborating the concept of interactive value creation with customers in context of the open innovation paradigm.[190]

---

182 Harryson 2008, p. 294. Also see Harryson 2000; 2006.
183 See e.g. Zaheer/Ventraman 1995; Nooteboom/Berger/Noorderhaven 1997; Hoecht/Trott 1999; Sydow 2000; Coulter/Coulter 2003.
184 See e.g. von Hippel 1986; 1988; Ulwick 2002; Dolan/Matthews 1993; Murphy/Kumar 1997; Brockhoff 2003.
185 See von Hippel 1988, pp. 96, 106.
186 See Prahalad/Ramaswamy 2004a; 2004b. For a detailed discussion regarding customer integration in services management also see e.g. Bruhn/Stauss 2009.
187 Prahalad/Ramaswamy 2004b, p. 5.
188 See Abraham 2005, pp. 10-11.
189 See Berger et al. 2005, p. 70.
190 See Reichwald/Piller 2006, pp. 105-148.

2.2.2.2 Conceptual Framework of Open Innovation

"The open innovation paradigm can be understood as the antithesis of the traditional vertical integration model where internal research and development activities lead to internally developed products that are then distributed by the firm."[191]

The open innovation paradigm states that corporations can increase their individual innovation potential by opening their boundaries and by interacting with corporate partners within the innovation process "using both internal and external ideas at all stages of new business development."[192] Consequently, understanding the corporate innovation process as a funnel beginning in the research phase and evolving via the development phase to the narrowed commercialization phase[193] its boundaries are interpreted as a permeable membrane enabling a reciprocal exchange of knowledge and technologies.[194] Figure 4 illustrates the open innovation construct visualizing the innovation funnel in the sense of a container of ideas, knowledge and technology. These partially have their origin inside the funnel and are transferred along the innovation process until their diffusion on current markets: This process is referred to as closed innovation.[195] Open innovation, in contrast, on the one hand, includes external sources of knowledge and technology into the innovation funnel, and on the other hand, also submits technology to collaboration partners to enter new markets. These perspectives can be understood as the outside-in and the inside-out process. Furthermore, in the literature a coupled process is introduced describing a combined approach:

- Outside-in process: The process is also referred to as 'inbound open innovation' and can be understood as a process based on the acquisition and exploitation of knowledge and technologies external to the corporate boundaries. Customers, suppliers, competitors, as well as corporations and institutions outside the respective industry sector and research institutions serve as potential carriers of ideas and knowledge which are analyzed for integration into the corporate innovation process.[196] Inbound processes can be understood as the internal processing and exploitation of originally externally located knowledge. The co-operation with external organizations such as universities, lead-users and complementary partners can be seen as a valuable source of impulses for technological development. Empirical studies show that the intensity of external

---

191 Chesbrough 2006, p. 15.
192 Kirschbaum 2005, p. 24.
193 See Bessant/Tidd 2011, p. 390.
194 See Chesbrough 2003a, p. XXV; Elmquist/Fredberg,/Ollila 2009, p. 327; Christensen/Olesen/Kjaer 2005, p. 1534; Sawhney/Prandelli 2000, p. 25.
195 See Chesbrough 2003a p. 21; Herzog 2008, p. 19.
196 See: Gassmann/Enkel 2006, p. 134; Baldegger 2007, p. 67.

knowledge integration varies from industry to industry. However, on an average of the 144 analyzed corporations about 80% utilize their customers as source of knowledge, 60% suppliers and 50% research institutions.[197] As core instruments for external technology integration research projects with external partners, venture investing, IP in-licensing and product in-sourcing are mentioned.[198] This allows for the deviation that the location where new knowledge is created does not necessarily accord to the location where innovations arise.[199] The capacity of a corporation to identify and absorb external knowledge appears to be a decisive aspect for its innovation performance and future competitiveness within the open innovation concept.

- Inside-out process: External commercialization and multiplication of technologies into new markets can be understood as the inside-out process, also referred to as 'outbound open innovation.'[200] This process is aligned to identifying collaboration partners for exploitation of internal knowledge and intellectual property (IP).[201] Compared to closed innovation, outbound open innovation follows the assumption that innovations do not necessarily have to be commercialized at the same location where they are developed. A common method for technology externalization is the foundation of corporate spin-offs in the form of technology start-ups to explore new markets outside the current market portfolio of corporate strategy.[202] Conscious communication of existing knowledge and knowledge gaps to stakeholders may consequently be of strategic nature to enable knowledge spillovers.

- Coupled process: The combination of inbound and outbound open innovation in a collaborative innovation process consisting of idea generation, development and commercialization can be understood as a coupled process. This approach aims at projects of high financial and market risk such as the establishment of new standards or technology designs.[203] The formation of strategic alliances based on complementary partners, joint ventures or the establishment of innovation networks serve as practical applications of the process. A decisive requirement for realizing inter-organizational innovation processes in the context of the coupled process is that, on the one hand, participating entities are capable of absorbing externally supplied knowledge and, on the other hand, are able to externalize internal knowledge to collaboration partners.[204] In most

---

197 See: Enkel 2009, p. 181.
198 A more detail discussion of open innovation instruments is given in Chapter 2.2.2.1.
199 See Gassmann/Enkel 2006, p. 134.
200 See Lichtenthaler 2009, p. 317.
201 See Enkel 2009, p. 182; Baldegger 2007, p. 67; Gassmann/Enkel 2006, p. 135.
202 See Enkel 2009, p. 182.
203 See Baldegger 2007, p. 67.
204 See Gassmann/Enkel 2006, p. 136.

cases the collaboration of the industrial partners requires a setting that is not directly related to the core competencies of the partners but meets a common goal such as the establishment of new industrial standards.[205]

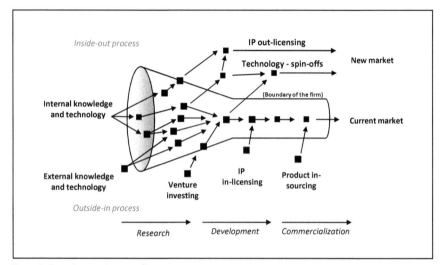

Figure 4: Open innovation paradigm
Source: Based on Chesbrough 2003a, pp. 183, 189; Mortara et al. 2009, p. 12; Gassmann/Enkel 2006, p. 134.

2.2.3 Instruments and Determinants of Open Innovation

2.2.3.1 Open Innovation Instruments

Open innovation can appear in different forms with reference to a set of several instruments.[206] Two main directions of knowledge and technology flows can be identified to

---

205 The intent to set new standards in retail and fast-moving consumer goods industry by a collaborative development of radio frequency identification (RFID) technologies by the strategic alliance of the corporations Henkel, Unilever and Metro serves as empirical example. Furthermore, pdb - Partnership for Dummy Technology and Biomechanics is another example from the automotive industry. pdb represents an alliance of German automotive manufacturers collaborating in the field of dummy technologies, biomechanics and simulation, which represents a neutral competitive area for the collaboration partners. The management of pdb coordinates this alliance and is consequently in charge of setting the basis for realizing high standards of passive passenger protection (See e.g. Gehre 2010; Scherer et al 2009; Bortenschlager et al. 2010).
206 See Figure 4.

systemize the scope of entrepreneurial opportunities within the open innovation construct. Technology exploitation requires instruments enhancing the ability to profit from internal knowledge resources such as out-licensing of IP or creating new ventures by spinning off technologies and venture teams.[207] Technology exploration instead focuses on the acquisition and utilization of external knowledge sources which refers to the in-sourcing of products and IP, and inter-organizational alliances for innovation based on collaborative R&D.[208] The set of open innovation instruments is constantly developing and corporations strive to identify new opportunities to integrate and exchange knowledge with external partners. Empirical studies show that corporations primarily refer to their customers before engaging in inter-corporate innovation mechanisms.[209] This means that open innovation instruments require an expertise and management skills to enable a mutual success of inter-corporate collaboration. To gain a deeper understanding of the mechanisms of open innovation, primarily technology spin-offs and the licensing of IP are discussed before drawing on technology in-sourcing and venture investing, and collaboration for innovation.

- Technology spin-offs: Venturing is defined as the process of starting up a new organizational entity based on internal knowledge which is transferred into a newly formed organization. The result of this process is mostly referred to as a corporate spin-off that can be enhanced by an additional transfer of financial as well as human resources.[210] Its reasoning is based on a strategic choice between leveraging internal competences to enter new markets or focusing on core competences and streamlining corporate development. Spinning off corporate ventures allows the initializing organization to reduce financial risk by integrating external investors and overcome potential misfits of the venture with corporate goals.[211] In this context, to have a share of a successful new venture is more profitable than owning an entire failed venture. Furthermore, as an advantage of corporate spin-offs an organic strong tie network creation can emerge in which knowledge flows among externalized and internal employees remain, whereas financial transactions are based on performance and value creation.[212]

- IP licensing: Licensing technologies in the form of IP rights such as patents enable the commercialization of specific technologies or knowledge by charging a license fee de-

---

207 See Chesbrough 2003a, pp. 135-176.
208 See van de Vrande/Vanhaverbeke/Duysters 2009, p. 427.
209 See van de Vrande/Vanhaverbeke/Duysters 2009, p. 435.
210 See van de Vrande et al. 2009, p. 428.
211 See Chesbrough/Garman 2009, p. 71.
212 Chesbrough/Garman (2009, p. 70) refer to Eli Lilly as an empirical example creating the online plattform InnoCentive.com as a spin-off from the project 'Bounty Chem.' Eli Lilly was the first customer to pay only for services required and sharing costs and risks of the project with customers and outside investors.

termined in a licensing contract.[213] Therefore a commercialization environment is required for protecting IP and offers the opportunity of a market setting to trade effectively ideas and technologies. "Commercializing through the market for ideas confers several benefits, allowing buyers and sellers of technology to soften downstream product market competition, avoid duplicative investment, and engage in complementary technology development."[214] Establishing a strategic management of IP, therefore, can be considered highly relevant to economically exploiting internal IP. Managing IP is connected to the identification of branches able to profit from established technologies in the given branch leading to comprehensive innovations and a multiplication of technologies.[215] Due to high dynamics and short innovation cycles in information technology (IT) markets, processor chips can be outdated quickly but deployed successfully to markets of lower IT intensity and longer product life cycles such as automotive industry, enabling a profitable technology transfer.[216] This example shows that the technology leverage to multiple branches opens up new sales markets for IP out-licensing corporations. Furthermore, in the case of technologies beyond corporate core markets corporations can save development costs and minimize development risk.[217] IP in-licensing in contrast, as in the automotive industry, enables the reduction of R&D costs while applying state of the art technologies to the product portfolio. In this case not only corporate partners but also public and private research institutions and universities can serve as suppliers of licenses.[218]

- Insourcing and venture investing: The mere acquisition of technologies transfers ownership rights of established products and services to the in-sourcing company. These are slightly modified and adapted for commercialization in existing market channels. This particular form of external technology sourcing is characterized by low transaction costs due to low market risk and instant diffusion, but it underlies a high negotiation power of the supplying corporation.[219] Conceptually the discussion meets the construct of innovation outsourcing within a provider-recipient framework.[220] Venture investing, in contrast can be understood as a strategic investment of a corporation by funding

213 For a detailed discussion on structuring licensing contracts see e.g. Lerner/Mergers 1998; Anand/Khanna 2000; Sarcho 2002.
214 Gans/Stern 2003, p. 337.
215 See Dahlander/Gann 2010, p. 704.
216 See Gassmann/Enkel 2006, p. 136.
217 Enkel (2009, p. 182) in an empirical example refers to, on the one hand, the pharmaceutical industry, in which substances such as Botox, Viagra and Erythropoitin have been leveraged in further application areas, on the other hand, as well as to IBM realizing additional profits of two billion $ via IP management.
218 See van de Vrande et al. 2009, pp. 424, 428.
219 See Chesbrough 2003, p. 183.
220 See Chapter 2.2.2.1.

start-up organizations. These investments can be paired, on the one hand, with pure fi-nancial strategies in the sense of venture capital investments and may follow, on the other hand, a relationship-based approach thriving for inter-organizational learning and competence development.[221] The engagement with young corporations may also be crucial to future radical innovation performance by creating an access to future busi-ness areas.[222]

- Collaboration for innovation: Systematizing the forms of inter-corporate collaboration enables a differentiated view of an analysis of collaboration for innovation. Three main categories of integrating external partners into the value creation process can be identi-fied: vertical, horizontal and branch integration.[223] Figure 5 illustrates these dimensions linked to specific potentials of open innovation along the value chain. Co-operation on a vertical scale refers to the customers and suppliers of the focal corporation which in this case is referred to as the original equipment manufacturer (OEM). The collabora-tion with customers can be applied using the customer as a source of innovative ideas and co-creator of innovation (1).[224] Depending on the industry structure, corporations might be operating in business to business (B2B) relations not directly linked to the end customer. In these cases interaction with the end customer can lead to valuable infor-mation regarding product modification and development (2). Based on the idea of 'wis-dom of the crowds'[225] latest research in this field shows that corporations can initiate innovation competitions among customers either for generating input in early stages of innovation processes or create new ideas for product development or problem-solving.[226] For customers despite being in contact with these innovative companies, in-centives to participate in such competitions arise from awards and prize money.[227] From this development arose the concept of crowdsourcing, introduced to discuss the potential of a broad range of customer knowledge for corporate innovation via digital channels.[228]

---

221 See Chesbrough 2003, p. 184; Zahra/Nielsen/Bogner 1999, p. 169.
222 Fueglistaller et al. (2008, pp. 219-224) elaborate the case of BASF corporate venturing activity. The role of the subsidiaries BASF Future Business and BASF Ventrue Capital is illustrated as striving for the estab-lishment of new technologies in new markets.
223 See Bea/Dichtl/Schweitzer 2000, pp. 391-396; Vahs/Schäfer-Kunz 2007, p. 123.
224 See for co-creation with customers e.g. von Hippel 1986; 1988; Ulwick 2002; Prahalad/Ramaswamy 2004a; 2004b.
225 See Surowiecki 2005.
226 See Reichwald/Piller 2009, p. 179; Terwiesch/Ulrich 2009; Piller/Walcher 2006.
227 For empirical examples see e.g. 'EconBiz Challenge: Ideas for Tomorrow's Economists' and IBM 'Innova-tionJam,' which generated 46.000 posts from worldwide clients and partners discussing the combination of new technologies to create market opportunities in 2006 (Østergaard 2008, p. 7).
228 See Howe 2006; Leimeister et al. 2009.

Collaboration with suppliers represents a rather traditional form of inter-corporate collaboration for innovation. On a transactional level, the OEM interacts primarily with its first-tier suppliers (3). In this case reciprocal proposals for innovation projects are elaborated and processed among the partners. Regularly, the first-tier supplier controls the complexity of coordinating competencies of second-tier suppliers and integrates these indirectly into the value creation process. In the case of technology scouting OEMs can identify trends of future business by opening up to second-tier technology corporations, facilitating the flow of information and ideas on the vertical scale (4).[229]

On a horizontal level, international corporations can profit from intra-organizational knowledge transfer by exploiting the broad scope of corporate boundaries (5).[230] Furthermore, the collaboration with competitors offers significant opportunities for inter-organizational innovation (6). Even though strategic alliances among competitors face severe challenges regarding the interaction and sharing of knowledge, they enable the realization of intense economies of scale by increasing volume intensities and economies of scope due to the access to complementary resources, capabilities and competencies, and inter-organizational learning.[231] The term 'co-opetition' has been mentioned in this context.[232] Knowledge and technology transfer between corporations of diverse braches and industries may increase innovation performance by reducing R&D costs and innovation risks if collaborating partners can equally profit from the innovation project. Such innovation-driven conglomerate collaborations (7) are rather difficult to establish concerning collaborative R&D since most technologies require branch-specific applications. In turn, as pointed out in the context of IP licensing corporations can optimize profitability of internal knowledge by commercializing IP to different branches.[233]

In addition to vertical, horizontal and branch integration, cooperation with universities and research institutes should be mentioned as a valuable source of external knowledge and innovation for corporations (8). University research can offer insight into technology trends and future development and enable early recognition of collaborating companies. The role of universities as knowledge-generating institutions receives

229 See Brenner 1996; Rohrbeck 2010, p. 171. For empirical evidence see e.g. Audi Electronics Venture GmbH, which operates as a subsidiary of AUDI AG and collaborates with technology corporations to start new ventures in specific fields of future business (see e.g. Reichelt 2008).
230 See e.g. Bergfeld 2009; Boutellier/Gassmann/ von Zedtwitz 2008; Türck 1998, pp. 221-224; Gerybadze 1998.
231 See Hamel/Doz/Prahalad 1989; Hamel 1991; Doz 1996a. Empirically, Star Alliance serves as a suitable example representing the alliance of 19 airline corporations and enabling a highly efficient worldwide network of aviation services (Kutschker/Schmid 2008, pp. 895-900).
232 See e.g. Nalebuff/Brandenburger 1997; Loebecke/van Fenema/Powell 1999.
233 See Chapter 2.2.3.1.

special attention in the discussion of regional innovation systems with reference to the triple helix of university-industry-government networks.[234] In this context, corporations profit from scientific research due to local knowledge spillovers.[235] Furthermore, the relevance of consultants and private research institutions as sources of knowledge on innovation within co-operative arrangements or informal sources of innovation should be mentioned.[236]

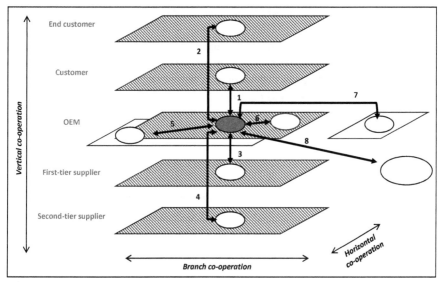

Figure 5: Potentials of open innovation along the value chain
Source: Based on Enkel 2009, p. 184.

2.2.3.2 Determinants of Open Innovation

Open innovation offers a high potential for corporations to realize competitive advantage by increasing the efficiency as well as the effectiveness of the innovation process. The different forms of open innovation practices may be found in the three types of innovators involved in an open innovation setting. These either innovate entirely from the inside 'core

---

234 See e.g. Etzkowitz 2002; Etzkowitz/Klofsten 2000; Cooke 2004; 2005. See for a detailed discussion Chapter 2.3.2.
235 See Franke 2002; Acs 2009; Audretsch/Aldrige 2009. Enkel/Gassmann/Chesbrough (2009, p. 313) show from an empirical study that 61% of the analyzed corporations collaborate with local universities.
236 See Tether/Tajar, 2008, p. 1079.

inside innovators,' innovate from the peripheral inside as 'peripheral inside innovators' or from the outside as 'outside innovators.'[237] In this context it should be mentioned that the potentials of open innovation cannot be equally transferred to all branches and industries alike. This may, on the one hand, be due to industry-specific clockspeed and, on the other hand, due to the degree of secrecy found in technology. Corporations operating in low-clockspeed industries such as primary industry products face less dynamic markets and therefore show less necessity for open innovation activity. Defense and atomic industries, for example represent fields in which the confidentiality and secrecy of technology take high relevance.

Consequently, the implementation of an open inter-organizational exchange of know-ledge flows is extremely limited.[238] These corporations, therefore, can be considered as core inside innovators focusing their innovation activity on internal R&D (closed Innova-tion). Peripheral inside innovators broaden their innovation scope to an intra-open innova-tion concept. In this case employees of the entire organization are asked to contribute to the innovation process by providing information drawn from experience and personal ide-as. In contrast to inside innovators, outside innovators integrate actors from outside the boundaries of the firm such as universities, research institutions, customers, suppliers and further stakeholders along the value chain. These innovators perform open innovation to achieve an inter-organizational exchange of knowledge and collaborative innovation.[239]

Collaborative innovation, as such, is certainly not the goal of open innovation instead of profiting from external knowledge and competences to increase effectiveness and effi-ciency of corporate innovation performance and consequently achieving a competitive advantage. Specifically, improving fit-to-market by meeting market demand and by inten-sifying the new-to-market effect emerging from highly perceived product attractiveness will increase innovation effectiveness due to an advanced access to demand information. Speeding up time-to-market by shortening the innovation process and cutting cost-to-market due to lower R&D costs will increase the efficiency of innovation projects caused by an improved access to available technologies.[240] Despite these opportunities for com-petitive advantage, further chances for profiting from the integration of external

---

237   See Möslein/Bansemir 2011, pp. 14-16.
238   See Gassmann 2006, 224, Enkel 2009, p. 183.
239   In the open innovation literature several examples of successful open innovation practices may be found. Enkel (2009, pp. 179-180) refers to IBM and its worldwide online brainstorming campaign in 2006, generating 46.000 new ideas. Furthermore the 'connect & development' strategy of Proctor & Gamble, the network of external inventors of Henkel, network initiatives by Bayer Material Science and continous creativity workshops by BASF are mentioned.
240   See Reichwald/Piller 2009, pp. 172-177. Mortara et al. (2009, p. 14) note in an empirical study that the reduction of time-to-market and access to additional competences and new ideas are the most realized competitive advantages due to open innovation.

knowledge can be identified in the literature. The reduction of R&D costs due to the realization of synergies reduces R&D capital intensity and therefore lowers innovation risk.[241] The accessibility of a broader basis of ideas increases corporate innovation potential by utilizing external knowledge to establish new business models,[242] "the best way to have a good idea is to have lots of ideas."[243] Furthermore, regarding internal innovation capability, the interaction with external partners broadens the view and prevents behavior blinded by routine, which may also influence corporate culture toward an open and dynamic climate for idea generation.[244] By collaborating with universities despite a technology transfer, also qualified employees may be transferred who integrate specific knowledge and competences into corporate boundaries.[245]

In contrast to these chances, the implementation of open innovation also bears strategic risks. The management of open innovation projects requires time and effort to cope with the complexity of the project caused by its multi-disciplinary and multi-institutional composition.[246] Since innovations show a failure rate of 25% to 40% on industrial goods markets and up to 60% on consumer markets, innovation costs may be reduced due to synergy effects but remain a sword of Damocles.[247] Opportunity costs arise for project members on the one hand due to individual investments into the project and on the other hand because of reciprocal dependencies creating a lock-in effect.[248] These perceived costs are influenced by the intensity of information and technology flows among the cooperating organizations causing a concern that knowledge spillovers in the form of unintended flows of knowledge may take place.[249] "Openness and free exchange of information, however, make companies more vulnerable to risks of information leakage."[250] Consequently, open innovation projects bear incentives for opportunistic behavior among the partners realizing free-rider profits by accessing and exploiting the common knowledge base without comparatively contributing.[251]

Innovation barriers in open innovation projects can also occur due to deficits in individual innovation capabilities. A collaborating corporation might "believe it possesses a monopoly of knowledge of its field, which leads it to reject new ideas from outsiders to the

---

241 See Gassmann 2006, p. 224; Rammer et al. 2005, p. 265.
242 See Ili/Albers/Miller 2010, p. 285.
243 Chesbrough 2006a, p. 2.
244 See Brockhoff 1994, p. 113; Ili/Albers/Miller 2010, p. 292; Chesbrough 2006b, pp. 33-34.
245 See Rammer et al. 2005, p. 88.
246 See Dahlander/Gann 2010, p. 706.
247 See Lüthje 2007, p. 41; Enkel, 2009, p. 187.
248 See Arthur 1989.
249 See Nooteboom 2000, p. 922.
250 Hoecht/Trott 1999, p. 258.
251 See van de Vrande et al. 2009, p. 428.

likely detriment of its performance,"[252] which defines the 'not invented here (NIH) syn-drome'. On the other hand, a 'not sold here syndrome' can be identified with reference to negative attitudes of employees toward the external commercialization of technology,[253] "if we don't sell the technology, no one should."[254] Furthermore, corporations lacking the capability to absorb external knowledge may decrease the innovation performance of the entire project.[255] The differentiating perspectives toward open innovation show that the integration of external knowledge sources offers corporations many opportunities to op-timize innovation performance. On the other hand an open exchange of firm-specific knowledge and technology with partnering corporations and institutions comes with an organizational risk. Consequently, the application and implementation of open innovation within corporate innovation activities requires a firm-specific approach and a structuring of management processes according to an individualized open innovation strategy.[256]

2.2.4 Structural Levels of Open Innovation and Inter-Organizational Networks

Open Innovation has primarily been researched on an organizational level analyzing the inflows and outflows of knowledge and technology of a focal corporation.[257] Further struc-tural levels of the concept can be identified within an inter-organizational network analysis ranging from an individual perspective to a national system level (see Figure 6). Individuals such as entrepreneurs, managers or employees may be involved in informal intra-organizational networks; also individual relations may reach beyond corporate boundaries and be embedded in inter-organizational networks.[258] Individual behavior, consequently, can be considered a highly relevant factor for the establishment of inter-organizational relations and the effectiveness of collaborative innovation performance.[259] From the or-ganizational level, bilateral relations between organizations can be analyzed on a dyad level with regard to the transaction processes between organizations. Conditions for inter-corporate collaboration between firms have been analyzed in past research, setting a foundation for more complex topologies. Evolving from economic analysis and the elabo-ration of concepts such as the principal-agent problem and game-theoretic prisoners' di-

---

252 Katz/Allen 1982, p. 7. Also see Lichtenthaler/Ernst (2006, pp. 370-371) for an overview of main empirical studies of the NIH syndrome.
253 See van de Vrande et al. 2009, p. 427; Lichtenthaler/Ernst 2006, pp. 375-379; Herzog 2008, p. 107.
254 Chesbrough 2003a, p. 186.
255 See Di Gangi/Wasko 2009, p. 307. Also see Chapter 2.2.2.1. for an introduction to the concept of ab-sorptive capacity.
256 See Chiaroni/Chiesa/Frattini 2010, p. 224; Enkel 2009, p. 189.
257 See Chesbrough 2003, p. 18.
258 See Vanhaverbeke 2006, p. 207; Harryson 2006; 2008.
259 See Enkel 2010.

lemma,[260] management research has discussed forms and mechanisms to overcome opportunism and elaborate conditions for the establishment of trust among collaboration partners.[261]

Complexity of analysis	• Individuals (intra- & inter organizational)
	• Corporations / organizations
	• Dyads
	• Inter-organizational networks
	• Regional innovation systems
	• National innovation systems

Figure 6: Analytical levels of open innovation
Source: Based on Vanhaverbeke/Cloodt 2006, p. 276.

Focusing on the procedures of an interactive innovation development among a set of collaboration partners, inter-organizational networks represent a more complex field of analysis that also can be applied to regional and national geographic structures.[262] The following subsections focus on the analytical level of inter-organizational networks and review the applicable concepts 'open innovation networks' and 'open innovation communities' before drawing on a regional analysis of open innovation within the forthcoming procedures of this work.

2.2.4.1 Open Innovation Networks

"The grand purpose of networking is to mobilize limited resources and strengthen the participating firms. Partners are now much more open and prepared for joint innovation, such that the network setting can be considered a natural arena for open innovation."[263]

Networks represent an organizational structure aiming at the realization of competitive advantages based on complex reciprocal and relatively stable relations among the participating actors.[264] Compared to bilateral cooperation, networks represent a constellation of

---

260 See for principal-agent problem e.g. Grossman/Hart 1983. For a prisoners' dilemma analysis, see e.g. Neyman 1985; Kreps et al. 1982.
261 See Nooteboom 1996; Hoecht/Trott 1999; Coulter/Coulter 2003; Sydow 2000.
262 See Vanhaverbeke/Cloodt 2006, p. 276.
263 Wincent/Anokhin/Boter 2009, p. 57.
264 See Sydow 1992, p. 79.

actors drawing on their resources and capabilities in which the sum of all direct and indirect relations enable a broader range of possible courses of action compared to single direct relations.[265] The establishment of networks represents a well-known strategy to improve corporate performance, specifically in the field of R&D.[266] Antecedents to this trend can be identified in early works predicting "networking between autonomous firms will grow still more important and will become the normal way of conducting product and process development."[267] Connecting this statement to the potentials of innovation in networks, an increase in patenting, product improvement, new product development, time-to-market velocity, and access to new markets are derived.[268] Networks offer the infrastructure to enable an exchange of information encouraging the combination of knowledge and therefore stimulating innovation.[269] Networks specifically oriented at the inter-organization realization of innovations may be referred to as 'innovation networks.' These can be defined as an economic mechanism of innovation activity among independent corporations based on complex-reciprocal and relatively stable social ties in which cooperatively economic advantages are generated, as expressed by innovative products and processes.[270]

The transfer of resources, inter-organizational relations and networking are crucial dimensions to enabling open innovation - even though they are rather implicitly present in the open innovation framework.[271] Consequently, the connection to knowledge-intensive organizations within a knowledge-based ecosystem context,[272] which contains widely spread knowledge and expertise, creates the opportunity for linked-in corporations to exploit the network within an outside-in and inside-out perspective.[273] A corporation might quickly close resource and competence gaps and integrate ideas by addressing the network without relying on internal R&D or vertical integration. Furthermore, such network structures may enhance opportunities for external technology commercialization such as joint-ventures, spin-offs, corporate venture investments and start-ups, all of which offer an attractive playground for entrepreneurial activity.[274] Therefore, a corporate involvement in innovation networks allows for the exploration of new business models by experimenting with new alternatives or the exploitation of the network's portfolio of re-

---

265 See Kutschker 1994, pp. 128-129; Kutschker 2005, p. 1131.
266 See e.g. Ozcan/Eisenhardt 2009; Powel, Koput/Smith-Doerr 1996; Hellström/Malmquist 2000.
267 Freeman 1991 p. 499.
268 See Powell et al. 1996; Gemünden et al. 1996; Almeida/Kogut 1999; Baum/Calabrese/Silverman 2000.
269 See Pittaway et al. 2004.
270 See Duschek 2002, p. 44.
271 See Chesbrough 2004, p. 25; Vanhaverbeke 2006, p. 210. Also see Chapter 2.2.1.2.
272 See e.g. van der Borgh/Cloodt/Romme 2012, pp. 151-152; Kirsch/Seidl/van Aaken 2010.
273 See Simard/West. 2006, pp. 231-232.
274 See Lichtenthaler 2006, p. 164; Simard/West 2006, p. 223.

sources and competences.[275] When approaching networks for exploitation a rather homogeneous share of expertise and technological knowledge is required for collaboratively developing new solutions. An exploration procedure, however, requires a heterogeneous share of knowledge among the partners to enable the identification of new projects.[276] The composition of the network consequently represents a decisive aspect of the network's innovation capacity.

Differentiating innovation networks from open innovation networks, the current discussion points out that the given innovation potentials of innovation networks are intensified in the era of open innovation.[277] Therefore, the spread of the concept can cause further advantages for existing innovation networks that did not utilize their entire scale of open innovation potential and rather concentrated on singular aspects such as upstream technology development.[278] As long as the networking corporations focus on utilizing internal resources for new product and service development as well as commercialization, they remain in a closed innovation context.[279] Open Innovation networks in comparison are not limited to upstream activities and include each aspect of the innovation process. Consequently, open innovation networks refer to "all activities to acquire and maintain connections with external sources of social capital to achieve innovation."[280]

A systematic literature review allows a more specific analysis of the concept of open innovation networks.[281] The analysis shows that the topic is discussed within a rather recent and evolving literature body (see Table 3). The contributions identified draw on a differentiated analysis of open innovation networks' dimensions (1), coordination of (2) and behavior in open innovation networks (3), and geographic parameters (4). Furthermore, related concepts are identified which are discussed in the following section with reference to the innovation community construct.

---

275 See March 1991, p. 85.
276 See Chesbrough/Prencipe 2008, p. 417; Harryson 2008, p. 297.
277 See Enkel 2010, p. 345; Lee et al. 2010.
278 See Vanhaverbeke/Cloodt 2006, p. 279.
279 See Vanhaverbeke 2006, p. 208.
280 de Jong et al. 2009, p. 425.
281 The databases EBSCO Host and Google Scholar were scanned for publications containing the terms 'open innovation' and 'network' in the title or abstract. 112 total matches were identified. These were reviewed by the selection criteria: publication in an academic journal, academic book or academic book chapter. A further selection process excluded contributions in the field of open source communities refering to West/Gallagher (2006, pp. 101-102), who identify open source as a specific application of open innovation, which requires a separate analysis.

Author	Year	Title	Source / publishing	Database
Simard/West	2006	Knowledge Networks and the Locus of Innovation	*Oxford University Press*	Google Scholar
Vanhaverbeke/Cloodt	2006	Open Innovation in Value Networks	*Oxford University Press*	Google Scholar
Dittrich/Duysters	2007	Networking as a Means to Strategy Change: The Case of Open Innovation in Mobile Telephony	*Journal of Product Innovation Management*	Ebsco Host
Harryson	2008	Entrepreneurship through relationships – navigating from creativity to commercialisation	*R&D Management*	Ebsco Host
Cardoso et al.	2008	Open Innovation Communities... or should it be "Networks"	*Springer*	Google Scholar
Wincent/Anokhin/Boter	2009	Network board continuity and effectiveness of open innovation in Swedish strategic small-firm networks	*R&D Management*	Ebsco Host
Kang/Kang	2009	How Do Firms Source External Knowledge For Innovation? Analysing Effects Of Different Knowledge Sourcing Methods	*International Journal of Innovation Management*	Ebsco Host
Melese/Lin/Chang/Cohen	2009	Open innovation networks between academia and industry: an imperative for breakthrough therapies	*Nature Medicine*	Ebsco Host
Fichter	2009	Innovation communities: the role of networks of promotors in Open Innovation	*R&D Management*	Ebsco Host
Lee et al.	2010	Open innovation in SMEs - An intermediated network model	*Research Policy*	Ebsco Host
Belussi/Sammarra/Sedita	2010	Learning at the boundaries in an "Open Regional Innovation System": A focus on firms' innovation strategies in the Emilia Romagna life science industry	*Research Policy*	Ebsco Host
Enkel	2010	Attributes required for profiting from open innovation in networks	*International Journal of Technology Management*	Google Scholar

Table 3: Systematic literature review of open innovation networks

- Dimensions of open innovation networks: With reference to network theory, open innovation networks literature draws on network formality, network strength, and net-
  work size to differentiate open innovation network dimensions.

Network formality refers to the intensity of organizational embeddedness of the networking partners. Formal ties represent contractual agreements of participating members and are the precise channels of knowledge transfer among organizations such as
strategic alliances or licensing. These enable the potential to formulate a specific open
innovation strategy structuring inter-organizational transaction processes and
knowledge flows.[282] Formal ties enable the establishment of inter-organizational value
creation based on complementary resources and therefore of realizing synergy effects.
In case of informal networks neither contractual regulations nor specific transactions
exist among organizations; rather, the co-operation is based on a reciprocal awareness
of mutual interests derived from social exchange.[283] Informal networks may result from
individual personal relations of employees, regional settings and communities, or

---

282 See Simard/West 2006, p. 224.
283 See Hakansson/Johansson 2002, p. 374.

membership in unions and can be interpreted as the origin of formal networks.[284] Flexibility in informal networks is consequently very high because the network structure is capable to respond quickly to external influences.[285]

Depending on environmental conditions and the intensity to strive for inter-organizational learning, it is a matter of corporate strategy to build strong or weak relations to network partners.[286] Strong ties are related to a high bonding intensity which mostly refers to reciprocal financial shares supporting the exploitation of a network structure. Weak ties in contrast aim at the exploration of new technological fields with a broad spectrum of network actors.[287] Offering access to a wide field of information sources, weak ties are highly relevant for realizing outside-in open innovation such as collaborative R&D or licensing arrangements.[288] A transfer from weak to strong ties among network partners may result in a shift from an inter-organizational resource exploration to an exploitation perspective.[289] Consequently, forms of inter-organizational linkages within networks are liable to dynamic change processes.

Following a network exploration approach a broad scope of ties to a variety of players within an informal network setting supports an exploration strategy aiming at the identification of new technological fields and business models.[290] Due to the low cost of direct information search and corporate absorptive capacity an involvement in several informal networks consequently creates a broader scope for information transfer increasing the individual potential of innovation performance.[291] An exploitation approach, in comparison, requires deep ties among network partners to enable access to decisive resources and competences and therefore extend the portfolio of core business operations. Hence, network structures based on deep ties may be a source of incremental innovation whereas broad networks have a higher potential to realize radical innovation due to the accessibility of specific knowledge and complementary resources.[292] "Networks are an inherent part of an organizational institutional environment and [...] are

---

284 See Vanhaverbeke 2006, p. 209.
285 See Kang/Kang 2009, p. 5.
286 See Chesbrough/Prencipe 2008, p. 417; Rowley/Behrens/Krackhardt 2000.
287 See Granovetter 1973, p. 1363.
288 See Chesbrough/Prencipe 2008, p. 417; Simard/West 2006, p. 230. Melese et al. (2009) emphasize the relevance of building open innovation networks among research institutions and industrial corporations in healthcare and the life sciences. Technology gaps could be overcome and R&D costs reduced by intensifying inter-organizational collaboration. Open innovation offers a potential for implementing biomedical research results into industrial products and health care services maximizing innovation performance.
289 See Harryson 2008, p. 303.
290 See Vanhaverbeke 2006, p. 209, 229; Kang/Kang 2009, p. 4.
291 See Kang/Kang 2009, p. 12-15.
292 See Vanhaverbeke 2006, p. 209.

key conduits through which knowledge travels from the environment to the firm."[293] Striving for an open innovation strategy corporations are asked to identify a balanced approach to network dimensions enabling exploitation as well as exploration of network resources to achieve inter-organizational innovation and competitive advantages.[294]

- Coordination of open innovation networks: Inter-organizational networks striving for value creation by "linking firms with different assets and competencies together in response to or in anticipation of new market opportunities"[295] require a certain form of coordination. A focal corporation such as an OEM may coordinate the value network aiming at the commercialization of innovation by focusing on downstream activities.[296] Therefore, balancing diverse interests and reducing tension among network partners may be considered crucial to inter-organizational innovation. An open innovation strategy, consequently, requires a network and relationship management considering all value creating and contributing components to realize a competitive advantage in contrast to competing value networks.[297]

Despite a hierarchical approach, for decentral network control network intermediaries and network boards can be identified. Innovation intermediaries are understood as knowledge brokers matching the demand of seekers with the supply of solvers striving for solutions to inter-organizational problems. Brokers increase open innovation efficiency by supplying relevant information and easing communication among network partners.[298] Especially within knowledge-intensive industries innovation intermediaries may stimulate inter-organizational knowledge flows "becoming pivotal facilitators in networks of research and technology co-production,"[299] creating a vital inter-organizational innovation system. Within such a system brokers may lie at the core of the network acting as proxies within an intermediated open innovation network model

293 Simard/West 2006, p. 220.
294 See Simard/West 2006, p. 235; Harryson 2008, p. 297; Vanhaverbeke 2006, p. 209. Dittrich/Duysters (2007) analyze in an empirical study the development of Nokia's innovation network. Evolving from a mere suplier-customer-relationship structure Nokia extended the number of its network partners to move ahead of former technology exploitation strategy toward a balanced model of exploitation and exploration. Building strategic alliances and joint ventures as well as corporate involvement in various innovation networks are consequences of an open innovation strategy causing the establishment of a number of innovations and establishing industry standards.
295 Vanhaverbeke/Cloodt 2006, p. 259.
296 Vanhaverbeke 2006, p. 214; Vanhaverbeke/Cloodt 2006, p. 279.
297 See Vanhaverbeke 2006, pp. 213, 216.
298 See Cardoso/Carvalho/Ramos 2008, pp. 54, 65. Chesbrough (2006c, p. 140-163) empirically examines the innovation intermediaries InnoCentive, NineSigma, Big Idea Group, InnovationXchange, SSIPEX, and Ocean Tomo, providing an overwiev of core fuctions and highlighting the challenges of accessing useful external knowledge.
299 Howells 2006b, p. 76.

(see Figure 7). To improve knowledge exploration and exploitation performance among networking corporations, trusted intermediaries are chosen for selecting and processing external information, structuring inter-organizational collaboration and building relations to networking partners over time.[300] Consequently, intermediaries that are linked in knowledge networks and connected to knowledge sources may speed and amplify innovation performance of assigned corporate partners.

Network boards may be installed to regulate inter-organizational activity as well as support joint R&D initiatives. "The board is appointed to coordinate and organize the network at an over-arching level and to ensure that R&D activities are performed in the best interests of the stakeholders."[301] The constitution of the board can be considered as decisive aspect for innovation performance of the network. A high fluctuation of members may increase innovation capacity by continuously integrating innovative impulses; on the other hand, continuity creates a stabilized climate among members promoting compliance and the establishment of shared trust. A consistent approach to network and board governance is recommended to maximize network performance.[302]

- Behavioral factors in open innovation networks: The degree of frankness and willingness to openly share information among co-operating actors can be identified as a decisive behavioral component on the individual level within open innovation networks. This intensity will directly influence the innovation capacity of the overall network structure.[303] The development of trust among interacting individuals is consequently derived as a critical success factor. The establishment of trust in bilateral co-operations has been the object of strategic management research.[304] The application of bilateral concepts to an innovation network model requires consideration of a more complex structure emphasizing trust as a relational capital[305] and therefore bonding perquisite for networked innovation.[306] On an organizational level the establishment of a democratic structure containing an equal share of rights and powers is seen as a compulsory criterion for sustaining inter-organizational knowledge transfer and thus a productive working atmosphere.[307]

---

300   See Lee et al. 2010, p. 293-294; Howells 2006a, p. 721; von Nell/Lichtenthaler 2011.
301   Wincent/Anokhin/Boter 2009, p. 57.
302   See Wincent/Anokhin/Boter 2009, p. 59, 64.
303   See Enkel 2010, pp. 350, 360.
304   See e.g. Zaheer/Ventraman 1995; Nooteboom/Berger/Noorderhaven 1997; Hoecht/Trott 1999; Sydow 2000; Coulter/Coulter 2003.
305   See Castelfranchi/Falcone 2006 p. 19.
306   See Campos/Pomeda 2007; Babcock-Lumish 2010; Rampersad/Quester/Troshani 2010.
307   See Enkel, 2010, p. 361.

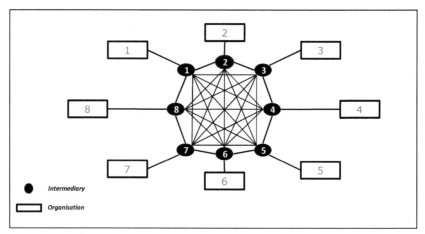

Figure 7: Intermediated open innovation network model
Source: Based on Chesbrough 2006c, p. 152.

- Regional structures and open innovation networks: A regional structure containing key organizations for knowledge generation and technology commercialization such as universities, research institutions and industrial corporations may be referred to as regional innovation system if an interrelationship can be identified among these organizations.[308] Geographic proximity consequently eases an inter-organizational transfer and the exchange of knowledge enabling the realization of local synergies. "It is beyond doubt that the external, geographically bounded innovation systems play a crucial role for companies' innovativeness."[309] Even though public institutions are involved in the creation and formation of regional and national innovation systems to increase location attractiveness, corporations are well aware of the necessity of a vital regional innovation network structure as a point of reference for achieving open innovation effectiveness.[310] To enable innovation performance on a global scale, evolving within a regional innovation system, the external flow of knowledge is required in a concept of open regional innovation system.[311] Here, the regional innovation structure is connected to

---

308 See Cooke 2004, p. 3; Chang 2002, p.487.
309 Vanhaverbeke 2006, p. 207.
310 See Simard/West 2006 p. 229; Vanhaverbeke 2006, p. 216.
311 See Belussi/Sammarra/Sedita 2010, p. 713.

both national and international cycles of knowledge flows for the creation and diffusion of innovation improving regional innovation output.[312]

2.2.4.2 Open Innovation Communities

Innovation communities "enable innovators to collectively share and develop ideas, discuss concepts and promote innovation."[313]

Innovation communities and innovation networks are identified as often similarly used terms and in fact, the concepts do show considerable parallels regarding the core alignment as to the specific form of inter-organizational cooperation for innovation.[314] Therefore, to enable a deeper understanding of the concept of open innovation communities, a systematic elaboration of the community construct allows for a more precise discussion of open innovation within structural settings.[315] The term innovation community comes from a combination of the sociological discussion of the community construct and innovation research with reference to a group of individuals "acting as universal or specialized promotors, often from more than one company and different organizations that team up in a project related fashion, and commonly promote a specific innovation, either on one or across different levels of an innovation system."[316] Table 4 provides an overview of the prevalent definitions. While prior contributions refer to an innovation community as the sum of organizations involved in an innovation process from idea generation to technology commercialization, later work understands the innovation community construct as a collective, topic-specific, and goal-oriented action of individuals toward problem-solving and innovation performance. Critics of the community construct differentiate it from networks from an emotional and a structural perspective.[317] "Communities are social containers for incremental innovation, whereas networks are the place for boundary-spanning learning

---

312 See Belussi/Sammarra/Sedita 2010, p. 718. In an empirical study the authors analyze the role of external research collaborations in the RIS of Emiia Romagna, Italy focusing on the life science industry. The results emphasize the relevance of knowledge flows beyond regional boundaries, striving for a vital balance of corporate transactions with regional and extra-regional organizations.

313 Möslein/Bansemir p. 18.

314 See West/Lakhani 2008, p. 225; Fichter, 2005, p. 287.

315 A systematic literature review was conducted, scanning the databases EBSCO Host, SpringerLink, and Emerald Management for academic publications containing the terms 'innovation community' and 'community of innovation' being mentioned in the title or abstract. After a selection process regarding topic affiliation and duplicats a total number of 71 matching contributions was identified and used as a basis for further analysis.

316 Fichter 2009, p. 360.

317 See Cardoso/Carvalho/Ramos 2008, pp. 70-71.

and as a consequence, for radical innovation."[318] Communities, therefore, emphasize a homogeneous climate creating an identity and allegiance among its members. They represent a unit lead by specific rules and behavioral conduct. Networks in comparison focus on tension due to differentiation and specification, and can be considered as less introverted and limited due to more flexible organizational structures.[319] However, based on empirical evidence showing that innovation communities mostly specifically strive for inter-organizational innovation and provide the capacity of realizing radical innovations,[320] a differentiated view of the concept is required.

As the current state of the discussion illustrates, the majority of contributions are located in the field of open innovation research, which understands a community as an open system promoting innovation. Consequently, innovation communities emphasize the interpersonal relations of members from a variety of organizations within the innovation process, while innovation networks primarily focus on inter-organizational relations.[321] Thus, networks are characterized by the exchange of information due to contact relations without precisely formulated goals and a common comprehension, whereas community members collaborate closely and strive for a collective goal, based on mutual understanding and a feeling of group identity.[322] To emphasize the perspective of an open system within the innovation community construct the term open innovation community will be applied further as it is referred to in the latest contributions.[323] Open innovation communities were predominantly researched within the structural settings of user-communities and user-manufacturer communities and refer to online contact networks and virtual communities as technical infrastructure for community-based innovation.[324] Furthermore, apart from virtual parameters transformational actors need to be considered to support other actors to perform open innovation.[325] These can be identified within innovation systems as building an open innovation community as a network of promotors.

318   Dal Fiore 2007, p. 857.
319   See Dal Fiore 2007, p. 860; Cardoso/Carvalho/Ramos 2008, p. 55.
320   See Fichter 2005; Fichter 2009.
321   See Fichter 2005, p. 289.
322   See Gerybadze 2007, p. 202; Fichter 2009, p. 361. Pisano/Verganti (2008, p. 81) define an innovation community as „a network where anybody can propose problems, offer solutions, and decide which solutions to use." They point to Linux open-source software community as an empirical example.
323   See Fleming/Waguespack 2007, p. 165; Cardoso/Carvalho/Ramos 2009; Zou/Yilmaz 2011. Also see Fichter 2009; West/Lakhani 2008.
324   See Fichter 2009, pp. 358-359.
325   See Winch/Courtney 2007, p. 751.

Innovation community	Author
"We propose the term 'innovation community' to refer to the organizations directly and indirectly involved in the commercialization of a new technology."	Lynn/Mohan/Aram 1996, p. 97
"I define 'innovation communities' as meaning nodes consisting of individuals or firms interconnected by information transfer links which may involve face-to-face, electronic, or other communication. These can, but need not, exist within the boundaries of a membership group. They often, but need not, incorporate the qualities of communities for participants, where 'communities' is defined as meaning 'networks of interpersonal ties that provide sociability, support, information, a sense of belonging, and social identity'."	von Hippel 2005, p. 96
User innovation communities are „distributed groups of individuals focused on solving a general problem and/or developing a new solution supported by computer mediated communication."	Dahlander/Wallin 2006, p. 246
"An innovation community is an informal network of likeminded individuals, acting as universal or specialised promotors, often from more than one company and different organisations that team up in a project related fashion, and commonly promote a specific innovation, either on one or across different levels of an innovation system."	Fichter 2009, p. 360
"The innovation community is a set of organizations with interest in the adoption, implementation, and assimilation of a specific IT innovation. Such a community emerges to make sense of the innovation and to develop an organizing vision for it. The collection of actors in the community evolves dynamically, as the collective attention evolves. The community dissolves once the collective attention disappears."	Wang/Ramiller 2009, p. 714

Table 4: Defining innovation communities

- Open innovation community as an online contact network: Based on the concept of lead user innovation that interprets a leading group of customers as trendsetters, problem solvers and consequently innovators,[326] the interaction process of individuals to achieve new developments within a certain field can be understood as community-based innovation representing the origin of the community innovation construct.[327] Online platforms serve as channels for communication among community members creating a virtual innovation marketplace. Participating individuals share an interest in a certain topic and therefore create a field for innovation. These can be differentiated by the group of innovation seekers and innovation providers striving for problem-solving and innovation based on collective intelligence.[328] In practice, several such platforms can be identified that highlight the empirical relevance of innovation communities for

---

326 See von Hippel 1988, pp. 96, 106; 2005, p. 22. Franke/von Hippel/Schreier 2006, p. 302.
327 See Franke/Shah 2003; Füller et al. 2006, pp. 60-64. Chu/Chan 2009. Open source software projects are popular examples of community-based innovation in which individuals voluntarily contribute to programming and development of software such as the Linux operating system. Furthermore, sports like kitesurfing and snowboarding have been identified as areas of community-based innovation (see Reichwald/Piller 2009, pp. 201-202; Franke/Shah 2003, pp. 160-164) emphasizing the applicability of the concept in various areas and industries to promote open innovation (von Hippel 2005, p. 93).
328 See Möslein/Bansemir 2011, p. 18; Fichter 2005, p. 289.

an exchange of ideas and expertise among individuals to achieve innovation.[329] "To increase the number of high-quality innovation ideas created by individuals, the possibility to interact with other people should be supported and facilitated."[330] Online community contact networks facilitate inter-personal interaction. Despite geographical conditions they enable global access to a diversified knowledge base beyond personal relations. The interaction with heterogeneous weakly connected individuals may lead to new impulses and perspectives toward idea development detached to personal filtering.[331]

One requirement, however, for enabling such knowledge intensive interactions based on specific capabilities is the establishment of a functioning market for ideas offering suitable institutional settings, operating requirements and efficiency.[332] Critics in turn argue that markets for technologies and ideas "are plagued by maladies, including asymmetric information, moral hazards, transaction costs, and strategic considerations that can even lead to the complete failure of markets."[333] Consequently, the amount of anonymity within such communities may inversely react to the existence and development of trust among individuals. Since trust is seen as the copula to establish relations for open idea and knowledge exchange a need for more intense inter-personal relations to establish breakthrough innovation can be identified.[334] Therefore, open innovation communities as online contact networks can be understood as access platforms to knowledge keepers and may offer impulses, though they require further steps apart from the platform to achieve collaborative radical innovations.

- Open innovation community as virtual community: A virtual community in comparison to an online contact network bundles "interested and specialized innovators for particular issues [...]. They originate from grouping together voluntarily and independently to create innovative solutions in a joint effort, embracing a family-like spirit."[335] Conse-

---

329 For an overview of innovation markets and idea plattforms, see Cardoso/Carvalho/Ramos (2009, pp. 14-16). The following selection provides some empirical insight within this contribution:
  - www.ideaconnection.com, the plattform organized by a Canadian corporation directly refers to the open innovation concept by stating 'Solve your open innovation challenges.' Here, a portfolio of problem-solvers based of scientists and engineers can be adressed by individuals or corporations to research and develop articulated problems.
  - www.ideawicket.com, which is run by an Indian company providing a plattform for innovators to share ideas designs and techniques within the worldwide web by posting comments and solutions to improve efficiency. Also networking features are available to enable a share of information only amoong selected partners.
330 Björk/Magnusson 2009, p. 662.
331 See Ohly/Kase/Skerlavaj 2010, p. 49; Perry-Smith 2006.
332 See Gans/Stern 2003, p. 334.
333 Fosfuri/Giarratana 2010, p. 767.
334 See Björk/Magnusson 2009, p. 668; Ohly/Kase/Skerlavaj 2010, p. 42.
335 Möslein/Bansemir 2011, p. 18.

quently, virtual community members' interact multi-directionally in reference to a specific topic creating a basis for reliable communication within a non-radically structured, ego-centered network.[336] A virtual community, therefore, can be understood as a collective, interacting within a virtual room created by social software and electronic media thriving for joint generation and evaluation of ideas and concepts for innovation.[337] Communication within virtual communities may be based on communication rings such as electronic messages enabling a direct communication among all members, whereas content trees allow for indirect communication by posting information on a central location as in a weblog. Such virtual communities may on the one hand, serve as a functional reason enabling acquisition and exchange of knowledge and on the other hand, as a hedonistic reason due to social interaction within the community.[338] Empirically, virtual communities are mostly initiated and coordinated by corporations aiming at the development of specific features within the product line or the solution of current problems.[339]

- Open innovation community as network of promotors: Pioneering contributions in innovation community research differentiated between a substructure and a superstructure within the inter-organizational innovation process. The superstructure refers to innovation-supporting institutions such as universities and public institutions. These may create R&D communities "working toward the solution of an interrelated problem-set [...] communicate their results to each other and hence participate in community 'networks'."[340] The substructure, however, is represented by the corporations mainly involved in the technology commercialization process. An intense interplay between these structural levels is decisive for achieving innovation.[341] Consequently, in addition to user communities and user innovation, a promoting unit of transformational leaders needs to be considered. These mainly enable other actors to innovate and can be understood as innovation promotors in regional or national innovation system, such as non-corporate R&D organizations, government agencies, industry associations or innovation brokers.[342] Within this perspective an innovation community can be considered as informal personal network of innovators collectively furthering specific innovation

---

336 See Weiber/Meyer 2002, p. 348.
337 See Fichter 2005, p. 289.
338 See Reichwald/Piller 2009, pp. 207-209.
339 In open innovation literature among others the following examples are referred to (see e.g. Möslein/Bansemir 2011, p. 12-13): InnovationJam by IBM (www.collaborationjam.com), IdeaStorm by Dell (www.dellideastorm.com), Virtual Innovation Agency by BMW (www.bmwgroup.com/via), and Factory-Concept by LEGO (www.factory.lego.com).
340 Debackere et al. 1994, p. 23.
341 See Lynn/Mohan/Aram 1996, pp. 97-102.
342 See Fichter 2009, pp. 358-359.

projects.[343] This perspective draws on the promotor theory of innovation research and the concept of multi-level innovation systems.

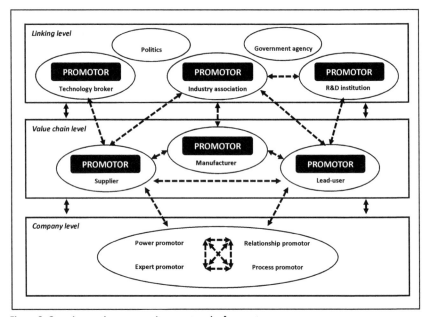

Figure 8: Open innovation community as network of promotors
Source: Based on Fichter 2009, p. 361.

Promotor theory emphasizes the relevance of key actors within an organization primarily to overcome intra-organizational innovation barriers and market challenges. These actors may be referred to as promotors if they actively and intensively further innovation projects and contribute to their execution.[344] A promotor may fulfill several characteristics depending on the source of the innovation barrier and may therefore take specialized roles that can be incorporated within different persons or only one individual, the 'universal promotor.' If a lack of experience and knowledge among the people involved in the innovation process exists, 'expert promotors' can draw on their specific knowledge and competences to close knowledge gaps and give impulses for

---

343 Fichter 2009, p. 360; Fichter 2005, p. 289.
344 See Witte 1973, p. 15; 1999, p. 15; Hauschild/Salomo 2011, p. 125.

advancements.[345] If a motivational denegation toward innovation projects prevails, 'power promotors' may force and motivate people due to their hieratical position and their ability to set sanctions or rewards.[346] A collaboration of expert and power promoters with the same goal is assumed as an augmentation of the effectiveness of promoting an innovation process.[347] Furthermore, to overcome administrative aspects due to system complexity 'process promotors' may speed innovation processes based on their expertise of the organizational flows, cycles and responsibilities of relevant actors and their communication skills to address and convince nodal points within an organization.[348] In the case of inter-organizational innovation projects the 'relationship promotor' relates to personal connections to key individuals within the innovation network by identifying potential collaboration partners and enabling an access to these organizations.[349]

These promotors may act on different levels within an innovation system. These levels can be differentiated as 'company level,' 'value chain level,' and 'linking level.' Figure 8 illustrates the interaction and informal relations of promotors on these levels creating a network of promotors within the innovation system. On a company level promotors fulfill the four roles of expert, power, process, and relationship promotor to overcome innovation barriers inside of the corporation. These are connected to promotors of networked corporations and actors on a value chain level such as suppliers, manufacturers and lead users. The interaction of promotors on the value chain level refers to the above- mentioned substructure concept. The linking level, accordingly, applies to the superstructure including promotors from institutions enabling other actors to innovate such as technology brokers, industry associations and R&D institutions.[350] Consequently, discussing open innovation communities requires an understanding of the relevance of transformational leaders collaborating informally and promoting mutual innovation above institutional boundaries and across all levels of the innovation system.[351] To differentiate an innovation community as a network of promotors from neighboring con-

---

345   See Witte 1973, p. 18; 1999, p. 17.
346   See Witte 1999, p. 16.
347   See Hauschild/Kirchmann 1997, p. 17.
348   See Hauschildt/Chakrabarti 1988, pp. 385-386.
349   See Gemünden/Walter 1995, pp. 973-974; 1999, pp. 119-120.
350   See Winch/Courtney 2007, p. 751; Lynn/Mohan/Aram 1996, pp. 97-102; Fichter 2009, p. 360.
351   As an empirical example Fichter (2005, pp. 291-296) elaborates on the 'add-value-to-paper community,' which was founded by actors from the paper industry to collectively achieve innovation projects and realize quality and efficiency improvements in paper and printing technologies. Based on the initiative of the head of paper chemicals at BASF, who referred to his informal personal network of key individuals as a network of promotors, which was created with representatives from the value chain level such as Axel Springer AG, UPM Kymmene, Omya AG and Voith AG. Furthermore, actors from the linking level were integrated as neutral competent authority to promote and moderate innovation processes.

structs, the following key criteria can be identified: "The community is always related to a specific innovation idea or project. All community members play a promotor role in this process. The community members collaborate closely and informally [...] with a feeling of group identity."[352]

2.3 Regional Innovation Structures

2.3.1 Regional Economics

"In these days, some experts argue that this century will be a century of regionalization. Nation-state has been losing its importance in economic, R&D, and innovation activities in the globalized society. Instead, region-state gains an importance as it is expected to bring up their regional economies more effectively in terms of systematical promotion of innovation activities."[353]

The term region considers a container of physical, social, political, and economic features.[354] Therefore, a regional structure determines a network of actors from different sectors of society. The regional structure may form an "operational environment of individuals, including certain physical and social elements."[355] The structure influences the individual behavior of its inhabitants and vice versa is influenced by individual actions, with reference to the concept of 'duality of structure.'[356] Also referred to as structuration theory it may be understood as "the essential recursiveness of social life, as constituted in social practices: structure is both medium and outcome of social practices. Structure enters simultaneously into the condition of the agent and social practices, and 'exists' in the generating moments of this constitution."[357] Consequently, human social actions can be considered as recursive and dynamically evolving the social structure.[358] Structures in this sense represent a recursively organized set of rules and resources building the foundation of individual behavior reconstituted by day-to-day activities.[359] Based on these elaborations the relevance of embeddedness within social structures was detailed by Granovetter (1985) with reference to the personal interactions within structural systems. Granovetter

---

352 Fichter 2009, p. 360.
353 Chung 2002, p. 485.
354 See Dicken/Malmberg, 2009, p. 345.
355 See Tuominen/Jussila/Saksa 2006, p. 11.
356 See Giddens 1976, p. 121. For an introduction and more precise elaboration of the sociological concept integrating various works by Giddens see e.g. Sarason/Dean/Dillard (2006, pp. 290-292); Kieser (2002, pp. 355-376).
357 Giddens 1979, p. 5.
358 See Jack/Anderson 2002, p. 470.
359 See Giddens 1979, p. 64.

criticizes Williamson's approach of transaction cost economics (1979) and emphasizes the influence of social structural effects on market behavior, "the anonymous market of neo-classical models is virtually nonexistent in economic life… there is sufficient social overlay in economic transactions across forms."[360] Based on these conceptual considerations, the following subsections discuss more specific attributes of structural economics based on geographic proximity.

2.3.1.1 Clustering and Regional Specialization

"Recent research on the world's 500 largest companies has established that the majori-ty of international business occurs within regional clusters in the three largest econom-ic regions of North America, Europe, and Asia."[361]

Cluster theory initialized an intense discussion among researchers of the fields of econom-ics, economic geography and strategic management to determine the relevance of region-al proximity for the innovative capacity of national and regional economies as well as cor-porate performance.[362] Within these fields further constructs and terminologies can be identified that tackle the issue of regional specialization and concentration such as 'inno-vative milieus'[363]. Behind the discussion on Marshall's work (1920) elaborating the con-struct of 'industrial districts' is an analytical overlap or a common point of view. Here, on the one hand, the relevance of knowledge acquisitions based on social and economic in-teraction processes is emphasized.[364] On the other hand, the embeddedness of individual actors and organizations within a network of formal and informal social relations, local institutions and infrastructure, suppliers, competitors, and collaboration partners is seen as a key to achieving new knowledge and innovation in regional structures.[365]

Based on an international trade analysis Porter identifies an interlinked system of de-terminants of national economic advantages (1998b, p. 72). A favorable specification of factor and demand conditions, the existence of related and supporting industries as well as firm strategy, structure and rivalry determine the evolvement of a specialized industry

---

360 See Granovetter 1985, p. 495.
361 Rugman/Brain 2004, p. 7.
362 See e.g. Porter 1998a; Porter 1998b; Porter 2000a; Porter 2000b; Furman/Porter/Stern 2002. For a review of innovation and space see Simmie (2005).
363 See for detailed discussions of the concept of innovative milieus Camagni (1995); Maillat (1995, pp. 161-162).
364 See Schamp 2005, p. 94.
365 See Breschi/Malerba 2005, p. 3.

within a regional structure.[366] Based on empirical investigation as in Western Germany, the role of geographic concentration is emphasized identifying the existence of regional industrial clusters.[367] "Clusters are geographic concentrations of interconnected companies and institutions in a particular field. Clusters encompass an array of linked industries important to competition."[368] Consequently, regional specialization occurs based on a set of determining factors allowing for a vital development of a specific industry within a geographic structure. Meanwhile, researchers argue that the cluster concept has produced minor research impact than raising public and political attention to regional specialization of industries to promote or sustain national competitive advantage.[369] The relevance of interorganizational interaction and the emergence of knowledge within these clusters are not precisely elaborated.

Malmberg/Maskell (2002) consider a knowledge-based approach on spacial clustering. Based on a firm's local capabilities regional specialization may occur depending on the interaction of actors from a horizontal and vertical level, and local institutions. Due to the local presence of competitors, direct comparison of performances is enabled, allowing for the rapid imitation of superior solutions. In the case of a deep vertical differentiation, an intense specialization process among regional firms is promoted, "the cluster can therefore develop knowledge far beyond the reach on any of its members. With the growth of knowledge, new economic activities become possible, the economy of the cluster progresses and the resulting extension of the internal market makes the process self-reinforcing."[370] Institutions are arranged differently within clusters. Depending on the specific mechanisms applied, institutions may cause a differentiation among clusters by promoting cognitive, organizational and social proximity in another way.[371] Resulting from the interaction of the horizontal and vertical level, and institutional arrangements, specific knowledge may arise within an industry. This process of intra-industrial knowledge transfer is consequently bound to the regional context and may be amplified due to structural dynamics.[372]

---

366 Porter refers to this system of determinants as 'diamond' (1998b, p. 72). Extensions of the concept include the role of the government as well as chance as influential components of national economic advantages (Porter 1998, p. 174).
367 See Porter 1998b, pp. 155-157; 154-156.
368 Porter 1998a, p. 78.
369 See Martin/Sunley 2003.
370 Malmberg/Maskell 2002, p. 440.
371 See Malmberg/Maskell 2002, p. 441.
372 See Glaeser et al. 1992, p. 1127. This phenomenon is referred to as 'Marshall-Arrow-Romer-Externalities.' The concepts of externalities as well as knowledge spillovers are presented in the following section.

2.3.1.2 Proximity, Knowledge Spillovers and Innovation

"The effect of networks on innovation is magnified by geographic proximity."[373]

As indicated above, regional concentration may positively influence corporate performance regarding innovation activities. Agglomeration advantages may occur, allowing
corporations to profit from one another based on their geographical proximity.[374] The concept of proximity can be understood as a basis for dynamic interaction among actors allowing for the establishment of interorganizational learning and knowledge spillovers.[375]
According to Boschma (2005) proximity directly relates to the innovation competence of a
firm, although one can differentiate between five dimensions of proximity. Cognitive, organizational, social, institutional and geographic proximity are inter-linked aspects causing
a reduction of uncertainty and therefore supporting the interaction of actors as well as
promoting inter-organizational learning. Geographic proximity serves as a promotor
among these dimensions facilitating the establishment of the other proximities.[376] This is
mainly caused by lower transaction costs in realizing face-to-face communication. Based
on frequent direct interactions, mutual practices represent a basis for building collaboration upon collective values and associations.[377] Depending on the intensity of inter-
organizational interaction circles of trust may emerge among the actors. These trust-based
relations provide strategic advantages for the linked-in corporations allowing for the formulation of a competitive network advantage due to embeddedness.[378] Consequently,
geographic proximity enables the establishment of informal relations among regional actors facilitating the evolvement of trust as a basis for inter-organizational and individual
cooperation.

As indicated, knowledge spillover effects are promoted by proximity.[379] The model of
knowledge spillovers is based on the concept of externalities[380] and describes a positive
external effect due to knowledge acquisition. Knowledge spillovers may occur if
knowledge that has been created within an organization is received by another external

---

373 Simard/West 2006, p. 225.
374 See Frenken/Van Oort/Verburg 2007, p. 687.
375 See Torre/Gilly 2000, pp. 173, 178.
376 In a case study of Silicon Valley, Saxenian 1990 elaborates on the relevance of geographic proximity as a
     facilitator to enable personal interaction in form of meetings, conferences and seminars to establish
     knowledge transfer. The case study refers to a collaborative action toward competitors from Japanese
     technology industries in the 1980's.
377 See Storper/Venables 2005, p. 322.
378 See Uzzi 1996, p. 676.
379 See Foray 2006, p. 101.
380 Externalities refers to a positive or negative effect of individual behavior toward another individuum or
     organization based on economic decisions.For a detailed introduction to the concept see
     Pindyck/Rubinfeld 2006, p. 879.

entity. The recipient of the spillover uses the received knowledge to gain a competitive advantage by integrating the knowledge component into the corporate R&D or overall innovation process.[381] Specific types of knowledge spillovers among corporations may be differentiated as follows: change of personnel, informal personal relations, similarities in value chain collaboration partners, and intended knowledge transfer such as consulting or public share of research results.[382] These types contribute to the overall intention to profit from knowledge spillovers by reducing R&D costs.[383]

Applying the concept of knowledge spillovers to regional structures, two perspectives can be identified: On the one hand, corporations may be situated within the same branch which allows for localization economies in terms of regional specialization; on the other hand, firms may be active within different branches realizing urbanization economies, with reference to a high diversity of the economic landscape.[384] The perspective of specialization draws from positive externalities within intra-industrial collaborations emphasizing strong synergy effects due to economic specialization within a regional structure.[385] Diversity, however, is seen as a source of positive externalities for corporations enabling a co-existence of multiple knowledge sources and consequently a basis for knowledge combination to cause innovation.[386] Both perspectives consequently argue for the existence of knowledge spillovers among actors within regional structures based on geographic proximity.[387] Based on a set of empirical studies regarding the effects of specialization and diversity toward economic growth, the relevance of a co-existence of diversified and specialized regional economies has been emphasized as precondition for a prospering economy.[388]

Depending on industry characteristics corporations show differentiating perspectives toward their regional knowledge spillover interests. High-tech corporations tend to prefer rather diversified regional settings in which technological similarities can be identified while mature industrial corporations aim for specialized surrounding realizing location externalities.[389] "Sectors that are related in terms of shared or complementary competences"[390] are referred to as the concept of 'related variety' which represents an amplification of the agglomeration economies construct. Within this concept the relevance of inter-

381 See Fischer 2006, pp. 1-2.
382 See Harhoff 2000, p. 240.
383 See De Bondt 1997, p. 12; Harhoff 2000, p. 246; Steurs 1995, p 250.
384 See Duranton/Puga 2000; Beaudry/Schiffauerova 2009.
385 See Marshall 1920.
386 See Jacobs 1969; Schamp 2002; Schamp/Rentmeister/Lo 2004; Corno/Reinmoeller/Nonaka 1999. Regarding the concept of combining explicit knowledge to create knowledge, see Nonaka/Konno (1998, p. 42).
387 See Glaeser et al. 1992; Jacobs 1969; Steurs 1995; Storper/Veneables 2004; Eriksson 2011.
388 See Duranton/Puga 2000, pp. 534, 553.
389 See Henderson et al. 1995; Neffke/Henning/Boschma 2011; Harhoff 2000.
390 Boschma/Iammarino 2009, pp. 292-293.

organizational relations among entities from different branches is introduced emphasizing the importance of cognitive proximity for enabling knowledge spillovers.[391] A region may profit from related variety if competences from different but associated industries leading to an amplification of research results for innovation due to collective research and branch-specific development.[392] In contrast to such mono structural regions, 'unrelated variety' refers to a high variety of disconnected branches within a region which increases the probability for the absorption of sector-specific shocks.[393]

To summarize in Porter's words: "Geographic, cultural, and institutional proximity leads to special access, closer relationships, better information, powerful incentives, and other advantages in productivity and innovation that are difficult to tap from a distance."[394]

2.3.2 Regional Innovation Systems

2.3.2.1 Conceptual Approach to Regional Innovation Systems

The evolutionary theory of economic change refers to dynamic processes within regional development and draws on endogenously created technological change as initiating momentum of economic change.[395] Furthermore, within the concept, corporate competences are understood as important reservoir of capabilities, experiences and knowledge representing the source of future technological development. Consequently, based on an understanding of chain-linked innovation processes, knowledge and individual as well as collective capabilities should not be seen as mere production factors, but rather as strategic assets for future competitiveness.[396] A system of innovation may be created that, above and beyond corporate competences, refers to all relevant economic, political, social, institutional and organizational factors influencing the evolvement and diffusion of innovation.[397] Derived from those elaborations, a discussion has emerged on the analysis of national and regional innovation systems.[398]

---

391 See Nooteboom 2000.
392 The co-existence of a automotive and an aviation industry within a region may serve as empirical example as is the case in the region of Ingolstadt, Germany. Here the headquarter of the automotive manufacturer AUDI as well as a subsidiary of EADS for military systems, Cassidian, is located. Joint research projects for lightweight construction materials will reduce individual research costs, and the results will be applied to branch-specific requirements allowing for inter-organizational cooperation for innovation.
393 See Boschma/Iammarino 2009, pp. 290.
394 Porter 1998a, p. 90.
395 See Nelson/Winter 1982.
396 See Schamp 2002; Schamp/Rentmeister/Lo 2004.
397 See Edquist 2005, p. 182.
398 See Asheim/Coenen 2005; Cooke 2004; Immarino 2005; Asheim/Isaksen 1997; Metcalfe 1995; Freeman 1987; Nelson 1993; Graf 2006.

The concept of national innovation systems (NIS) refers to the creation of innovation within national economies and can be defined as "the networks of institutions in the public and private sector whose activities and interactions initiate, import, modify, and diffuse new technologies."[399] NIS also may be seen in a wider sense as "all interrelated institutional actors that create, diffuse, and exploit innovations" as well as "organizations and institutions directly related to searching and exploring technological innovations, such as R&D departments, universities, and public institutes" with reference to a more narrow perspective of the concept.[400] The interaction of technology development and national institutional surrounding conditions, therefore, intensively influence the economic development of an economy. Innovation-based competitive advantages draw on an optimal interplay of technology innovation and corresponding structural development.[401] This point of view emphasizes the relevance of individual organizational characteristics to innovation and change such as the reduction of insecurity within innovation processes and the intensity of path dependencies.[402] Performance factors of NIS rely on the achievement potential and capabilities of substructures that can be identified on a sectoral or regional level.

The sectoral perspective draws on the similarities in techniques and demands as well as strategic interdependencies among related organizations and may be structured due to concentration, vertical integration and diversification.[403] "Sectoral systems of innovation have a knowledge base, technologies, inputs and a (potential or existing) demand. They are composed of a set of agents carrying out market and non-market interactions for the creation, development and diffusion of new sectoral products."[404] Sectoral systems of innovation, consequently, are composed of knowledge and technology, actors and networks, and institutions that shape the interaction of participating agents within a dynamic and transformational context. Geographical boundaries due to these sectoral dynamics do not necessarily determine the sectoral structure, yet they are considered an important element in the analysis of sectoral systems.[405] The concept of regional innovation systems (RIS), in contrast, specifically emphasizes the relevance of regional structures as a bounding element for inter-organizational innovation.

Based on NIS research explaining general macroeconomic interests of national economies in establishing and financing university education and fundamental research, the

---

399   Freeman 1987, p. 4.
400   Chung 2002, p. 486.
401   See Freeman 1987, p. 330.
402   See Lundvall 1992, p. 10.
403   See Malerba 2002, p. 247.
404   Malerba 2005, p. 65.
405   See Malerba 2002, p. 260.

analysis of RIS refers to more specific investments to promote innovation.[406] An RIS is defined as a sub-system based on interaction, knowledge generation and exploitation which is linked to global, national and other regional systems for commercializing new knowledge.[407] Table 5 provides an overview of definitions of a RIS emphasizing inter-organizational interactions within all levels of the regional structure. A RIS, consequently, differs to an NIS besides size aspects because of the regional connection and interplay of industrial and educational structure as well as research and technology competences.[408] This relates to an understanding of an RIS as a chain-linked innovation model emphasizing the interaction among actors within the innovation process.[409]

RIS, therefore, can be characterized as a concept uniting the aspects of regional context, networks, interaction, institutional learning, and innovation.[410] A region can be considered a political unit on a meso-level which lies between the national and local level of governmental activity. Organizational actors within a region establish networks due to regional proximity and interact by exchanging knowledge causing an inter-organizational knowledge transfer.[411] Depending on the intensity of knowledge flows organizations can profit from their regional embeddedness by exploiting the knowledge sources of the regional network for organizational learning and innovation. Furthermore, the concept of RIS can be described from a historical, institutional, evolutionary as well as social perspective.[412] From an historical point of view, the efficiency of a system is determined by social values and norms that are related to the historical trajectories of the region. Since production and institutional factors as well as inter-regional relations may vary according to the historic development of a region experience and culture can be interpreted as an influencing factor in regional innovation potential.[413] Determined by the historical development the characteristics of regional institutions may be decisive for the existence of a RIS. Institutions can be seen as social relations framing the activities of economic value creation, consumption and interaction building the substance of social life and an enhancing factor for human interactions.[414] The relationship of organizations and the institutional environment, therefore, can be considered decisive for the promotion of innovation performance.[415]

---

406 See Cooke 2009, p. 93.
407 See Cooke 2004, p. 3.
408 See Diez/Kiese 2009, pp. 247-248.
409 See Tappeiner/Hauser/Walde 2008, pp. 862-863; Chung 2002, p. 484.
410 See Cooke 2009, pp. 94-95.
411 See Frenken/Van Oort/Verburg 2007, p. 687.
412 See Doloreux 2002, pp. 251-253; Doloreux/Parto 2005; Doloreux/Dionne 2008; Iammarino 2005.
413 See Lundvall 1992.
414 Setterfield 1993, p. 756; Hodgson 1988, p. 134; North 1990, pp. 3-4.
415 See Nelson 1993.

Rergional innovation system	*Author*
„An (regional) innovation system consists of a production structure (technoeconomic structures) and an institutional infrastructure (political-institutional structures)."	Asheim/Isaksen 1997, p. 302
„We define a RIS as a complex of innovation actors and institutions in a region that are directly related with the generation, diffusion, and appropriation of technological innovation and an interrelationship between these innovation actors."	Chung 2002, p. 487
"A regional innovation system consist of interacting knowledge generation and exploitation sub-systems linked to global, national an other regional systems for commercializing new knowledge."	Cooke 2004, p. 3
"A (RIS) may thus be defined as the localised network of actors and institutions in the public and private sectors whose activities and interactions generate, import, modify and diffuse new technologies within and outside the region."	Iammarino 2005, p. 4

Table 5: Definitions of regional innovation systems

According to evolutionary economics the process of change determines organizational development. Due to inter-organizational relations path-dependencies prevail implementing socio-economic imperatives for innovation within the system.[416] This evolutionary perspective can be aligned according to the understanding of innovation as a social process of interaction and interorganizational learning, which allows for a social perspective of RIS. Technological innovation is based upon intra-regional collective knowledge flows and inter-regional linkages enhancing organizational access to a variety of innovation capabilities.[417] This point of view "underscores organizational innovation in the promotion of interaction and collaboration through partnership, flexibility, innovation support, networks, and interactive learning."[418]

2.3.2.2 Application and categorization of regional innovation systems

Based on the assumption of a continuous evolution toward a knowledge based society the concept of RIS has been applied to further conceptual as well as empirical research.[419] This aims at identifying key organizational and institutional dimensions within RIS, the determinants for innovation potential, dependencies among organizations within a region to per-

---

416 See Nelson/Winter 1982; Cooke/Boekholt/Todling 2000.
417 See Camagni 1999, p. 6.
418 Doloreux 2002, p. 253.
419 See Leydesdorff/Fritsch 2006, p. 1539. For an comparitive overview of empirical studies on RIS see Doloreux/Parto 2005.

form innovation, and the identification of similarities and differences among regional clusters.[420] The 'triple helix' model, which analyzes inter-dependencies and dynamic interaction of knowledge-producing institutions within a region such as universities, industry, and
government institutions, represents a specification in the discussion of RIS.[421] The model
refers to the emergence of university-industry-government interactions based on tri-
lateral networks and hybrid organizations in contrast to a laissez-faire and etatistic model.[422] The triple helix model consequently characterizes a regional knowledge infrastructure based on overlapping institutional arrangements and relying on an intensive interaction of regional knowledge intensive organizations in the form of collaborative relationships.[423]

Within this perspective universities play a decisive role in the regional knowledge production and innovation creation process. They „are extending their teaching capabilities
from educating individuals to shaping organizations in entrepreneurial education and incubation programmes."[424] As a locus of knowledge creation, universities embody the decisive power to trigger innovation. On the one hand, they provide academics employing
their knowledge for business, and on the other hand, they may provide additional resources to transfer research results into practice. In this case the concept of 'entrepreneurial universities' arises, with reference to the university as an incubator for entrepreneurial opportunities.[425] The intensity of university-industry interaction, therefore, offers a
great potential to create a knowledge-intensive entrepreneurial climate.[426] Corporations
as counterparts to the entrepreneurial university depend on specifically educated human
capital as well as state-of-the-art research results for commercialization. Consequently,
especially knowledge-intensive corporations can profit from investing in inter-
organizational relations with universities. The state in the form of public institutions is
meant to support the development of economic opportunities by providing a framework
of consultative and financial services as well as judicial and tax incentives.[427]

Based on the conceptualization of RIS, an empirical investigation demands a specification of the concept by identifying subcategories to classify regions due to their individual
configuration. Emphasizing the role of knowledge-creating institutions in addition to uni-

---

420   See Cooke/Boekholt/Todling 2000; Sternberg 2000; Asheim/Coenen 2005; Asheim et al. 2003.
421   See Etzkowitz/Klofsten 2005, p. 245; Antonelli 2008, p. 2.
422   See Etzkowitz 2002, p. 118; Etzkowitz/Klofsten 2005, p. 243.
423   See Etzkowitz/Leydesdorff 2000, p. 111.
424   Etzkowitz/Dzisah 2008, p. 655. Dzisah/Etzkowitz 2012.
425   See Etzkowitz/Klofsten 2005, p. 245.
426   Common examples for entrepreneurial universities are Stanford University for Silicon Valley and the
      Massachusetts Institute of Technology (MIT) for the Boston region.
427   Etzkowitz/Dzisah 2008, p. 656. Institutions such as United Nations, OECD, World Bank, and European
      Union emphasize within their initiatives the relevance of university-industry-government collaborations
      to improve economic development (Etzkowitz/Leydesdorff 1997, p. 4).

versities and industrial enterprises, public research institutions are highly relevant innovation actors and need to be included for further considerations. Within this point of view
regions may be categorized as 'advanced RIS' if an appropriate number of innovation actors are identified. Regions missing a component to be added in near future can be named
'developing RIS'. Regions that lack one component such as public research institutes may
be referred to as 'less developed RIS.'[428] This approach underlines that the classic concept
of RIS represents a rather idealized model that is not quite capable of capturing the complexity of existing systems in reality, mainly because of path dependencies and network
relations.[429] This cognition requires a broader approach to innovation systems with reference to "all parts and aspects of the economic structure and the institutional set-up affecting learning as well as searching and exploring,"[430] that is, based on the variety of inter-
organizational value creation oriented interactions within regional structures. Different
logic can be applied to conceptualize RIS depending on the regional knowledge infrastructure and industry specific knowledge intensity:[431]

• Territorially embedded regional innovation system: Based on geographic proximity corporations draw on inter-corporate learning processes to stimulate innovation without
  specific interactions with knowledge-creating organizations. SME networks in industrial
  districts represent a pertinent example for such RIS offering a network-based variety of
  territorially embedded experts promoting the "adaptive technological and organizational learning in a territorial context."[432]

• Regionally networked innovation system: Resulting from policy intervention to increase
  regional innovation capacity and inter-organizational collaboration, this intentional
  strengthening of regional infrastructure can be identified within regionally networked
  innovation systems. Due to the placement of organizations relevant for corporate innovation processes, collaboration of public and private institutions is promoted. In this
  context SMEs can draw on knowledge-intensive institutions sourcing their expertise
  and competencies to generate radical innovation. Technology transfer agencies may
  amplify these collaborations by reducing information barriers, increasing the collective
  innovation capacity of the region.[433]

• Regionalized national innovation system: This concept integrates extra-regional organizations into regional innovation-activity-accessing experts outside the region for cooperation. Based on personal relations due to similarities in expertise and occupation

428 See Chung 2002, p. 489.
429 See Cooke 2009, p. 94; Cooke/Boekholt/Tödtling 2000, p. 5.
430 Lundvall 1992, p. 12.
431 See Asheim/Coenen 2005, p. 1179-1180.
432 Storper/Scott 1995, p. 513.
433 See Asheim/Coenen 2005, p. 1180.

'epistemic communities' are created across regional boundaries enabling the flow of knowledge among its members.[434] The installation of 'science parks' and corporate R&D laboratories represents a planned innovative climate based on specific expertise and competencies but lacking inter-organizational relations. Due to missing regional embeddedness these institutions contribute to the national innovation system rather than providing knowledge to local institutions.[435]

Based on these elaborations characterizing various forms and specific characteristics of RIS, regional innovation structures will be used as an umbrella term within this work. This is understood as a defined geographic area forming an operational environment of individuals and containing knowledge producing, knowledge-processing, and knowledge-exploiting organizations to interactively generate innovation.

2.4 Synopsis

This chapter presents the state of discussion regarding the critical components of this work by introducing core concepts and essential definitions as a basis for further analysis. By reviewing the literature in the fields of strategic entrepreneurship, open innovation and regional innovation structures, a sound foundation is elaborated for approaching an integrated discussion toward a strategic approach of entrepreneurship in regional innovation structures. This section summarizes relevant aspects of the topics presented and points out coherencies as well as decisive areas of further investigation to approach an understanding of critical components of entrepreneurship in regional innovation structures.

- Strategic entrepreneurship: Based on an understanding of entrepreneurship as a process of the discovery, evaluation and exploitation of economic opportunities[436] to achieve market innovation, entrepreneurial behavior relates to the attributes of innovativeness, risk-taking, proactiveness, and competitive aggressiveness.[437] The aspect of competitive aggressiveness emphasizes the relevance of strategically approaching market conditions to achieve entrepreneurial performance. Entrepreneurship, consequently, contains a strategic component related to the ability of the entrepreneur to exploit market opportunities. The concept of strategic entrepreneurship emphasizes this aspect by balancing the opportunity-based behavior of entrepreneurship with a strategic

---

434   See Coenen/Moodysson/Asheim 2004, p. 1009.
435   See Henry/Massey/Wield 1995, pp. 724-725; Asheim/Coenen 2005, p. 1180.
436   See Shane/Venkataraman 200, p. 218.
437   See Lumpkin/Dess 1996, p. 152. Note: The first component of the entrepreneurial orientation construct, 'autonomy,' is considered a precondition for the ability to execute the mentioned attributes.

advantage-seeking behavior.[438] The implementtation of strategic entrepreneurship requires a functioning interplay of an entrepreneurial mindset of the people, an entrepreneurial culture and leadership, and a strategic resources management within the
organization to successfully perform innovation and achieve a competitive advantage.[439] This perspective allows for a definition of the entrepreneurial firm as an organization, regardless of age and size, following an opportunity-based firm behavior.[440]
The pursuit of this attitude requires an entrepreneurial management based on an organizational structure aiming at the continuous exploitation of entrepreneurial opportunities.[441]

- Open innovation: Defining innovation as the adoption of change new to an organization
  and its corresponding environment,[442] core components of innovation competence can
  be identified.[443] Based on the technological base of the corporation understood as innovation resources, innovation capabilities create the dynamic component to successfully interact with the corporate environment to explore knowledge sources and exploit
  market opportunities. The open innovation concept refers to this interactive approach,
  postulating an internal as well as external flow of ideas, knowledge and technology to
  advance an interactive value creation.[444] Aware of established concepts such as absorptive capacity, outsourcing of innovation, innovation networks, and co-creation of innovation a conceptual framework is elaborated differentiating knowledge flows external
  to the boundaries of the firm based on inter-organizational collaboration from the outside-in and from the inside-out.[445] Within an understanding of collaboration for innovation several potentials for open innovation can be identified along the vertical and horizontal scale as well as outside a particular sector of industry.[446] This illustration allows
  for a differentiated approach to the analytical levels of open innovation toward a complex structural setting as in 'open innovation networks' and 'open innovation communities'.[447] These perspectives demonstrate various forms of dimensions, coordination and
  behavior within such complex structures uncovering determinants of open innovation.
  Driven by the opportunities of the concept such as the reduction of R&D costs, speeding the commercialization process, and amplifying IP commercialization corporations

---

438   See Hitt et al. 2001, p. 481; Ireland/Hit/Sirmon 2003, p. 963.
439   See Ireland/Hit/Sirmon 2003, p. 963.
440   See Brown/Davidsson/Wiklund 2001, p. 953; Stevenson/Jarillo 1990, p. 21.
441   See Stevenson/Jarillo 1990, p. 23.
442   See knight 1967, p. 478.
443   See Bergfeld 2009, p. 14.
444   See Chesbrough 2003a, p. 15; Kirschbaum 2005, p. 24.
445   See Chesbrough 2003a, pp. 183, 189; Gassmann/Enkel 2006, p. 134.
446   See Enkel 2009, p. 184.
447   See Vanhaverbeke/Cloodt 2006, p. 276.

engage in inter-organizational innovation. Nonetheless, an open exchange of firm-specific and critical knowledge, on the one hand, is characterized as a decisive component to enable open innovation; on the other hand, it is considered as essential risk within open innovation projects.[448]

- Regional innovation structures: The region can be defined as a container of physical, social, political and economic features[449] forming an operational environment of individuals.[450] Based on cluster theory the relevance of a regional setting containing a variety of connected industries and institutions for achieving economic advantage has been emphasized.[451] Based on regional specialization regarding industrial competencies, corporations may profit from their physical surrounding due to proximity.[452] In this regard, a decisive component to achieve competitive advantage is based on the realization of positive externalities in the form of knowledge spillovers. Corporations may acquire valuable knowledge to reduce R&D costs or initiate innovation processes based on spillovers.[453] For a conceptual approach to regional structures promoting the emergence of innovation, 'regional innovation systems' are introduced. These are based on the interaction of knowledge generating and exploiting organizations connected to global, national and further regional systems for commercialization.[454]

Applying the concept to empirical settings demands a differentiated approach allowing for a categorization of regional RIS as territorially embedded, regionally networked and regionalized NIS.[455] As an umbrella term regional innovation structures, therefore, may be defined as a geographic area forming an operational environment of individuals and containing knowledge-producing, knowledge-processing, and knowledge-exploiting organizations to interactively generate innovation. The exploitation of regional structures, however, does not rely exclusively on geographic proximity but on its effects in promoting the development of cognitive, organizational, social and institutional proximity.[456] The social embeddedness within regional structures is therefore emphasized as decisive component within the discussion of geographical proximity and knowledge spillovers.[457]

---

448 See van de Vrande et al. 2009, p. 428.
449 See Dicken/Malmberg 2009, p. 345.
450 See Touminen/Jussila/Saksa 2006, p. 11.
451 See Porter 1998a; 1998b, pp. 154-157.
452 See Frenken/van Oort/Verburg 2007, p. 687.
453 See Harhoff 2000, p. 246; De Bondt 1997, p. 12.
454 See Cooke 2004, p. 3.
455 See Asheim/Coenen 2005, pp. 1179-1180.
456 See Boschma 2005; also see Porter 1998a, p. 90; Nooteboom 2000.
457 See Granovetter 1985.

Studies on influential factors of entrepreneurial performance emphasize the relevance of contextual elements as decisive component for sustainable corporate success.[458] In particular knowledge-intensive corporations striving for innovation performance rely on the existence of a vital regional economic climate, which enables the extensive flow of knowledge and resources such as capital and skilled labor among regional actors.[459] Due to regional proximity, positive spillover effects may occur among these organizations allowing corporations to profit from one another[460] and to identify entrepreneurial opportunities based on knowledge transfer.[461] On the other hand, due to a share of asymmetric information with reference to technological distance, a principal agent problem may occur creating opportunities to unequally exploit potential collaboration partners.[462] In this connection, the resolving uncertainty may be of twofold nature. On the one hand, uncertainty may be exogenous and therefore unaffected by actions of the firm due to environmental turbulence or technological newness. On the other hand, uncertainty may be endogenous and consequently based on the inter-organizational relationship, which can be influenced by actions of the collaborating organizations.[463] "Prior to a relationship, one does not know how opportunistic the partner is."[464] Especially for young entrepreneurial firms knowledge drainage of firm-specific information may be critical to future competitiveness.[465] Due to the limited possibilities of protection of IP based on its intangibility,[466] entrepreneurial firms get into a prisoner's dilemma of inter-corporate innovation.[467]

The regional environment of an entrepreneurial firm, therefore, can be considered crucial for its potential to detect and pursue entrepreneurial opportunities by drawing on proximity to reduce uncertainty. Regional embeddedness "enables co-operative managers to engage in direct long term interaction with significant parties participating in the construction of the entrepreneurial environment."[468] Understanding the regional innovation structure as a network of actors from various organizations and institutions striving for inter-organizational innovation allows for a transfer to the presented constructs of 'open innovation networks' and 'open innovation communities.' Here, forms of coordination can, on the one hand, be identified in order to reduce uncertainty and establish trust among

---

458   See e.g. Lumpkin/Dess, 1996; Eriksson, 2011; Lerner/Haber, 2000.
459   See Sternberg 2009, p. 23.
460   See Frenken et al. 2007, p. 687.
461   See Audretsch/Aldridge, 2009; Acs et al. 2009.
462   See Akerlof 1970.
463   See Folta 1998, pp. 1010-1011.
464   Nooteboom 2000, p. 919.
465   See Hoecht/Trott 1999, p. 266.
466   See Tether/Hipp 2002, p. 165.
467   See Trott 2008, p. 239; Bergfeld/Doepfer 2009, p. 3.
468   Touminen et al. 2006, p. 16.

network members in the form of innovation intermediaries;[469] on the other hand, to promote the overcoming of innovation barriers in the form of innovation promotors.[470] Within this perspective entrepreneurs are asked to create capabilities enabling the recognition of value of external information, its assimilation and application to commercial ends, in the sense of absorptive capacity.[471] Consequently, entrepreneurial firms are required to identify knowledge keepers, knowledge brokers, and innovation promotors, and to establish a dynamic-knowledge based strategy[472] that is strongly connected to a relational capacity[473] to perform knowledge exploration and exploitation for entrepreneurial activity.

469 See Chesbrough 2006c, p. 152.
470 See Fichter 2009, p. 361.
471 See Cohen/Levintal 1990, p. 128.
472 See Lichtenthaler 2006, pp. 56-63.
473 See Dyer/Singh 1998.

"As innovation capability continues to globalize, networks are becoming increasingly important. An entrepreneur can now access resources on a worldwide basis - and thus realize competitive advantage well beyond her weight class. Networks accord an important role to so-called brokers: individuals and companies that are able to link talents and assets… and business practice in ways that generate value."[474]

3. Theoretical Basis

3.1 Social Capital Theory and Entrepreneurial Networks

3.1.1 Social Capital Theory

"Networks of civic engagement are an essential form of social capital: The denser such networks in a community, the more likely that its citizens will be able to cooperate for mutual benefit."[475]

The concept of social capital can be identified in a broad array of scientific fields ranging within the spectrum of social sciences. Despite early publications drawing on the term and, as in case of Granovetter, considering social capital as decisive resource for inter-organizational collaboration (1985, p. 524), a remarkable increase of attention in the social sciences disciplines can be found since the 1990s.[476] The emergent multi-disciplinary elaboration of social capital hampers a comprehensive understanding of the concept. Consequently, a variety of definitions may be identified in the literature.[477] The intense discussion of the concept emphasizes the importance of considering socio-institutional structures to corporate analysis.[478] From a business administrative perspective, therefore, the definition by Nahapiet/Ghoshal can be identified as the one most referred to in research papers applying the concept to specific problem statements such as the relevance of social capital for entrepreneurial firm performance.[479] According to the authors social capital can

---

474 Kao 2009, p. 114.
475 Putnam 1993, p. 173.
476 See Woolcock/Narayan 2000, p. 225; also see Lee 2009, p. 248.
477 For an overview of definitions of social capital see Adler/Kwon 2002, p. 20.
478 See Bathelt/Glückler 2003, p. 189.
479 See e.g. Maurer/Ebers 2006; Martínez-Cañas/Saez-Martinez/Ruiz-Palomino 2012. Using Google Scholar, a number of 6392 citations of the contribution by Nahapiet/Ghoshal (1998) can be identified at current state of investigation. Despite a contribution by Coleman (1998) which has received more popularity due to 17701 listed citations, elaborating the concept from a sociological perspective regarding the crea-

be understood as "the sum of the actual and potential resources embedded within, available through and derived from the network of relationships possessed by an individual or social unit. Social capital comprises both the network and the assets that may be mobilized through that network."[480] This perspective enlarges the previously presented view of social capital as valuable organizational resource by also interpreting social capital as factor for the provision of access to resources. Within a network perspective this leads to the understanding that "social capital thus comprises both the network and the assets that may be mobilized through the network."[481]

A systematic review of social capital across the business and management fields by Lee 2009 provides a helpful contribution to systemize the concept as a suitable theoretical background for this work. Here, on the one hand a fourfold view of social capital as a comprehensive approach is identified as providing a systemized overview of the multiple perspectives on the concept. On the other hand, a dimensions model of social capital is seen as decisive for enabling an application of the concept to a business and management context. Therefore, within the following subsections an overview of social capital perspectives and dimensions is elaborated. Based on these aspects a conceptual approach to social capital is presented.

3.1.1.1 Multilayer Perspective of Social Capital

The characterization of social capital is hindered due to its intangibility and tacit nature, as which is emphasized by Coleman: "If physical capital is wholly tangible, being embodied in observable material form, and human capital is less tangible, being embodied in the skills and knowledge acquired by an individual, social capital is less tangible yet, for it exists in the relations among persons."[482] In this context the emergence of a multidisciplinary discussion of the concept has caused the evolution of a broad array of perspectives. Woolcock/Narayan (2000) consider the common denominator of these perspectives by presenting a fourfold perspective of social capital drawing on a communitarian, networks, institutional and synergy view.[483]

---

tion of human capital in society. The contribution by Nahapiet/Ghoshal (1998), however, draws on an organizational perspective discussing the concept from a business administrative point of view allowing for an application of the concept for further elaboration in the field of strategic management (also see Lee 2009, p. 254).

480   Nahapiet/Ghoshal 1998, p. 243.
481   See Weterlund/Svahn 2008, p. 493.
482   Coleman 1998, pp. 100-101.
483   See Woolcock/Narayan 2000, pp. 229-235.

- Communitarian view: This perspective of social capital draws on a normative value system serving as a 'kit' of human interaction toward a productive outcome. This is based on a community perspective with reference to a high density of social ties among local organizations.[484] A local context (region), therefore, can be interpreted as a physical and social environment, influencing the individual mindset and ways of behavior of its inhabitants.[485] Within this view social capital represents a set of norms that encourage inter-organizational co-operation including aspects such as honesty, meeting obligations and reciprocity.[486] By understanding co-operation as a process, trusted relationships among collaborating actors are developed as well as shared values to achieve a common goal drawing on frequent communication.[487] The intense interaction among community members may also be characterized as 'thick social capital,' serving as a differentiator to less intensive forms of interaction conceptualized as 'thin social capital'.[488] A development of "benevolence-trust and solidarity" is amplified by the environmental conditions acting upon the community such as economic and structural dynamics.[489] "The social capital embodied in networks of civic engagements seems to be a precondition for economic development."[490] Thus, if the interplay of economics and society is based on shared values which is based on intense interaction, social capital may positively influence the economic climate and the creation of welfare.[491]

- Networks view: Based on the approach by Granovetter (1973) one may differentiate between strong and weak ties among people and organizational entities within network structures the perspectives of bonding and bridging social capital are elaborated.[492] The aspect of bonding refers to intra-network linkages containing actors who communicate frequently and establish trust among the network members. 'Bonding social capital,' consequently, refers to the establishment of 'strong ties' within communities based on frequent interaction and a value-based proximity.[493] Whereas bridging draws on an open network approach and the establishment of 'weak ties' to a wide array of characters and organizations via infrequent communication. 'Bridging social capital', therefore, can be understood as vehicle to sources new information.[494] Social capital primari-

---

484   See Woolcock/Narayan 2000, p. 229.
485   See Touminen/Jussila/Saksa 2006, p. 11.
486   See Fukuyama 1997, p. 5.
487   See Putnam 2000, p. 19; Porter/Kramer, 2011, p. 66.
488   See Putnam/Goss 2002, p. 10.
489   See Putnam 1993, p. 37; Lee 2009, p. 250; Woolcock/Narayan 2000, p. 230.
490   See Putnam 1993, p. 37.
491   See Cohen/Fields 2000, p. 179; Putnam/Goss 2002, p. 3.
492   See Gittell/Vidal 1998.
493   See Putnam/Goss 2002, p. 3; Grafton 2005, p. 756.
494   See Burt 1997, p. 340.

ly is determined by network structures that lead to individual advantages based on their positioning within a network.[495] Thus, from an economic perspective, social capital within a networks view may provide advantages based on decreased transaction costs and access to resources. However, "there are also costs in that these some ties can place considerable noneconomic claims of members' sense of obligation and commitment, with negative economic consequences."[496] This critical remark emphasizes that building social capital within networks does not directly create a utility but rather the potential for interactive value creation. Therefore, the identification of social capital efficiency requires further and case-specific analysis.

- Institutional view: The creation of social capital within communities, networks and civil society at large may be seen as a product of its institutional environment. The emergence of social capital within this understanding, consequently, may be influenced by macro conditions such as political and market interventions. Institutions have the power to establish trust in a functioning economic environment, enabling the evolvement of entrepreneurial opportunities and flourishing free market trade by providing the conditions required.[497] Based on the establishment of formal structures, 'formal social capital' is created serving as a stabilizer of a complex social system.[498]

- Synergy view: Here, the realization of synergies between governmental institutions and private entities is emphasized. The cornerstones of this view are complementarity, understood as a supporting relation between public and private actors and embeddedness which refers to the quality of ties between these actors. The aspect of complementarity allows for the realization of advantages based on the interaction with actors located in different fields of expertise. Based on relations to complementary actors opportunities may be identified based on inter-disciplinary knowledge transfer.[499] This perspective may be conceptualized as 'outward-looking social capital.'[500] If synergy persists, expressed by a vital economic climate and individual liberty to participate in society, then high levels of 'bridging social capital' can also be identified.[501]

---

495 See Portes 2000, p. 48.
496 Woolcock/Narayan 2000, p. 231.
497 See Skocpol/Ganz/Munson 2000, p. 541. The establishment of a market for ideas, protecting intellectual property serves as suitable example for this perspective (see Ganz/Stern 2003).
498 See Putnam/Goss 2002, p. 10. In contrast to formal social capital the authors mention the existence of 'informal social capital' which relates to continuous habitual social interaction.
499 See Burt 1992, p. 9; Adler/Kwon 2002, p. 19.
500 See Putnam/Goss 2002, p. 11. Per contra 'inward-looking social capital' may be defined as "social capital of a collectivity (organization, community, nation, and so forth) is not so much in that collectivity's external ties to other external actors as it is in its internal structure - in the linkages among individuals or groups within the collectivity and, specifically, in these features that give the collectivity cohesiveness and thereby facilitate the pursuit of collective goals." (Adler/Kwon 2002, p. 20).
501 See Woolcock/Narayan 2000, p. 237.

Based on these views presented, it becomes apparent that social capital theory addresses a spectrum of differentiable phenomena. Within the introduction chapter to "Democracies in Flux: The Evolution of Social Capital in Contemporary Society" Putnam/Goss (2002) the authors emphasize the challenge in establishing reliable classifications of the concept. Based on an understanding of social capital as "social networks and the norms of reciprocity associated with them"[502] the authors suggest the following distinctions, being aware of conceptual interference: (1) thick versus thin social capital; (2) bridging versus bonding social capital; (3) formal versus informal social capital; (4) inward-looking versus outward-looking social capital. These aspects are contained in the four views of social capital presented above, which supports the suggestion of these categories serving as suitable perspectives to approach and systemize the complex and multilayer phenomenon.

3.1.1.2 Dimensions of Social Capital

Social capital may be understood as "the number of people who can be expected to provide support and the resources these people have at their disposal."[503] Furthermore, in addition to this resource perspective, the concept may emphasize the relevance of relations and networks to set the preconditions for the access to these resources. This leads to an understanding of social capital as "features of social organization such as networks, norms and social trust that facilitate coordination and cooperation for mutual benefit. Social capital enhances the benefits of investment in physical and human capital."[504] As indicated within the 'networks view' the development of social capital from an economic point of view does not directly relate to the creation of increased utility but rather serves as the potential for interactive value creation. Therefore, the concept of social capital needs to be discussed in a more precise manner that systemizes the variety of attributes assigned to the concept within a business and management context (to serve as suitable theoretical basis for the analytical procedures of this work). Based on the elaborations of Nahapiet/Ghoshal (1998), which is the most cited article discussing social capital as influential factor to develop intellectual capital within a management context,[505] social capital may be determined by a (1) a structural dimension, with reference to the existence, size and density of relationships within a network; (2) a cognitive dimension comprising shared understanding and the relevance of common cognitive schemes; and (3) a relational di-

---

502 Putnam/Goss 2002, p. 3.
503 Boxman/de Grant/Flap 1991, p. 52.
504 Putman 1995, p. 36.
505 See Lee 2009, p. 254.

mension, drawing on the elements characterizing the quality of relationships such as trust and prevalence of norms and obligations.[506]

- Structural dimension: The network structure is emphasized as the core element influencing the effects and development of social capital and can therefore be considered its essential component.[507] "The structure of social nets is crucial to understanding the opportunities and restrictions of actors, in accordance with their positions in them."[508] Understanding the structure of a network as a result of social interactions of actors, various forms of configurations within a network for an interactive exchange of resources among individuals and organizations can be identified. The network configuration is based on the share of bonding and bridging social capital among its members. Therefore, the character of network ties determines the infrastructural architecture of the networks' channels for information transfer.[509] As indicated in the networks view of social capital,[510] 'strong ties' relate to frequent interactions among network members and the establishment of a value-based proximity.[511] 'Weak ties,' in contrast, are based on infrequent communication and loose connections to a wide spectrum of characters and organizations located in separate network clusters.[512]

Consequently, configuration patterns can be identified determining the structural embeddedness of actors.[513] These are characterized by the network size, which refers to the number of ties in a network, the level of the network's centrality toward a core actor, and the level of constraints of network relations.[514] Regarding network constraints, actors may profit most intensively from their social capital by bridging and consequently coordinating information transfer between separate networks with reference to the idea of structural holes.[515] "The structural hole argument defines social capital in terms of the information and control advantages of being the broker in relations between people otherwise disconnected in the social structure."[516] Figure 9 displays a simulated network structure, which considers the reader as focal actor bridging between three network clusters. These clusters show strong ties among its members, whereas the reader is used as broker connecting the clusters due to weak ties. Within this constella-

---

506   See Nahapiet/Ghoshal, 1998, pp. 251-256.
507   See Portes 2000, p. 48; Lin 2001, p. 14.
508   See Garcia 2006, p. 7.
509   See Nahapiet/Ghoshal, 1998, p. 252.
510   See Chapter 3.1.1.1.
511   See Putnam/Goss 2002, p. 3; Grafton 2005, p. 756.
512   See Granovetter 1973, p. 1363.
513   See Granovetter 1985, pp. 481-483.
514   See Gilsing/Nooteboom 2005, pp. 181-185; Scott 1991.
515   See Burt 1992.
516   Burt 1997, p. 340.

tion structural holes occur between, on the one hand, between you and your cluster and actor A and, on the other hand, you and your cluster and actor B. Furthermore, a structural hole persists between the actors A and B.[517]

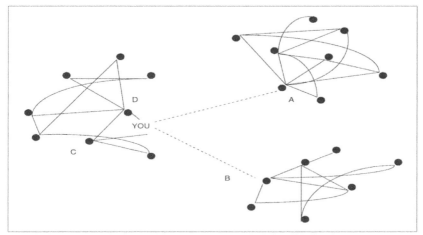

Figure 9: Network structure, structural holes and weak ties
Source: Lee 2009, p. 255, based on Burt 1992, p. 27.

As the concept of structural holes shows, networks vary in character and actors may profit from the multitude of network clusters by building bridges and therefore broker-ing knowledge among them. The existence of such clusters may result from the strong relations of actors involved in a rather strong and stable network structure. Based on this structure the evolvement of collective values among the network members and commitment toward a common goal is promoted which is also referred to as 'network-ing capital.'[518] "While recognizing that the structural facets also may be systematically associated with other conditions for the exchange and combination of knowledge, we believe that these associations are primarily derived indirectly, through the ways in which structure influences the development of the relational and cognitive dimensions of social capital."[519]

• Cognitive dimension: The cognitive dimension emphasizes the relevance of a shared understanding and common cognitive schemes among network actors. Their synergy is intensified in the case of cultural congruence with reference to a shared base of values

517 See Lee 2009, pp. 255-256.
518 See Mandell/Keast 2008, p. 693.
519 See Nahapiet/Ghoshal, 1998, pp. 251-252.

whose emergence is facilitated by a common language.[520] "Personal knowledge can be transmitted because a set of values are learned, permitting a shared language by which to communicate."[521] The language and codes used to communicate are emphasized as the decisive component to exchange knowledge within a sender-recipient context.[522] Consequently, an interactive process of knowledge creation by combining existent forms to create new knowledge requires a sound basis for information transfer.[523] Furthermore, Nahapiet/Ghoshal (1998, pp. 254) draw on the relevance of shared narratives improving reciprocal cognition and serving as facilitator in exchanging experiences and practices.

- Relational dimension: Certain elements characterize the quality of relationships among network actors. This quality is determined by the accessibility of resources through the network leading to the potential of realizing 'relational rent'.[524] The relational dimension, consequently, draws on the ability of actors to source knowledge via network channels by receiving access to relevant network partners, as well as a mutual anticipation and motivation to engage in interactive knowledge and value creation.[525] The existence of norms and obligations as well as identity within the network are emphasized as critical aspects for the establishment of network quality trust:

  - "Some see trust as a source of social capital, some see it as a form of social capital, and some see it as a collective asset resulting from social capital."[526] Trust, consequently, can be understood and interpreted from multiple angles, even though comprehensively it is a facilitator for the exchange of resources and information,[527] determining a trustworthy actor as popular partner of exchange.[528]

  - Norms can be understood as a 'relational value system' affecting the appropriate and acceptable behavior of individuals within the social context and therefore providing certain goodwill. "Its effects flow from the information, influence, and solidarity it makes available."[529] Thus, norms represent a foundation of interac-

---

520 See Cameron/Freeman 1991, p. 28.
521 Kogut/Zander 1992, p. 389.
522 See Nahapiet/Ghoshal, 1998, pp. 253.
523 See Nonaka/Konno 1998, p. 42.
524 See Dyer/Singh 1998, p. 662. Here, the authors define a relational rent as "a supernormal profit jointly generated in an exchange relationship that cannot be generated by either firm in isolation and can only be created through the joint idiosyncratic contributions of the specific alliance partners."
525 See Nahapiet/Ghoshal, 1998, p. 254.
526 See Adler/Kwon 2002, p. 26.
527 See Uzzi 1996, p. 678.
528 See Tsai/Ghoshal 1998, p. 467. For a more detailed discussion of the role of trust in inter-organizational relations, see Chapter 3.1.2.2.
529 Adler/Kwon 2002, p. 23.

tive knowledge creation influencing the willingness to openly share resources such as knowledge and information with network partners.[530]

- Obligations rely on a set of pre-determined rules creating a committed focus to undertake action.[531] Obligations consequently serve as expectations which are based on a certain personal relationship. These expectations draw on the willingness of actors to achieve a repeatable experience within the interaction process with network partners.[532]

- Based on the logic of strong ties, similar emotional intimacy is developed toward the structural system. These emotions may turn out into a feeling of identity. "Identification is the process whereby individuals see themselves as one with another person or group of people."[533] As discussed within the communitarian view, a social system such as a regional structure may influence the individual mindset and the behavior of its inhabitants.[534] Therefore, a specification of identity among network actors may mobilize the perceived opportunities to interact and amplify the frequency of cooperation due to an anticipation of mutual advantage.

3.1.1.3 Conceptual Aproach to Social Capital

"Social capital is the goodwill available to individuals or groups. Its source lies in the structure and content of the actor's social relations. Its effects flow from the information, influence, and solidarity it makes available to the actor."[535]

Based on previous elaborations the creation of social capital may relate to an interpersonal action in which one actor provides a favor to a network contact without direct compensation. Applying the structural, relational and cognitive dimensions[536] to the context of social capital creation, three elements that have to be mutually prevalent within social relations can be identified and therefore serving as source of social capital: (1) the existence of opportunities for social relationship creation, (2) the motivation of individuals to cooperate with each other either intrinsically inspired, or driven by norms of reciprocity, and (3) the existence of certain abilities essential for a cooperation's success.[537] Opportu-

---

530 See Nahapiet/Ghoshal, 1998, p. 255.
531 See Lee 2009, p. 257.
532 See Tsai 2000, p. 927.
533 See Nahapiet/Ghoshal, 1998, p. 256.
534 See Touminen/Jussila/Saksa 2006, p. 11.
535 Adler/Kwon 2002, p. 23.
536 See Nahapiet/Ghoshal, 1998, pp. 251-256. Also see for a discussion of these dimensions the previous Chapter 3.1.1.2.
537 See Adler/Kwon 2002, p. 27.

nities arise when structures of exchange exist (structural dimension); trust and valid norms facilitate motivation (relational dimension). The cognitive schemes and value patterns shape the ability to combine individual and social values (cognitive dimension). This sub-section presents a conceptual model introduced by Adler/Kwon (2002) summarizing previous elaborations of social capital theory and offering a sound basis for a continuative discussion of entrepreneurial networks. The model aims to explain social capital by drawing on its sources, its benefits and risks as well as the contingencies influencing its value.[538] Figure 10 illustrates the conceptual model and the inter-relations of the components mentioned which are discussed in more detail:

- Sources of social capital: Opportunity, motivation and ability are identified as essential sources of social capital creation. Opportunities emerge based on the social ties of an actor's network. Here, the quality and the configuration of the network structure are decisive in serving as a vital medium for opportunity creation. Special emphasis is placed on the existence of a balanced specification of strong and weak network ties to provide access to a broad spectrum of resources.[539] Furthermore, in this context the brokerage of knowledge is characterized as a decisive source of profiting from social capital.[540] The intrinsic aspect of motivation to engage in such transactions is connected to the individual belief that social exchange does not require an immediate return, which contradicts the thought pattern of the 'homo economicus.'[541] The motivational aspect is coined by norms of general reciprocity within the network and a shared value base such as trust among network actors.[542] The establishment of trust draws on the "the willingness and ability of individuals to define collective goals that are then enacted collectively."[543] Understanding ability as the package of capabilities and resources obtained by a network actor, it is the individual who actively participates in exchange processes based on specific resources and the potential to source these via network ties. Ability, consequently, strongly depends on the motivation of network contacts to interact and the opportunities resulting from the network structure.[544]

- Benefits and risks of social capital: Since the creation of social capital requires an investment, as in other forms of capital, a positive return on investments in social relationships may occur, but risk may also be present and needs to be considered. "There are also costs in that these some ties can place considerable noneconomic claims of

---

538   See Adler/Kwon 2002, p. 23.
539   See Granovetter 1973, p. 1363.
540   See Burt 1992, p. 27.
541   See Adler/Kwon 2002, p. 24.
542   See Putnam 1993, pp. 182-183; Putnam 2000, p. 19; Woolcock/Narayan 2000, p. 230.
543   Leana/Van Buren 1999, p. 542.
544   See Adler/Kwon 2002, p. 27.

members' sense of obligation and commitment, with negative economic consequences."[545] The effectiveness of social capital draws on the benefits realized through it regarding information, influence and control, and solidarity.[546] Information benefits may arise from an intense exchange of information within network clusters of strong ties and an outreach to separate clusters based on weak ties causing positive externalities. Based on the concept of structural holes the brokering of knowledge within structures as such may amplify the diffusion of information based on reciprocal flows between network clusters.[547] A hypothetical vice versa constellation would provoke inefficiencies due to high investment requirements in establishing strong ties to separate network clusters.[548] Furthermore, the establishment of a reliable network structure based on strong ties may provide power benefits regarding the assurance of direct accessibility to resources required. Nonetheless, one should critically mention that "the ties that bind may also turn into ties that blind."[549] Solidarity benefits may intensify reciprocal trust and loyalty among actors, but they may also lead to inefficiencies when overembeddedness neglects the dynamics and flow of new ideas.[550] Contracts of exclusiveness need to be mentioned in this context which aim for the prevention of unintended knowledge spillovers to competitors but may exclude the accessibility of complementary resources for future innovation.[551]

- Contingencies and value of social capital: This is based on the understanding that the ability of a network's actor is decisive for creating social capital. The possession of complementary capabilities may be essential to creating opportunities for social capital development. Hierarchical structures within large organizations or network clusters determining the extent of resources, skills and mindset contained, may provide a demand for complementary capabilities, which can be identified in close range network clusters.[552] Consequently, to approach social capital efficiency the networking intensity

---

545 See Woolcock/Narayan 2000, p. 231.
546 See Sanderfur/Laumann 1998, p. 481.
547 See Burt 1992, p. 27.
548 See Granovetter 1973, p. 1363.
549 Powell/Smith-Doerr 1994, p. 393.
550 See Uzzi 1997, p. 59; Stam/Elfring 2008, p. 109; Florida/Cushing/Gates 2002, p. 20.
551 See Segal/Whinston 2000; Azoulay/Shane 2001, pp. 338-339.
552 The discussion of specialization as applied in Chapter 2.3.1.1 may serve as example to illustrate the interaction of hierarchical relations and complementary capabilities. Large corporations such as OEMs focus their operations and apply specific norms and culture within their organizational structure. Small entrepreneurial firms may offer complementary capabilities by specializing in fields outside of the OEM's focus and more flexibly applying new solutions to prevailing tasks. For example, the application of new software may be a critical aspect in the implementation of large corporations due to formal constraints, whereas it is a capability of small firms to react quickly to changing market conditions.

must be aligned to the organizational goals.[553] Task contingencies align to this perspective that the configuration of relations to market actors regarding the investment in strong and weak ties should be congruent with goals defined. Furthermore, symbolic contingencies need to be mentioned regarding the establishment of social capital in global market economies. Cultural congruence determines the applicability of the described forms of social capital development. Therefore, in the context of international business studies a differentiation of cultural conditions within networked interactions need to be considered.[554]

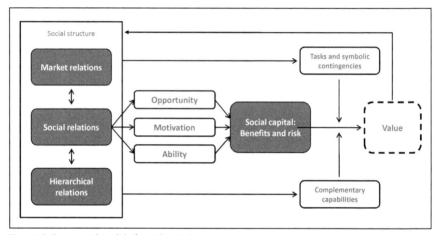

Figure 10: Conceptual model of social capital
Source: Adler/Kwon 2002, p. 23.

3.1.2 Entrepreneurship and the Relevance of Social Capital

"Specifically, early in venture's development, entrepreneurs often face high risks resulting from limited protection for their developing ideas. Resource providers also face risks from information asymmetry, and, in turn, adverse selection, arising from the entrepreneur's unwillingness or inability to fully communicate information."[555]

As this statement indicates, the commercialization process of entrepreneurial goods and services includes severe challenges. Especially entrepreneurs in the field of KIBS face high

---

553 See Krackhardt/Hanson 1993, p. 110.
554 See Hofstede 1994; Trompenaars/Prud'homme 2004.
555 Smith/Lohrke 2008. p. 316.

uncertainties regarding the collaboration with external partners due to a fear of unintended knowledge spillover reducing the value proposition of the products offered. In return, following the character of knowledge-intensive firms, these entrepreneurial firms offer the application of advanced knowledge to solve prevailing challenges of established organizations,[556] which causes an information asymmetry to potential customers.[557] Consequently, a 'paradox of disclosure' becomes persistent within entrepreneurial activity. "Simply put, when trading in ideas, the willingness-to-pay of potential buyers depends on their knowledge of the idea, yet knowledge of the idea implies that potential buyers need not pay in order to exploit it."[558] This section draws on the identified conflict relating entrepreneurship to social capital.

To identify the relevance of social capital for entrepreneurial performance the literature was screened for contributions to the field of research. This focused on works analyzing the impact of social capital within an empirical investigation and relating specific components to entrepreneurial performance. The following corresponding contributions were identified:[559]

- Brüderl/Preisdörfer (1998): Based on 1700 responses of new business ventures in Upper Bavaria, Germany, the authors empirically test the 'network success hypothesis'[560]. The results indicate that entrepreneurs are able to receive support for establishing entrepreneurial performance based on their strong ties. The analysis of weak ties, however, showed less relevance. Furthermore, the hypothesis that the social capital of entrepreneurs might compensate for shortfalls of human and financial capital was not confirmed in this investigation.[561]

- Liao/Welch (2003): The authors elaborate eight hypotheses based on the dimensions of social capital,[562] regarding their effects on growth endeavors of entrepreneurial firms. The attributes of entrepreneurial orientation (innovativeness, pro-activity and risk-taking) are determined as variables characterizing the innovative character of the en-

---

556 See Hipp 1999, p. 94.
557 See Akerlof, 1970.
558 Gans/Stern 2003, p. 338. For insight into the origin of the concet of 'paradox of disclosure,' see Arrow 1962.
559 The selction of contributions identified does not guarantee completeness but may serve as a sufficient basis for further elaborations.
560 See Aldrich/Zimmer 1986a. The 'network success hypothesis' refers to the assumption that the performance of an entrepreneurial firm in terms of survival and growth depends on the personal network of the entrepreneur.
561 See Brüderl/Preisdörfer 1998, p. 224. Therefore, the authors draw on further research projects to contribute to further research within the discussion of networked entrepreneurship.
562 For an elaboration of the structural, relational and cognitive dimensions of social capital see Chapter 3.1.1.2.

trepreneurial firm venture performance.[563] The analysis draws on a sampling of the 'Panel Study of Entrepreneurial Dynamics" containing 150 technology-oriented and 312 non-technology-oriented start-ups. Based on equation modeling technique, the authors found no evidence for significant effects of structural social capital for growth endeavors of technology-oriented start-ups. "The presence or absence of extensive social ties is not a pre-condition for the growth of technology ventures."[564] For non-technology-oriented entrepreneurs, on the other hand, the accessibility of resources via networks has been identified as critical for venture growth. With regard to the relational dimension trust and trustworthiness have been identified as mutually relevant. "Trust and trustfulness greatly increase entrepreneurs' accessibility and appropriatability of external resources."[565] Since trust evolves from strong ties, a case-specific approach toward network structuring is required to enable social capital efficiency, with reference to an economic discussion of structural embeddedness.[566] This perspective is emphasized by the significance of cognitive social capital in the form of shared values as transmitter of efficient exchange and assimilation of knowledge.

- Davidsson/Honig (2003): The study aims to determine factors of success of human and social capital in order to explore and exploit entrepreneurial opportunities. Based on a data set of 380 nascent entrepreneurs the relevance of strong and weak ties with reference to bridging and bonding social capital is empirically analyzed. With regard to human capital, the authors show that organizational support by institutional representatives such as entrepreneurship coaches may only provide significant support within the entrepreneurial process if these have much experience and expertise to share with nascent entrepreneurs. With regard to social capital, however, the findings prove the relevance of social contacts obtained in formal networks such as business clubs and associations to increase the probability of sales or profitability.[567]

- Mosey/Wright (2007): Within a 12-month timeframe the authors use a longitudinal approach to analyze 24 academic nascent technology entrepreneurs. Based on 45 interviews the relevance of entrepreneurship experience is seen in the capability to establish social capital. The results show that entrepreneurs with higher experience draw on wider social network structures and also show a higher capability in effectively establishing network ties. In contrast, less experienced entrepreneurs encounter structural holes between research networks and business networks constraining opportunity

---

563   See Liao/Welch 2003, p. 152. Also see Chapter 2.1.1.
564   See Liao/Welch 2003, p. 165.
565   Liao/Welch 2003, p. 166.
566   See Krackhardt/Hanson 1993, p. 110; Stam/Elfring (2008, p. 109) emphasize in thier contribution the possibility of negative effects on performance based on an over-embeddedness.
567   See Davidsson/Honig 2003, p. 325.

recognition.[568] The formation of ties consequently is emphasized as decisive for nascent technology entrepreneurs to achieve entrepreneurial performance by transferring specific technological knowledge into business networks.

The studies briefly presented allow for a meta-analytical approach toward influential components of social capital regarding entrepreneurial performance. The following subsections, therefore, elaborate these components in an aggregated perspective emphasizing the relevance of tie-formation and the relevance of establishing trust as essential factors of social capital influencing the performance of the entrepreneurial firm.

3.1.2.1 The Relevance of Tie Formation

The previous elaborations emphasize the relevance of tie formation as a decisive aspect for the future development of an entrepreneurial venture. However, by going into detail contradictory perspectives can be identified regarding the balance of weak and strong ties. Whereas Smith/Lohrke (2008) highlight that "the network's structure should consist of an even higher number of weak, rather than strong, ties,"[569] Liao/Welch (2001) conclude from their findings that "a sparse social network is actually a beneficial factor for technology entrepreneurs in that they can access rich non-redundant information and knowledge and also lower costs in maintaining few ties."[570] Consequently, the formation of network structures has to be adapted to case-specific analysis to achieve social capital efficiency.[571] Depending on the characteristics of the entrepreneurial firm, individual implications can be drawn from empirical studies. A decisive component within the analytical process is the ambition of the corporation to either explore new knowledge for developing new capabilities and innovations, or to exploit the prevailing portfolio of organizational knowledge.[572] Also, the possibility persists that firms strive for a combined approach of knowledge and idea sourcing and IP commercialization as characterized by the coupled-process of open innovation.[573] The implementation, however, may cause severe organizational challenges requiring intensive investments in multiple network clusters simultaneously.[574]

---

568 See Mosey/Wright 2007, p. 932.
569 Smith/Lohrke 2008, p. 319. The authors base their statement on an empirical envestigation by Schutjens/Stam 2003.
570 Liao/Welch 2003, p. 166. Also see Brüderl/Preisdörfer 1998, p. 224.
571 See Krackhardt/Hanson 1993, p. 110; Stam/Elfring 2008, p. 109.
572 See Harryson 2008, p. 295.
573 See Gassmann/Enkel 2006, p. 136. Also see Chapter 2.2.2.2.
574 See He/Wong, p. 492.

Based on the initial definition of entrepreneurship as a process of discovery, evaluation and exploitation[575] in which individuals pursue opportunities to create market innovations[576] a combined perspective of exploration and exploitation appears to be a precondition of entrepreneurial behavior. Striving for a tie formation which maximizes the yield per contact, the superficiality character of weak ties has to be considered. This may amplify knowledge and technology scouting but slow down the process of knowledge transfer. Understanding strong ties as facilitator for exploitation of innovation, one may conclude that the "commercialization of radical innovation requires management of both weak and strong relationships for transfer and transformation of information into innovation across multiple types of networks."[577] Consequently, depending on the respective step within the entrepreneurial process, a specific mix of weak and strong ties can be characterized as most beneficial allocation. Being aware that the entrepreneurial process in knowledge-intensive fields represents a highly interactive procedure with multiple actors from a variety of corresponding network clusters, an entrepreneurial firm will develop a specific set of strong and weak ties within an evolutionary process over time.[578]

3.1.2.2 Reciprocity and the Relevance of Trust

Reciprocity refers to the mindset of "not 'I'll do this for you, because you are more powerful than I, nor even I'll do this for you now, if you do that for me now, but I'll do this for you now knowing that somewhere down the road you'll do something for me'"[579]

The concept of reciprocity can be understood as a norm binding a social structure of strong ties and guiding collective action.[580] As indicated by Putman (1993), reciprocity neglects the guideline of efficient utility maximization and refers to a long-term oriented thought pattern of social interaction. By following a commitment to a common goal actors are required to transform their egocentric mindset into a community member perspective.[581] Reciprocity, therefore, can be defined as "a set of motivationally interrelated gifts of favours."[582] The critical element within this construct the aspect of trust in a return for a

---

575 See Shane/Venkataraman 2000, p. 218.
576 See Stevenson/Jarillo 1990 p. 23; Krackhardt 1995, pp. 53-55.
577 Harryson 2008, p. 295.
578 See Elfring/Hulsink 2007, p. 1853, 1866. For a process-based perspective of the evolution of entrepreneurial networks, see Hansen 1995; Schultjens/Stam 2003.
579 Putnam 1993, p. 182-183.
580 See Goulder 1960, p. 161.
581 See Adler/Kwon 2002, p. 25.
582 Kolm 2009, p. 13.

favorable action in the form of a social credit.[583] Consequently, an actor investing in the establishment of social capital trusts in receiving a future return on investment based on the norm of reciprocity.[584]

As indicated in previous aspects of this work, the establishment of trust is as a key component for a long-term development of social relations and to enable the reciprocal exchange of resources.[585] Trust, therefore, may be understood as "the willingness of a party to be vulnerable to the actions of another party based on the expectation that the other will perform a particular action important to the trustor, irrespective of the ability to monitor or control that other party."[586] This statement relates the trust construct to the characteristic of the trustworthiness of an actor, which can be conceptualized by a combined perception of honesty and predictability toward the interaction partner.[587] Transaction cost economics (TCE), drawing on the precondition of rational behavior in transaction processes,[588] found a broad range of criticism serving as suitable construct to explain inter-organizational behavior due to a neglection of social components.[589] "Variability of trustworthiness, and hence of its opposite, propensity toward opportunism underlines the need to extend TCE with considerations of trust."[590] These contributions have highlighted the relevance of trust among collaboration partners to reduce the perception of opportunistic behavior and thus of transaction costs.[591]

The inter-personal relationships between exchange partners are critical for the development of trust. Here, scholars distinguish between, on the one hand affective trust, which is based on an instant intrinsic virtue leading to a genuine concern toward the partner, and on the other hand cognitive trust which relates to a conscious decision process.[592] Whereas in the case of affective trust a high level of reciprocal goodwill can be found, the latter requires a more complex analysis. Within this perspective "trust develops successively; it is the result of a gradual deepening of the relationship through a process of mutual adaptation to the needs of the other party."[593] The establishment of reputation may,

---

583   See Lin 2003, p. 151.
584   See Putnam/Goss 2002, p. 7.
585   See Cohen/Fields 2000, p. 189; Chiles/McMackin 1996, p. 88.
586   Mayer/Davis/Schoorman 1995, p. 712; also see Lin 2003, p. 147.
587   See McKnight/Chervany 2006, p. 35.
588   See Williamson 19975, p. 40.
589   See e.g. Granovetter 1985, p. 495; Krugman 2000, p. 49.
590   See Nooteboom 1996, p. 993.
591   See Chiles/McMackin 1996, p. 88; Nooteboom 2007, pp. 35-39.
592   See McAllister 1995. Also see Johnson/Grayson (2005) for an applied discussion to service relationships.
593   Gounaris 2005, p. 127.

therefore, positively influence cognitive trust based on publicly communicated honors signalizing trustworthiness.[594]

For entrepreneurs building a reputation represents an immense challenge due to a lack of experience.[595] But also established corporations are challenged to create an image of 'fairness' to openly interact with entrepreneurial firms guaranteeing mutual advantage from the acquisition of external knowledge and technology. Corporations that can be identified as institutions of integrity strategically invest in their reputation to receive access to external technologies.[596] Entrepreneurs, therefore, might explicitly engage in relations with organizations in order to allow for an instant establishment of a high level of cognitive trust. This perspective allows for the thorough pattern of the deliberate action view that "entrepreneurs [can] pro-actively develop their exchange relationships so as to acquire social capital and overcome liability of newness."[597]

3.1.3 Synopsis

"As we gain a deeper understanding of the drivers of entrepreneurship, we see an opening of innovation processes that are getting increasingly networked."[598]

The liabilities that young and specifically nascent entrepreneurs face when entering product and service markets may be severe. Based on social capital and network theory, research in entrepreneurship has strived to identify the critical components necessary to overcome those liabilities and to enable the survival and flourishing of entrepreneurial firms. Aldrich/Zimmer (1986a) pioneered in the field by formulating the 'network success hypothesis' which refers to the assumption that the performance of an entrepreneurial venture in terms of survival and growth depends on the personal network of the entrepreneur. Whereas several studies confirmed this hypothesis by concluding that the personal network of the entrepreneur may lead to the realization of cost advantages in comparison to competitors,[599] an 'oversocialization' within the discussion can be identified. "Actors are oversocialized when portrayed as governed exclusively by values and norms and undersocialized when portrayed as isolated, rational economic units."[600] Consequent-

---

594 See Lin 2001, p. 19. See also Burt (2005, p. 209) who describes the reputation of an actor within network
    structures as content of 'echos' characterized as communication processes within networks.
595 See Witt 2004, p. 394.
596 See Gans/Stern 2003, p. 344.
597 See Smith/Lohrke 2008, p. 315.
598 Harryson 2008, p. 290.
599 See Starr/MacMillan 1990, pp. 83-85.
600 Larson 1992, p. 97.

ly, among experts networking has been emphasized as a panacea, whereas the economic point of view as actual origin of the discussion has been kept in the backseat.[601]

In contrast, recent empirical studies can be identified as drawing on the realization of social capital efficiency by analyzing the influence of social capital components' on entrepreneurial performance.[602] To summarize this chapter in this regard, entrepreneurial networks strive to reduce the liabilities of young entrepreneurial firms and to enable the exploration and exploitation of knowledge among network actors. Entrepreneurial networks, therefore, can be understood to result from activities by an entrepreneur to build, sustain and extend the individual network structure. The structure of the network setting is based on the extent of networking partners, the diversity of characters within the network and the quality of relations to these actors. The structure, consequently, can be interpreted as the determining variable creating the framework requirements for the dependent variables. These are, on the one hand, activities that are necessary for sustaining and establishing network contacts with reference to the effort invested in the network, in terms of time and frequency of interactions. On the other hand, lie the extent and quality of resources in the form of information and services that are potentially provided by network partners (see Figure 11).[603]

The literature highlights the importance of the establishment of trust as the essential aspect to overcome prevailing liabilities.[604] Since trust evolves with the establishment of strong ties inside network clusters, an involvement within dense network structures is seen as crucial for start-up success.[605] This perspective is emphasized by the significance of cognitive social capital in the form of shared values as the transmitter of efficient exchange and assimilation of knowledge. On the other hand, an over-structural embeddedness may hinder the exploration of entrepreneurial opportunities and the potential for establishing growth.[606] Therefore, a case-specific approach to network structuring is emphasized to enable an optimal return on social capital investments.[607] This leads to the conclusion that the question "what entrepreneurs can do to improve their chances of success in terms of networking and influence the structural characteristics of their personal network"[608] offers a broad field for further analysis.[609]

---

601 See Witt 2004, p. 409.
602 See e.g. Brüderl/Preisdörfer 1998; Liao/Welch 2003; Martinez-Canas/Saez-Martinez/Ruiz-Palomino 2012.
603 See Witt 2004, pp. 395-396.
604 See Liao/Welch 2003, p. 166.
605 See Davidsson/Honig 2003, p. 325.
606 See Stam/Elfring 2008, p. 109.
607 See Elfring/Hulsink 2007, pp. 1853, 1866.
608 Witt 2004, p. 396.
609 Also see Hoang/Antoncic 2003, pp. 181-182.

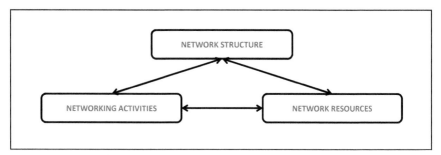

Figure 11: Dependency factors of entrepreneurial networks
Source: Based on Witt 2004, p. 395.

3.2 Competence-Based Approach to Co-Innovation

To enable a more profound understanding of the concept of co-innovation competence, a discussion in a wider context within the competence-based view of the firm will serve as the conceptual basis of this work. "Competences are not off-the-shelf products but are embedded in the heads and hands of people in teams, organizational structure and procedures, and organizational culture. They have a strong tacit dimension, especially in innovation."[610] Drawing on a basic understanding of the competence-based view and terms used within, the conceptual application to explain the corporation as an open system offers a suitable point of reference for further analysis. In this regard, the management of firm-specific resources and capabilities inside and outside of the boundaries of the firm receive more detailed attention. Especially a dynamic management of the knowledge and technology base is seen as the critical capacity of the firm to evolve within dynamic conditions drawing on the concept of 'dynamic capabilities.'[611] Based on those elaborations the concept of co-innovation competence is approached by reviewing the corresponding literature in the field and attempting a definition. Furthermore, path dependencies of the concept are discussed before drawing implications for further investigation regarding co-innovation competence of the entrepreneurial firm.

---

610   Notteboom 2006, p. 32.
611   See Teece/Pisano 1994; Teece/Pisano/Shuen 1997.

3.2.1 Competence-Based View of the Firm

3.2.1.1 Toward an Understanding of the Competence-Based View of the Firm

"Unlike physical assets, competencies do not deteriorate as they are applied and shared. They grow."[612]

Much of the discussion of the competence-based view of the firm suffers from a multiple application of terms that lack a comprehensive definition.[613] Especially a clarification of the terms 'competence,' and 'capability' seems necessary to select precise definitions and avoid confusion. In this regard, this work refers to the elaborations of Sanchez/Heene/Thomas (1996), who define capability as "repeatable pattern of action in the use of assets to create, produce, and/or offer products to the market," whereas competence is defined as "an ability to sustain the co-ordinated deployment of assets in a way that helps a firm to achieve its goals."[614] Consequently, a capability may be understood as an intangible re-source such as the knowledge and skill to operate a given tangible resource or intangible system.[615] A combined number of assets aligned for value creation, however, constitutes a competence.[616]

Based on the elaborations of the resource-based view of the firm, which serves as the conceptual origin of the competence-based view, resources refer to both tangible and intangible assets such as capabilities and knowledge enabling the firm to implement strat-egies to improve performance.[617] These resources are of strategic relevance to the firm if they are valuable, rare, imperfectly imitable and non-substitutable.[618] The competence-based perspective, in turn, perceives the corporation's resources as such, as insufficient to achieve a competitive advantage. Competences draw on the combination of resources for value creation by creating core products that serve customer requirements and show mar-ket-leading performance.[619] As Grant (1991) indicates: "Productive capacity requires the cooperation and coordination of a team of resources. A capability is the capacity for a team of resources to perform some task or activity."[620] Consequently, individual capabili-ties serve as the basis of organizational competences,[621] and it requires a 'higher-order

---

612 Prahalad/Hamel 1990, p. 82.
613 See Sanchez 2004, p. 519; Hansen 2009, p. 148.
614 See Sanchez/Heene/Thomas 1996, pp. 7, 11.
615 See Sanchez/Heene 1996 p. 41.
616 See Coombs (1996, p. 346) for a graphical display.
617 See Barney 1991, p. 101.
618 See Barney 1991, pp. 106-112.
619 See Coombs 1996, p. 346; Amit/Shoemaker 1993, p. 35; Hamel/Prahalad 1994b, p. 206.
620 Grant 1991, pp. 118-119.
621 See Doz 1996b, p. 157.

capability' to coordinate and configure the prevailing components to achieve corporate performance.[622] Therefore, building up competences as well as their leverage are seen as decisive to enabling future competitiveness.[623]

The term 'competence building' refers to a development or establishment of a competence base of a corporation, whereas 'competence leveraging' indicates the optimized utility of available competences.[624] The process of competence leveraging includes the exploitation of new corporate fields, which requires a moderate adaptation of the competence base. This indicates that an interdependent relationship between the terms can be identified. Competence building strongly relates to the qualitative changes of value creation and commercialization capacity of the actors within the corporation. To maintain competitiveness corporations are therefore required to effect an efficient leverage of prevailing competences and to simultaneously pursue continuous competence building. Management may invest in internal assets such as intellectual capital and individual capabilities to improve the competence base as well as draw on a wider extent to leverage the competence base of the firm.[625]

As the interplay of competence building and competence leverage indicates, a corporation as a specialized form of a social organization, characterized by the necessity to achieve rents for its actions to sustain the organization, is arranged in and depends on its environmental context.[626] On the one hand external forces drive continuous development, whereas, on the other hand, the environment offers a supply of knowledge sources to cope with these forces of change. Consequently, to establish a valuable knowledge base corporations rely on the internal evolution of its assets as well as on the external accessibility of specific resources to enable new knowledge creation by combining existing knowledge.[627] This perspective requires capabilities that "evolve over time and ... deliberate firm-level investments in learning and making improvements."[628] The competence of the corporation may be seen in an effective and efficient coordination and application of corporate assets as well as in the accessibility of external resources combined with specific capabilities to enable value creation and to deliver competitive products and services to the market.

---

622   See Collis 1994, p. 144; Grant 1996, pp. 377-378.
623   For a discussion of innovation competence see Chapter 2.1.2.2.
624   See Sanchez/Heene 2002, p. 71.
625   See Teece/Pisano/Shuen 1997, pp. 509-512; Sanchez/Heene 2002, p. 89.
626   See Lichtenthaler 2009, p. 317; Laursen/Masciarelli/Prencipe 2012.
627   See Gibb 2002, pp. 253-254.
628   Ethiraj et al. 2004, p. 28.

3.2.1.2 Conceptualizing the Firm as an Open System

Based on the understanding of the competence-based view of the firm, the achievement of future competitiveness involves goal-oriented and focused competence building as well as a competence-leveraging process. These strive for the optimization of the prevailing competence base and the development of new competences, based on the interplay with market conditions and further influential factors external to corporate boundaries. Continuous interaction processes with the external surrounding of the firm, consequently, are seen as decisive for corporate survival and future competitiveness.[629] In this perspective Sanchez/Heene (1996) discuss a dynamic, systemic, cognitive, and holistic conceptual approach, interpreting the corporation as an open system.[630]

Figure 12 illustrates the concept, where the dotted lines are the boundaries of the firm inducing permeable walls and therefore an open system interacting with components external to the firm. A value creation process serves as the basis for the concept initiated by the interplay of the 'strategic logic' with management processes and with the environmental context. "Strategic logic refers to the rationale(s) employed (explicitly or implicitly) by decision makers in the firm as to how specific deployments of resources are expected to result in an acceptable level of attainment of the firm's goals."[631] Since the strategic logic, consequently, can be understood as a collective mindset of the individuals involved in the formation of the value creation process, its characteristics may depend on the organizational structure and the corresponding attributes of an entrepreneurial management.[632] The cognitive capabilities of corporate leaders, thus specifically structure the basis of corporate decision-making.[633] In contrast, a lack of cognitive capability within strategic logic may negatively influence the exploration of market changes and the corresponding alignment of corporate assets.[634] In this case the recognition of the environmental context is decisive to either directly drawing implications based on scanning and benchmarking or source external experts such as consultants to offering corporate advisory.[635] "Managerial perceptions of possible technological, organizational or market changes may stimulate

---

629   See Sanchez/Heene 1996 pp. 39, 47.
630   See Sanchez/Heene/Thomas 1996, p. 11; Sanchez 2004, p. 521. Also see: Hansen 2009, pp. 187-189.
631   Sanchez/Hene/Thomas 1996, p. 10. The 'strategic logic' concept draws on the term 'dominant logic' as it was coined by Prahalad/Bettis (1986, p. 490). It is defined as "the way in which managers conceptualize the business and make critical resource allocations decisions."
632   See Chapter 2.1.1.2.
633   See Sanchez/Heene 2002, p. 88.
634   Sanchez/Hene/Thomas (1996, p. 7) define assets as "anything tangible or intangible the firm can use in ist processes for creating, producing, and/or offering ist products (goods or services) to a market."
635   See Sanchez/Hene 1996, p. 56.

decisions to build up qualitatively new stocks of resources in anticipation of environmental changes in the future."[636]

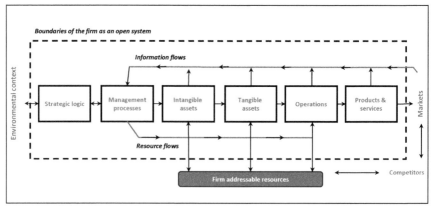

Figure 12: The corporation as an open system
Source: Based on Sanchez/Heene 1996, p. 41; 1997, p. 24.

To achieve the efficient use of prevailing resources and capabilities as well as their aligned development to exploit market opportunities, management processes need to be defined. These are influenced by the strategic logic and set the ground for future decision-making. Based on data and information flows from internal firm-specific resources and external sources such as 'firm addressable resources,' these processes are characterized by the evaluation and interpretation of data serving as a systemized foundation for decision-making. Specifically, intangible assets are understood as a set of capabilities, knowledge and social capital which enable the deployment of tangible assets for value creation. By leveraging knowledge and capabilities across corporate processes the use of tangible assets may be optimized.[637] In addition corporations may draw on an extra source of resource and competency base to close internal gaps by establishing ties to 'firm addressable resources'.[638] These refer to the sourcing of products and services offered by corporate partners allowing for an increase in efficiency and flexibility.[639] These partnerships may be

---

636 Sanchez/Hene 1997, p. 34.
637 See Quinn/Anderson/Finkelstein 1996. Sanchez/Heene (1996 p. 51) in this context refer to 'lower-order control loops' drawing on a feedback information flow.
638 See Sanchez/Heene 1996 p. 42; Sanchez/Hene/Thomas 1996, p. 7.
639 See Espino-Rodríguez/Padrón-Robaina 2006, p. 54. For a discussion on outsourcing and its effects on innovation performance see Chapter 2.2.2.1.

of formal character and are based on contractual agreements or may refer to habitual informal collaboration and network contacts.

Thus, flexibility is seen as critical to defining an alternative strategic logic regarding the perceived opportunities for value creation and to identifying a way to approach the definition of alternative management processes required for the pursuit of these opportunities. Furthermore, flexibility is required within the configuration and deployment of value chains integrating single components at need to achieve efficiency. To enable such a 'coordination flexibility' instant access to a broad array of suitable resources and capabilities is a necessary precondition.[640] Flexibility, therefore, may increase corporate potential and allow for an early reaction to market changes or even causing creative destruction.[641] The open system view of the firm, therefore, offers a dynamic perspective including the relevance of considering continuously changing context and market conditions. The achievement of competitive advantages, consequently, depends on the cognitive capabilities of corporate leaders to flexibly engage in new opportunity exploration and exploitation. Besides firm-specific resources the access to firm-addressable resources represents the initial point in configuring value creation processes that refer to an interaction with external stakeholders. Due to these considerations the open system view may be seen as a holistic approach to modelling corporate value creation processes looking beyond the boundaries of the firm and considering corporate behavior within its environmental context.[642]

3.2.1.3 Dynamic Knowledge and Technology Management Capacity

"(Market) leadership changes hands in about seven out of ten cases when discontinuities strike."[643]

Different industries show dissimilar speeds of renewal, characterized by "the rate at which capital equipment becomes obsolete, the pace of organizational restructuring, or the rate at which brand names are established."[644] Therefore, the length of product lifecycles and the intensity of market pressure for continuous innovation are determined by the particular industry's clock speed. Especially knowledge-intensive sectors in the field of consumer electronics are known for their high speed, whereas heavy industrial manufacturing such

---

640   See Sanchez 2004, p. 520.
641   See Schumpeter 1996, p. 81-87.
642   See Sanchez/Hene/Thomas 1996, p. 11; Sanchez 2004, p. 521; Morecroft/Sanchez/Hene 2002, p. 6.
643   Utterback 1996, p. 162.
644   Perrons/Platts 2004, p. 624. Also see Fine 2010.

as the oil and gas industry show rather slow rates of technological advance.[645] To maintain competitiveness corporations are required to anticipate future market dynamics and align their resources and capabilities accordingly.[646] The evaluation of branch structure's future development and market characteristics necessitate a managerial analysis based on specific knowledge of technology trends, regulations, demographics, and lifestyle to allow for a rational foresight.[647] To participate in future competition, corporations are required to establish core competences that are relevant to those competences relating to the fundamental business of the firm.[648] "Core competences are the collective learning in the organization, especially how to coordinate diverse production skills and integrate multiple streams of technologies."[649] Derived from this definition, the streaming of corporate operations toward a higher efficiency of available assets serve as sources of achieving higher value creation. Therefore, core competencies create a unique value for the customer and allow for the establishment of a competitive advantage.[650]

In times of vertical disintegration and specialization,[651] small entrepreneurial organizations aim for niche markets to differentiate themselves from established firms and to develop core competences across organizational boundaries.[652] Due to structural and industry dynamics these conditions may be a subject to change based on market-pull and technology-push factors.[653] In this regard, the relevance of the establishment of capabilities has been emphasized, which ensure a competitive alignment of corporate assets under dynamic conditions, known as 'dynamic capabilities.'[654] These can be defined "as a firm's ability to integrate, build, and reconfigure internal and external competences to address rapidly changing environments. Dynamic capabilities thus reflect an organization's ability

645 See Perrons/Platts 2004, p. 630. Forn an empirical example, see note 3 referring to the historical development of the Apple iPhone.
646 See i.e Sirmon/Hitt/Ireland 2007, p. 275.
647 See Hamel/Prahald 1994a, pp. 127-128.
648 See Teece/Pisano/Shuen 1997, p. 516.
649 Prahalad/Hamel 1990, p. 82.
650 See Hamel/Prahalad 1994b, p. 206. Regarding core competences it is to be mentionaed that scholars have argued about the stability of the concept: "All resources and capabilities of an organization must be aligned and balanced in order to create competence, and in this sense none can actually be said to be more 'core' than others" (Sanchez/Heene 2004, p. 37). Based on the systemic view of the corporation as an open system, this perspective holds out. Therefore, this work follows the point of view accordingly.
651 See Doellgast/Greer 2007; Chen 2005; O'Farrell/Moffat/Hitchens 1993.
652 In this context Prahalad/Hamel (1990, p. 91) refer to core competences as "the wellspring of new business development."
653 See Sanchez 2004, p. 530. Also see Brem/Voigt (2009) for an integrated discussion of market-pull and technology-push factors referring to the German software industry.
654 See Teece/Pisano 1994, p. 538; Teece 2007, p. 1319; Teece/Pisano/Shuen 1997, p. 521; Teece 2009.

to achieve new and innovative forms of competitive advantage given path dependencies and market positions."[655]

Based on a review of the broad field of discussions regarding the relevance and characteristics associated with dynamic capabilities Zahra/Sapienza/Davidsson (2006) elaborated on an integrative model allowing for a blueprint systemizing the aspects mentioned within a process-related approach (see Figure 13). Based on the perspective of entrepreneurship as an activity destined to discover, evaluate, and exploit opportunities,[656] entrepreneurial activity functions as initial within the model. On the one hand, the activity influences the prevailing resources and skills of the organization due to their utilization and leverage, on the other hand, organizational learning processes are promoted to employ external knowledge sources as new opportunities occur. The aspect of organizational learning is also seen as a decisive component to evaluate risks and to protect or reconfigure tangible and intangible corporate assets.[657] In combination these elements cause a momentum toward the creation of new substantive capabilities and the organizational knowledge and technology base.[658] The dynamic capabilities required to adapt to changing conditions are determined by the substantive capabilities and the knowledge base. As the reciprocal arrows indicate, dynamic capabilities are not only affected but also vice versa cause a transformation of the substantive capabilities and of the knowledge base. In combination, they affect the performance of the firm, which in turn influences future entrepreneurial activity.[659]

Dynamic knowledge and technology management capacity, therefore, relates to the ability of the firm to align its knowledge and technology base over time. This refers to a process of knowledge generation, accumulation and exploitation within and outside of corporate boundaries.[660] Because of changing business environments corporations are required to constantly adapt and renew their knowledge and technology base to the corresponding conditions. Based on the understanding of organizational capabilities, they are formed by the integration of knowledge into an organizational unit. To achieve a "competitive advantage in dynamically-competitive environments" Grant (1996) identifies three decisive components for knowledge integration: (1) efficiency, drawing on the extent of accessibility of specific knowledge in comparison to its utilization; (2) the scope of specific

---

655 Teece/Pisano/Shuen 1997, p. 516. For an overview of prevailing definitions of the term see Zahra/Sapienza/Davidsson 2006, p. 922.
656 See Shane/Venkataraman 2000, p. 218.
657 See Teece/Pisano/Shuen 1997, p. 521; Teece 2007, p. 1319; Zahra/Nielsen/Bogner 1999, p. 179.
658 Zahra/Sapienza/Davidsson (2006, p. 926) define substantative capabilities as "the set of things that the firm can do" and organizational knowledge as "the set of all that is known or understood by the organization and its members."
659 See Zahra/Sapienza/Davidsson 2006, pp. 925-926.
660 See Lichtenthaler 2006, p. 61.

knowledge the organizational capability refers to; (3) flexibility of integration - the possibility of reconfiguring existing knowledge and the accessibility of new knowledge.[661] In addition, the organizational capabilities themselves require reconfiguration and renewal which leads to the cognition that knowledge and technology management capacity itself should be seen as a dynamic organizational capabilities.[662] "The implication is that managers (both in young and established firms) do not and probably should not, create 'once-and-for-all' solutions or routines for their operations but continually reconfigure or revise the capabilities they have developed."[663]

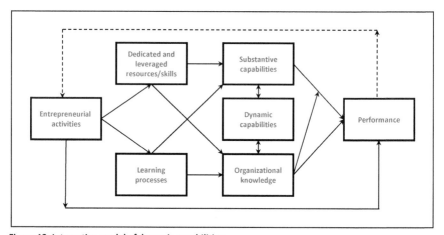

Figure 13: Integrative model of dynamic capabilities
Source: Based on Zahra/Sapienza/Davidsson 2006, p. 926.

To conclude, dynamic capabilities are essential to enabling a prosperous future development of the corporation. However, the continuous transformation of the knowledge and technology base requires on the one hand investments in human capital within corporate boundaries as well as, on the other hand, investments in social capital to assure access to critical resources external to the firm. These investments form the basis for pursuing entrepreneurial opportunities and causing an impact on the evolvement of substantive capabilities and knowledge. Since dynamic capabilities are interlinked with these components they reconfigure the corporate potential of value creation and are as well subject of change.

---

661 See Grant 1996b, pp. 380-382.
662 See Lichtenthaler 2006, p. 63.
663 Zahra/Sapienza/Davidsson 2006, p. 920.

3.2.2 Co-Innovation Competence of the Entrepreneurial Firm

3.2.2.1 Defining Co-Innovation Competence

"The capability of organizations to co-innovate with other organizations can be of crucial importance in sustaining and strengthening competitive positions in markets. Organizations create new products, processes and organizations by sharing complementary resources, knowledge and competencies and go through several stages of strategy making in which they interactively explore, develop and realize their co-innovative ambitions."[664]

In recent management literature a number of contributions highlight the relevance of accessing sources of knowledge external to corporate boundaries via strategic alliances to overcome the increasing complexity of R&D projects which may exceed the capabilities of the individual organization.[665] Therefore, "external resources for innovative renewal can complement endogenous capabilities and enable companies to cope with complex technologies through shared resources for increased learning capacity and improved innovative skills."[666] The concept of co-innovation reflects these considerations and aims for the realizing synergies from inter-organizational collaboration (co) resulting in higher efficiency based on a reduction of time spent and resources and capabilities leveraged to perform an innovation. Based on the product lifecycle curve Beelaerts van Blokand/Verhagen/ Santema (2008) introduce a value-time curve to illustrate theses effects graphically (see Figure 14). The authors' co-innovation refers to "the creation of a partnership between companies and/or institutes and/or customers on sharing knowledge, costs and benefits in order to create unique value for the customers."[667]

As the figure indicates innovation projects create negative value at the beginning, due to R&D investments. Once released to market a successful product creates a positive value in terms of cash-flow, reaching breakeven (BE) after exceeding the costs required for product release. After going through a rapid growth stage a maturity level is reached that may end in stabilization or decline.[668] In the figure two curves can be identified, differentiating a co-innovation project from an internal, closed innovation project, which is represented by the dotted line. The varying amplitudes of the curves indicate three effects:

---

664 Bossink 2002, p. 311.
665 See e.g. Gassmann 2006, p. 224.; Kang/Kang 2009; Tsai/Wang 2009; van de Vrande/Vanhaverbeke/ Duysters 2009; Laursen/Masciarelli/Prencipe 2012.
666 Hagedoorn/Duysters 2002, p. 169. Also see Teece/Pisano/Shuen 1997.
667 Beelaerts van Blokand/Verhagen/Santema 2008, p. 7.
668 See Beelaerts van Blokand/Verhagen/Santema 2008, p. 8. Note: A decline stage is not indicated in this figure, presuming a stable cash-flow evolvement over time.

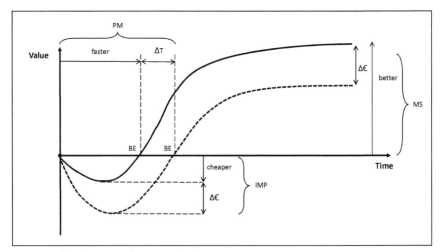

Figure 14: Value-time curve of co-innovation impact
Source: Beelaerts van Blokand/Verhagen/Santema 2008, p. 10.

- Innovation investment multiplier (IMP): The indicator can be understood as the total innovation investments of the co-operating partners, divided by the investment taken by one of the partners.[669] Based on the guiding thought of collaboration to share innovation risk among partners and cooperatively create value by combining mutual innovation competence, synergies can be realized to decrease the negative amplitude and thus realize a financial delta ($\Delta€$).[670]

- Production multiplier (MP): In the case of production-intensive innovation projects, co-operating partners may impact time-to-market velocity by co-producing specific components.[671] The parameter therefore may be determined by the time required to achieve the total production of the project divided by the individual time spent (ΔT).

- Market share (MS): Customer integration into new product or service development processes may reduce market risk at the diffusion of innovations.[672] Based on this perspective the identification of innovative ways to co-create value with customers is a de-

---

669   See Beelaerts van Blokand/Verhagen/Santema 2008, p. 8.
670   Also see Gassmann 2006, p. 224; Rammer et al. 2005, p. 265; Chesbrough/Schwartz 2007, p. 55; Bossink 2002, p. 311.
671   See Powell et al. 1996; Gemünden et al. 1996; Almeida/Kogut 1999; Baum et al. 2000; Jones 2000, p. 341. Reichwald/Piller 2009, pp. 172-177; Mortara et al. 2009, p. 14. Also see Chapter 2.2.3.2.
672   See von Hippel 1988, pp. 96, 106.

cisive aspect in strategic management to create a unique competitive advantage.[673] Therefore, co-producing innovation with customers may offer a higher market share and in turn profit growth ($\Delta \in$).

As elaborated earlier in this work, innovation competence of the corporation constitutes an effectively combined alignment of innovation resources and innovation capabilities.[674] "All resources and capabilities of an organization must be aligned and balanced in order to create competence."[675] From a strategic management perspective, therefore, core components configuring a co-innovation competence need to be identified.

The technology base of a corporation, which builds upon firm-specific knowledge combined with the corresponding skills to employ and configure these technologies, symbolizes the skeleton of innovation resources by providing the core capabilities of the corporation to create value.[676] In a networked innovation context the ties to potential collaboration partners, as expressed by social capital of the organization represent a decisive component to enrich this skeleton.[677] "Social capital is a resource and a factor that provides access to resources."[678] In the literature, contributions may be found positively relating social capital to innovation performance. Here, the network structure of organization regarding the exploration and exploitation of knowledge, is seen as an indicator for the inducement of entrepreneurial opportunities.[679] Within a relational context the establishment of trust and mutual norms among network partners is emphasized as decisive to promoting innovation.[680] This perspective is supported by the cognitive level emphasizing a positive connection between shared vision and inter-organizational innovation.[681] Social capital as the higher-order construct of the structural, relational, and cognitive dimension, therefore, can be understood as a decisive innovation resource contributing to the capacity of the corporation to perform innovation in collaboration with external actors.[682]

Thus, the technology base and social capital of a corporation constitute the framing components of corporate co-innovation resources. According to the discussion of the relevance of tie formation it requires specific capabilities to coordinate and align the co-

---

673 See Abraham 2005, pp. 10-11.
674 See Chapter 2.1.2.2.
675 Sanchez/Heene 2004, p. 37.
676 See Coombs 1996, p. 351-352; Chesbrough/Schwartz 2007, p. 56.
677 See Harryson 2008, p. 295.
678 Martinez-Canas/Saez-Martinez/Ruiz-Palomino 2012, p. 63. For a more detailed elaboration of social capital theory, see Chapter 3.1.1.
679 See Ahuja 2000, p. 335.
680 See Tsai/Ghoshal 1998, p. 467; Smith/Lohrke 2008, p. 315; also see Chapter 3.1.2.2.
681 See García-Morales/Moreno/Llorens-Montes 2006, p. 207.
682 See Zheng 2010, p. 151; Martinez-Canas/Saez-Martinez/Ruiz-Palomino 2012, p. 64; Nooteboom 2007, pp. 33-34.

innovation resources to efficiently explore and exploit innovation opportunities within an array of weak and strong ties.[683] In this context, the components absorptive capacity, being the ability of a corporation to explore external knowledge and desorptive capacity, the ability to exploit internal knowledge is identified in the literature as constituting elements of co-innovation capabilities.[684] Based on the structuring of innovation competence a corresponding structure of co-innovation competence can be derived (see Figure 15). To gain a deeper understanding of co-innovation capabilities the constituting components absorptive capacity and desorptive capacity as foundation for effectively exploring and exploiting opportunities and their links to co-innovation resources require further analysis:

- Absorptive capacity: The concept of 'absorptive capacity' has received much attention in the latest innovation research and has been seen as a decisive ability of a corporation to explore and subsequently integrate external knowledge as sources of innovation, creating a conceptual basis for continuative studies in the field.[685] The term was coined by Cohen/Levintal (1990) and can be defined as "the ability of a firm to recognize the value of new, external information, assimilate it, and apply it to commercial ends."[686] The concept draws on previous work relating corporate innovation performance to the accessibility of complementary assets.[687] This implies that corporations lacking a specific technological knowledge required for pursuing an opportunity need to have the capability to identify potential carriers of the required knowledge within the external surrounding of the corporation. In a second step they need the ability to absorb relevant knowledge by co-operating with the identified actor. Third, achieve an internal integration by applying that knowledge to the innovation project.[688]

This threefold process of absorptive capacity shows the necessity for a multitude of capabilities to successfully implement the concept. A core component represents the capability of exploring external knowledge sources. A connection to the technology base and social capital must be present within this capability to, on the one hand, identify and access and, on the other hand, to evaluate potential knowledge sources within the firm's environment.[689] Furthermore, as a cornerstone of the concept assimilation or absorption of the knowledge identified as suitable for collaborative innovation is required.

---

683 See Elfring/Hulsink 2007, pp. 1853, 1866; also see Chapter 3.1.2.1.
684 See Lichtenthaler 2006, pp. 64-70; Lichtenthaler/Lichtenthaler 2010; Müller-Seitz 2012, pp. 90-91.
685 See Chapter 2.2.2.1.
686 Cohen/Levintal 1990, p. 128. For an overview of conceptualizations of absorptive capacity see Hughes/Wareham 2010, pp. 342-343.
687 See Teece 1986, p.289; Harryson 2006, pp. 354-355. The primary use of the term lies in economics literature in a contribution by Adler (1965) referring to an absorptive capacity on a nation-state macro level as a concept within the theory of international capital movements.
688 See Lichtenthaler 2006, p. 68; Zahra/George 2002, p. 192.
689 See Cohen/Levintal 1990, p. 129; Lichtenthaler/Lichtenthaler 2009, p. 1319; Müller-Seitz 2012, p. 91.

This comprises a capability "to put new knowledge into memory, what we would refer to as the acquisition of knowledge, and the ability to recall and use it."[690] This capability is aligned with the integration of new knowledge into the knowledge base due to organizational learning leading to the ability to transform and dynamically evolve innovation capabilities.[691] This emphasizes that firms need to draw on a profound base of co-innovation ressources and a set of higher-order capabilities to successfully perform absorptive capacity.[692]

- Desorptive Capacity: Based on the absorptive capacity construct Lichtenthaler (2006) introduces the desorptive capacity concept with reference to the ability of an organization to exploit external knowledge.[693] "Desorptive capacity describes a firm's capability of external knowledge exploitation, which is complementary to internal knowledge application in a firm's own products."[694] The capability to exploit internal knowledge primarily requires a knowledge base attractive to potential collaboration partners and, second, intensive network ties to identify opportunities in order to securely offer knowledge for commercialization. "The more complex the knowledge, the stronger the ties required to support its transfer."[695] Furthermore, to successfully commercialize knowledge the corporation has to draw on a mindset and a culture of the organizations' people involved in the process, to willingly offer internal knowledge, technologies and ideas to network partners for integrating these within their value creation structure.[696] Therefore, a capability is required that enables a suitable knowledge transfer to the recipient.[697] The concept of desorptive capacity completes the spectrum of capabilities for an integrative perspective of knowledge exploration and exploitation offering a comprehensive understanding of capabilities required to pursue the full range of entrepreneurial opportunities resulting from a networked innovation perspective.

Co-innovation competence, therefore, can be defined as an efficient interplay of on the one hand co-innovation resources drawing on the technological base of a corporation con-

---

690 Cohen/Levintal 1990, p. 129.
691 See Teece/Pisano/Shuen 1997, p. 521; Teece 2007, p. 1319; Lane/Koka/Pathak 2006; Lichtenthaler/ Lichtenthaler 2009, p. 1320.
692 Here, it is to be noted that absorptive capacity as such does not directly relate to successfully commercializing innovation, but rather represents a capability-based approach to inter-organizational R&D as in the outside-in process of open innovation (see Chapter 2.2.2.2).
693 See Lichtenthaler 2006, pp. 65-75; Lichtenthaler/Lichtenthaler 2009, pp. 1321-1322; Müller-Seitz 2012, p. 91.
694 Lichtenthaler/Lichtenthaler 2009, p. 1321.
695 Harryson 2008, p. 295.
696 In contrast to the NIH syndrome also a 'only-sold-here' syndrome may exist, referring to a negative attitude to commercializing knowledge externally (Lichtenthaler/Ernst 2006, p 372; Boyens 1998).
697 See Lichtenthaler/Lichtenthaler 2009, p. 1322.

taining core capabilities for value creation and the value of its external ties expressed by social capital, and on the other hand co-innovation capabilities aligning these resources within the corporate network for the exploration of assets external to the corporation and exploitation of internal assets for inter-organizational value creation. From the inter-dependencies among corporations resulting from successful collaborative innovation projects, mutual capabilities to perform future innovation may evolve. "Mutual understanding and trust emerge in a process of interaction."[698] Consequently, this evolvement can be expressed by inter-organizational learning[699] changing the knowledge base as well as an evolvement or deepening of mutual trust among collaboration partners, which creates an impact on efficiently coordinating co-innovation resources for future co-innovation projects. Co-innovation competence, therefore, has to be seen as a dynamic concept liable to path dependencies resulting from co-innovation projects.

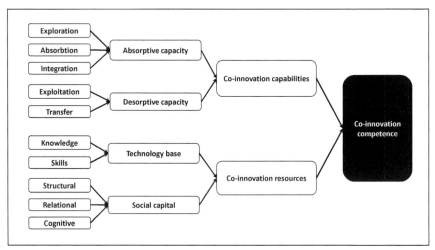

Figure 15: Structure of co-innovation competence
Source: Based on Bergfeld 2009, p. 14; Coombs 1996, p. 346.

---

698   See Notteboom 2006, p. 32.
699   See Grant 1996b, pp. 380-382; Lane/Lubatkin 1998; Lichtenthaler 2009.

3.2.2.2 Path Dependence of Co-Innovation Competence

"The higher the complexity of the project due to high uncertainty of success, the more likely is a mutual cooperation for innovation."[700]

Previous elaborations in this work of co-innovation competence drew on the alignment of capabilities and resources of a corporation within a network context to systematically explore and exploit opportunities of innovation. Here, the focus lies primarily on the individual corporation acting within its economic environment. As indicated above, the concept need not be understood as a static structure, but as a dynamic concept following path dependencies that require the consideration of interaction patterns among collaboration partners in a co-innovation competence evolvement. The concept of path dependence relates to the likelihood of past developments influencing future events.[701] For example, an early decision in technology development cycles may cause grounding preconditions for future developments due to a 'lock-in' effect.[702] In these cases selecting a specific good may result in increasing economies of scale while alternatives lead to higher costs causing a 'squeeze-out' effect of alternatives.[703] A lock-in may also occur in inter-organizational collaboration. As transaction costs economics indicates, due to reciprocal knowledge and social capital links based on previous collaborations, switching costs may appear unreasonable, bearing the uncertainty of change.[704] Therefore, certain paths may show future developments of a corporation based on past events.[705] This perspective also has been indicated within the open system view in which the strategic logic of a corporation determines the corporate value creation process - and vice versa is influenced by the information's drawing from interactions of the corporation with external factors.[706]

Even though the goals and likely effects of co-innovation appear to be established the implementation of required corporate behavior in the form of a co-innovation competence needs further investigation. In this regard, sequences and patterns of co-innovation in a dyad perspective can be identified in the literature.[707] These concentrate on the establishment of on the one hand formal framing conditions of the collaboration such as the negotiation of contracts and agreements and on the other hand organizational structuring

---

700 Notteboom 2002, p. 33.
701 See Martin/Sunley 2006, p. 399.
702 See David (1985) who elaborates that early decisions in technology development may cause a lock-in resulting in an irrevocable precondition for further developments based on the example of QWERTY keypad.
703 See Arthur 1989, p. 119.
704 See Williamson 1979; Williamson 1987; Nooteboom 1999.
705 See Teece/Pisano/Shuen 1997, p. 522.
706 See Sanchez/Heene 1996, p. 41.
707 See e.g. Kreiner/Schultz 1993, pp. 193-195; George/Farris 1999, pp. 381-382; Bossink 2002, p. 313.

of the collaboration such as governance mode, management methods and responsibilities. Furthermore, communication and commercialization strategies for the resulting products and services can be identified.[708] Based on these findings and an empirical investigation, Bossink (2002) proposes a four stage model for the development of co-innovation strategies (see Figure 16):

1. Autonomous strategy development (quadrant I): A number of independently operating organizations is represented by a set of circles. These are forced by market dynamics and changes of context conditions to establish strategies to improve innovation performance.[709] In this context the organizations examine opportunities to achieve innovation in collaboration with potential partners. Based on the establishment of weak ties among the actors, the organizations collectively explore possibilities for co-innovation.

2. Co-operative strategy development (quadrant II): Based on these weak ties a part of these organizations engage in a proof of potentials for co-operation by elaborating co-innovation strategies (indicated by the arrows between the circles). The evaluations draw on the mixture of complementary assets and the resulting capacity of realizing synergies to increase innovation performance.[710] The value of the individual assets and social capital among the actors are decisive components to establish a co-operation. "Organizations that successfully co-innovated before try to work with the same team of partners again."[711]

3. Co-innovation venturing (quadrant III): Based on a successful assessment the organizations initiate a co-innovation venture project (symbolized by an overlapping circle connecting the collaborating parties). Here, formal aspects such as contracts and agreements are signed as well as governance and management modes defined. With reference to those aspects a venture unit is created which receives an autonomous position.

4. Co-innovation performance (quadrant IV): The co-innovating organizations establish strong ties among each other via the venture unit and strive for performing innovation and creating economic value by commercializing the products and services developed.[712] If the project has been carried out successfully, the collaborating partners continue to pursue new opportunities autonomously aiming for an exploitation of the capabilities developed within the co-innovation project.[713]

---

708   See Bossink 2002, pp. 313-314. The author summarizes these interaction patterns in the development of co-innovation strategies based on an extensive literature review.
709   See Sanchez/Heene 1996, p. 56; Sirmon/Hitt/Ireland 2007, p. 275.
710   See Teece 1986, p.289; Hagedoorn/Duysters 2002, p. 169; Harryson 2006, pp. 354-355.
711   Bossink 2002, p. 315.
712   See Beelaerts van Blokand/Verhagen/Santema 2008, p. 7.
713   See Bossink 2002, p. 316.

The stage model indicates that decisive components for the establishment of co-innovation projects are on the one hand the portfolio of assets a corporation can contribute to the project and, on the other hand, the social capital collaborating partners can draw on for the establishment of a co-innovation venture. This leads to path dependencies because co-innovating organizations will gradually evolve their co-innovation competence based on the establishment of strong ties to former collaboration partners and co-innovation capability development. This cognition underlines the basic statement by Teece/Pisano/Shuen (1997): "The notion of path dependencies recognizes that 'history matters.'"[714]

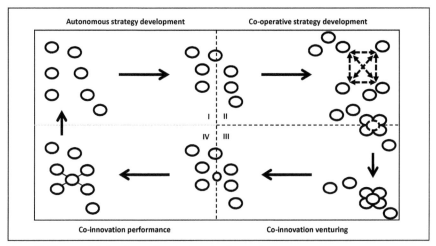

Figure 16: Stage model of co-innovation strategy development
Source: Based on Bossink 2002, p. 314.

3.2.2.3 Entrepreneurial Implications of Co-Innovation Competence

The elaborated approach toward a definition of co-innovation competence and its path dependencies indicate the relevance of social capital to engaging in co-innovation that may draw on previous co-innovation projects. Furthermore, despite this resource perspective which is aligned to the possession of strategic resources, co-innovation capabilities are emphasized and understood as the firm's capacity to explore and exploit their environmental surroundings. These components within an integrative concept of co-innovation competence are subject to a dynamic evolvement if applied to transaction processes and

---

714   Teece/Pisano/Shuen 1997, p. 522.

corporate value creation. This perspective bears certain difficulties for entrepreneurial firms to gain access to evolving co-innovation cycles constituted by strong-tie connections among independent corporations forming multi-actor innovation alliances.[715] As discussed with regard to entrepreneurial networks the establishment of strong and weak ties may be essential for the entrepreneurial firm to engage in exploration and exploitation processes to pursue opportunities and achieve entrepreneurial performance.[716] However, for entrepreneurial firms the liabilities of newness and smallness remain a barrier for co-innovation, as emphasized by the transaction cost argument of lock-in effects among established collaboration partners due to perceived switching costs.[717] Consequently, it remains questionable how the establishment of social capital can effectively contribute to entrepreneurial performance if the development of strong ties to relevant collaboration partners is challenged by a lack of accessibility.

With reference to this consideration there are two paths to gaining access to potential co-innovation partners: The first one relates to the argument of complementary assets as core initiator of collaboration for innovation.[718] Based on the cognitive capabilities of the entrepreneur, the organization may be capable of reacting rather flexibly to structural dynamics and adapt the alignment of its assets accordingly.[719] Young entrepreneurial firms may show a higher flexibility in integrating external knowledge into their knowledge base,[720] leading to a reconfiguration of its innovation competence. On behalf of these capabilities in combination with its strategic resources the entrepreneurial firm might be capable of offering state-of-the-art critical assets complementary to the portfolio of assets of an established alliance of co-innovation partners. In this case it remains an open question whether the value of the assets presented by the entrepreneur for integration into a co-innovation alliance will overcome the liabilities of newness and smallness toward the entrepreneurial firm.

A second pathway for entrepreneurial firms to access established co-innovation alliance structures lies in collaboration with innovation promotors and network intermediaries to bridge structural holes.[721] The development of ties to knowledge brokers embedded in network structures may amplify the potential of indirectly establishing links to potential collaboration partners. The regional context as direct environmental surrounding of the entrepreneurial firm may provide a variety of organizations and individuals who by profession support the establishment of network ties for entrepreneurial firms. These may have

---

715   See Hagedoorn/Duysters 2002; Stuart 2000; Wassmer/Dussauge 2011. Also see Bossink 2002, p. 316.
716   See Davidsson/Honig 2003, p. 325. Also see Chapter 3.1.2.
717   See Liao/Welch 2003, p. 166.
718   See See Teece 1986, p.289; Harryson 2006, pp. 354-355; Bossink 2002, p. 315; Sternberg 2007, p. 654.
719   Sanchez/Heene 2002, p. 88.
720   See Grant 1996b, p 382.
721   See Fichter 2009, p. 361; Chesbrough 2006c, p. 152; Burt 1992, p. 27.

sufficient relational capital to reduce the liabilities of the entrepreneurial organization by setting up ties among potential collaboration partners and creating an infrastructure for co-innovation and inter-organizational knowledge flows.[722]

The following sections of this work aim at establishing an empirical analysis of the interplay of entrepreneurial firms within their regional context to achieve entrepreneurial performance. Based on the characteristics of regional innovation structures,[723] a strategic approach will be elaborated specifying co-innovation strategy development. In this context the characteristics of the regional economic and specifically entrepreneurial climate need to be considered as critical factor for the promotion of entrepreneurial behavior. Therefore the interplay of entrepreneurs of knowledge-intensive firms and regional innovation promotors represent the focus of the following analytical approach.

---

722   See Sternberg 2007, p. 654; 2009, p. 23.
723   See Chapter 2.3.

"Co-creation involves both a profound democratization and decentralization of value creation, moving it from concentration inside the firm to interactions with its customers, customer communities, suppliers, partners, and employees, and interactions among individuals."[724]

4. Conceptual Framework and Dimensions of Analysis

4.1 Conceptual Framework of the Investigation

This chapter aims for an integrative discussion of the concepts previously elaborated. In this regard, the entrepreneurial firm is the focal object of the investigation striving for economic value creation within its environmental context. In the literature several contributions can be identified analyzing the influence of external factors and conditions on firm performance.[725] These contributions serve as point of reference for conceptualizing a basic framework of analysis. Specifically, the well-known contribution by Lumpkin/Dess (1996) in entrepreneurship research "Clarifying the entrepreneurial orientation construct and linking it to performance" presents a conceptual approach relating the entrepreneurial orientation construct and its characterizing components to the performance of the firm.[726] This linkage, however, is influenced by environmental factors characterized inter alia by industry characteristics as well as organizational factors such as firm resources, structure and corporate culture.[727]

Following the proposed intention of elaborating a strategic approach to entrepreneurship in regional innovation structures three constituting components can be identified as influencing the process of value creation of the entrepreneurial firm. The primary factor of the capacity of the firm to achieve performance requires consideration. Referring to an understanding of entrepreneurship as opportunity-driven behavior aiming for the exploitation of opportunities identified,[728] entrepreneurship relates to an innovation process initiated by entrepreneurial activity.[729] Therefore, the capacity of the entrepreneurial firm

---

724 Ramaswamy/Goullart 2010, p. 7.
725 See e.g. Lumpkin/Dess 1996; Pelham 1999; Lichtenthaler 2009.
726 For a more detailed of the entrepreneurial orientation construct see Chapter 2.1.1.
727 See Lumpkin/Dess 1996, p. 154. The citation index of the 'Google scholar' database indicates a number of 2725 citations of the contribution on the current state of analysis, emphasizing the value of the contribution.
728 See Littunen 2000, p. 295; Shane/Venkataraman 2000, p. 218.
729 See Sharma/Chrisman 1999, p. 17.

to achieve innovation and consequently improved entrepreneurial performance must be seen as critical element of analysis. Second, drawing on the title of this work, the concept of co-innovation competence introduced is applied to the investigation representing the organizational dimension. Since co-innovation competence can be understood as an inter-active approach toward inter-organizational innovation performance and value creation,[730] external factors and the environmental context need to be considered. Therefore, third, the relevance of climatic conditions regarding the structural setting for the pursuit of en-trepreneurial opportunities based on inter-organizational collaboration need to be ex-plored. Based on the elaborations of regional innovation structures,[731] an analysis of the regional entrepreneurial climate as environmental dimension may, therefore, offer an insight into the conditions necessary for co-innovation. These may be based on a geo-graphically bounded democratic flow of knowledge among actors establishing a system that promotes the pursuit of entrepreneurial opportunities.[732]

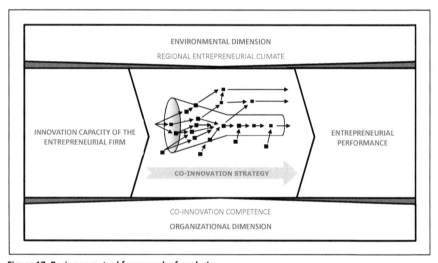

Figure 17: Basic conceptual framework of analysis

These factors show reciprocal characteristics and therefore need to be analyzed in an inte-grated structure. An analysis of the interplay of these dimensions relates to a complex multi-factor approach offering a variety of sub-components relevant for formulating a

---

730 See Chapter 3.2.
731 See Chapter 2.3.
732 See Sternberg 2007, p. 654; 2009, p. 23.

strategic approach to entrepreneurship in regional innovation structures. Based on the conceptual approach to open innovation,[733] in this regard, the term of 'co-innovation strategy' is elaborated, considering the factors influencing entrepreneurial performance within an economic market setting based on inter-organizational value creation. Figure 17 illustrates the basic conceptual framework of this investigation relating the three factors presented to entrepreneurial performance based on the establishment of a co-innovation strategy.[734] The following subsections elaborate these components constituting the framework in more detail before implications for a co-innovation strategy are discussed.

4.1.1 Innovation Capacity and Entrepreneurial Performance

4.1.1.1 Innovation Capacity of the Entrepreneurial Firm

"Entrepreneurship can be conceptualized as a function of opportunity structures and motivated entrepreneurs with access to resources."[735]

Despite external conditions and attributes shaping the environmental context of the entrepreneurial firm the organizational or the personal level should be considered as a critical component inter-relating with the firm's environment. "Personal preferences, for example, a particular regional 'climate' or environment (soft location factors), greatly influence the decision of creative people to migrate" and participate in the regional economic system.[736] Personal traits of character consequently influence the individual intention and decision- making process to pursue entrepreneurial opportunities within a given context.[737] Especially the motivation of an entrepreneur to engage in the foundation of a corporation with reference to a certain need for achievement, desire and passion is to be mentioned as decisive for the future development of the firm.[738]

In the literature several contributions can be identified that analyze the motivational aspects of entrepreneurship leading to a twofold perspective of the phenomenon. On the one hand entrepreneurial motivation may draw on economic necessities to find an alter-

---

733 See Chapter 2.2.
734 The framework introduced and illustrated in Figure 17, on the one hand, draws on the conceptual model elaborated by Lumpkin/Dess (1996, p. 154) and on the other hand refers to the illustration of the open innovation paradigm (Chesbrough 2003a, pp. 183, 189) symbolizing co-innovation strategy.
735 Aldrich/Zimmer 1986b, p. 3.
736 Sternberg 2007, p. 658.
737 See Koe Hwee Nga/Shamuganathan 2010, p. 259; Littunen 2000, p. 295.
738 See Shane/Locke/Collins 2003, p. 263-269. Also see Löfsten/Lindelöf 2003, p. 53; Koe Hwee Nga/ Shamuganathan 2010, p. 261.

native solution to employment.[739] Furthermore the aspect of self-fulfillment is mentioned meeting satisfactory necessities by aiming at the establishment of more flexible working conditions and autonomy.[740] On the other hand, there is a discussion of entrepreneurship as opportunity-based behavior can be identified.[741] This perspective in its origin follows a Schumpeterian sense by linking entrepreneurial motivation to the personal skills of the entrepreneur in the form of technological or specific knowledge applied to the market causing creative destruction.[742] Within a market-based approach the capability of the entrepreneur to identify a market niche combined with the skills at hand may be seen as working to trigger the motivation to engage in entrepreneurial activity.[743] In this regard, with reference to the relevance of networks, entrepreneurs may build upon previous experiences and established personal networks to exploit opportunities emerging within these structures.[744] Furthermore, based on the range of professional experience gathered in previous projects or employment, the entrepreneur may refer to a certain set of knowledge and capabilities as well as a personal network facilitating the pursuit of entrepreneurial opportunities.[745] Consequently, the identification of a market demand aiming for exploitation based on a given set of resources such as knowledge and social capital may serve as a basis to initiate entrepreneurial processes. The latter perceptions of entrepreneurial motivation understood as the willingness to exploit opportunities,[746] clearly connect this concept to an innovation process initiated by entrepreneurial activity aiming for growth creation.[747]

"The discovery of opportunities - to positively evaluate opportunities, to pursue resources, and to design the mechanisms of exploitation - also depend on the willingness of people to 'play' the game."[748] As elaborated earlier, the motivation of an entrepreneur to pursue opportunities based on a given set of resources focusing on the knowledge base is linked to the concept of entrepreneurial orientation emphasizing the relevance of innovativeness and the willingness to take risks as decisive components of innovative entrepreneurial behavior.[749] Consequently, entrepreneurial motivation may be influenced by several personal factors; however, this work follows the stream of literature that posits en-

---

739   See e.g. Caliendo/Kritikos 2010.
740   See Block/Koellinger 2009, p. 191; Bergmann/Sternberg 2007, p. 207.
741   See Stevenson/Jarillo 1990; Brown/Davidsson/Wilkund 2001.
742   See Schumpeter 1996, p. 132.
743   See Kirzner 1973, p. 68.
744   See Sternberg 2009, p. 227.
745   See Wagner/Sternberg 2004, p. 223; Bergmann/Sternberg 2007, p. 207; Brixy/Hundt/Sternberg 2009, p. 20.
746   See Littunen 2000, p. 295; Shane/Venkataraman 2000, p. 218.
747   See Sharma/Chrisman 1999, p. 17; Alvarez/Barney 2002, p. 89.
748   Shane/Locke/Collins 2003, p. 258.
749   See Lumpkin/Dess 1996, pp. 140-149. Also see Chapter 2.1.1.

trepreneurial motivation as initiating preconditions to exploit entrepreneurial opportunities and to create innovation.

Based on the contribution by Shane/Locke/Collins (2003), who coined the term 'entrepreneurial motivation,' a framework can be presented systemizing the inter-relationship of the three components environmental conditions, intellectual capital (IC), and entrepreneurial motivation in connection with the process of recognition, evaluation, and exploitation of entrepreneurial opportunities (see Figure 18). Linking these attributes in turn allows for a comprehensive understanding of the innovation capacity of the entrepreneurial firm. As the graphic shows, environmental conditions serve as source of opportunity emergence and influence the future development of the exploitation process lead by a combination of IC and entrepreneurial motivation (indicated by the dotted line). The authors emphasize the role of motivation in this regard as the most relevant to exploit opportunities within a given environmental context to enable the transition of the entrepreneurial process.[750] However, as described above the resource base of the entrepreneurial firm especially with reference to its IC needs to be considered providing the critical attributes for opportunity exploitation. IC refers to "the sum of everything everybody in a company knows that gives it a competitive edge... IC is intellectual material knowledge, experience, IP, information... that can be put to use to create wealth."[751] IC consequently draws on the intangible assets of an entrepreneurial firm embodied in its human capital. Understanding IC as higher-order construct contributions can be seen as integrating human capital, IC and social capital in the form of structural and relational capital within the IC construct.[752] The contribution by Pena (2002) emphasizes the relevance of IC for entrepreneurial firms by elaborating its impact on business start-up success. The author positively relates the educational level and the horizon of experiences made by the entrepreneur and its source of contacts in the form of social capital to venture performance.[753]

To conclude, the innovation capacity of the entrepreneurial firm is strongly dependent on the motivation of the entrepreneur to pursue opportunities resulting in innovation performance. The motivational aspect serves as the carrier of transition within the process that draws on the IC embodied within the people involved in the venture as source of entrepreneurial activity. This leads to the recognition that innovation capacity show a highly intangible character implying that the quality of the resource base with reference to the concept of IC and the entrepreneurial motivation to pursue opportunities emerging in the

---

750 See Shane/Locke/Collins 2003, p. 276.
751 Stewart 1997, p. 67.
752 See Pena 2002, p. 181; Hayton 2005, p. 140. For a presentation of the diemensions of social capital see Chapter 3.1.1.2.
753 See Pena 2002, pp. 194-195. Also see Wagner/Sternberg 2004, p. 223; Bergmann/Sternberg 2007, p. 207; Brixy/Hundt/Sternberg 2009, p. 20.

environmental context drawing on a certain passion as well as innovativeness and risk-taking can be identified as core components constituting the innovation capacity of the entrepreneurial firm.

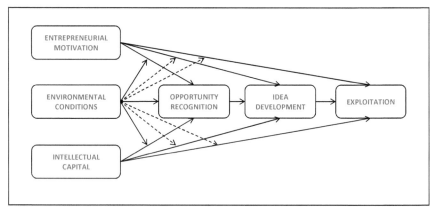

Figure 18: Inter-related components of entrepreneurial capacity
Source: Based on Shane/Locke/Collins 2003, p. 274.

4.1.1.2 Entrepreneurial Performance

"There are many different ways to achieve high entrepreneurial performance."[754]

There is no standard concept in the literature to determine and measure the performance of a corporation. Instead it is recognized as a rather challenging task.[755] Strategic management literature offers several contributions relating corporate activity to performance. A review shows that there is a large body of literature linking the management of internal and external elements such as organizational and environmental factors to performance.[756] Here it is argued that the usage of a wide spectrum of performance indicators is a necessary precondition for receiving reliable results when researching the influence of attributes to performance. However, most of these contributions lack a precise elaboration of the term, rather interpreting performance in terms of 'success' as a general form of positive development of the corporation based on the creation of economic value.[757] The

---

754   Brown/Davidsson/Wiklund 2001, p. 965.
755   See Covin/Slevin 1998, p. 83.
756   See e.g. Lumpkin/Dess 1996, p. 154; Pelham 1999; Lichtenthaler 2009.
757   See Lichtenthaler 2009, p. 319.

challenge is based on its multi-dimensional nature[758] and is the subjective perspective of performance. Therefore, the term mainly can be considered as a relative component to the competitive surrounding of the corporation.[759] Performance consequently may refer to a broad spectrum of corporate activity results ranging from survival to sustainable development to the realization of high profits. With reference to the basic understanding of profit as "the difference between a monetary measure of outputs (revenues) and a monetary measure of resources (expenses)"[760] performance generally draws on a positive balance of expenditures and returns based on an economic value creation allowing for future corporate activity.

Specifically the field of R&D and innovation management indicates a high correlation between innovation and corporate performance.[761] Innovation as such is understood as the outcome of corporate activity in the form of new product or service development as well as the implementation of new processes.[762] This serves as a performance characteristic leading to the term of 'innovation performance.'[763] Following the thought of a positive balance of expenses and returns, innovation performance leads to higher returns in the phase of commercialization compared to the investments required for R&D.[764] Here, literature contributions can be identified with reference to the exploitation of external knowledge sources to increase innovation performance drawing on the concept of knowledge spillover to amplify effectiveness within the innovation process.[765] However, this performance aspect may also be related to elements such as an increase in efficiency leading to profit maximization or growth rates in terms of assets gained from corporate activity.

Especially in the case of young entrepreneurial firms it is rather difficult to gather specific data to determine their performance despite of a lasting existence of the firm. This is due to the fact that there is no legislation on publishing corporate figures of any kind. An analytical approach also may also be hampered because these firms consider relative performance data as highly confidential.[766] The term 'entrepreneurial performance' has gained certain popularity in the entrepreneurship literature,[767] although these contribu-

---

758 See Chakravarthy, 1986, p. 437.
759 See Pelham, 1999, p. 33.
760 Cordero 1990, p. 187.
761 See e.g. Damanpour/Evan 1984; López-Nicolás/Meroño-Cerdán 2011.
762 See Moore/Tushman 1982, p. 132; Roberts 1987, p. 3; Damanpour 1991, p. 556. Aslo see Chapter 2.1.2.1.
763 See Cordero 1990.
764 See Cordero 1990, pp. 187-189.
765 See e.g. Ahuja/Katila 2001; Battor/Battor 2010; Hsueh/Lin/Li 2010; Lichtenthaler 2009;; Stuart 2000; Tsai/Wang 2009.
766 See Fiorito/LaForge 1986; Flatten/Greve/Brettel 2011, p. 144; Butler/Saxberg 2001, p. 420.
767 See e.g. Larson 1991; Bellu 1993; Hayton 2003; Chatterji 2009.

tions do not present a more precise elaboration of the term despite the general reference to an economic understanding of performance within an entrepreneurship context. Based on the idea that "high revenue growth is the result of a complex array of market forces, environmental conditions, and organizational decision making,"[768] the term may be considered a positive result of entrepreneurial activity enabling the future development of the corporation. "Thus, a small, privately owned firm may regard its continued existence as a satisfactory indicator of high performance."[769] A contribution by Murphy/Trailer/Hill (1996) sheds light on the array of components to be considered when talking about entrepreneurial performance. Based on an extensive literature review of empirical studies in entrepreneurship literature the authors identify the realization of efficiency in terms of return on investment, equity and assets as well as growth in terms of a change in turnover and employees as the most relevant dimensions of entrepreneurial performance.[770]

Consequently, this work relates to the understanding of entrepreneurial performance as a positive economic development of the firm assuring the basis of its future economic activity. Because it is recognized that "survival rates are an important consideration, but may be misleading if not examined with care,"[771] the attribute of growth with reference to the sum total of turnover and the human capital employed leading to an increase of the corporate resource base should be considered. Furthermore, by drawing on the understanding of entrepreneurship as a process of opportunity exploitation to achieve innovation, entrepreneurial performance can be considered in connection with the innovation performance of the firm.[772]

4.1.2 Organizational Dimension - Co-Innovation Competence

An analysis of the organizational dimension draws on the introduced approach to the concept of co-innovation competence. This is understood as an efficient interplay of co-innovation resources drawing on the technological base of a corporation containing core capabilities for value creation and the value of its external ties expressed in social capital as well as co-innovation capabilities to align these resources within the corporate network to exploration assets outside corporate boundaries and exploitation of internal assets for cooperative value creation.[773] This chapter elaborates on an extension of the concept. On

---

768   Larson 1991, p. 186.
769   Lumpkin/Dess 1996, p.154.
770   See Murphy/Trailer/Hill 1996, pp. 16-17.
771   Murphy/Trailer/Hill 1996, p. 21.
772   See Littunen 2000, p. 295; Shane/Venkataraman 2000, p. 218; Sharma/Chrisman 1999, p. 17; Cordero 1990, pp. 187-189.
773   See Chapter 3.2.2.

the one hand, the aspect of co-innovation resources is discussed more deeply, linking social capital theory to a dynamic perspective of technology base development. On the other
hand, the aspect of co-innovation capabilities is discussed in connection with the introduced concept of open innovation networks.[774] The transfer and connections of these topics contribute to a comprehensive view of co-innovation competence as the organizational
dimension of this investigation.

4.1.2.1 Co-innovation Resources

"A dynamic theory of organizational learning provides a means of understanding the
fundamental tension between exploration (feed forward) and exploitation (feedback).
Although one may be tempted to equate organizational learning solely with the innovative feed-forward process, in doing so one fails to recognize that the feedback process
provides the means to exploit what has been learned."[775]

Co-innovation resources refer to a combined perspective of the technology base and the
social capital obtained by the corporation. The technology base is characterized by the
firm-specific knowledge linked to the corresponding skills to employ and configure the
firm's stock of technologies, providing the core capabilities of the corporation for value
creation.[776] Within an understanding of an economic system based on specialization, vertical disintegration and chain-linked value creation processes, serving as basis for an economic understanding of an innovation system,[777] the technology base provides the essential attribute of a corporation within a landscape of complementary assets.[778] The exploitation of technology-based core capabilities within a corresponding system requires accessibility to potential collaboration partners Based on the resource of social capital, seen as a
factor providing the access to resources beyond corporate boundaries.[779] Thus, social capital can be understood as a decisive innovation resource promoting the capacity of the firm
to perform innovation in collaboration with external partners.[780]

Furthermore, the inter-relatedness of social capital with the development of the technology base needs to be considered within a dynamic comprehension. Therefore, the ca-

---

774   See Chapter 2.2.4.1.
775   Crossan/Lane/White 1999, p. 534.
776   See Coombs 1996, p. 351-352; Chesbrough/Schwartz 2007, p. 56.
777   See Edquist 2005, p. 182. Precisely, an innovation system refers to all relevant economic, political, so-
      cial, institutional and organizational factors influencing the evolvement and diffusion of innovation.
778   See Teece 1986, p.289; Chen 2005; Doellgast/Greer 2007; Sternberg 2007, pp. 653, 654.
779   See Nahapiet 2008, p. 580; Martinez-Canas/Saez-Martinez/Ruiz-Palomino 2012, p. 63. Also see Chapter
      3.1.1.
780   See Zheng 2010, p. 151; Nooteboom 2007, pp. 33-34; Martinez-Canas/Saez-Martinez/Ruiz-Palomino
      2012, p. 64.

pacity of the firm to dynamically align its technology base over time may be seen as a critical component connected to the concept of co-innovation resources. This refers to the capability to generate and accumulate knowledge within the firm based on transaction processes by consistently adapting and renewing its technology base to remain competitive within a likewise dynamic system.[781] The initial for corporate development can be interpreted as either a first-mover or a follower behavior. Thus, on the one hand, development may be the result of market pressure forcing the organization to adapt its processes and knowledge base to market standards via adoption.[782] On the other hand, the pursuit of entrepreneurial processes aiming for the exploitation of identified opportunities serves as a trigger for organizational change.[783]

The environment of the firm should be considered a source of opportunities influencing the transition of the entrepreneurial process.[784] The environmental context of the firm, however, has a twofold character. Primarily, general market conditions that apply to each actor participating in the market such as legal aspects framing the market setting can be identified, offering a democratic perspective toward the pursuit of entrepreneurial behavior. Second, the environmental conditions created by the corporation in the form of the establishment of ties and relations to organizations and individuals interacting with the firm need to be considered. The latter may be decisive for the capacity of the firm to exploit opportunities within an innovation system. This indicates the relevance of social structures first as source of opportunity emergence and second as enabler to pursue the entrepreneurial process.

Floyd/Woolridge (1999) systemize the presented context by linking the aspect of technology base development to knowledge and social network theory.[785] Based on their contribution, a framework can be presented indicating an opportunity-based co-innovation resource development process (see Figure 19). As the figure shows, entrepreneurial opportunities emerge from the existing technology base and the social structure surrounding the firm relating to its social capital. The co-innovation resource development process draws on a dynamic perception of organizational learning with reference to a stage process that considers the individual, group and organizational level.[786] Initialized at the individual level, subjective criteria in the form of cognitive capabilities produce ideas that are combined with information provided from weak social ties.[787] These ties are considered as

781 See Teece/Pisano/Shuen 1997, p. 521; Grant 1996b, pp. 380-382; Lichtenthaler 2006, p. 61. Also see
     Chapter 3.2.1.3.
782 See e.g. Rothwell/Bessant 1987; Kitchell 1995.
783 See Zahra/Sapienza/Davidsson 2006, p. 926.
784 See Shane/Locke/Collins 2003, p. 274; Stevenson/Jarillo 1990, p. 25; Sanchez/Heene 1996, p. 41.
785 See Floyd/Woolridge 1999, p. 132.
786 See Crossan/Lane/White 1999, pp. 525, 532.
787 See Sanchez/Heene 2002, p. 88.

"important for penetrating the social and cognitive rigidities embedded in the organization's existing capability set. Bridging relationships thus create competing ideas within the organizational ecology."[788] A transfer to the group level emerges within the pursuit of the opportunity when central actors are involved by taking entrepreneurial initiatives and stimulating developmental efforts. Within this level the organization starts to expand its empirical knowledge. In the third stage, empirical knowledge is processed within the organization creating pragmatic knowledge expressed by new knowledge, skills and capabilities. At the organizational level individual weak social ties relevant for pursuing the opportunity are strengthened leading to the emergence of formalized network structures. These formalized ties draw on contractual agreements as the basis for inter-organizational knowledge transfer and collaboration.[789] This process consequently leads to an enrichment of the co-innovation resources due to the integration of the newly created knowledge, skills and capabilities into the technology base and an extension of the social capital of the firm based on the establishment of formalized network structures with collaborating partners.

The framework presented emphasizes the relevance of social capital for corporate competitiveness in accordance with previous concepts presented in this work.[790] Based on the discussion of accessibility of co-innovation partners for young entrepreneurial firms,[791] the framework indicates that an entrepreneur should focus already in early stages of the corporate lifecycle on building co-innovation resources to gain entry into established innovation alliances. Based on critical resources and a set of social ties the corporation bears the chance of gradually developing its base of co-innovation resources and increasing its potential of a prosperous future development. Due to market dynamics, innovation networks show likewise show a dynamic character. The establishment of strong ties to a given set of actors located in an innovation network may serve as initial step for gaining access to this network regarding the collaboration in future innovation projects. "Some firms expand their portfolios as this deterministic account suggests - that is, they use existing ties as stepping-stones to new ties."[792] However, this implies a continuous systemized alignment of corporate resources aiming for the pursuit of entrepreneurial opportunities.

---

788 Floyd/Woolridge 1999, p. 132.
789 See Simard/west 2006, p. 224; Vanhaverbeke 2006, p. 209.
790 See e.g. Adler/Kwon 2002, p. 23. Also see Chapter 3.1.2.
791 See Chapter 3.2.2.3.
792 Ozcan/Eisenhardt 2009, p. 260.

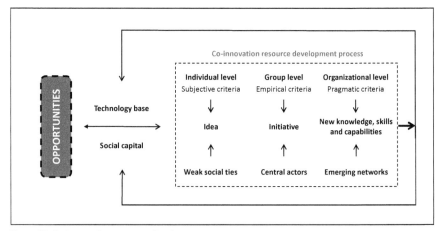

Figure 19: Co-innovation resource development process
Source: Based on Floyd/Woolridge 1999, p. 132.

4.1.2.2 Co-Innovation Capabilities

"In transforming ideas into initiatives, entrepreneurs pursue opportunities by circum-venting existing arrangements and creating novel social structures. In doing so they be-come the center of change processes."[793]

Aligned to the discussion of co-innovation resource development, the capabilities of the firm for effectively managing ties to organizations within its environmental context with reference to the corporate network need to be considered. This network offers a support-ing infrastructure enabling an inter-organizational transfer of competences and therefore serves as the basis of co-innovation.[794] Based on the definition of innovation networks, referred to as an economic structure of inter-organizational innovation activity based on complex-reciprocal and relatively stable social ties in which new products and services and processes are created,[795] the relevance of social ties for innovation performance can be identified.[796] Consequently, the inter-connectedness of organizations within a knowledge-based environment, containing a broad range of competences in terms of firm-specific resources and capabilities,[797] for linked-in organizations pitches a filed for the emergence

---

793 Floyd/Woolridge 1999, p. 139.
794 See Pittaway et al. 2004.
795 See Duschek 2002, p. 44.
796 See Elfring/Hulsink 2007, pp. 1853, 1866. Also see Chapter 3.1.2.1.
797 See van den Bosch/Volberda/ de Boer 1999, pp. 552, 558-565.

of entrepreneurial opportunities by exploring and exploiting the given network struc-ture.[798] This accounts for „all activities to acquire and maintain connections with external sources of social capital to achieve innovation."[799]

Innovation networks, therefore, allow for exploring new business models and an ex-ploiting the network's portfolio of competences for co-innovation.[800] Transferring this network analytical perspective to the organizational level allows the interpretation that a broad scope of ties to a spectrum of actors may support an exploration strategy by widen-ing the field of potential collaboration partners aiming at the identification of new tech-nologies and business models.[801] "In today's business landscape, most firms no longer rely on a single alliance: many firms maintain entire alliance portfolios compromised of multi-ple simultaneous strategic alliances with different partners in order to access a broad range of resources."[802] By lowering the search costs due to an increase of market knowledge and accessibility an involvement in several informal networks, consequently, broadens the scope of potential knowledge transfer and increases the likelihood of co-innovation performance.[803] This attribute relates to the absorptive capacity of the firm to recognize and evaluate information external to corporate boundaries.[804] The concept therefore is based on the co-innovation resources of the firm by requiring social capital in the form of the accessibility to weak ties as well as the technology base by being capable of evaluating the competences with the network portfolio as suitable for collaborative innovation.[805] "Ties lower relational uncertainty about the quality of potential partners."[806] Furthermore, co-innovation resource development processes need to be established to absorb and integrate external competences identified.[807] This relates to a dynamic set of capabilities to establish and maintain week ties as well as organizational learning process-es.

The bottom part of Figure 20 illustrates the absorptive capacity as a component of co-innovation capabilities within an open innovation framework. Here, the process from op-portunity identification to innovation performance is characterized by the three stages research, development and commercialization. Within these stages actors external to the firm can be identified, located within the corporate network. These are characterized as

798   See Simard/West. 2006, pp. 231-232.
799   de Jong et al. 2009, p. 425.
800   See March 1991, p. 85.
801   See Vanhaverbeke 2006, pp. 209, 229; Kang/Kang 2009, p. 4.
802   Wassmer/Dussauge 2011, p. 47.
803   See Kang/Kang 2009, pp. 12-15.
804   See Cohen/Levintal 1990, p. 128.
805   See Lichtenthaler 2006, p. 68; Zahra/George 2002, p. 192; Chesbrough/Prencipe 2008, p. 417; Harryson 2008, p. 297.
806   Ozcan/Eisenhardt 2009, p. 260. Also see Granovetter 1973; Uzzi 1997.
807   See Lane/Lubatkin 1998, p. 462; Gray 2006, p. 347. Also see Chapter 4.1.2.1.

carriers of specific competences suitable for the corresponding stages such as universities primarily in research and R&D institutes covering the research as well as the development stage. Knowledge-intensive firms may possess competences in all stages of the innovation process but specifically refer to the commercialization phase. A co-innovative approach in this regard will go beyond the sourcing of technologies by also drawing on the capabilities of networking partners as the critical asset for achieving co-innovation performance.

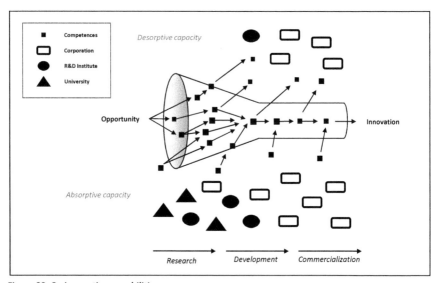

Figure 20: Co-innovation capabilities
Source: Based on Chesbrough 2003a, pp. 183, 189.

The upper part of the figure indicates an exploitation approach. Here the establishment of rather strong ties among network partners is seen as decisive for openly exploiting the corporate competence base. This approach refers to the desorptive capacity of the firm to transfer its competences to network partners and therefore, to maximizing value crea-tion.[808] Recent contributions can be identified with reference to this approach as 'out-bound open innovation' emphasizing the exploitation of the technology base inside and outside of corporate boundaries.[809] Approaching networks for exploiting the necessity of rather strong ties can be identified for achieving co-innovation depending on the complex-

---

808   See Lichtenthaler 2006, p. 65-75; Lichtenthaler/Lichtenthaler 2009, p. 1321. Also see Chapter 3.2.2.1.
809   See Lichtenthaler 2009, p. 319.

ity of the knowledge transferred.[810] Specifically, if capabilities are a matter of exploitation, because of their tacit character requirements and suitable conditions for their transfer need to be considered. "The monetary and strategic benefits from outbound open innovation do not necessarily overcompensate negative effects from selling 'corporate crown jewels.'"[811] This indicates the necessity of high market knowledge to drawing on relational capital to trusted collaboration partners to enable the most efficient exploitation of corporate competences.

To pursue entrepreneurial opportunities within a co-innovation context, an accessibility of complementary assets and specific competences is decisive.[812] The composition of the corporate network, characterized by a set of strong and weak ties, therefore, represents a critical factor for achieving co-innovation by enabling a simultaneous exploration of network competences and the exploitation of internal competences among network partners.[813] Understanding the composition as a dynamic process within changing environments, a network and relationship management considering all value creating and contributing components to realize competitive advantage is required.[814] To overcome the negative effects of network dependencies such as knowledge saturation among the actors, the capability to establish and maintain corporate ties demands a strategic approach aligned with the technology base. In this regard, the relevance of the regional context to establishing social capital for external knowledge acquisition represents an accessible pool of competences and embedded collaboration partners.[815] Furthermore, an effective network composition may reach beyond regional structures and bridge structural holes between network clusters by mediating these ties.[816]

The ability of the firm to effectively compose a network structure enabling co-innovation is a critical capability of a highly dynamic character. Consequently, compared to the open innovation paradigm which specifically draws on the sourcing of technologies within an outside-in and inside-out process,[817] co-innovation capabilities relate to the identification, transition and transfer of competences within the environmental context of the firm to pursue opportunities based on a collaborative approach of value creation.

---

810 See Harryson 2008, p. 295.
811 Lichtenthaler 2009, p. 319. Also see Fosfuri 2006.
812 See Vanhaverbeke/Cloodt 2006, p. 259.
813 See Simard/West 2006, p. 235; Harryson 2008, p. 297; Vanhaverbeke 2006, p. 209.
814 See Vanhaverbeke 2006, pp. 213, 216.
815 See Laursen/Masciarelli/Prencipe 2012, p. 177.
816 See Ozcan/Eisenhardt 2009, p. 260.
817 See Chesbrough 2003a, pp. 183, 189; Mortara et al. 2009, p. 12; Gassmann/Enkel 2006, p. 134.

4.1.3 Environmental Dimension - Regional Entrepreneurial Climate

"Without an environment that fosters the detection of opportunities, no entre-preneurship will emerge."[818]

As indicated in the previous stages of this work the environmental context of a firm has been considered as a highly relevant component regarding its possibilities to pursue en-trepreneurial processes and realize corporate performance.[819] In strategic management literature this dimension is mainly reduced to the consideration of market dynamics, in-dustry characteristics, flexibility and systemic complexity.[820] These aspects, however, may require a more precise determination to analyze the regional environment of an entrepre-neurial firm as an influential factor to its development. Therefore, in the following subsec-tions an understanding of the environmental context as a supporting climate for the pur-suit of entrepreneurial behavior will be elaborated following the quest for "ideal geogra-phies for entrepreneurship."[821] Specific factors are presented contributing to the charac-teristics of an entrepreneurial climate. Based on this construct, the question remains how entrepreneurial firms may draw on surrounding elements to speed and amplify entrepre-neurial performance. Therefore, the role of regional networks as source of a regional knowledge base and their contribution to knowledge spill-over effects are elaborated in more detail, integrating entrepreneurship within the concept of RIS. Furthermore, the relevance of regional promotors of innovation framing the RIS by supporting entrepre-neurial firms to engage in regional knowledge networks is elaborated. The presentation of these topics will offer a sound basis for discussing a strategic approach to entrepreneur-ship conceptually linking the relevance of the environmental context to entrepreneurial performance.

4.1.3.1 Toward an Understanding of the Entrepreneurial Climate

"Local and regional determinants are much more relevant than national or suprana-tional framework conditions for explaining the number of start-ups in a given region and the growth or survival of young firms."[822]

Configurations of social, political, and economic conditions within regional structures may create an economic climate that significantly influences the likelihood of prosperous de-

---

818   Stevenson/Jarillo 1990, p. 25.
819   See e.g. Sanchez/Heene 1996, p. 41; Stevenson/Jarillo 1990, p. 25; Lichtenthaler 2009.
820   See Lumpkin/Dess 1996, p. 154.
821   See Thornton/Flynn 2003, pp. 420-421.
822   Sternberg 2007, p. 656.

velopment of firms located within.[823] The business environment consequently can be understood as a decisive component affecting corporate development.[824] Especially regional clusters provide supporting conditions for young entrepreneurial firms due to the existence of inter-organizational networks.[825] The entrepreneur therefore may draw on regionally embedded structural capital to engage with regional actors and establish relational capital as a foundation for future collaboration. Aside from various regional case studies which can be identified in the economic and geographic literature,[826] Silicon Valley, California, USA, predominantly serves as the empirical example for the relevance of the regional context as source of competitive advantage.[827] Here, a setting can be identified that is characterized by a high knowledge density creating a regional infrastructure of various complementarily knowledge providing actors. The infrastructural configuration of institutions such as universities, R&D institutes, technology parks and business incubators, therefore, may be seen as the structural preconditions for the stimulation of knowledge accumulation and creation. Furthermore, it is not the mere existence of knowledge sources but the interaction and knowledge exchange among these regional actors that is considered decisive to amplifying new knowledge creation and commercialization. Such conditions may create a specific climate allowing for the development of new ideas for business, living and working models,[828] which can be termed a 'regional entrepreneurial climate.'

A more precise analysis of factors influencing the entrepreneurial climate would go well beyond a discussion of infrastructural configuration. Also 'soft-factors' such as norms and beliefs may be decisive to establishing a vital entrepreneurial climate.[829] Based on data drawing from the Global Entrepreneurship Monitor (GEM) Brixy/Hundt/Sternberg (2009) introduce in their report of entrepreneurship in Germany a set of characteristics influencing the framing conditions of a regional entrepreneurial climate.[830] Aligned to a systematic review of additional contributions with reference to the term as well as its synonym 'entrepreneurial milieu' a set of components can be identified as dominant factors constituting the characteristics of an entrepreneurial climate (see Table 6). The identified set of components indicates the relevance of considering the inter-relations of regional conditions guided by the political framing. This leads to an understanding of the vitality of the

---

823 See Goetz/Freshwater 2001, pp. 64-65.
824 See Porter 1998c, p. 198.
825 See Rocha/Sternberg 2005, p. 268.
826 See e.g. Asheim/Coenen 2005; Doloreux/Dionne 2008; Belussi/Sammarra/Sedita 2010. Also see Rocha/Sternberg (2005, p. 278-380) for an overview on empirical studies on clusters and development.
827 See e.g. Saxenien 2000; Lee et al. 2000.
828 See Lee et al. 2000, p. 7.
829 See Goetz/Freshwater 2001, p. 67.
830 See Brixy/Hundt/Sternberg 2009, p. 21. The majority of aspects listed within the report draw on previous work by Wagner/Sternberg (2004).

entrepreneurial climate as an alternating concept. On the one hand the regional entrepreneurial climate may be based on components of rather general nature, promoting the pursuit of entrepreneurial opportunities seen as a guideline for public policy. On the other hand a critical amount of individual skills, capabilities and knowledge must be provided by the organizations and individuals within the corresponding structure to exploit these favorable conditions that in turn create a vital entrepreneurial climate.[831]

Constitutional factors of an entrepreneurial climate	
Factors	**Author**
Political framing conditions and taxation	Wagner/Sternberg 2004, p. 237; Bergmann/Sternberg 2007, pp. 209-210; Fritsch/Müller 2007, p. 299; Armington/Acs 2002, p. 37
Regional financing and venture capital	Acs/Szerb 2007, p. 115; Thompson 1989; Zook 2002; Chen et al. 2010; Wagner/Sternberg 2004, p. 223
Physical infrastructure	Wagner/Sternberg 2004, p. 230; Hackett/Dilts 2004, p. 57; Löfsten/Lindelöf 2003, p. 56
Regional networks and knowledge spillovers	Etzkowitz/Klofsten 2005, p. 245; Wagner/Sternberg 2004, p. 222; Iammarino 2005, p. 4; Cooke 2004, p. 3; Acs et al. 2009; Audretsch/Lehmann 2005; Audretsch/Aldridge 2009
Regional knowledge intensity and human capital	Cooke 2009, p. 94; Cooke/Boekholt/Tödtling 2000, p. 5; Sternberg 2007, p. 655; Bergmann/Sternberg 2007, pp. 205-206
Regional prosperity and entrepreneurial activity	Fritsch/Müller 2007, p. 309; Wagner 2007, p. 205; Wagner/Sternberg 2004, p. 230
Social norms and values	Goetz/Freshwater 2001, p. 67; Armington/Acs 2002, p. 39; Fritsch/Müller 2007, p. 309

Table 6: Dominant factors constituting the entrepreneurial climate

On a national as well as on a regional level political framing conditions have a critical influence on the decision of an entrepreneur to establish a corporation within a specific geographic setting.[832] By providing a legal framework and the institutional power to coordinate market behavior constitutional conditions can be defined creating the basis for entrepreneurial market participation such as the protection of IP.[833] Public policy, consequently, may positively influence an entrepreneurial climate by creating incentives facilitating and promoting entrepreneurial performance. In this regard, several contributions are directed at policy makers to vitalize and optimize the regional entrepreneurial cli-

831 In this regard it is to be mentioned that the literature used from economic geography differentiates between a macro- and a micro-level perspective regarding the constitutional factors of an entrepreneurial climate. The presented factors refer to the macro-level, whereas the micro-level components such as entrepreneurial motivation and intellectual capital, are integrated into the discussion of the innovation capacity of the entrepreneurial firm following a strategic management thought pattern (see Chapter 4.1.1.1.).

832 See Wagner/Sternberg 2004, p. 237; Bergmann/Sternberg 2007, pp. 209-210; Fritsch/Müller 2007, p. 299. Also see Porter 1998, p. 174.

833 See Gans/Stern 2003, pp. 338-339. Also see Nooteboom 2000a.

mate.[834] The aspect of political framing conditions, therefore, serves as higher-order construct including or inter-dependent with further aspects such as taxation as a specific tool of public policy. Empirical evidence shows that nations or regions in the case of political sovereignty show higher rates of newly founded firms if economic incentives in the form of comparably lower corporate tax rates are provided.[835] Furthermore, from a financial perspective, the existence of public funding or state-aided subsidized loans for providing start-ups with seed money needs to be considered.[836] Even though financial capital can be seen as a resource of high mobility transferred on a global scale, a geography of venture capital can be identified.[837] Consequently, the characteristics of a regional infrastructure of financial institutions and their capability of promoting entrepreneurial firms are highly relevant for the establishment of a vital regional entrepreneurial climate.[838]

The physical infrastructure provided within a geographic setting may represent a rather basic, albeit nonetheless an important aspect within the process of choice of location for founding a corporation. Transport facilities allowing the entrepreneur to efficiently travel to potential collaboration partners and vice versa an uncomplicated reachability of the entrepreneurial firm shows certain relevance. In the sector of knowledge-intensive firms providing corporate services the technical infrastructure regarding I&C technologies such as high-speed internet accessibility represents an inevitable precondition for such firms within their choice of location. Furthermore, the availability of economically priced office and industrial real estate leads to lower financial capital intensity of the start-up which may be crucial in receiving external funding and reaching profitability of the firm.[839] In this context, the existence of business incubators can be identified. "A business incubator is a shared office space facility that seeks to provide its incubatees (i.e. 'portfolio-' or 'client-' or 'tenant-companies') with a strategic, value adding intervention system (i.e. business incubation) of monitoring and business assistance. This system controls and links resources with the objective of facilitating the successful new venture development of the incubatees."[840] These incubators seemingly may provide, on the one hand, fairly condi-

---

834 See e.g. Baldacchino/Dana 2009; Etzkowitz 2002; van Johnston 2000; Tsai/Kuo 2011.
835 See Armington/Acs 2002, p. 37. In this regard the term 'tax haven' has been coined referring to countries such as Mauritius and Monaco or regions such as the Cayman Islands and the Virgin Islands.
836 See Acs/Szerb 2007, p. 115. In the case of Germany the Ministry of Economics and Technology provides several programs for start-up financing such as the EXIST program which directly aims at promoting university spin-offs. For an overview of public start-up financing programs by the state of Germany, see: www.foerderdatenbank.de.
837 See Thompson 1989; Zook 2002; Chen et al. 2010; Thornton/Flynn 2003, pp. 419-420.
838 See Wagner/Sternberg 2004, p. 223. Acs/Szerb 2007, p. 116.
839 See Wagner/Sternberg 2004, p. 230. In this context the term 'burn rate' can be identified in entrepreneurship literature referring to the amount of money needed by a start-up to support its operations (Sapienza/de Clercq 2000, p. 57).
840 Hackett/Dilts 2004, p. 57.

tioned physical infrastructure and services to support administrative processes and, on the other hand, access to established networks to entrepreneurial firms located within the incubator and collaboration partners such as established firms and suppliers and research institutes. Depending on the character of the entrepreneur these conditions may positively influence the start-up process by reducing the risk involved.[841]

The accessibility of established networks stemming from business incubators indicates the relevance of regional networks as a potential source of collaboration partners to initiate value creation processes. The existence of regional networks of multiple actors such as corporations, politicians and research institutions is mentioned as decisive component to lock into those prevailing structures and profit from the structural capital given due to the regional context.[842] These regional networks draw on the establishment of a RIS emphasizing the creation and modification of knowledge and its commercialization based on the interaction of its actors.[843] The relevance of knowledge-producing institutions in this regard is emphasized within the introduced 'triple helix model.'[844] "While industry and government have traditionally been conceptualized as primary institutional spheres, what is new in the triple helix model is that the university is posited to be leading sphere along with industry and government."[845] The transfer of knowledge and technology within these structures may therefore cause regional knowledge spillovers creating entrepreneurial opportunities.[846]

The critical resource for the evolvement of RIS lies in the individual knowledge base by the actors contributing to the system which may be extended within inter-organizational knowledge transfer.[847] This implies, however, the necessity for knowledge-intensive and knowledge producing organizations to be located within the regional structure.[848] These organizations rely upon the human capital available to productively engage in the knowledge creation process. A high rate of qualified, skilled and specialized human capital within a region may offer the entrepreneur the opportunity to expand organizational operations and achieve growth in terms of innovations performed and number of employees employed.[849] The prosperity of the region characterized by the high quality of physical infrastructure, human capital and regional networks, consequently, may highly impact

---

841   See Löfsten/Lindelöf 2003, p. 56; Pena 2002, pp. 192-194.
842   See Etzkowitz/Klofsten 2005, p. 245; Wagner/Sternberg 2004, p. 222.
843   See Iammarino 2005, p. 4; Cooke 2004, p. 3.
844   See Chapter 2.3.2.2.
845   Cooke 2002, p. 117.
846   See Acs et al. 2009; Audretsch/Lehmann 2005; Audretsch/Aldridge 2009. The brief introduction to entrepreneurship within regional innovation systems as a component of the entrepreneurial climate is elaborated in more detail within the following section 4.1.3.2.
847   See Frenken/Van Oort/Verburg 2007, p. 687.
848   See Cooke 2009, p. 94; Cooke/Boekholt/Tödtling 2000, p. 5.
849   See Fritsch/Müller 2007, p. 299; Sternberg 2007, p. 655; Bergmann/Sternberg 2007, pp. 205-206.

entrepreneurial activity. Based on the dualism of structure,[850] entrepreneurial behavior therefore may contribute to shaping the characteristics of the entrepreneurial climate while being influenced by the conditions given. This causes a spiral effect attracting new firms, leading to the cognition that the intensity of entrepreneurial activity itself serving as testimonial must be considered as highly relevant factor characterizing the quality of the entrepreneurial climate.[851] Audretsch/Keilbach (2004) define this circumstance as 'entrepreneurship capital' of a geographic setting and indicate a positive relation of entrepreneurship capital to economic performance.[852]

In addition, as indicated above, the relevance of 'soft-factors' such as the norms and values of society toward entrepreneurial behavior needs to be considered as an influential factor of the regional entrepreneurial climate.[853] "Norms and beliefs in the surrounding environment influence the value of a given stock of social capital. For example, entrepreneurship may be seen as legitimate in one context, whereas in another context it might be seen as opportunistic and self-seeking."[854] Social values create a tacit context influencing entrepreneurial behavior. Especially the appreciation of entrepreneurs as driving forces of innovation and economic growth cause a positive attitude toward entrepreneurs. This attitude may be expressed by the willingness of established institutions to cooperate with young entrepreneurial firms and regional institutions providing supporting services.[855] Furthermore, in this context, the exposure to entrepreneurial failure has received attention in entrepreneurship literature.[856] Cultures that understand failure as a process of learning may encourage entrepreneurial behavior among its inhabitants.[857] The entrepreneurial spirit of a region characterized by the norms and values of its inhabitants, therefore, serves as a decisive attribute to completing the spectrum constitutional factors characterizing the entrepreneurial climate.[858]

---

850 See Giddens 1979, p. 64. Also see Chapter 2.3.1.
851 See Fritsch/Müller 2007, p. 309; Wagner 2007, p. 205; Wagner/Sternberg 2004, p. 230.
852 See Audretsch/Keilbach 2004, p. 949.
853 Also see Goetz/Freshwater 2001, p. 67.
854 Adler/Kwon 2002, p. 33.
855 See Armington/Acs 2002, p. 39.
856 See McGrath 1999; Also see Pechlaner/Stechhammer/Hinterhuber 2010.
857 See Shepherd 2004, p. 274.
858 See Fritsch/Müller 2007, p. 309.

4.1.3.2 Entrepreneurship in Regional Innovation Structures

"Innovative firms (and innovative entrepreneurs leading such firms) are the most important players within an RIS."[859]

A complex approach to analyze entrepreneurship within a regional context is provided by
the perspective of regional innovation structures. Based on previous elaborations in this
work, regional innovation structures may be understood as an innovation system within a
geographic setting creating an operational environment of knowledge producing, processing and exploiting organizations aiming for an interactive approach to perform innovation.[860] The concept draws on the establishment of an ecosystem of knowledge in which
the creation of new knowledge and its commercialization are connected to a cyclical and
systemic structure.[861] The dynamics within these structures may lead to the establishment
of 'regional knowledge capabilities' with reference to a continuous development of the
regional knowledge base.[862] Due to the process of specialization of competences and the
necessity of inter-organizational collaboration based on complementary assets,[863] corporations aim at exploiting regionally embedded knowledge by in turn contributing to the local
knowledge base.[864] This attitude is based on reciprocity causing a consistent development
of the system. Several industries can be identified which practice this form of regional
open innovation "in order to overcome intra-firm knowledge asymmetries by tapping in to
the regional knowledge capabilities and systemic innovation strength of accomplished
regional and local clusters."[865] Core element of the discussion, consequently, is a regionally
based establishment of knowledge flows that offer a wide spectrum for commercialization
based on knowledge spillovers and therefore create entrepreneurial opportunities.

Knowledge spillover theory applied to entrepreneurship draws on the perception that
"all knowledge is economic knowledge,"[866] and can be differentiated into non-rival, codified knowledge and rival, tacit knowledge. The emergence of new knowledge and its
commercialization, however, may require an additional perspective with reference to endogenous and exogenous knowledge considering its value over time.[867] An entrepreneurial
venture, consequently, may increase its potentials of success by having new and rival

---

859 Sternberg 2007, p. 654.
860 See Asheim/Isaksen 1997, p. 302; Cooke 2004, p. 3; Iammarino, p. 4. Also see Chapter 2.4.
861 See Kirsch 2001; Kirsch/Seidl/van Aaken 2010; van der Borgh/Cloodt/Romme 2012, pp. 151-152.
862 See Cooke 2005, pp. 1134-1139.
863 See Teece 1986, p.289; Dahlander/Wallin 2006, p. 1243; Boschma/Iammarino 2009, pp. 292-293.
864 See Vanhaverbeke 2006, p. 216.
865 Cooke 2005, p. 1147.
866 Acs et al. 2009, p. 17.
867 See Romer, 1986; 1991; 1996, p. 204.

knowledge at its disposal profiting from knowledge asymmetries.[868] In this regard, entre-preneurial firms may, on the one hand, draw on endogenous knowledge as an initiating impulse or, on the other, hand have been capable of exploiting exogenous knowledge sources for their entrepreneurial pursuit.[869]

Based on specialization and firm-specific competences the creation of new knowledge may not fit the prevailing technological base leading to an excess, or spillover, of knowledge contained within an organizational unit. This spillover may occur most inten-sively in primarily knowledge-producing organizations such as universities and R&D institu-tions not aiming for the commercialization of their knowledge produced.[870] Knowledge spillover theory within an entrepreneurial context "posits that it is new knowledge and ideas created in one context but left uncommercialized or not vigorously pursued by the source actually creating these ideas, such as a research laboratory in a large corporation or research undertaken by a university, that serves as the source of knowledge generating entrepreneurial opportunities."[871] Consequently, the exploitation of knowledge produced by one organization within commercial means by an entrepreneurial organization trans-ferred at lower rates than knowledge generation costs refers to the knowledge spillover theory of entrepreneurship.

Although the literature indicates that knowledge spillovers may be promoted by geo-graphic proximity due to a reduction of costs for accessing and absorbing knowledge,[872] a crucial factor for the effectiveness of regional innovation structures for entrepreneurial firm performance is the establishment of ties to these knowledge-producing organizations and respectively their embeddedness in the regional innovation network. Consequently, physical embeddedness within a regional structure based on geographic proximity may not be sufficient for accessing regional network structures but serve as an initiating com-ponent to allow for the establishment of social embeddedness within these structures.[873] "Any business activity is embedded in a broader socio-institutional context, and therefore the economic dimensions or relationships cannot be separated from socio-institutional ones."[874]

Especially in knowledge-intensive fields does the evolvement of trust as a consequence of social embeddedness serve as critical resource for collaboration.[875] Based on the norm of reciprocity this may require an active participation by individual actors within the sys-

---

868 See Scott 2006, pp. 7-8.
869 See Acs et al. 2009, p. 28.
870 See Stephan 2001; Antonelli 2008; Tether/Tajar 2008.
871 Audretsch/Lehmann 2005. p. 1193.
872 See Foray 2006, p. 101; Audretsch/Lehmenn 2005, p. 1194.
873 See Boschma 2005, p. 70; Sternberg 2007, p. 660.
874 Sternberg 2007, pp. 656-657.
875 See Uzzi 1996, p. 676; Lin 2003, p. 151.

tem asking for an investment to establish relational capital and hereupon accessing the regional knowledge base.[876] Based on the works by Sternberg (2007; 2009) potential fields of interaction for entrepreneurial firms within regional innovation structures can be identified (see Figure 21). These may be seen as particular entry options or as an aggregate of options to engage in and exploit the potentials of regional innovation structures.

As the concept of knowledge spillover indicates, the interaction of entrepreneurial firms with knowledge-producing organizations such as universities and R&D institutions should be considered as a source of exogenous knowledge and exploitation of entrepreneurial opportunities. Audretsch/Lehman (2005) identify two potential types of knowledge spillovers regarding the university-industry relationship, emphasizing the heterogeneity of university knowledge output.[877] Here, the authors, on the one hand, differentiate between disciplines of clearly defined scientific methodology such as the natural sciences producing predominantly codified knowledge and disciplines of less standardized methodology such as the social sciences producing less codified and rather implicit knowledge.[878] With regard to the relevance of proximity one may conclude that knowledge spillover in the form of technology transfer may show higher effectiveness due to proximity if an increased amount of implicit knowledge is involved. Consequently, the research results in the natural sciences if published in scientific journals may not require social ties for knowledge spillover whereas the transfer of less codified knowledge than in social sciences or off-stream research results may be amplified by social ties.[879] On the other hand, knowledge spillovers may occur in this constellation based on the inter-organizational transfer of human capital. Specific knowledge embodied in graduating university students may serve as a powerful channel of integrating university knowledge into the corporate knowledge base.[880] This transfer may be amplified due to regional proximity because of lower search costs for corporations finding appropriate knowledge keepers as well as for university students finding matching corporations to contribute as employees to value creation processes based on their specific knowledge acquired.[881]

Universities in turn may profit from collaborating with corporations by gaining a reputation as being capable of providing relevant knowledge to serve economic interests. Entrepreneurial firms in this case receive the role of 'knowledge filters' by applying specific

---

876   See Putnam/Goss 2002, p. 7. Also see Chapter 3.1.2.2.
877   See Audretsch/Lehmann 2005, p. 1194.
878   Also see Stephan 1996, pp. 1229-1231.
879   See Sternberg 2007, p. 655.
880   See Varga 2000, p. 303; Schartinger/Schibany/Gassler 2001, p. 259. Also see Saxenien (2000) describing
      the relevance of regional advantages in case of human capital transfer from Stanford University to firms
      located in the Silicon Valley.
881   See Audretsch/Lehmann 2005, p. 1194; Sternberg 2007, p. 655.

components of the university' knowledge base to commercial ends.[882] This will affect the attractiveness of the university as an industrial research collaboration partner and increase the attractiveness for students to enroll at the university aiming for future industrial employment. As the previous statement regarding the necessity of an investment into the establishment of ties to knowledge-producing institutions indicates, to obtain these spillovers corporations should initiate this process by providing financial capital to universities. This may be done by the financing collaborative research endeavors which in its highest peculiarity may lead to the establishment of new centers and subdivisions within the university or the provision of employment within established centers and institutes.[883]

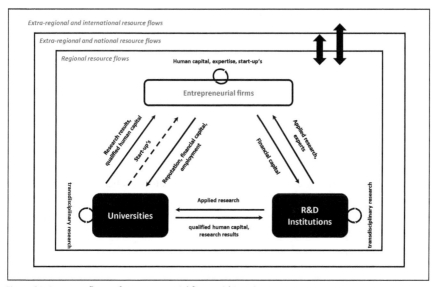

Figure 21: Resource flows of entrepreneurial firms within RIS
Source: Based on Sternberg 2007, p. 654; 2009, p. 23.

---

882   See Mueller 2006, p. 1499.
883   Empirically several examples of corporate financed chairs and research centres within universities may be found globally (e.g. UBS endowed chair of finance and asset pricing at Goethe University Frankfurt, Germany). With regard to the provision of employment within a formalized university-industry collaboration the 'Ingolstadt Institutes' can be mentioned as an empirical example. Here the automotive manufacturer AUDI AG has established several links to geographically adjacent universities to collaborate in technological as well as social sciences. By financing the employment of Ph.D candidates working on a collaboratively developed research questions, the corporation, on the one hand, profit of the results obtained and, on the other hand, from binding highly qualified future employees to the corporation. See e.g. www.ini-ku.de.

This reciprocal flow of resources and specifically knowledge transfer within a regional uni-versity-industry relationship is indicated on the left hand side of Figure 21. Entrepreneurial firms with lower financial resources, however, are challenged to lock-in to cooperations as such, but may draw on their innovativeness and potential future development promising future reciprocities. The collaboration of universities with entrepreneurial firms, conse-quently, requires a mutual first-stage investment to establish a fruitful future collaboration and resource transfers. An additional aspect is to be mentioned in this regard with respect to the discussion of the 'entrepreneurial university' within RIS.[884] Universities may also actively contribute to the regional base of entrepreneurial firms by promoting the founda-tion of new ventures (indicated by the dotted line).[885] In this case both parts can refer to established ties kick-starting a process of reciprocal resource flows.

Furthermore, as the right hand side of the graphic shows public, semi-private, and pri-vate R&D institutions are relevant sources of exogenous knowledge.[886] Based on the provi-sion of financial capital by corporations, those collaborations provide firms with the oppor-tunity to outsource R&D and to drawing on high expertise of researchers within these in-stitutions.[887] The expertise of these institutions may be of endogenous character devel-oped within previous industrial research collaborations and also of exogenous character drawing on a network of knowledge sources at their hands.[888] The graphic indicates this perspective by the loop with reference to transdisciplinary research projects among knowledge-producing institutions.[889] In this regard, the collaboration of R&D institutions with universities needs to be considered which may lead to a transfer of human capital and research results to R&D institutions and vice versa knowledge gained within industrial research projects. Entrepreneurial firms, consequently, may profit from collaborating with R&D institutions by accessing their base of applied research and realizing knowledge spill-over due to the acquisition of specific knowledge at a lower cost than internally produced and receiving access to additional knowledge keepers based on the establishment of ties to collaborating R&D institutions.

In addition to the discussion of knowledge transfer between industry and primarily knowledge-producing institutions, the flow of resources among entrepreneurial firms

---

884   See Etzkowitz/Klofsten 2005, p. 245.
885   See Ndonzuau/Pirnay/Surlemont 2002; Pirnay/Surlemont/Nlemvo 2003; Walter/Auer/Ritter 2006.
886   Also See Denti 2009.
887   See e.g. Quinn 2000; 2002; Howells 2000. Also see Chapter 2.2.2.1.
888   See Freeman 1991, p. 510.
889   Nowotny (2003, pp. 48-49) comments on the idea of transdisciplinarity: "the loss to what is felt to have been a former unity of knowledge. ... [the] expectation that transdisciplinarity contributes to a joint problem solving that it is more than juxtaposition; more than laying one discipline alongside another. ...If joint problem solving is the aim, then the means must provide for an integration of perspectives in the identification, formulation and resolution of what has to become a shared problem."

needs to be considered. As elaborated earlier collaboration among firms based on an infrastructure of complementary assets is a precondition during times of specialization and
chain-linked innovation processes.[890] Inter-firm collaboration, therefore, may be an essential source of new knowledge creation processes based on knowledge transfer causing
inter-organizational learning. "Entrepreneurial behavior in a learning framework involves
search activities such as expending resources on the exploration of alternative possibilities,
attempting to understand the relationship between organizational characteristics and outcomes, and determining the viability of organizational change. Thus, entrepreneurial learning includes these activities directed toward discovering possibilities for change at organizations."[891] Therefore, specifically the innovation performance of young firms may be influenced by knowledge flows among networked firms.[892] This perception, however, needs
to be considered within the discussion of unintended knowledge spillover requiring for
mechanisms of protection of IP preventing opportunistic behavior.[893] Furthermore, start-
up's may emerge from inter-firm collaboration, in the form of spin-offs transferring
knowledge and technology and/or human capital into a newly founded venture.[894] As in
case of university spin-offs these organizations may draw on a competitive advantage
compared to rather organic entrepreneurial firms by being locked into established network structures.

To date, the aspect of extra-regional links has not been considered within the discussion of entrepreneurship in regional innovation structures. These have been described as a
dynamic system of multiple actors based on interaction collectively contributing to the
development of the regional knowledge base. Comparing these regional structures reveals
an asymmetric share of specific regional knowledge capabilities.[895] These capabilities refer
to capacity of regional actors to integrate exogenous knowledge form extra-regional
sources into the regional innovation structure (indicated by the strong arrows reaching out
of the regional context). As discussed for the categorization of RIS,[896] epistemic communities may exist across regional boundaries and transfer knowledge among its members.[897]
Specifically universities and R&D institutes require these communities to exchange their
specific knowledge in the form of research results with globally located experts within
their field of research.

890 See Teece 1986, p.289; Sternberg 2007, pp. 653, 654.
891 Lant/Mezias 1990, p. 149. Also see Gibb 2002.
892 See Shan/Walker/Kogut 2006, p. 387.
893 See Nooteboom 2000, p. 919; Hoecht/Trott 1999, p. 266.
894 See Dahlstrand 1997. Also see Bossink 2002, p. 315.
895 See Cooke 2005, pp. 1134-1139.
896 See Asheim/Coenen 2005, pp. 1179-1180; Chung 2002, p. 489. Aslo see Chapter 2.3.2.2.
897 See Coenen/Moodysson/Asheim 2004, p. 1009.

Although the regional environmental context of entrepreneurial firms has been empha-sized as highly relevant, corporate links beyond geographic proximity are considered as fundamental preconditions for the achievement of entrepreneurial performance. This as-pect serves as a source to contribute to the regional knowledge base offering complemen-tary assets based on exogenous knowledge and therefore preventing negative conse-quences of a too intense regional lock-in.[898] The downside of strong ties binding actors to the regional system in a knowledge context is a leveling of the regional knowledge base due to a lack of interaction with the extra-regional environment. Hence, drawing on the theory of structural holes[899] entrepreneurial opportunities may emerge due to the func-tion of entrepreneurial firms as 'transmission channels' integrating economically useful knowledge from external networks into the regional innovation structure.[900] In this regard, one may speak of 'open regional innovation systems' enabling global competitiveness of the RIS.[901]

Consequently, a set of options can be identified for entrepreneurial firms to engage in, exploit and profit from the economic potentials of regional innovation structures. This leads to the cognition that entrepreneurial activity may be a result of mutual investments of regional actors into the regional knowledge base promoting the emergence of entre-preneurship "localized within close geographic proximity to the knowledge source."[902] These investments as in the case of spin-offs may draw on a transfer of knowledge gener-ated in one organization to be commercially exploited within a new venture. According to the concept of knowledge spillover, these investments may refer to the willingness of es-tablished corporations and institutions to build ties with young entrepreneurial firms inte-grating them within regional resource flows. The establishment of these ties, however, may requires strong networking capabilities by the entrepreneur or the existence of re-gional actors promoting the development of entrepreneurial firms.

4.1.3.3 Regional Promotors of Innovation

"The facilitation and support of business networks and associations may provide the most consistent and effective support for emerging businesses."[903]

---

898   See Sternberg 2007, p. 657.
899   See Burt 1992. Also see Chapter 3.1.1.2.
900   See Sternberg 2007, p. 657.
901   See Belussi/Samarra/Sedita 2010, p. 713.
902   Audretsch/Lehmenn 2005, p. 1179.
903   Davidsson/Honig 2003, p. 325.

The presentation of the current state of discussion regarding the structural levels of open innovation and inter-organizational collaboration has shown that intermediaries may serve as coordinators of open innovation networks.[904] Furthermore, the role of promotors as enablers of inter-organizational innovation has been presented in the concept of innovation communities.[905] Based on these elaborations a transfer to an analysis of the environmental conditions surrounding the entrepreneurial firm and contributing to its potential for value creation can be realized.

This chapter has emphasized the aspect of economic specialization leading to chain-linked innovation processes of cooperating organizations.[906] Connecting this perspective to the discussion of RIS allows for a more precise analytical approach characterizing an economic structural setting. By understanding the corporate transaction process that aims for economic value creation as focal element of an economic infrastructure, a set of organizations can be identified that contribute to those value-creation processes. These organizations, consequently, can be understood as promotors by enabling corporations to achieve economic performance,[907] by providing and/or diffusing knowledge within the RIS.[908] As discussed with regard to RIS, a transferring resources from knowledge-producing institutions to entrepreneurial firms can be identified as enhancing their capacity to perform innovation.[909] Universities and public R&D institutions, therefore, may primarily be seen as promotors of specific expertise,[910] by supporting corporate innovation capacity due to the provision of research results suitable for commercialization.[911]

With reference to the term 'linking level' which was introduced by Fichter (2009), in this regard further actors can be identified within the regional environmental context of the firm such as government agencies, industry associations and innovation brokers.[912] These, on the one hand, also may possess specific expertise offered by consultative support and, on the other hand, they may serve as 'relationship promotors' by brokering ties to potential collaboration partners and thus providing access to keepers of specific competences to pursue interactive value creation.[913] Understanding these actors as institutional representatives they can contribute to the regional conditions for economic value crea-

---

904 See Chesbrough 2006c, p. 152. Also see Chapter 2.2.4.1.
905 See Fichter 2009, p. 361. Also see Chapter 2.2.4.2.
906 See ie. Tappeiner/Hauser/Walde 2008, pp. 862-863; Chung 2002, p. 484; Sternberg 2007, p. 653.
907 See Witte 1999, p. 15; Hauschild/Salomo 2011, p. 125.
908 See Doloreux 2003, p. 71.
909 See Sternberg 2007, p. 654; 2009, p. 23. Also see Chapter 4.3.1.2.
910 See Witte (1973, p. 17) elaborating the term 'expert promotors.'
911 See Mason/Wagner 1999, pp. 97-100.
912 See Fichter 2009, p. 360; Winch/Courtney 2007, p. 751.
913 See Gemünden/Walter 1999, pp. 119-120.

tion, consumption and organizational interaction and thus innovation performance.[914] Regional institutional representatives within a RIS, consequently, may act as promotors of innovation by providing expertise as well as establishing knowledge flows among regional actors and thus serve as mediators enhancing inter-organizational collaboration for innovation.

Following the framework of an ideal entrepreneurial region, the following structures prevail: supporting the linkage of organizations and technology, universities offer expertise for commercialization, incubators exist to support business development, and established corporations intensively collaborate with entrepreneurial firms.[915] "In a region like this one would expect to see entrepreneurship flourishing."[916] Regional innovation promotors can impact the entrepreneurial climate by amplifying the effects of regional proximity. In other words, innovation promotors can be considered co-creators of regionally embedded structural capital and may have the capacity to establish new ties and therefore to promote the establishment of relational capital among regional actors.

Relating the elaborated factors constituting an entrepreneurial climate to the list of promotors mentioned above requires for an extension to display a more complete spectrum of actors influencing regional economic development with regard to entrepreneurship and innovation.[917] Apparently the term 'innovation brokers' offers access to a range of actors who in some way serve as brokers of innovation by either offering expertise how to or with whom to pursue opportunities. Specifically managers of business incubators need to be considered aiming for the promotion of a successful venture development of entrepreneurial firms.[918] These may provide an access to a network of entrepreneurial firms located within the incubator as well as to the incubator's network of collaboration partners. Furthermore, the aspect of geographically bounded venture capital needs to be considered.[919] Accordingly, the regional infrastructure of financial institutions and their willingness toward knowledge-intensive venture investing is decisive.[920] This financial infrastructure may provide formal and informal venture capital markets differentiating between institutionalized organizations and private investors termed 'business angels.'[921] These actors follow an economic interest in promoting the successful development of their

914 Setterfield 1993, p. 756; Hodgson 1988, p. 134; North 1990, pp. 3-4; Nelson 1993. For a discussion on institutions and co-ordination of innovation systems see Notteboom 2000a.
915 See Asheim/Cooke 1998, p. 235.
916 Thornton/Flynn 2003 p. 421.
917 See Chapter 4.1.3.1.
918 See Hackett/Dilts 2004, p. 57.
919 See Thompson 1989; Zook 2002; Chen et al. 2010; Thornton/Flynn 2003, pp. 419-420.
920 See Wagner/Sternberg 2004, p. 223. Acs/Szerb 2007, p. 116.
921 See Harrison/Mason 2000, p. 224; Black/Gilson 1998.

invested ventures and therefore need to be regarded as decisive regional innovation promotors.

Based on the statement of an ideal entrepreneurial region the role of established corporations as collaboration partners for entrepreneurial firms has been emphasized.[922] In
addition, corporate actors should be considered promotors of innovation by providing
relevant knowledge-intensive services for entrepreneurial firms. In this case empirical examples can be identified of experts in the fields of law, taxes and consulting organizing a
regional network of experts to promote the development of entrepreneurial firms following a professional interest.[923] Furthermore on a corporate level entrepreneurial firms as
such require consideration. Based on the concept of 'corporate venturing' which can be
understood as "the creation of new businesses within existing firms,"[924] entrepreneurial
firms capable of practicing corporate venturing may take a multi-character innovation
promotor role by providing venture capital, expertise as well as access to regional networks in the form of an incubator to a venture.

An empirical study by Rabe (2007) analyzes the infrastructure of promotors in the area
of Karlsruhe, Germany. The author identifies several promotor categories existing within
the region of analysis.[925] Following the stream of components presented above financial,
infrastructural and consultative support containing the brokering of contacts can be identified as most influential aspects to promote entrepreneurial performance. Drawing from
the empirical results, however, the author identifies differentiating user profiles of the
regional infrastructure of innovation promotors. Hence, depending on the entrepreneurial
motivation young entrepreneurs may show varying demand for and awareness of supporting institutions.[926]

The relevance of regional networks as a potential source of collaboration partners to initiate value creation processes has already been emphasized, specifically drawing on the
role of regional innovation promotors enabling access as well as providing resources to
entrepreneurial firms. However, despite the existence of a vital infrastructure of innovation promotors, the effects of their performance rely on the willingness and capability of
the entrepreneur to exploit these exogenous knowledge sources for entrepreneurial pur-

---

922 See Asheim/Cooke 1998, p. 235.
923 An empirical example for such a regional network can be found in the region of Ingolstadt, Germany,
     termed 'Beraterpool' - a pool of consultants. A set of lawyers, tax advisors, and consultants connected
     to the local business incubator offer their services specifically for entrepreneurial firms aiming for a fu-
     ture collaboration with the evolving corporations. See www.beraterpool-ingolstadt.de
924 Burgers et al. 2009, p 207.
925 See Rabe 2007, pp. 249-251.
926 See Rabe 2007, pp. 273-274. Differentiating behavior may be identified among the groups of entrepre-
     neurs aiming for a direct transfer of knowledge from university by starting a business and entrepreneurs
     drawing on a range of professional experiences obtained as employee. These show less interaction with
     regional innovation promotors due to their prevailing expertise.

suit.[927] Therefore, the innovation capacity of the entrepreneurial firm may be seen as decisive counterpart to this infrastructure to exploit the competences offered by innovation promotors for achieving entrepreneurial performance.[928]

4.2 Synthesis and Implications for Empirical Analysis

4.2.1 Synthesis - Co-Innovation Strategy of the Entrepreneurial Firm

"Every company has a network of relationships ... few companies in our experience take the time to articulate their own business model. Fewer have any clear idea about the business models of their external relationships. By assessing other's business models, understanding one's own business needs, and degree of their alignment with one's own business model, one can turn these relationships into more valuable co-development partnerships."[929]

This work has emphasized the relevance of the environmental context of the firm for identifying and pursuing entrepreneurial opportunities. In this regard, the embeddedness of the entrepreneurial firm in a regional context characterized by a set of attributes constituting a regional entrepreneurial climate serve as the decisive influential factor for the potentials of opportunity emergence and exploitation. "Geographical proximity and geographical clustering provide the resources necessary to the flourishing of entrepreneurial ventures including knowledge, services, and money."[930] The concept of co-innovation competence presented may be understood as a mixture of resources and capabilities necessary for the entrepreneurial firm to engage in inter-organizational value creation and consequently profit from its environmental context.[931] However, as the elaborated framework of investigation illustrates, a linking these components to entrepreneurial performance may require the formulation of strategic considerations allowing for an application of co-innovation competence within a regional entrepreneurial climate (see Figure 17).

Pena (2002) concludes: "The ability to establish and benefit from business networks is an important intangible asset that entrepreneurs must take into account during the gestation period of a firm."[932] Nonetheless, it is to be emphasized that even though a large body of literature can be identified claiming networking as panacea to boost entrepreneurial

---

927   See Acs et al. 2009, p. 28; Littunen 2000, p. 295; Shane/Venkataraman 2000, p. 218. Stevenson/Jarillo
      1990, p. 25.
928   See Löfsten/Lindelöf 2003, p. 56; Pena 2002, pp. 192-194.
929   Chesbrough/Schwartz 2007, p. 59.
930   Thornton/Flynn 2003, p. 426.
931   See Chapter 3.2.2.1.
932   Pena 2002, p. 194.

performance, constraining factors still persist.[933] These may be of exogenous character expressed by the characteristics of the regional entrepreneurial climate but also of endogenous character hindering the entrepreneurial firms to engage in intensive network relations.[934] As the concept of duality of structure indicates, exogenous and endogenous factors may be inter-linked and influence one another.[935] Two key elements of constrains can be identified in this regard. On the one hand, there is the apprehension of opportunistic behavior hampering the willingness of organizations to openly exchange knowledge.[936] On the other hand, misgivings might occur that prevailing network structures and resources embedded within may not lead to an amplification of corporate performance and therefore cause inefficient investments.[937]

Young entrepreneurial firms, specifically in knowledge-intensive industries face severe barriers in openly sharing knowledge and cooperating in innovation projects with corporate and institutional partners due to potential knowledge and technology drainage.[938] Consequently, strategic risk arises from openness and the free exchange of information in the form of unintended knowledge spillovers.[939] Among such entrepreneurs this perception is magnified due to the relevance of firm-specific knowledge as a critical component for competitiveness and therefore the future existence of the firm.[940] The regional entrepreneurial climate may contribute to a reduction of apprehending opportunistic behavior by offering access to regional knowledge flows that draw on regional-based structural capital allowing for a transfer into cognitive capital, and in turn create relational capital.[941] In this regard, the necessity of mutual investments in the establishment of reciprocal ties is a precondition for a locking-in entrepreneurial firms into regional innovation structures.[942] These investments, however, are challenged from an entrepreneurial perspective by limitations on available resources. Furthermore, due to the necessity of complementary assets asymmetric shares of information exist causing uncertainty about the quality of potential collaboration partners which refers to the liability of newness of the entrepreneurial firm but may also apply vice versa. In the case of a lock-in to a network the aspect of overembeddedness or oversocialization has been emphasized in the literature with reference to strong ties among a set of actors hindering the emergence of new knowledge and entre-

---

933 See Witt 2004, p. 409.
934 For an empirical investigation in the region of Ingolstadt, Germany, see Thierstein et al. (2011, pp. 94-104). Also see Chapter 1.2.
935 See Giddens 1979, p. 64. Also see Chapter 2.3.1.
936 See e.g. Hoecht/Trott 1999, p. 258; Gans/Stern 2003; Keupp/Gassmann 2009, p. 338.
937 See Witt 2004, p. 395; Woolcock/Narayan 2000, p. 231.
938 See Gans/Stern 2003; Keupp/Gassmann 2009, p. 338.
939 See Hoecht/Trott 1999, p. 258; van de Vrande et al. 2009, p. 428.
940 See Smith/Lohrke 2008, p. 316.
941 See Liao/Welch 2001, p. 167.
942 See Putnam/Goss 2002, p. 7.

preneurial opportunities.[943] Thus, inefficiencies may arise due to extensive network investments to establish reciprocity which may not impact corporate performance. This indicates that the characteristics of the environmental dimension may have the capacity to diminishing co-innovation constrains in terms of perceived opportunistic behavior if an open knowledge infrastructure and inter-organizational knowledge flows can be identified. In this regard, the role of intermediaries and innovation promotors should be considered decisive actors providing expertise and specifically relational capital to entrepreneurial firms.[944] Furthermore, economic incentives need to be visible for the entrepreneur to engage in a system that may be present if assets embedded in a regional innovation structure are transparent and dynamic regional knowledge capabilities persist to overcome network inefficiencies.[945] Drawing form this cognizance, the interplay of the external dimension with organizational competences needs to be considered to achieve economic performance. Therefore, on the one hand, co-innovation resources to evaluate regional knowledge capabilities and, on the other hand, co-innovation capabilities to absorb and desorb regional innovation structures are required.[946]

Based on the positive impact of relational capital on entrepreneurial performance,[947] networking efficiency in this context, may be seen as decisive for enabling access to critical ressources and reducing the likelihood of opportunistic behavior,[948] while the investments into social capital are balanced along organizational goals.[949] In regard to a strategic discussion of co-innovation competence the concept needs to be discussed within a more precise analysis of the establishment of inter-organizational relations drawing on 'the relational view.'[950] Based on the contribution by Chesbrough/Schwartz (2007) this may allow for formulating a four step strategic approach toward co-innovation alliance development:

1. Co-innovation alignment: Co-innovation draws on considerations for realizing synergies resulting in higher effectiveness of innovation performance.[951] Consequently, depending on the characteristics of the opportunity identified, the entrepreneurial firm should define specific objectives and goals to be obtained by taking a collaborative approach. These objectives may include a reduction of R&D costs, an increase in flexibility due to leveraged capabilities and/or an expansion of market access for diffusion. Based on

---

943 See Uzzi 1997, p. 59; Stam/Elfring 2008, p. 109; Florida/Cushing/Gates 2002, p. 20; Larson 1992, p. 97; Powell/Smith-Doerr 1994, p. 393.
944 See Fichter 2009, p. 361; Gemünden/Walter 1999, pp. 119-120.
945 See Cooke 2005, pp. 1134-1139.
946 See Chapter 4.1.2.
947 See Pena 2002, pp. 192-194.
948 See Baum/Calabrese/Silverman 2000, p. 267.
949 See Krackhardt/Hanson 1993, p. 110.
950 See Dyer/Singh 1998.
951 See Beelaerts van Blokand/Verhagen/Santema 2008, p. 10. Also see Chapter 3.2.2.1.

these objectives implications for the co-innovation alignment can be drawn such as the spread of fixed costs and the leverage of complementary assets.[952] In this regard, the relevance of proximity and industry characteristics needs to be considered. Depending on the objectives defined, co-innovation in complex technological fields and projects of highly tacit knowledge may be optimized by geographical proximity.[953]

2. Assessment of internal and external capabilities required: To pursue the objectives defined the entrepreneurial firm needs to be aware of its own capabilities to successfully align a co-innovation approach. Core capabilities in this case are understood as "key sources of a company's distinctive advantages and value added."[954] Within collaborations based on complementary assets the firm has to engage in market research to identify and evaluate potential collaboration partners.[955] The intensity of the prevailing social capital of the firm allows for a higher accessibility of asset-keepers leading to the awareness that strong and weak ties may be essential for the entrepreneurial firm to engage in exploration and exploitation processes to pursue opportunities and achieve entrepreneurial performance.[956] Furthermore, innovation promotors may support the process of finding an appropriate partner for co-innovation due to their relational capital.[957] A co-innovation alliance within the area of one's core capabilities, however, should be considered as a risky venture requiring an extensive a priori analysis due to the risk of capability drainage.[958]

3. Co-innovation structuring: The desired benefits of cooperation may occur only if the partners are capable of contributing complementary assets. This requires a collaborative structuring of the alliance. Here, critical components, responsibilities and working processes need to be aligned allowing for the realization of synergies.[959] In this regard, the necessity of inter-organizational knowledge-sharing routines needs to be mentioned,[960] leading to an individual co-innovation resources development.[961]

4. Dynamic co-innovation governance: "Governance plays a key role in the creation of relational rents because it influences transaction costs, as well as the willingness of alli-

---

952 See Chesbrough/Schwartz 2007, p. 56.
953 See Saxenian 1990, p. 101.
954 Chesbrough/Schwartz 2007, p. 56.
955 See Dyer/Singh 1998, p. 668.
956 See Davidsson/Honig 2003, p. 325. Also see Chapter 3.1.2.
957 See Gemünden/Walter 1999, pp. 119-120.
958 "An example of co-dev in the 'core' gone wrong is the classic case of IBM's partnership deal to develop its personal computer operating system with a small software startup called Microsoft" (Chesbrough/Schwartz 2007, p. 56).
959 See Teece 1986, p.289; Hagedoorn/Duysters 2002, p. 169; Harryson 2006, pp. 354-355; Chesbrough/ Schwartz 2007, pp. 57-58.
960 See Dyer/Singh 1998, p. 664.
961 See Chapter 4.1.2.1.

ance partners to engage in value-creation initiatives."[962] Collaborating successfully within dynamic fields requires a continuous assessment of one's own capabilities and these of the collaborating partners. The value of the individual assets and social capital among the actors are decisive components to establish and maintain a co-operation.[963] To overcome a negative lock-in effect, dynamic co-innovation governance among the alliance partners needs to be applied enabling the emergence of new opportunities for future successful co-innovation within a network context.[964] Specifically, the active bridging of structural holes by taking 'long jumps' into new networks may offer high potentials of realizing co-innovation performance.[965]

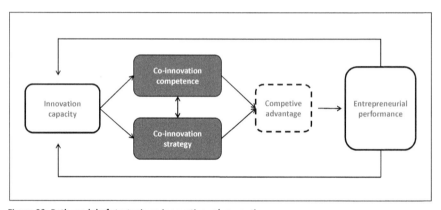

Figure 22: Path model of strategic co-innovative value creation

This approach to co-innovation strategy demonstrates, on the one hand, a systemized alignment of internal assets and capabilities as precondition to establish a co-innovation competence, which is capable of effectively pursuing opportunities and performing innovation. On the other hand, innovation profit can be exaggerated by drawing on innovation competences of potential collaboration partners and aligning these toward a mutual co-innovation strategy. Based on the elaborations of strategic entrepreneurship and the conceptual approach of Ireland/Hitt/Sirmon (2003),[966] a path model of strategic co-innovative entrepreneurial performance can be presented. It is initiated by the innovation capacity of the firm realizing entrepreneurial performance via an achievement of a competitive ad-

962 Dyer/Singh 1998, p. 669.
963 See Bossink 2002, p. 315.
964 See Chesbrough/Schwartz 2007, p. 59.
965 See Ozcan/Eisenhardt 2009, p. 260; Burt 1992, p. 27.
966 See Ireland/Hitt/Sirmon 2003, p. 967. Also see Chapter 2.1.1.1.

vantage based on the interplay of co-innovation competence and co-innovation strategy (see Figure 22). Once more, co-innovation competence is understood as a dynamic concept that successfully applied, increases the innovation capacity over time (as indicated by the back loop). Consequently, a co-innovation strategy strives for an economic exploitation of the firm's environmental context to increase effectiveness and efficiency of innovation performance to achieve a competitive advantage.

4.2.2 Implications for Empirical Analysis

The elaborations and paths taken in this chapter allow for an expansion of the conceptual framework of the investigation presented in chapter 4.1. Based on the four constituting elements 'innovation capacity of the entrepreneurial firm,''regional entrepreneurial climate,' 'co-innovation competence' and 'entrepreneurial performance' specific characteristics of these can be identified implicating the establishment of a more precise framework suitable for empirical analysis (see Figure 23). By summarizing the elements presented, the corresponding attributes of each element relevant for further analysis are specified:

- Innovation capacity of the entrepreneurial firm: The element emphasizes the relevance of the personal characteristics of the entrepreneur or the entrepreneurial team and their intention to pursue opportunities.[967] Specifically the motivation of these actors to engage in innovation processes is seen as decisive for a positive future development of the venture.[968] In this regard, entrepreneurial motivation, therefore, is characterized by an entrepreneurial orientation that refers to innovativeness and the willingness to take risks.[969] Apart from motivational considerations IC and thus the resource base of the entrepreneurial firm provide the critical attributes for opportunity exploitation.[970] Consequently, entrepreneurial motivation and corresponding behavior constitute the decisive components of the mindset of the entrepreneur which linked to the resource base serve as conceptual basis for the innovation capacity of the firm.[971]

- Regional entrepreneurial climate: Researching the environmental context of a firm as a supporting climate for the pursuit of entrepreneurial behavior, specific factors need to be considered constituting such an entrepreneurial climate. Furthermore, considering the role of regional networks as source of the regional knowledge base and their con-

---

967   See Koe Hwee Nga/Shamuganathan 2010, p. 259; Littunen 2000, p. 295.
968   See Shane/Locke/Collins 2003, p. 263-269. Also see Löfsten/Lindelöf 2003, p. 53; Koe Hwee Nga/ Shamuganathan 2010, p. 261.
969   See Lumpkin/Dess 1996, pp. 140-149.
970   See Pena 2002, pp. 194-195. Also see Wagner/Sternberg 2004, p. 223; Bergmann/Sternberg 2007, p. 207; Brixy/Hundt/Sternberg 2009, p. 20.
971   See Chapter 4.1.1.1.

tribution to knowledge spill-over affects, the role of entrepreneurial firms in RIS is to be analyzed. In this regard, regional promotors of innovation framing the RIS can be identified as accelerators of regional knowledge transfer:

-   Regional context: Configurations of social, political and economic conditions within regional structures may significantly influence the likelihood of prosperous development of firms located within its geographic boundaries.[972] Such conditions can be characterized by a specific climate allowing for the pursuit of entrepreneurial opportunities,[973] which can be termed a 'regional entrepreneurial climate'. On a national as well as a regional level political framing conditions critically influence the decision of an entrepreneur to establish a corporation within a specific geographic setting.[974] Public policy, consequently, may positively influence an entrepreneurial climate by creating incentives facilitating and promoting entrepreneurial performance. In addition, the 'soft-factors' such as norms and values of society toward entrepreneurial behavior are influential factors for the regional entrepreneurial climate.[975] The entrepreneurial spirit of a region serves as the decisive attribute of constituting factors characterizing the entrepreneurial climate.[976]

-   Regional innovation structure: Regional innovation structures draws on the establishment of an ecosystem of knowledge in which the creation of new knowledge and its commercialization are connected to a cyclical and systemic structure.[977] The core element of the concept, consequently, is a regionally based establishment of knowledge flows that offer a wide spectrum for commercialization based on knowledge spillovers and therefore create entrepreneurial opportunities. In this context, entrepreneurial firms embedded within the regional structure may be able to exploit regional knowledge sources for their entrepreneurial pursuit.[978] The emergence of spin-offs may indicate high innovation intensity within the structure draw on a transfer of knowledge generated in one organization to be commercially exploited within a new venture. Following the concept of knowledge spillover, these investments may refer to the willingness of established

---

972   See Goetz/Freshwater 2001, pp. 64-65.
973   See Lee et al. 2000, p. 7.
974   See Wagner/Sternberg 2004, p. 237; Bergmann/Sternberg 2007, pp. 209-210; Fritsch/Müller 2007, p. 299. Also see Porter 1998, p. 174.
975   Also see Goetz/Freshwater 2001, p. 67.
976   See Fritsch/Müller 2007, p. 309. Also see Chapter 4.1.3.1.
977   See Kirsch 2001; Kirsch/Seidl/van Aaken 2010; van der Borgh/Cloodt/Romme 2012, pp. 151-152.
978   See Acs et al. 2009, p. 28.

corporations and institutions to build ties with young entrepreneurial firms and integrating these within regional resource flows.[979]

- Regional promotion of innovation: Within a RIS regional institutional representatives can be identified located in a 'linking level' acting as promotors of innovation by providing expertise as well as establishing knowledge flows among regional actors and thus serving as mediators enhancing inter-organizational collaboration for innovation.[980] These, on the one hand, may possess specific expertise which is offered by consultative support and, on the other hand, they may serve as 'relationship promotors' by brokering ties to potential collaboration partners and thus providing access to keepers of specific competences to pursue interactive value creation.[981] Furthermore, actors need to be considered to provide financial capital enabling the pursuit of entrepreneurial opportunities.[982] Promotors consequently, enable corporations to achieve economic performance[983] by providing and/or diffusing knowledge, contacts and resources within the RIS,[984] and therefore enhance firm capacity to perform innovation.[985]

- Co-innovation competence: Understanding co-innovation competence as a dynamic concept directed at an efficient interplay of co-innovation resources and co-innovation capabilities the components need to be considered as evolving elements within the pursuit of entrepreneurial opportunities:

  - Co-innovation resources: Co-innovation resources refer to a combined perspective of the technology base and the social capital obtained by the corporation. The technology base is characterized by firm-specific knowledge connected to the corresponding skills to employ and configure the stock of technologies of the firm and therefore provide the core capabilities of the corporation for value creation.[986] In turn, social capital in this regard represents a decisive innovation resource promoting the capacity of the firm to exploit these technologies by performing innovation in collaboration with external partners.[987] Therefore, the environment of the firm should be considered a source of opportunities influencing

979 See Chapter 4.1.3.2.
980 See Fichter 2009, p. 360; Winch/Courtney 2007, p. 751.
981 See Gemünden/Walter 1999, pp. 119-120.
982 See Wagner/Sternberg 2004, p. 223; Acs/Szerb 2007, p. 116.
983 See Witte 1999, p. 15; Hauschild/Salomo 2011, p. 125.
984 See Doloreux 2003, p. 71.
985 See Sternberg 2007, p. 654; 2009, p. 23. Also see Chapter 4.1.3.3.
986 See Coombs 1996, p. 351-352; Chesbrough/Schwartz 2007, p. 56.
987 See Zheng 2010, p. 151; Nooteboom 2007, pp. 33-34; Martinez-Canas/Saez-Martinez/Ruiz-Palomino 2012, p. 64.

the prevailing range of entrepreneurial opportunities.[988] This indicates the relevance of social structures as a source of opportunity emergence drawing on the existing technology base. This refers to the capability of the firm to generate and accumulate knowledge based on transaction processes by consistently adapting and renewing its technology base, understood as an opportunity-based co-innovation resource development process.[989] This process leads to the enrichment of the co-innovation resources and the extension of the social capital of the firm requiring a continuous systemized alignment of corporate resources aiming for the pursuit of entrepreneurial opportunities.[990]

- Co-innovation capabilities: To pursue entrepreneurial opportunities within a co-innovation context, an accessibility of complementary assets and specific competences is decisive.[991] Co-innovation capabilities aim for an effective management of ties creating an infrastructure that enables an inter-organizational transfer of competences.[992] The resulting composition of the corporate network represents a critical factor for achieving co-innovation by enabling a simultaneous exploration of network competences and exploitation of internal competences among network partners.[993] Co-innovation capabilities, therefore, relate to the identification, transition and transfer of competences within the environmental context (absorptive and desorptive capacity) of the firm to pursue opportunities based on a collaborative approach of value creation.[994]

• Entrepreneurial performance: The analysis of entrepreneurial activity related to performance is difficult due to a lack of suitable data despite the existence of the firm over time.[995] A more specific approach to entrepreneurial performance emphasizes the realization of efficiency in terms of return on resources invested as well as growth with reference to a change in turnover and employees as most relevant dimensions of entrepreneurial performance.[996] Furthermore, drawing on the understanding of entrepreneurship as a process of opportunity exploitation to achieve innovation, entrepreneuri-

---

988   See Shane/Locke/Collins 2003, p. 274; Stevenson/Jarillo 1990, p. 25; Sanchez/Heene 1996, p. 41.
989   See Teece/Pisano/Shuen 1997, p. 521; Grant 1996b, pp. 380-382; Lichtenthaler 2006, p. 61.
990   See Chapter 4.1.2.1.
991   See Vanhaverbeke/Cloodt 2006, p. 259.
992   See Pittaway et al. 2004.
993   See Simard/West 2006, p. 235; Harryson 2008, p. 297; Vanhaverbeke 2006, p. 209; Lichtenthaler 2006, pp. 64-70; Lichtenthaler/Lichtenthaler 2010; Müller-Seitz 2012, pp. 90-91.
994   See Chapter 4.1.2.2.
995   Lumpkin/Dess 1996, p. 154.
996   See Murphy/Trailer/Hill 1996, pp. 16-17.

al performance is related to the innovation performance of the venture.[997] Consequently, entrepreneurial performance can be understood as a positive economic development of the firm assuring the basis of its future activity by achieving innovation and
growth (increase of turnover and corporate resource base).[998]

The assumption of an innovation capacity of the entrepreneurial firm which draws on a
substantial resource base characterized by firm specific assets and an entrepreneurial motivation striving for the pursuit of opportunities to achieve innovation and growth may be
seen as precondition for empirically analyzing the presented framework. In this regard,
connecting the specific elements of the framework to the elaborated approach of a co-
innovation strategy of the entrepreneurial firm, the following research questions (RQ)
arise:

- RQ 1: Does co-innovation competence positively relate to entrepreneurial performance?

    - RQ 1a: Do entrepreneurs perceive networking and the establishment of social re-
      lations as relevant resource for identifying and pursing entrepreneurial opportu-
      nities?

    - RQ 1b: How do entrepreneurial firms approach their environmental context to
      engage in inter-organizational collaboration and to overcome reciprocally per-
      ceived barriers of co-innovation?

- RQ 2: Does the regional entrepreneurial climate positively influence entrepreneurial
  performance?

    - RQ 2a: Do specific characteristics of a regional entrepreneurial climate critically
      impact entrepreneurial performance?

    - RQ 2b: Do entrepreneurs recognize the value of regional knowledge sources to
      amplifying their scope of entrepreneurial activity?

    - RQ 2c: Are regional promotors of innovation perceived as collaboration partners
      to source specific knowledge and critical resources to overcome entrepreneurial
      challenges?

---

997 See Littunen 2000, p. 295; Shane/Venkataraman 2000, p. 218; Sharma/Chrisman 1999, p. 17; Cordero
     1990, pp. 187-189.
998 See Chapter 4.1.1.2.

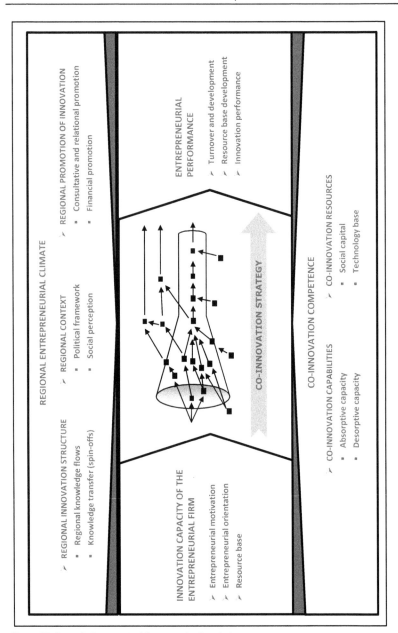

Figure 23: Extended conceptual framework of analysis

"The focus on geographical proximity and intra-regional linkages of RIS leaves several questions unanswered that are crucial for regions competing with each other. Research gaps exist, especially with respect to empirical studies."[999]

5. Methodology and Operationalization of Empirical Analysis

5.1 Procedure and Area of Analysis

"The understandable tendency to follow the line of least mathematical resistance has biased trade theory toward static, perfectly competitive, constant returns stories. Unfortunately it is not possible to use these stories to address most of the interesting questions in economic geography."[1000]

As this statement by the Nobel Prize winning scholar Krugman indicates, social phenomena may hardly be grasped by limiting their complexity to defined models allowing the application of standardized procedures of analysis. Being aware that the selected phenomenon of investigation applies to this challenge a suitable approach has to be identified within the possibilities of scientific analytical procedures to achieve cognizance. The following section, therefore, presents the concept of triangulation as multi-component analytical concept allowing for an approach toward the investigation of strategically pursuing entrepreneurship in regional innovation structures.

As the investigation requires a regional setting for analysis, selection criteria need to be considered to allow for the detection of an appropriate point of reference. Being aware of the circumstance that regional case studies may lack comparability and transferability due to complexity and regional specifics, the various regional studies, first and foremost the popular example of the Silicon Valley, emphasize the relevance of these studies to reflect the prevailing view and state of discussion on empirical conditions.[1001] Based on the presented characteristics of regional innovation structures, the term can be understood as a defined geographic area forming an operational environment of individuals and containing knowledge-producing, knowledge-processing, and knowledge-exploiting organizations to interactively generate innovation.[1002] The regional setting for analysis, consequently, has

---

999   Sternberg 2007, p. 655.
1000   Krugman 2000, p. 49.
1001   See e.g. Saxenien 2000; Lee et al. 2000; Asheim/Coenen 2005; Doloreux/Dionne 2008; Belussi/Sammarra/Sedita 2010.
1002   See Chapter 2.3.2.2.

to provide a set of infrastructural as well as institutional components to meet selection criteria. Furthermore, sustainable economic development and vibrant growth rates expressed by high structural dynamics need to be considered as decisive regional characteristics to allow for the application of the dynamic concept of co-innovation competence. Therefore, following the methodological approach framing the analytical procedures of this work, the selected area of investigation is presented.

5.1.1 Triangular Approach of Cognisance Emergence

In academic research a broad range of methodologies can be identified that analyze empirical phenomena. Economic analysis which can be understood as a disciplinary advancement of mathematics has focused on applying mathematical procedures to systematically explain market developments or individual, respectively corporate behavior. As the introductory statement by Krugman (2000) indicates these procedures rely on a reduction of empirical complexity by establishing models assuming predefined conditions such as rational behavior drawing on the concept of the 'economic man'. In these models based on mathematical procedures cognizance can be achieved regarding the influence of changing parameters toward the established system within a ceteris paribus assumption. While economic theory in its origin has determined the corporation to be a 'black box' creating value based on rational behavior within given market structures, the discipline of business administration and specifically strategic management has emerged which considers the relevance of social phenomena selecting the corporation as object of investigation.

Strategic management, which can be seen as an inter-disciplinary advancement of economics and sociology, has contributed to explaining the corporation and its constituting components, as the stream of literature of 'the resource-based view of the firm' indicates.[1003] The discipline harnesses a broad spectrum of methodological procedures applied to an analysis of corporate behavior and processes. This spectrum is characterized by the opposing components of quantitative and qualitative analytical procedures. While quantitative research and its range of statistical and precisely multivariate analytical methods[1004] has received high acceptance in producing representative results, "the work of qualitative scholars is termed unscientific, or only exploratory, or subjective."[1005] Due to a lack of standardized procedures to establish objective significant results the quality and rigor of qualitative research the results has been questioned although various contributions can be identified elaborating methodological concepts and approaches for data generation and

---

1003   See Grant 1991; Barney 1991.
1004   See e.g. Kachigan 1991; Janssens 2008; Esbensen 2006; Backhaus et al. 2003.
1005   See Denzin/Lincoln 2005, p. 8.

processing .[1006] However, contributions such as "Open Innovation: The new imperative for creating and profiting from technology" by Chesbrough (2003a), drawing on a set of qualitative case studies, have created a decisive impact on strategic management research. Consequently, depending on the characteristics of the selected phenomenon of investigation, case-specific analytical procedures within the spectrum of methodological procedures may be required to achieve valuable results.

Researching a complex phenomenon may require the usage of a set of multiple methodological approaches to improve the process of cognizance by gaining a more accurate perspective of the phenomenon selected for analysis.[1007] This work therefore draws on the concept of triangulation considering the linkage of three methodological components (see Figure 24). Triangulation can be understood as "the combination of methodologies in the study of the same phenomenon."[1008] As the figure illustrates the concept as it is applied in this work is constituted by the two levels of 'literature review' and 'empirical investigation.' The conceptual framework elaborated in chapter 4 represents the first component by analyzing the identified phenomenon from multiple disciplinary angles drawing on a systematic review of corresponding literature identified. Based on these contributions, predominantly originating from the disciplines of strategic management and economic geography a comprehensive view of entrepreneurship in regional innovation structures is presented within a multi-disciplinary approach.[1009] This implies that works in the field of economic geography are interpreted and transferred to a strategic management thought pattern that considers the entrepreneurial firm as the focal object of investigation rather than the regional context. The knowledge drawn from the review serves as a basis for approaching the empirical investigation. This level refers to a mixture of a qualitative and a quantitative analysis aiming at transcending of methodological limitations via 'cross validation.'[1010] As the reciprocally directed arrows in the figure indicate, the particular analytical results are inter-linked and reflected to achieve a holistic cognizance.

The presented procedure of triangulation presented as applied to this work indicates a linear cognitive process following a basic understanding of empirical research of a Popperanian sequence to achieve a progressive understanding.[1011] This chapter, therefore, aims

---

1006   See Denzin/Lincoln 2005, p. 3. Also see e.g. Creswell 1998; Lamnek 1995; Denzin 2003; Fikfak/ Adam/Garz 2004; Berg 2004.
1007   See Todd 1979, p. 602.
1008   Denzin 1978, p. 291.
1009   See Choi/Pak 2006, p. 351.
1010   See Todd 1979, p. 602. Also see Srnka 2007.
1011   See Popper, 2005. Apposing to this linear cognitive process contributions can be identified that provide information for this procedure. Specifically, the concept of 'grounded theory' suggests a nonlinear approach to overcome this aspect by introducing an approach of multiple investigative paths leading toward rather unforeseeable outcomes (see Glaser/Strauss 1967).

to establishment a sound basis for the empirical investigation. Here, the procedures of data selection and analysis within the qualitative and quantitative components are elaborated before the subsequent Chapter 6 presents the findings drawing on the concept of triangulation.

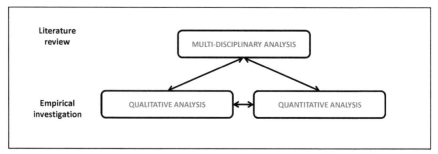

Figure 24: Triangular approach of holistic cognizance

5.1.2 Selection of the Area of Empirical Investigation

For an empirical analysis a regional setting needs to be identified aligned to the conceptual approach of regional innovation structures and therefore considered suitable for this investigation. In this regard, a balance of knowledge-intensive firms and research institutions is considered a precondition providing the infrastructural basis of a RIS in the form of the regional knowledge base. Furthermore, high regional economic development intensity expressed by structural dynamics may be seen as decisive characteristics of the region to allow for an application of the concept of co-innovation competence. In the process of selecting a suitable region for analysis, the country of Germany was chosen due to the availability of federal data regarding regional economic performance and the availability of recent studies evaluating the data and linking it to regional dynamics. These studies show that Germany consists of 412 regional districts which are evaluated on structural dynamic intensity.[1012] Despite most intensively dynamic regions are spread over the country, a triangular cluster of three highly dynamic regions surrounding the city of Ingolstadt can be identified in the federal state of Bavaria.[1013] This area is referred to as the region of Ingol-

---

1012   See Prognos 2010a, p. 8-10.
1013   See for a graphical display Appendix 1.

stadt, consisting of the districts Eichstätt, Neuburg-Schrobenhausen, Pfaffenhofen a.d. Ilm and the city of Ingolstadt.[1014]

An analysis of the region in the context of the introduced concept of regional innovation structures indicates that the region of Ingolstadt contains a broad variety of corporations and knowledge-producing institutions. Based on federal data, the region shows high economic prosperity and is predominantly characterized by the automotive industry.[1015] The main driver of regional economic development is the automotive OEM AUDI AG employing 31344 people at its headquarters in Ingolstadt.[1016] As the company's annual report indicates, the recent development of the corporation needs to be considered as engine of regional structural dynamics: "Record year 2010 ... the AUDI Group displayed its international competitiveness impressively and achieved historic peak figures for production, deliveries and in all key financial performance indicators."[1017] Furthermore, the region contains a consistently growing number of SMEs; among them many knowledge-intensive technology-based firms.[1018] The activities of AUDI AG, consequently, have been stimulating suppliers to consider further investments in the region, as well as attracting new firms to locate within the area.

These developments cause a twofold impact on the regional entrepreneurial climate. On the one hand, entrepreneurial opportunities may emerge specifically in the field of engineering; on the other hand, people may rather strive for employment at prosperous established corporations. Table 7 illustrates this perception by comparing the enterprise formation intensity in technology-intensive industries in the region of Ingolstadt and its districts to the state of Bavaria. The statistical analysis with reference to the reference years of 2005 to 2008 indicates that the Ingolstadt region shows overall lower rates of enterprise formation than the federal state of Bavaria and in the field of corporate services lies below the average of Germany equaling 100.

Since the data presented may not capture the latest economic developments, the impact of recent regional prosperity on the enterprise formation intensity represents a matter of further empirical analysis. However, implications can be drawn from the data presented regarding the characteristics of the regional entrepreneurial climate questioning the existence of relevant infrastructure promoting entrepreneurship. A more detailed structural analysis conducted by Thierstein et al. (2011, pp. 94-104) provides an overview regarding the prevailing regional conditions. Based on their elaborations, critical compo-

---

1014   See Bavarian Ministry of Economics, Infrastructure, Traffic and Technology 2011, p. 19; Federal Bureau of Statistics Bavaria 2010.
1015   See Thierstein et al. 2011; Prognos 2010b.
1016   See AUDI AG 2010, p. 159.
1017   AUDI AG 2010, pp. 128-129.
1018   See Pechlaner/Bachinger, 2010, p.1748.

nents may be identified allowing for a selection of the region as suitable for further analysis. Here it is stated that the region offers a set of actors that can be classified as promotors of entrepreneurship.[1019] These are institutional representatives of organizations such as industry associations, government agencies, research as well as finance institutions following the presented discussion of innovation promotors.[1020] Specifically the existence of two local business incubators is to be mentioned offering apart from infrastructural support and business services, consulting and access to experts in the fields of tax, law and finance. Furthermore, two universities can be identified collectively covering a broad spectrum of disciplines. Both institutions offer centers for entrepreneurship which accompanies by a high expertise in the field and entrepreneurship education.[1021]

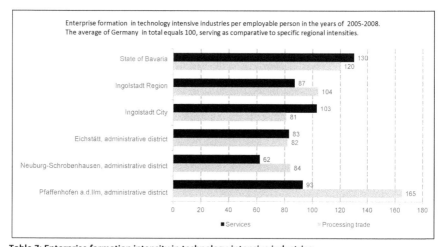

Table 7: Enterprise formation intensity in technology-intensive industries
Source: Brandt 2010, p. 28. Based on Mannheimer Unternehmenspanel (ZEW).

The selection of the Ingolstadt region, Germany, consequently is justified by the attributes presented that meet the requirements for analyzing entrepreneurship in regional innovation structures. Even though empirical research indicates that the region may not be characterized by a highly entrepreneurial climate and serve as a best practice example such as the Silicon Valley;[1022] the potential for identifying valuable insights to detect a strategic

1019   See Thierstein et al. 2011, p. 96.
1020   See Fichter 2009, p. 360. Also see Chapter 4.1.3.3.
1021   See Thierstein et al. 2011, p. 99.
1022   See Saxenian 1990; 2000; Lee et al. 2000.

approach regarding the interplay of the entrepreneurial firm with its environmental con-text remains. Moreover, since such highly entrepreneurial regions remain scarce, the im-plications from this work may lead to a higher applicability for likely structured regions characterized by a focal corporation and dynamic development.

5.2 Qualitative Research Approach

5.2.1 Qualitative Data Analysis

„Qualitative research is a situated activity that locates the observer in the world... quali-tative research involves an interpretive, naturalistic approach to the world. This means that qualitative researchers study things in their natural settings, attempting to make sense of, or to interpret, phenomena in terms of the meanings people bring to them."[1023]

Qualitative research tends to be confronted by skepticism regarding the validity of results due to the subjective process of individual verbal interview data generation and interpre-tation.[1024] This characteristic may lead to the criticism that qualitative research results may lack representativeness which also is influenced by oftentimes missing explanations re-garding the procedure of interpreting verbal data.[1025] Nonetheless, contributions can be identified establishing research procedures and emphasizing the potentials of qualitative research drawing on the relevance of establishing detailed and differentiated results with-in case-specific analysis.[1026] Specifically, the research of complex social phenomena draw-ing on multiple perspectives aiming for an understanding of individual behavior as a basis for reflecting the academic discussion and establishing a new conceptual approach may require the application of qualitative analytical procedures.[1027] Hermeneutics serve as the basic principle of such a research process striving for the establishment of the context and a reconstruction of the phenomenon selected for analysis based on the perceptions of the people involved.[1028]

Due to their involvement in and specific knowledge of the phenomenon these people can be considered experts,[1029] who need to be selected by considering of specific criteria

---

1023   Denzin/Lincoln 2005, p. 3.
1024   See Denzin/Lincoln 2005, p. 8.
1025   See Welsh 2002.
1026   See Reuber/Pfaffenbach 2005, p. 35. Also see Creswell 1998; Lamnek 1995; Denzin 2003; Fikfak/
        Adam/Garz 2004; Berg 2004.
1027   See e.g. Flick 2000, p. 14; Meier Kruker/Rauh 2005, pp. 14, 62.
1028   See Schnell/Hill/Esser 1995, pp. 79-80.
1029   See Flick 2000, p. 139; Meuser/Nagl 2009, p. 37.

in order to achieve plausibility within the research process.[1030] By accessing and combining the perspectives of experts the goal of establishing an image of reality can be approached. Especially the analysis of complex inter-related structures requires the reception of a broad spectrum of information from these actors including in addition to case-specific knowledge, context-specific knowledge and perceptions.[1031] Therefore, to receive this information, interviews need to be conducted.

Qualitative research offers several methodological forms to approach the process of verbal data generation based on a question-answer structure.[1032] In this regard, the level of standardization of the interview may be of decisive character determined by the interview design.[1033] This work applies guideline-supported interviews aiming for the discussion of a precise topic within an open frame drawing on a set of in advance elaborated questions as guiding elements during the interview. Correspondingly, the accomplishment of a rather open discussion is aimed to be based on a flexible structure allowing for an accentuation of dominant aspects perceived by the interviewee emerging within the discussion. The course of the interview, therefore, may be guided by the interviewer - but is configured by the answers of the interviewee requiring a dynamic adaptation of the process.[1034] This format is considered suitable for collecting verbal data regarding a complex specific social topic which applies to the selected phenomenon of investigation.[1035]

The application of analytical procedures of the data collected primarily requires a direct transformation of the interviews conducted into a text format in the form of a transcript. Furthermore, a systemized process of analysis needs to be established to allow for an inter-subjective presentation of the results.[1036] Consequently, a structured analytical approach longs for a systemized filtering of information and a deductive establishment of a comprehensive examination. In this regard, the data material is analyzed for specific aspects specifically contributing to a selected field of interest. Bundling of these aspects identified enables the construction of an image of reality.[1037] This procedure requires a coding system providing for a systemized data evaluation process that highlights the information relevant for approaching a given research question.[1038] The coding may be operationalized manually or can be performed in support of computer-assisted application.

1030   See Reuber/Pfaffenbach 2005, p. 150.
1031   See Bogner/Menz 2009, pp. 70-75.
1032   See Reuber/Pfaffenbach 2005, p. 131.
1033   See Kromrey 2002, pp. 3378-379.
1034   See Reuber/Pfaffenbach 2005, p. 133.
1035   See Flick 2000, pp. 139, 143-145.
1036   See Mayring 2002, p. 63.
1037   See Flick 2000, pp. 281-282.
1038   See Gläser/Laudel 2010, p. 45.

To react to criticism toward qualitative research, recently it was recently emphasized that computer-assisted analysis may be capable of contributing to an increase of rigor of the qualitative research process and the reliability of its results. By following a systemized procedure of data generation, processing and interpretation, computer-aided analysis may lead to a more transparent and objectively comprehensible process of establishing qualitative research results.[1039] However, software analytical results of interview data are not statistical results meeting standardized methodological criteria such as significance. Instead, they serve as point of reverence for data interpretation within the methodological procedures of qualitative research. Therefore, a combination of computer-assisted and conventional analysis needs to be applied.[1040]

5.2.2 Semantical Network Analysis

„Language is not a neutral tool used to express our concepts of life and society, but, rather, linguistic forms shape our perceptions of what is possible and what is desirable."[1041]

Innovation networks and open innovation have become buzz words in corporate strategy and are discussed among academics as well as practitioners as panacea to improve corporate and specifically innovation performance. Nonetheless, entrepreneurs also take a critical stance and withdraw from networking and open innovation due to perceived high transaction costs, not guaranteeing an amplification of corporate performance,[1042] and concerns of opportunistic behavior leading to unintended knowledge drainage.[1043] However, due to the popularity of these terms true perceptions may be hard to detect because of a bias of social desirability. Consequently, to determine profound perceptions of entrepreneurs toward co-innovation within regional structures a methodology for analysis is required reaching beyond explicit research procedures and allowing for an implicit but systematic analysis. Furthermore, regional studies may be biased by a certain loyalty toward the regional context and influenced by political consideration which in case of this analysis may be predominantly present among regional innovation promotors. In this regard, qualitative studies have been identified applied semantical network analysis as methodological tool to analyze implicit opinions and value patterns of interviewees using

---

1039   See Fielding, 2002, p.162. Also see Kuckartz 2005.
1040   See e.g. Fielding 2002; Welsh 2002; Zelger/Oberprantacher 2002, p. 1.
1041   Mokre 2006, p. 307.
1042   See Witt 2004, p. 395; Woolcock/Narayan 2000, p. 231.
1043   See Hoecht/Trott 1999, p. 258; Gans/Stern 2003; Bergfeld/Doepfer 2009; Keupp/Gassmann 2009, p. 338.

the software-based method GABEK/WinRelan.[1044] This work follows these contributions and applies the method of semantical network analysis as a software-based analytical procedure to overcome the described criticism regarding qualitative research and serve as an analytical tool to detect explicit as well as implicit thought patterns of entrepreneurs as well as innovation promotors. The following sections therefore introduce the concept and its computer-assisted application allowing for a systemized approach of qualitative data interpretation.

5.2.2.1. Methodology

The method of semantical network analysis takes its origin in the discipline of philosophy and linguistic studies considering syntactical as well as semantic aspects to structure verbal data.[1045] A systematic approach to data interpretation is established by defining a set of rules and data coding allowing for a meta-analysis of interview data and the identification of common knowledge and opinions in the form of a comprehensive view.[1046] Following the linguistic concept of a 'gestalt' indicating complex relations among a set of expressions,[1047] collected interview data needs to be organized in text units containing a number of three to nine lexical expressions indicating the content of the corresponding text unit.[1048] In this regard, "verbal data are understood not as isolated concepts but as coherent linguistic complexes, that is, groups of statements forming meaningful wholes."[1049] Based on the establishment of these meaningful wholes the textual analysis is based on the development of a data network as in the form of graphical arrangements, which equally considers syntactical as well as semantical aspects and therefore enable the organization of knowledge based on individual statements of interviewees.[1050] The graphical arrangements form a meta-evaluation profile by establishing a transparent perception of the interviewees' assertions and display conceptual structures and causal assumptions in a mind map format.[1051] In these graphs, every line and arrow is documented by the collected data and expresses the number of connections of expressions applied to the same context which allows for an identification of a certain relationship among these terms. Here, spe-

---

1044   See e.g. De Wet/Pothas/De Wet 2001; Pothas/De Wet/De Wet 2001; Raich 2008; Doepfer et al. 2011.
1045   See Zelger/Oberprantacher 2002, pp. 3, 23.
1046   See e.g. Zelger 2004, pp. 236-237, 246, 248.
1047   See Smith 1988, p. 11.
1048   See Zelger 2002, p. 24.
1049   Zelger 2004, p. 237.
1050   See Zelger 2002, p. 24; 2004, p. 237; Raich 2008, p. 28.
1051   See Zelger 2002, p. 94; Zelger/Oberprantacher 2002, p. 10.

cial emphasis is put on terms strongly connected within a cyclical relation forming a cluster that indicates a thought pattern of interviewees.[1052]

From an operational point of view the process of knowledge systemization within semantical network analysis drawing on the method GABEK can be described in a conceptual framework.[1053] Figure 25 graphically displays the process of knowledge analysis with GABEK based on the motivation to gain an understanding of actions and behavior of actors within a given social structure. The process is initiated by the collection of interview data based on open questions directed at selected interviewees to acquire perceptions and opinions toward a specific social context (displayed on the left-hand side).[1054] The selection of these interview partners and the design of a guiding interview structure are based on previous experience with the social phenomenon to be analyzed which also may draw on a literature analysis.

The interview data collected represents the verbal database in the form of explicit knowledge about the social structure and is therefore referred to as 'knowledge systems and attitudes.'[1055] Within the following steps the database is processed and organized to display a meta knowledge structure. To reduce complexity, the data are systemized by applying the range of methodological tools via the software application WinRelan to determine essential aspects and therefore create a set of 'conceptual knowledge systems.'[1056] Here, on the one hand, knowledge is integrated by bundling text units and, on the other hand, knowledge is selected by analyzing the data regarding specific fields of interest. The selection process allows for a systemized approach based on data coding to search and recall for a knowledge system by zooming in on the given aspect within the verbal database resulting in the establishment of constructs such as gestalts and semantical network graphics.[1057] The corresponding aspect of selection may draw on the formulation of goals and means to determine the social structure of analysis. These conceptual knowledge systems are based on the knowledge systemization processes and may contribute to an understanding of actions and behavior in social structures via interpreting and reflecting the elaborated results on the given context.[1058]

1052   See Zelger/Oberprantacher 2002, p. 23.
1053   See for English literature regarding the method GABEK: Zelger 2000; 2002; 2004a; 2004b; Zelger/
        Oberprantacher 2002.
1054   See Zelger 2000, p. 205.
1055   See Zelger 2000, p. 215.
1056   The analytical procedure via the software application WinRelan are presented in more detail in the
        subsequent section 5.2.2.2.
1057   See Zelger 2004, pp. 233-234.
1058   See Zelger 2000.

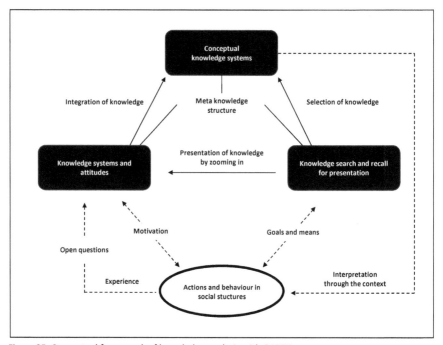

Figure 25: Conceptual framework of knowledge analysis with GABEK
Source: Based on Zelger 2000, p. 215.

5.2.2.2. Analytical Procedure

The analytical procedure of semantical network analysis applied in this work utilizes the software application WinRelan which was developed by the conceptual father of the method GABEK. Based on the basic understanding of the methodology as introduced above, this section provides an overview of analytical tools of the software used within this work.[1059] This overview refers to the contribution by Zelger (2004a) and corresponds to the outline of operations here presented illustrating operational processes and corresponding intermediate results within a hierarchical structure (see Figure 26).

1059   The software provides an array of analytical tools a selected set of which was applied to this work
        suitable for gaining an understanding of the investigated social structure.

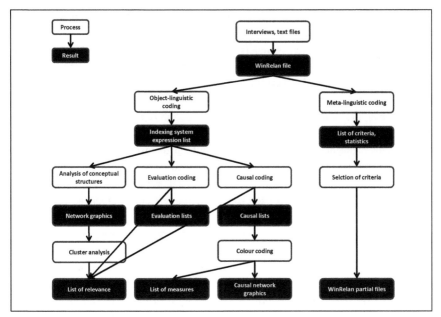

Figure 26: Procedure of WinRelan analysis
Source: Based on Zelger 2004a, p. 6.

Based on the collected verbal data in the form of openly structured interviews, the text documents are transformed into a WinRelan data file which representing the precondition for initiating analytical procedures (displayed at the top of the illustration). The texts are manually separated into text units containing three to nine lexical expressions highlighted in the corresponding unit.[1060] In the second step the prevailing data are applied to a coding process which, on the one hand, is named object-linguistic coding and, on the other hand, meta-linguistic coding. Meta-linguistic coding refers to the connection of specific criteria to the corresponding text unit such as the demographic characteristics or the position of the interviewee as well as predefined text-related criteria.[1061] Within a broad data sample this procedure allows for the systematic selection of text units meeting specific criteria to determine the perceptions of a group of interviewees sharing certain characteristics such as

---

1060   See Zelger 2002, p. 24.
1061   See Zelger 2004a, p. 27.

location and occupation.[1062] These selections also need to be applied to object-linguistic coding to enable further analysis.

Object-linguistic coding can be understood as the set of processes required to enable a content analysis of the collected data. In this regard, a standardized indexing system has to be established when identifying expressions within the text units to reduce the number of synonyms and homonyms to a minimum.[1063] The resulting list of expressions is applied to further coding procedures such as causal and evaluation coding. With regard to evaluations, expressions can be marked by a positive, negative and neutral evaluation index if the text explicitly highlights the corresponding attribute of the expression.[1064] This procedure allows for a statistical overview of attitudes of interviewees toward certain expressions on a positive-negative spectrum. Furthermore, causal coding should be considered. Causal relations can be indicated among expressions within a text unit if dependencies between terms are identified.[1065] These dependencies can be displayed in a semantical causal network graphic. Here relations are indicated by arrows if components likewise influence each other in the form of a green arrow (positively perceived effect), black arrow (neutral effect) and a red arrow (negatively perceived effect). Inverse effects may also occur with reference to the same color coding but are indicated by a lance (see Figure 27). Despite displaying these relations in the form of graphics a list of measures can be established providing an overview of the causal relations within the total data set.

In addition to the presented coding procedures the prevailing data can be analyzed within conceptual structures leading to the establishment of semantical network graphics. Within these graphics "the meaning of important terms that emerge in the course of discussion can be reconstructed on the basis of all the interview texts in which the term was used."[1066] Consequently, a given term can be selected for analysis leading to the establishment of a corresponding semantical network offering a basis to understand the meaning of the term in connection with its surrounding expressions. The establishment of a total verbal data semantical network graphic may allow for the identification of clusters, respectively gestalts, within such a cloud indicating the existence of relevant topics in the data.[1067] These clusters in connection to the evaluation and causal coding procedures con-

1062   In this investigation therefore, text units of entrepreneurs can be anlyzed separately from these of innovation promotors (see Chapter 5.2.3).
1063   See Zelger 2004a, p. 16.
1064   See Zelger 2004a, p. 32.
1065   See Zelger 2004a, p. 35.
1066   Zelger 2004a, p. 19.
1067   Furthermore, a hierarchical order of gestalts can be performed leading to the establishment of hyper and even hyper-hyper gestalts that summarize the collected data (see Zelger 2004, p. 241; Zelger/Oberprantacher 2002, p. 23). Due to the variety of components identified within the conceptual framework, this work refers to the analytical procedures presented to gain an understanding of the perceptions regarding these specific components.

tribute to the establishment of a statistical overview allowing for the identification of important topics within the data. "In this way it is not only ensured that we continue to process important topics and keep an eye on them during their implementation, but it is also made possible that we include the important context of these topics and thus understand the problem situation in greater detail."[1068]

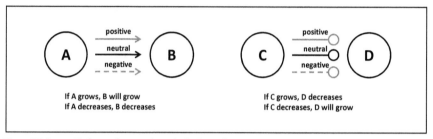

If A grows, B will grow
If A decreases, B decreases

If C grows, D decreases
If C decreases, D will grow

Figure 27: Semantical causal network analysis - legend
Source: Based on Zelger 2002, p. 130; Raich 2008, p. 32.

5.2.3 Interview Guideline Design and Data Selection

5.2.3.1 Entrepreneurs of Knowledge-Intensive Firms

Empirically analyzing the elaborated framework of investigation based on a qualitative research procedure demands identification of young entrepreneurial firms arranged in knowledge-intensive industries within the selected region of analysis serving as object of investigation. Following the concept of young entrepreneurial firms characterized as newly established operating entities situated in an early stage of the corporate lifecycle aligned to entrepreneurship literature a threshold of six years was chosen for selection.[1069] At the time of investigation this referred to a founding date ranging from 2005 to 2010. Furthermore, despite the location of the firm in the geographic setting of Ingolstadt region, the analysis aims at entrepreneurial firms founded by an entrepreneur or entrepreneurial team and operating in an industry sector which can be considered as knowledge-intensive.[1070] For the systematic identification of firms matching these criteria membership data of the German Chamber of Industry and Commerce, Munich, Upper Bavaria was analyzed. In order to improve data quality, addi-

---

1068   Zelger 2004a, p. 65.
1069   See Bouwen/Steyaert 1990; Kroll/Walters 2007.
1070   For a definition and classification of knowledge-intensive industry sector, see Legler/Frietsch 2006, pp.5-10.

tional research was required. After applying selection criteria a total number of 258 corporations were identified suitable for further analysis. Via a random selection process these corporations were addressed for interview arrangements by telephone. Aiming for a range of interviews exceeding the number of 30 to achieve a sufficient data basis for semantical network
analysis, 33 interviews could have been conducted.

The design of the interview guideline directed at entrepreneurs of knowledge-intensive
firms draws on the presented procedures of semantical network analysis aligned to the elaborated framework of investigation. Thus, following this methodology, to achieve an optimal
data quality, the aim was to generate a fluent discussion between interviewer and interviewee. The formulation of open questions therefore, needs to be considered regarding the interview preparation.[1071] Here, the interviewer may slightly guide the discussion focusing on core
aspects of information needed. However, to receive a more profound impression regarding the
perceptions of the interviewee toward the phenomenon selected for analysis a rather free
conversation is to be achieved.[1072] Therefore, to receive a firsthand insight into the perceived
entrepreneurial climate of the Ingolstadt region related to the aspect of co-innovation the
following structure of interview questions was established for the interviews with entrepreneurs of knowledge-intensive firms serving as initiators and sustainers of the conversation:[1073]

• Business model: The initial questions aim at establishing a conversation which is dominated by the interviewee. Therefore, on the assumption that entrepreneurs are willing
  to share their story regarding their business model and current activities they are asked
  to briefly introduce their corporation.[1074] From an analytical point of view this questions
  aims for the assessment of the innovation capacity of the entrepreneurial firm regarding its knowledge-intensity and IC.[1075]

• Enterprise formation in the Ingolstadt region: Aligned to the question regarding the
  business model to determine the innovation capacity of the firm the motivations for
  enterprise formation are asked.[1076] Furthermore, in this regard the reason for selecting
  the region of Ingolstadt as corporate location is identified, necessary to a discussion of
  the perceived regional entrepreneurial climate.[1077] Here, the challenges for entrepre-

---

1071   See Zelger/Oberprantacher 2002, p. 7; Zelger 2004b, p. 231; Pothas/De Wet/De Wet 2001, p. 85.
        Also see Mayring 2002, p. 67.
1072   See Lamnek 2005, p. 39.
1073   Due to the recommended open discussion format the conducted interviews do not neccessarily
        follow the elaborated structure in detail. In turn the transcripts show that interviewees have estab-
        lished connections among the aspects within the conversation leading for a dynamic adaptation of
        the interview procedure. In this regard see Reuber/Pfaffenbach 2005, p. 133.
1074   See Gläser/Laudel 2009, pp. 114-115.
1075   See Pena 2002, pp. 194-195; Wagner/Sternberg 2004, p. 223. Also see Chapter 4.1.1.1.
1076   See Shane/Locke/Collins 2003, p. 263-269; Löfsten/Lindelöf 2003, p. 53.
1077   See Lee et al. 2000, p. 7; Bergmann/Sternberg 2007, pp. 209-210; Fritsch/Müller 2007, p. 299.

neurship in the region are assessed as well as the knowledge of the entrepreneur concerning the range of regional institutions promoting entrepreneurial activities.[1078]

- Innovation: To gain an understanding of whether the selected interview partner is suitable for analyzing the concept of co-innovation competence the general perspective toward the innovativeness of the firm is established by discussing the perceived relevance of innovation performance.[1079] By relating the conversation to the buzz word 'open innovation' the perception of the entrepreneur toward inter-organizational value creation is assessed.[1080]

- Networking and cooperation: Based on the topic of open innovation a discussion about the relevance of networking and alliances is initialized. In this context, the interviewee is analyzed regarding the social capital of the firm applied to inter-organizational value creation.[1081] Specifically, the collaboration with R&D institutes and universities is emphasized to gain an understanding of the ability of the firm to engage in regional innovation structures and exploit potential knowledge spillovers.[1082] Taking a critical stance toward the buzz topic drawing on the danger of knowledge drainage and unintended spillovers,[1083] the entrepreneur is asked for an alliance and network management to overcome the barriers of co-innovation.[1084]

- Future development: The interview ends by determining expected entrepreneurial performance based on estimates by the entrepreneur regarding future development goals.[1085]

Applying the presented procedures of semantical network analysis to the interview data gathered allows for a presentation of the composition of the data sample. Figure 28 illustrates the resulting data cloud representing the intensity of connections. In accordance with the listed descriptive statistics indicating a number of 851 sentences and a containing number of 1666 expressions, the cloud shows a strong connectedness among the most frequently used terms. This may be quantified by the 52030 detected direct relations among the expressions and a total of 57743 connections within the data sample. Leading

1078   See Fichter 2009, p. 360; Winch/Courtney 2007, p. 751.
1079   See Littunen 2000, p. 295; Shane/Venkataraman 2000, p. 218; Sharma/Chrisman 1999, p. 17; Cordero 1990, pp. 187-189.
1080   See Chesbrough 2003a; Gassmann 2006; Enkel/Gassmann/Chesbrough 2009; Gassmann/Enkel/ Chesbrough 2010.
1081   See Zheng 2010, p. 151; Nooteboom 2007, pp. 33-34; Martinez-Canas/Saez-Martinez/Ruiz-Palomino 2012, p. 64.
1082   See Acs et al. 2009, p. 28; Sternberg 2007, p. 654; 2009, p. 23.
1083   See Hoecht/Trott 1999, p. 258; Gans/Stern 2003; Keupp/Gassmann 2009, p. 338.
1084   See Chesbrough/Schwartz 2007; Dyer/Singh 1998.
1085   See Murphy/Trailer/Hill 1996, pp. 16-17.

terms are highlighted by a colored background and are connected to thick lines representing a high number of sentences constituting the corresponding connection. Within the following procedures these thick lines remain neutral, whereas the precise number of connections will is listed. Furthermore, topic-specific clusters within the data cloud are extracted serving as basis for a comprehensive interpretation of the prevailing interview data.

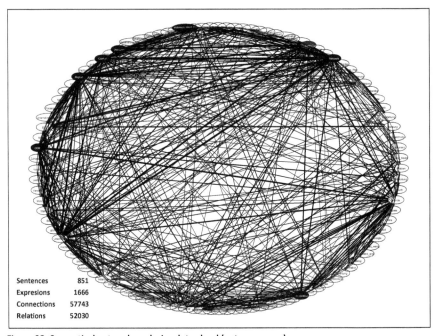

Sentences	851
Expresions	1666
Connections	57743
Relations	52030

Figure 28: Semantical network analysis - data cloud (entrepreneurs)

5.2.3.2 Regional Promotors of Innovation

Within the prevailing procedures of this work the relevance of the environmental context of the firm to achieve performance was discussed. In this regard, contributions were identified emphasizing the role of promotors of innovation within an economic structure located within a 'linking level' respectively a 'super structure' of the corresponding system.[1086]

1086   See Fichter 2009, p. 360; Winch/Courtney 2007, p. 751.

Promotors, enable corporations to achieve performance,[1087] by providing and/or diffusing knowledge, contacts and resources within the corresponding system,[1088] and consequently enhance the capacity of firms to perform innovation. These actors can be considered active elements contributing to the establishment and maintenance of a regional entrepreneurial climate and therefore serve as relevant interview partners to assess the constitution of the entrepreneurial climate in the selected region of analysis. Based on the elaborations in chapter 4.1.3.3 promotors can be seen as institutional representatives of organizations such as industry associations, government agencies, research and finance institutions as well as established firms.[1089] In the region of Ingolstadt 15 of these actors were identified and contacted for an interview. These actors contain representatives of regional banks, universities, business incubators, industry associations, government agencies, public-private regional development organizations and corporations engaged in entrepreneurial venturing.

Aligned to the course of action applied to the design of the interview guideline directed at entrepreneurs of knowledge-intensive firms following the procedures of semantical network analysis in connection with the presented framework of investigation the interview guideline for regional innovation promotors was established.[1090] Likewise aiming for a fluent discussion dominated by the interviewee open questions were prepared to gain an insight into the perception of the regional entrepreneurial climate by the identified innovation promotors.[1091] These serve as comparative to the data collected of entrepreneurial firms to gain a more profound understanding of the entrepreneurial climate of the selected region:[1092]

- Institution/organization: By asking the interviewee about her/his range of activities as representative of the corresponding institution, on the one hand, it is aimed for initializing the conversation and, on the other hand, to receive a verification regarding the classification of the interviewee as regional innovation promotor.

- Ingolstadt region: Showing a high degree of connectedness to the region as basis of professional activity the interviewee is questioned regarding a characterization of the region specifically relating to the economic structure.

1087   See Witte 1999, p. 15; Hauschild/Salomo 2001, p. 125.
1088   See Doloreux 2003, p. 71.
1089   Also see Fichter 2009, p. 360.
1090   See Chapter 5.2.3.1.
1091   See Zelger/Oberprantacher 2002, p. 7; Pothas/De Wet/De Wet 2001, p. 85. Also see Mayring 2002, p. 67.
1092   Also in this case the interviews conducted do not neccessarily follow the elaborated structure in detail because of the recommended open discussion format requiring a dynamic adaptation during the interview process. In this regard see Reuber/Pfaffenbach 2005, p. 133.

- Regional entrepreneurial climate: The discussion of the regional economic structure is continued by directing the conversation at the entrepreneurial climate asking for a perception and identification of main actors contributing to its development.

- Knowledge transfer: Based on the relevance of knowledge flows within regional innovation structures and consequently its transfer among regional actors,[1093] the regional infrastructure of promotors is elaborated by identifying core actors as well as prevailing challenges.

- Regional innovation networks: Based on the identification of regional innovation promotors with regard to entrepreneurship and knowledge transfer the existence of a regional innovation network is discussed[1094] as well as potentials to develop and/or extend prevailing structures.

- Future development: The interview ends with a conversation regarding future development perspectives of the regional entrepreneurial climate.

Applying the above-presented procedure of semantical network analysis to the prevailing interview data of regional innovation promotors leads to the presentable establishment of the data sample composition. Figure 29 shows the resulting intensity of connections within the data cloud. Conforming to the listed descriptive statistics indicating a number of 271 sentences and a containing number of 626 expressions, the cloud illustrates the connectedness among most frequently used terms. This can be quantified by identified 6337 direct relations among the expressions and a total of 7485 connections within the data sample. In line with the presented data cloud of entrepreneurial firms,[1095] the coloring of leading terms and their intensity of connectedness to related expressions is shown. The selection of specific clusters within the data allows for an interpretation of the prevailing perceptions of the innovation promotors toward a comprehensive understanding of the regional entrepreneurial climate.

1093   See van der Borgh/Cloodt/Romme 2012, pp. 151-152; Sternberg 2007, p. 654; 2009, p. 23.
1094   See Fichter 2009.
1095   See Chapter 5.2.3.1.

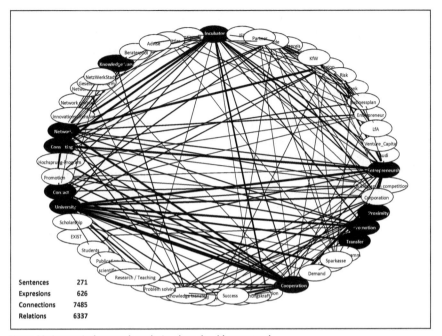

Sentences	271
Expresions	626
Connections	7485
Relations	6337

Figure 29: Semantical network analysis - data cloud (promotors)

5.3 Quantitative Research Approach

"The relationship between a given independent variable and performance is likely to depend upon the particular performance measure used. It is quite possible for an independent variable to be positively related to one performance measure and negatively related to another. Thus, research finding support for an effect on one performance variable cannot justify the assumption that the effect is similar across other measures of performance."[1096]

This statement indicates the challenge of applying quantitative data analysis to the elaborated framework of investigation due to the multitude of components introduced which may affect entrepreneurial performance. To approach this matter from a quantitative research perspective contributing to the triangular process of cognizance a field study was designed. The following subsections present the sample analyzed within the quantitative

---

1096   Murphy/Trailer/Hill 1996, p. 21.

research approach as well as the data selection process serving as basis for analytical procedures. Furthermore, based on the elaborated framework of investigation variables and survey design are presented before the potentials of analytical procedures are discussed.

5.3.1 Sample and Data Selection

To approach the presented research framework from a quantitative analytical perspective young entrepreneurial firms operating in knowledge-intensive fields within the economic structure of the Ingolstadt region had to be identified to participate in a survey to collect relevant data for statistical analysis. Therefore, in accordance with the qualitative data selection process, a set of categories was established in order to systematically narrow the field of potential survey participants. With regard to the age of the corporation a threshold of six years was chosen in order to only consider young entrepreneurial organizations, thus to a founding date ranging from 2005 to 2010.[1097] Furthermore, despite the necessity of being located in the area of Ingolstadt region, the survey was aimed at entrepreneurial organizations that had been founded by an entrepreneur or entrepreneurial team, operating in an industry sector considered as knowledge-intensive.[1098]

To identify corporations that meet these criteria a data sheet was set up based on regional membership data of the German Chamber of Industry and Commerce, Munich, Upper Bavaria. Additional research was necessary to improve data quality to determine whether the corporations can be considered appropriate for analysis which was conducted via D&B database and further individual research. Based on the data available the defined criteria were applied to the data sheet. After the selection process, the data sample was reduced to a total number of 258 corporations not infringing upon the defined criteria. These corporations were addressed via postal mailings with an invitation to participate in the survey which was fielded in print. Consequently, a paper pencil self administered interviewing was applied.[1099] To boost the response rate, the entrepreneurs were addressed individually and/or via regional innovation promotors such as the managing director of the local business incubator. Non-respondents were once more invited within a second cycle leading to an open timeframe to participate in the study from November 2010 to February 2011. In the end, a response rate of 23.25% was realized. However, once more filtering the received data via the defined selection criteria six respondents had to be disregarded and further eleven respondents did not meet data quality requirements in terms of survey

1097   See Bouwen/Steyaert 1990; Kroll/Walters 2007. Also see Chapter 5.2.3.1.
1098   See for a definition and classification of knowledge-intensive industry sector Legler/Frietsch 2006, pp. 5-10.
1099   See Kotler et al. 2011, p. 367; Eckey/Kosfeld/Türck 2008, p. 18; Kuß/Eisend 2010, p. 118.

completeness. Consequently, a total number of 43 surveys accounted for further analysis.[1100] Considering the number of returns mismatching the selection criteria the data sample was reduced to a total of 248 corporations, thus a response rate of 17.34%. Being aware that the number of usable surveys cannot be considered as very high and may cause an exclusion of multivariate analytical analysis,[1101] the achieved response rate can be assumed as suitable for further analysis amending the process of cognizance within a triangular perspective.[1102]

Detailed information regarding the final composition of the data sample provides Table 8. Following federal statistics, services contributing to manufacturing as in engineering and energy are officially assigned to the manufacturing industry. However, in practice they may be referred to as knowledge-producing and service-providing rather than manufacturing corporations. Consequently, the sample represents entrepreneurial firms situated in knowledge-intensive fields providing business services. The table illustrates a high composition in the fields of consulting, media, and I&C services, whereas 44% relate to a broader range of services such as insurance and tax advisory categorized as 'miscellaneous.' As requested, the participating corporations can be considered young entrepreneurial firms, predominantly founded between 2007 and 2010. With regard to the origin of these firms, about 80% can be characterized as entrepreneurial start-ups, whereas the reaming 20% originate from universities or established firms in the form of spin-offs. This ratio aligns to the polled aspects indicating the size of the entrepreneurial firm at current state; about 77% made less than EUR 1 million total revenues in 2010 and 70% employed less than ten people. The residual firms exceed these figures which either may draw on a rapid growth rate and high entrepreneurial performance or a resource transfer from the originating organization.

1100   Survey-based analytical procedures in the field of entrepreneurship are challenged by the fact that entrepreneurs either do not have the capacity in terms time to fully engage in such interviews or are not willing to communicate critical information (see Fiorito/LaForge 1986; Flatten/Greve/Brettel 2011, p. 144; Butler/Saxberg 2001, p. 420).

1101   See e.g. Bühner 2003, p. 17.

1102   See Albers et al. 2009, p. 54; Kuß/Eisend 2010, p. 118.

Industry sector		Size		Age and origin	
Manufacturing	9,30%	Total revenue		Founding year	
- Engineering	6,98%	< 1 million €	76,74%	2005-2006	25,58%
- Energy	2,33%	1 - 5 million €	9,30%	2007-2008	39,53%
		> 5 million €	4,65%	2009-2010	34,88%
Business Services	90,70%	Number of Employees		Origin	
- I&C services	11,63%	< 10	69,77%	- Startup	79,07%
- Media	13,95%	10 - 25	11,63%	- Spin-off	20,93%
- Consulting	13,95%	25 - 50	9,30%		
- Logistics	6,98%	> 50	4,65%		
- Miscellaneous	44,19%				
					N=43

Table 8: Composition of quantitative data sample

5.3.2 Variables, Survey Design and Analytical Procedures

In accordance with the elaborated extended framework of investigation the corresponding variables of the empirical investigation are determined.[1103] The survey applied for this investigation begins with general information regarding the location of the firm, its founding year and branch categorization to allow for a systemized selection process of participants.[1104] Aiming for the analysis of young entrepreneurial firms in the Ingolstadt region operating in knowledge-intensive industries federal classifications were applied.[1105] Due to growing service capacities in industrial sectors manufacturing industries were considered in addition to the field of business services. Verifications whether corporations belong to the desired classification are established by asking for the main fields of corporate activity allowing for a more detailed categorization of participating firms.

To gain an insight into the innovation capacity of the entrepreneurial firm, entrepreneurs were questioned regarding their entrepreneurial motivation.[1106] Specifically, personal motivations, identification of an opportunity, prevailing contacts, or specific knowledge and competences have been considered as valuable information in this regard.

1103   See Chapter 4.2.2.
1104   It is to mention that the survey design relates to previous studies conducted in the selected area of analysis, see Thierstein et al. 2011.
1105   See Legler/Frietsch 2006, pp.5-10.
1106   See Shane/Locke/Collins 2003, p. 263-269; Löfsten/Lindelöf 2003, p. 53; Koe Hwee Nga/ Shamuganathan 2010, p. 261.

While the first ones in the form of motivation and identification of an entrepreneurial opportunity may indicate the personal characteristics of the entrepreneur and the intention to pursue opportunities,[1107] the latter ones draw on the prevailing resource base of the firm. The existence of established contacts refers to previous experience and embeddedness in networks serving as an indicator for social capital and expertise.[1108] Furthermore, the existence of specific knowledge or technological competences serving as attributes of the entrepreneurial pursuit point to the quality of the resource base.[1109] Since IC is embedded in the people working for an organization,[1110] the number of employees and specifically of highly qualified employees has been asked.

The number of employees also may serve as an indicator of entrepreneurial performance when analyzed over time. Following the literature identified, growth rates in turnover as well as people employed can be considered points of reference to determine entrepreneurial performance.[1111] Therefore, firms have been asked to assess the latest and future employee developments. In accordance, total turnover and latest as well as potential future developments were asked to be estimated. Furthermore, emphasizing the relevance of innovation based on entrepreneurial behavior, entrepreneurial performance is to be related to the innovation performance of the firm.[1112] In this regard, corporations were addressed whether they have performed service innovations and/or released new products or services to the market within the last two years.

With regard to innovation performance connected to the discussion of co-innovation competence the participants were questioned whether these innovations were achieved in-house or in collaboration or via outsourcing. Based on the relevance of specific technological and market knowledge as well as market accessibility to perform co-innovation,[1113] the perception of these aspects as barriers to achieve innovation was assessed. Furthermore, in this regard the question whether a lack of internal capabilities to explore, transform and exploit innovation processes was raised with reference to the concept of co-innovation capabilities.[1114] In turn, co-innovation resources were explored by determining the networking activities in addition to the received information regarding the knowledge

---

1107 See Koe Hwee Nga/Shamuganathan 2010, p. 259; Littunen 2000, p. 295.
1108 See Sternberg 2009, p. 227.
1109 See Pena 2002, pp. 194-195. Also see Wagner/Sternberg 2004, p. 223; Bergmann/Sternberg 2007, p. 207; Brixy/Hundt/Sternberg 2009, p. 20.
1110 See Stewart 1997, p. 67.
1111 See Murphy/Trailer/Hill 1996, pp. 16-17.
1112 See Littunen 2000, p. 295; Shane/Venkataraman 2000, p. 218; Sharma/Chrisman 1999, p. 17; Cordero 1990, pp. 187-189.
1113 See Teece 1986, p.289; Chen 2005; Doellgast/Greer 2007; Sternberg 2007, pp. 653, 654; Nahapiet 2008, p. 580; Martinez-Canas/Saez-Martinez/Ruiz-Palomino 2012, p. 63.
1114 See Simard/West 2006, p. 235; Harryson 2008, p. 297; Vanhaverbeke 2006, p. 209; Lichtenthaler 2006, pp. 64-70; Lichtenthaler/Lichtenthaler 2010; Müller-Seitz 2012, pp. 90-91.

base. Here, the firms were asked about their engagement in formal networks and whether they have been capable of exploiting corporate relations to entrepreneurial firms for organizational learning.[1115] In addition, the question of the intensity of perceived economic risk to pursue innovation projects may provide an insight into co-innovation competence from a resource as well as capability perspective. This is due to the deduction that high innovation risk occurs when corporations do not collaborate for innovation (social capital) or do not have the capability to effectively exploit co-innovation projects.[1116]

With regard to the perception of the regional entrepreneurial climate the influence of the regional political framing in the form of regulations,[1117] as well as the influence of social values,[1118] were addressed toward the pursuit of entrepreneurial opportunities and innovation. Furthermore, the characteristics of the regional innovation structure were assessed by the perception of the entrepreneurs regarding the willingness of established corporations to engage in inter-organizational collaboration and the accessibility of the regional market for young entrepreneurial firms.[1119] Also, the number spin-offs participating in the survey may serve as additional indicator for the quality of the regional entrepreneurial climate, if understood as an outcome of either entrepreneurial universities or (inter-) organizational venturing.[1120] In this regard, it is interesting to identify whether these organizations have received a resource transfer in any kind which leads to the aspect of regional promotion of innovation. Understanding innovation promotors as institutional actors providing expertise, contacts and resources in the form of consulting, financial capital, and infrastructure they enable the pursuit of entrepreneurial opportunities.[1121] Therefore, entrepreneurs have been asked, on the one hand, if they have received support, and, on the other hand, if they perceive regional financial and institutional support as sufficient to overcome market entry barriers.

Methodologically, the survey is designed to receive precise answers from the participating firms regarding the variables presented. In connection with the aim of this work to assess a strategic approach to entrepreneurship in regional innovation structures aligned to the introduced framework and its variables, the majority of aspects require the procedure of direct question leading to yes/no answers or the selection of a given option. In case of the perceptions on the regional barriers to pursue entrepreneurial opportunities

1115   See Simard/west 2006, p. 224; Vanhaverbeke 2006, p. 209; Floyd/Woolridge 1999, p. 132.
1116   See Hoecht/Trott 1999, p. 258; van de Vrande et al. 2009, p. 428.
1117   See Wagner/Sternberg 2004, p. 237; Bergmann/Sternberg 2007, pp. 209-210; Fritsch/Müller 2007, p. 299. Also see Porter 1998, p. 174.
1118   See Goetz/Freshwater 2001, p. 67.
1119   See Acs et al. 2009, p. 28.
1120   See Etzkowitz/Klofsten 2005, p. 245; Dahlstrand 1997; Bossink 2002, p. 315.
1121   See Witte 1999, p. 15; Hauschild/Salomo 2011, p. 125; Wagner/Sternberg 2004, p. 223. Acs/Szerb 2007, p. 116; Sternberg 2007, p. 654; 2009, p. 23.

and innovation a four-point scale was applied. Aligning these variables for empirical testing in connection with the presented framework, the components constituting the innovation capacity of the entrepreneurial firm may be understood as independent variables, whereas entrepreneurial performance serves as higher-order construct as dependent variable. The regional entrepreneurial climate and co-innovation competence represent constructs of latent variables influencing entrepreneurial performance.[1122] However, due to the survey design required for this specific analysis, the measure of 1-7 Likert-type scales as most commonly used in innovation research,[1123] at this stage of investigation did not apply and may indicate an option for further analysis. Therefore, the intent to relate multivariate analytical procedures to the analysis is challenged. Furthermore, due to the number of 43 complete surveys the attempt to apply a factor analysis could not be pursued.[1124]

Consequently, the received quantitative data are presented based on descriptive statistics. Despite cross-analytical procedures this format of data presentation does not allow for statistically relating latent variable constructs such as co-innovation competence to performance. However, in addition to the semantical network analysis of the 33 interviews with entrepreneurs and 15 interviews with innovation promotors conducted the descriptive data may serve as amending component to the qualitative data.

1122   See Pinnekamp 2008, p. 149.
1123   See e.g. Lichtenthaler 2006, p. 155.
1124   See Bühner (2003, p. 17) naming a sample size of 60 a minimum requirement to perform a factor analysis. Furhtermore, it is to be noted that only the questions using a 1-4 scale may apply to this procedure. In this regard the KMO-Criterion may serve as indicator to apply a factor analysis (see Backhaus et al. 2003, p. 276). However, the prevailng data offers a KMO of 0,555 which does not classify for further analysis (see Kaiser/Rice 1974 p. 111).

"Innovation is enacted through webs of social relations, rather than isolated events associated with heroic scientists or entrepreneurs."[1125]

6. Empirical Study Results

6.1 Innovation Capacity and Entrepreneurial Performance

The innovation capacity of an entrepreneurial firm has been emphasized as a precondition for empirically analyzing the presented framework of investigation. This is based on the assumption that firms refer to a substantial resource base in the form of firm-specific assets and an entrepreneurial motivation characterized by opportunity-based firm behavior to achieve performance. In this regard, knowledge-intensive firms were selected as objects of investigation, assuming the existence of critical resources specifically in terms of knowledge as basis of entrepreneurial motivation. Therefore, the first section of the empirical results discusses the innovation capacity of the firms analyzed before drawing on the data collected to determine entrepreneurial performance. The elaboration of these components characterizing the selected entrepreneurial firms offers the basis for approaching the established research questions by investigating the interplay of co-innovation competence and regional entrepreneurial climate as influential factors on the achievement of entrepreneurial performance.

6.1.1 Innovation Capacity

The innovation capacity of the entrepreneurial firm refers to the personal characteristics of the entrepreneur - or the entrepreneurial team and their intention to start a business and establish its positive future development.[1126] In this regard, the motivation of these actors to engage in innovation processes is seen as a decisive component for the future development of the firm.[1127] Entrepreneurial motivation, on the one hand, can be characterized by innovativeness and the willingness to take risks with reference to an opportuni-

---

1125   Bunell/Coe 2001, p. 570.
1126   See Koe Hwee Nga/Shamuganathan 2010, p. 259; Littunen 2000, p. 295.
1127   See Shane/Locke/Collins 2003, pp. 263-269. Also see Löfsten/Lindelöf 2003, p. 53; Koe Hwee Nga/Shamuganathan 2010, p. 261.

ty-based behavior[1128] and, on the other hand, the resource base of the entrepreneurial firm may serve as source of entrepreneurship providing the critical attributes for opportunity identification and exploitation.[1129] Consequently, entrepreneurial motivation and the corresponding behavior constitute the decisive components of the mindset of the entrepreneur which are linked to the resource base serve as conceptual basis for the innovation capacity of the firm.[1130]

As Table 9 illustrates the quantitative empirical results show that the participating entrepreneurs of knowledge-intensive firms in the region of Ingolstadt primarily draw on their resource base as a source of their entrepreneurial motivation and future corporate development. This is indicated by about 70% of the entrepreneurs drawing on a highly qualified team (including the entrepreneur) in terms of academic education and the allegation of specific knowledge as most relevant factor of enterprise formation (65%). Furthermore, the resource of social capital in the form of contacts to potential customers is prioritized as the second element (63%) whereas the possession of certain technological competences receives 53%. Interestingly, personal motivation and the identification of an entrepreneurial opportunity turn out to be the least mentioned aspects.

Entrepreneurial motivation		*Resource base*	
Specific knowledge	65,12%	Highly qualified employees	69,77%
Contacts to potential customers	62,79%		
Technological competences	53,49%		
Personal interests	48,84%		
Idification of an opportunity	44,19%		

Table 9: Quantitative results - innovation capacity

These results may indicate a rather rational entrepreneurial behavior which is influenced by personal interests (49%) and the pursuit of entrepreneurial opportunities (44%) but is dominated by the focus on the resources available, specifically in terms of knowledge and social capital. This perspective may be enlarged by drawing on the results from the qualitative data analysis in the form of a semantic network analytical procedure. The semantical network illustrated, which represents a data cluster of terms in cyclical relation to the ex-

---

1128   See Lumpkin/Dess 1996, pp. 140-149; Stevenson/Jarillo 1990; Brown/Davidsson/Wilkund 2001.
1129   See Pena 2002, pp. 194-195. Also see Wagner/Sternberg 2004, p. 223; Bergmann/Sternberg 2007, p. 207; Brixy/Hundt/Sternberg 2009, p. 20.
1130   See Chapter 4.1.1.1.

pression 'motivation' shows that entrepreneurship is characterized by an array of components relating to motivational components as well as prevailing resources (Figure 30). Due to the connection to the term 'network' understood as source to exploit specific knowledge via entrepreneurship and to achieve innovation quantitative results can be confirmed. Furthermore, the relevance of expertise to establish a business plan and experience as constituting element of the knowledge base underlines the perceived relevance of the resource base as the central aspect to engaging in an entrepreneurial process.[1131] However, the upper part of the network indicates the relevance of personal attributes expressed by the willingness and the interest in being independent and to take a challenge in the form of entrepreneurship to achieve a personal development as well as a financial gain and perform innovation. "In the beginning it was clearly the challenge to start a business and to be successful with it... Honestly speaking, I have to admit that the opportunity to earn money certainly was a motivation that has caused me to go on."[1132]

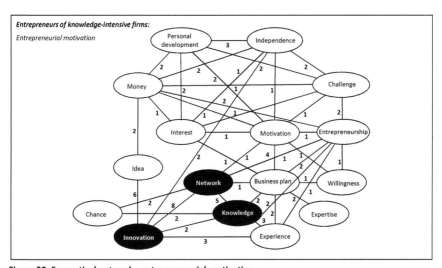

Figure 30: Semantical network - entrepreneurial motivation

1131   Aslo see Sternberg 2009, p. 227; Bergmenn/Sternberg 2007, p. 207.
1132   Interviewee 33. The quotes presented here drawn from the interview transcripts, the text passages have been converted from a spoken to a written structure to improve understandability. Furthermore, since the interviews were conducted in German, the quotes represent a direct translation of the original German statements.

In relation to the introduced framework of entrepreneurial capacity,[1133] the findings con-firm the relevance of the inter-relationship of IC and entrepreneurial motivation for oppor-tunity recognition and exploitation in connection with environmental conditions. Specifi-cally, the entrepreneurs note motivational aspects to engage in entrepreneurial activity as relevant component but predominantly emphasize the relevance of their specific knowledge which in connection with the corporate network is applied to achieve innova-tion. Consequently, the prevailing selection of knowledge-intensive firms can be character-ized by a strong resource base as essential element of their innovation capacity which in connection with personally affected motivational aspects is applied to pursue opportuni-ties and perform innovation. This implies that the firms can be considered as innovative striving for a positive future development.

6.1.2 Entrepreneurial Performance

The analysis of entrepreneurial performance has been emphasized as the challenging task due to the multitude of components related to the construct.[1134] With reference to the literature, as the most relevant dimensions of entrepreneurial performance the realization of efficiency in terms of return on resources invested as well as growth in the form of a change in turnover and employees can be identified.[1135] Furthermore, entrepreneurial performance is related to innovation drawing on the understanding of entrepreneurship as a process of opportunity exploitation to achieve innovation.[1136] Thus, entrepreneurial per-formance is seen as a positive economic development of the firm assuring the basis of its future activity by achieving innovation and growth regarding an increase of turnover and/or the corporate resource base.[1137]

An overview of the quantitative database regarding these components to determine entrepreneurial performance shows that the analyzed firms can be considered as high-performance ones (see Table 10). Here, with regard to recent turnover and employee de-velopment the firms clearly note a dominating positive development. This perspective is amplified by the statements regarding the expected future development in terms of growth. Thus, the majority of the firms predict an increase in turnover and number of em-ployees in the near future. Furthermore, drawing on the aspect of innovations performed

1133   See Figure 18. Also see Shane/Locke/Collins 2003, p. 274.
1134   See Brown/Davidsson/Wilkund 2001, p. 965.
1135   See Murphy/Trailer/Hill 1996, pp. 16-17.
1136   See Littunen 2000, p. 295; Shane/Venkataraman 2000, p. 218; Sharma/Chrisman 1999, p. 17; Cordero 1990, pp. 187-189.
1137   See Chapter 4.1.1.2.

within recent corporate activity, 58% claim to have released a new product or service to the market while 72% have applied a new process to corporate activity.

Entrepreneurial performance					
Turnover development		**Employee development**		**Innovation performance**	
- increase	58,14%	- increase	48,84%	- Product/service innovation	58,14%
- constant	25,58%	- constant	34,88%	- Process innovation	72,09%
- decrease	2,33%	- decrease	2,33%		
Future turnover development		**Fututre employee development**			
- increase	83,72%	- increase	69,77%		
- constant	11,63%	- constant	25,58%		
- decrease	4,65%	- decrease	0,00%		

Table 10: Quantitative results - entrepreneurial performance

These results indicate that the firms analyzed do fulfill the criteria established to characterize entrepreneurial performance. Nonetheless, qualitative research results can contribute to widening our understanding of entrepreneurial performance by systematically analyzing causal relations among the terms mentioned with regard to 'success,' which can be identified within the data set as a strongly related component.[1138] Figure 31 illustrates the resulting semantical causal network indicating the structure of components influencing the achievement of success within a sequential process leading to the realization of profits. In detail nine components can be identified that are linked to success. On the upper right hand side, on the one hand, the relevance of knowledge flows and thus the provision of information from outside of corporate boundaries and, on the other hand, internal processing of knowledge are indicated as influential factors. Furthermore, below, promotors and the reception of funding are positively related to achieve corporate success. These aspects refer to the relevance of the accessibility to knowledge networks,[1139] the capability to transform new knowledge,[1140] and the support of institutional actors.[1141]

The remaining components form a rather complex inter-related structure Based on the terms innovation, know-how, image, contacts and network. This illustrates the relevance

---

1138   Furthermore, contributions can be identified directly relating the term to performance (see e.g. Lichtenthaler 2009, p. 319).
1139   See Simard/West 2006, p. 235; Harryson 2008, p. 297.
1140   See Cohen/Levithal 1990, p. 128; Floyd/Wooldridge 1999, p. 132.
1141   See Fichter 2009, p. 360; Winch/Courtney 2007, p. 751.

of IC as corporate basis to achieve success.[1142] "It is incredibly important to possess good know-how. If that is present, one is always one step ahead of the competitors, and one can establish a reputation or image in the corresponding branch."[1143] Social capital, however, in the form of corporate contacts and involvement in networks, are indicated as aspects that improve efficiency and gain new customers contributing to a successful development of the firm. Furthermore, a triangular relationship can be identified among success, innovation and networks, which indicates a positively perceived influence of networks regarding the emergence of innovation which in turn leads to growth. "Innovations are the most decisive aspects. They do not necessarily influence the future existence of the firm but they do influence its growth. Future existence can be achieved via standard operations, but if you want to grow, you need innovations."[1144] This implies that among entrepreneurs of knowledge-intensive firms based on their firm-specific knowledge and network relations the achievement of innovation is considered a decisive element of entrepreneurial performance leading to future growth rates. In turn, efficiency emerges from inter-organizational collaboration and therefore indirectly contributes to corporate success.[1145]

6.2 Co-Innovation Competence

The concept of co-innovation competence was introduced as a dynamic construct directed at an efficient interplay of co-innovation resources and co-innovation capabilities.[1146] This section empirically approaches the concept by first drawing on the resource base of the entrepreneurial firm, emphasizing the relevance of social capital in terms of entrepreneurial networking and its influence on technology base development. In the second step empirical evidence regarding co-innovation as such is discussed and related to the attributes of co-innovation capabilities. These elaborations aim at an analysis of the relations between co-innovation competence and entrepreneurial performance.[1147]

1142   See Pena 2002, p. 194.
1143   Interviewee 7.
1144   Interviewee 28.
1145   A more detailed analysis of causal relations regarding the terms innovation and network are given in
        the subsequent section.
1146   See Chapters 3.2.2.1; 4.1.2.
1147   See Chapter 4.2.2, RQ 1.

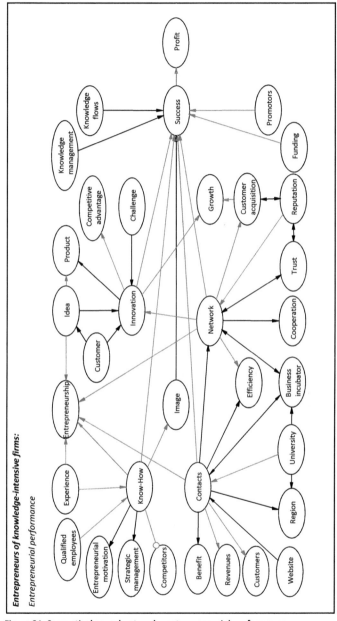

Figure 31: Semantical causal network - entrepreneurial performance

6.2.1 Co-Innovation Resources and Entrepreneurial Networking

Co-innovation resources can be understood as a multi-component construct constituted by the social capital and the technology base obtained by the entrepreneurial firm. The technology base is characterized by firm-specific knowledge connected to the corresponding skills to employ and configure the corporate stock of technologies and therefore providing the core capabilities of the corporation for value creation.[1148] Social capital, in turn, represents a decisive innovation resource promoting the capacity of the firm to exploit these technologies by performing innovation together with collaboration partners.[1149] In this regard, the environment of the firm can be considered a source of opportunities that influence the prevailing range of entrepreneurial opportunities.[1150] This indicates the relevance of social structures as source of opportunity emergence aligned to the technology base. Here, the capability of the firm to generate and accumulate knowledge within inter-organizational transaction processes is considered a relevant factor for consistently adapting and renewing the corporate technology base.[1151] This process furthermore, leads to an enrichment of co-innovation resources by extending the social capital of the firm which requires a dynamic systemized alignment of corporate resources to engage in the pursuit of new entrepreneurial opportunities.[1152]

The establishment of social capital, consequently, refers to a long-term process requiring continuous investments to initiate and sustain relationships with corporate partners. In this regard, it was stated that networking may cause inefficiencies due to an imbalance of the investments required and potentials of network exploitation.[1153] Furthermore, these investments may be characterized by offering critical knowledge that bears the emergence of opportunistic behavior in terms of unintended knowledge drainage.[1154] This perception occurs primarily if firms draw on firm-specific knowledge as basis of its entrepreneurial activity. Therefore, entrepreneurs take a critical stance regarding entrepreneurial networking initiatives questioning their relevance as influential factor on performance.

The perception is confirmed by the quantitative data. As previously presented, the results indicate the knowledge-intensive entrepreneurial firms analyzed refer to a profound technological base as the elementary component of entrepreneurial activity.[1155] Table 11

1148   See Coombs 1996, pp. 351-352; Chesbrough/Schwartz 2007, p. 56.
1149   See Zheng 2010, p. 151; Nooteboom 2007, pp. 33-34; Martinez-Canas/Saez-Martinez/Ruiz-Palomino 2012, p. 64.
1150   See Shane/Locke/Collins 2003, p. 274; Stevenson/Jarillo 1990, p. 25; Sanchez/Heene 1996, p. 41.
1151   See Teece/Pisano/Shuen 1997, p. 521; Grant 1996b, pp. 380-382; Lichtenthaler 2006, p. 61.
1152   See Chapter 4.1.2.1.
1153   See Witt 2004, p. 395; Woolcock/Narayan 2000, p. 231.
1154   See Hoecht/Trott 1999, p. 258; Gans/Stern 2003; Bergfeld/Doepfer 2009; Keupp/Gassmann 2009, p. 338.
1155   See Table 9.

in this context, indicates on the top left-hand side that only 26% of entrepreneurs state being frequent participants in formal networks. However, it is interesting that, when cross-linking this result to the statements regarding recent turnover development the spread reflects the average of the whole data sample, though concern for future growth rates of all of these firms increases. A similar impression creates the question regarding the ability of the firms to exploit corporate relations to entrepreneurial firms for organizational learning (18%) which draws on the introduced co-innovation resource development process.[1156] These corporations indicate comparably higher recent as well as future growth rates. Based on these findings this allows for positively relating entrepreneurial networking to performance.

Entrepreneurial networking and performance				
Frequent participation in formal networks	25,58%	Inter-organizational learning		18,60%
of those		*of those*		
Turnover development		Turnover development		
- increase	45,45%	- increase		75,00%
- constant	27,27%	- constant		12,50%
- decrease	9,09%	- decrease		0,00%
Future turnover development		Future turnover development		
- increase	100,00%	- increase		100,00%
Fututre employee development		Fututre employee development		
- increase	100,00%	- increase		62,50%
		- constant		25,00%

Table 11: Quantitative results - entrepreneurial networking

The statistically indicated positive relationship between networking and performance raises the question why only a minor part of the entrepreneurial firms are involved in networking activity. Furthermore, it appears to be questionable if entrepreneurial firms relate certain attributes to networking which may lead to the perception of the establishment of social relations as critical resource to pursuing entrepreneurial opportunities. Qualitative data analysis provides a more detailed insight into the terms causally related to the aspect of networking. Figure 32 presents a semantical causal network that puts the corresponding expressions in a process structure. The figure illustrates that networking as such may not be understood as a result but rather as an intermediate component allowing for the transformation of business ideas into market innovations.

1156   See Figure 19; Floyd/Wooldridge 1999, p. 132.

With regard to the skepticism toward networking the aspect of knowledge drainage can be confirmed as perceived negative result of networking as well as cooperation.[1157] In addition, the graphic indicates that industry and network structure characteristics need to be considered within the economic context regarding the motivation of entrepreneurs to engage in networks. In the case of the Ingolstadt region, which is characterized by the automotive industry, networks are dominated by industry-specific relations among established firms creating a structure directed at providing specific services to the OEM rather than pursuing entrepreneurial opportunities by combining knowledge sources and closing structural holes.[1158] "We access networks outside of the region because of their wider structure and variety of topics. Here, in the big automotive networks, entrepreneurial innovation is rather kept in the back seat."[1159]

Concerning the necessity to invest in networks perceived as a burden leading to inefficiencies,[1160] one entrepreneur contradicts this perception by stating: "If I had more time and less to do, I would invest more intensively in our network. But if I had more time, it would mean that I would need the network because I do not have so much to do."[1161] Consequently, the entrepreneurial perception of networking relates to demand-based investments that in turn indicates that entrepreneurs perceive networking as source of contacts and a field to pursue entrepreneurship and to obtain new orders, drawing only on networking when the capacity, or demand, is given. This perspective contributes to an understanding of the statistical results indicating a lack of necessity for the majority of the firms to be involved in formal networks. Furthermore, results indicate that social components take a decisive position to establish the linkage of contacts and networking leading to innovation, entrepreneurship and success. Here, values, reputation and trust serve to enable one to acquire new customers and therefore to reciprocally have a positive influence on the potentials of networking. This confirms the relevance of relational capital as a decisive soft component in entrepreneurial networking.[1162] However, apparently the establishment of relational capital among entrepreneurial firms does not relate to continuous investments in networking relations but rather the development of a positive reputation that draws on successfully accomplished cooperation projects.[1163] This perception

1157   See Hoecht/Trott 1999, p. 258; Gans/Stern 2003; Keupp/Gassmann 2009, p. 338.
1158   See Ozcan/Eisenhardt 2009, p. 260; Burt 1992, p. 27.
1159   Interviewee 11.
1160   See Witt 2004, p. 395; Woolcock/Narayan 2000, p. 231.
1161   Interviewee 6.
1162   See Liao/Welch 2001, p. 167; Pena 2002, p. 181; Hayton 2005, p. 140; Putnam/Goss 2002, p. 7. Also see Chapter 3.1.2.2.
1163   Also see Lin 2001, p. 19; Burt 2005, p. 209.

directly relates to the co-innovation resource development process considering social capital as a dynamic resource resulting from corporate activity.[1164]

As a source of reputation, specific knowledge is emphasized that is positively linked to a
cooperative relationship with a university. This indicates that entrepreneurs of knowledge-
intensive firms value the connection to knowledge-producing institutions as positively
influencing their corporate knowledge base.[1165] Furthermore, with regard to institutional
actors the relevance of business incubators as inter-related component creating access to
networks, influencing the establishment of contacts, and brokering promotion can be
identified.[1166] Consequently, this indicates that regional institutions positively contribute
to entrepreneurial networking.[1167] Overall, despite the mentioned achievement of success
and innovation through networking with reference to rather broad terms the potentials of
identifying qualified employees, pursuing business development, and gaining an overview
as well as access to market actors are named as positive outcomes of networking investments. "Understanding innovation as continuous change and a corporation as a system -
how do changes emerge within the system? Clearly, because of external influences!"[1168]

Consequently entrepreneurs of knowledge-intensive firms value the potentials of networking and are willing to invest in the establishment and maintenance of social relations
to increase corporate success and perform innovation in collaboration with external partners if the demand is perceived to acquire new resources and/or collaboration partners to
pursue entrepreneurial activity. Being aware of the likelihood of opportunistic behavior,
entrepreneurs focus on the establishment of trusted relations by building a reputation
based on firm performance which leads to a continuous development of the corporate
knowledge and technology base as well as its social capital. This interpretation of the empirical data allows for an approval of the introduced concept of co-innovation resources.

1164   See Figure 19; Floyd/Wooldridge 1999, p. 132.
1165   See Sternberg 2007, p. 654; 2009, p. 23.
1166   See Hackett/Dilts 2004, p. 57.
1167   For a more detailed discussion regarding these aspects in relation to regional innovation networks
        see Chapter 6.3.
1168   Interviewee 6.

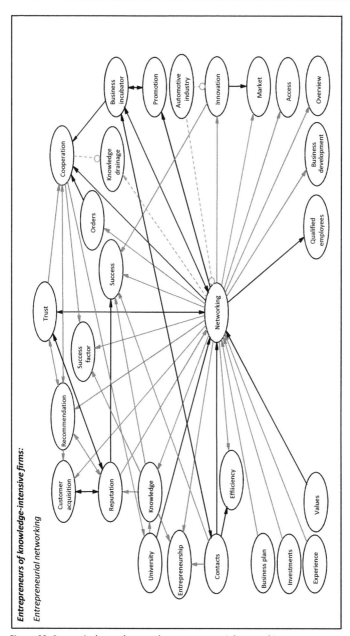

Figure 32: Semantical causal network - entrepreneurial networking

6.2.2 Co-innovation and Co-Innovation Capabilities

Co-innovation was introduced as a concept aiming for an increase in innovation performance by cooperating with external partners possessing complementary assets and specific competences leading to the achievement of synergies.[1169] In this regard, the construct of
co-innovation capabilities was presented in this works serving as an enabling component
to engage in co-innovation activity. Co-innovation capabilities, consequently, aim for the
effective management of ties creating an infrastructure that encourages an inter-
organizational transfer of competences to achieve innovation.[1170] The resulting composition of the corporate relations forms a critical factor for achieving co-innovation by enabling the simultaneous exploration of network competences and exploitation of internal
competences among network partners.[1171]

The empirical investigation of co-innovation resources which constitute the partnering
element of co-innovation capabilities has shown that entrepreneurs primarily refer to a
corporate network of trusted collaboration partners which draws on previous successful
collaborations.[1172] This may lead to the perception that young entrepreneurial firms possess only a limited number of relations suitable to performing co-innovation. Quantitative
results confirm this perception by indicating that innovation performance in the form of
new processes applied and/or new products and services released to the market by the
firms is dominantly produced in-house, though to a reasonable degree is performed in
collaboration (see Table 12, upper part). However, an outreach to the establishment of
new relations has been indicated as an option to achieve innovation. To assess the capacity of these firms to engage in co-innovation, entrepreneurs were asked for their perception of potential innovation barriers (see Table 12, lower part).

Their knowledge about prevailing market structures and corresponding networks as
well as their accessibility may be seen as relevant aspects to detecting collaboration partners appropriate for future collaboration.[1173] The graphic indicates that less than 10% of
the entrepreneurs see these aspects as high innovation barriers and about 50% see them
as either low or no barrier at all. This may agree with the statement of the majority of entrepreneurs that the corporate technological base as well as internal innovation capabili-

---

1169   See Beelaerts van Blokand/Verhagen/Santema 2008, p. 10; Vanhaverbeke/Cloodt 2006, p. 259.
        Teece1986, p . 289. Also see Chapter 3.2.2.1.
1170   See Pittaway et al. 2004. Also see Chapter 4.1.2.2.
1171   See Simard/West 2006, p. 235; Harryson 2008, p. 297; Vanhaverbeke 2006, p. 209; Lichtenthaler
        2006, pp. 64-70; Lichtenthaler/Lichtenthaler 2010; Müller-Seitz 2012, pp. 90-91.
1172   See Chapter 6.2.1.
1173   See Teece 1986, p.289; Chen 2005; Doellgast/Greer 2007; Sternberg 2007, pp. 653, 654; Nahapiet
        2008, p. 580; Martinez-Canas/Saez-Martinez/Ruiz-Palomino 2012, p. 63.

ties cannot be considered innovation barriers.[1174] These findings may lead to the conclusion that entrepreneurs do not see the necessity to initiate collaboration processes if external as well as internal characteristics are not considered innovation barriers. In turn, the
question of the intensity of perceived economic risk to pursue innovation projects offers
an opposing view. Approximately 70% consider strategic risk as high or medium barrier to
innovation. This statement raises the question whether entrepreneurial firms lack the capability to structure and engage in innovation alliances to share innovation risk and amplify innovation performance.[1175]

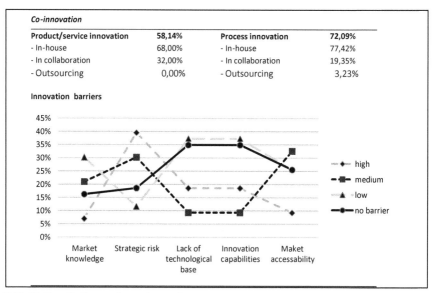

Table 12: Quantitative results - co-innovation

To gain a more precise insight into prevailing thought patterns of entrepreneurs regarding
co-innovation, an analysis of the qualitative results may serve as suitable basis. A semantical network analysis of the inter-related terms network, cooperation and innovation indicates strong connections among these terms creating a range of cyclical relations (see Figure 33). Here, in connection with the terms mentioned a set of potential collaboration

---

1174   This aspect aligns to the discussion of co-innovation capabilities. See Simard/West 2006, p. 235;
        Harryson 2008, p. 297; Vanhaverbeke 2006, p. 209; Lichtenthaler 2006, pp. 64-70; Lichtentha-
        ler/Lichtenthaler 2010; Müller-Seitz 2012, pp. 90-91. Also see Chapter 4.1.2.2.
1175   See van de Vrande et al. 2009, p. 428; Beelaerts van Blokland/Verhagen/Santema 2008, p. 10.

partners, as well as mediating institutions can be identified which are linked to associations indicating these relations. Consequently, a network of co-innovation actors persist which includes partners, customers, the OEM, and the university which also may be accounted for a mediating institution in alliance to the business incubator.[1176] Apparently the region takes a critical position in connecting the corporate network to the OEM and the achievement of innovation. In this regard, the statement of an entrepreneur can be identified: "Usually, SME's accomplish the biggest innovations, but there are innovations SMEs cannot cope with because of their capital intensity and time required."[1177] This implies that entrepreneurs are well aware of establishing innovation alliances to approach large volume innovation projects. Entrepreneurial firms in this context, seem to be drawing on mediating institutions within the regional context offering support to gain an access to established corporations.

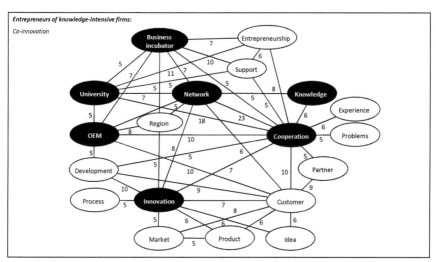

Figure 33: Semantical network - co-innovation

Furthermore, the value of customers as cooperation partners is emphasized. With reference to the concept of co-creation new ideas may emerge from these cooperations leading to innovations and an extension of the product and market portfolio.[1178] A dynamic component in the network structure represents the term development which linked to the

---

1176   See Fichter 2009, p. 360; Winch/Courtney 2007, p. 751.
1177   Interviewee 24.
1178   See Hippel 1986; 1988; Ulwick 2002; Prahalad/Ramaswamy 2004a; 2004b.

actors OEM and customer may, on the one hand, indicate the necessity to engage in cooperation projects to perform innovation and therefore cope with market developments
and, on the other hand, draw on previous cooperations to amplify future innovation potentials based on a dynamic co-innovation resource development. "The network represents a pipeline for innovation. Once new technologies are in the network you have to
adopt and develop something new to stay competitive. Technical developments continuously set new standards."[1179]

Co-innovation resources in the form of specific knowledge and experience can be confirmed as relevant connectors within the network construct. However, in contrast to these
positively related perceptions toward co-innovation, identification of the term problem
requires further consideration. In this regard, the following statement can be quoted: "In
the end, each corporation needs to be entrepreneurial on its own. Especially when it's
about arranging duties. Here, the emergence of problems is quite likely. Cooperation
therefore is possible only when you know that there will be no cannibalism among the
partners. If these problems occur every corporation will act egoistically."[1180] This assertion
indicates that despite the awareness of the range of potentials to successfully engage in
and exploit co-innovation projects critical aspects remain that may contribute to the highly
perceived innovation risk. A semantical causal network analysis drawing on the term innovation, therefore, may provide additional information regarding the perceptions of inter-
organizational innovation of knowledge-intensive entrepreneurial firms (see Figure 34).

The figure demonstrates aspects influencing innovation and its effects. Thus dynamic
components as change, diffusion (of new technologies) and organizational learning are
listed causing innovation and may lead to the achievement of growth and a competitive
advantage. Furthermore, from a critical point of view, innovation is perceived as a challenge to realizing continuous improvements of efficiency, which is influenced by large
firms forcing this process. In accordance with the semantical causal network of entrepreneurial networking presented,[1181] the regional industry-specific characteristics create a
negative relationship to the decisive terms innovation and network. Even though the automotive industry longs for continuous technological improvements, its structure is clearly
hierarchical, leaving a limited space for entrepreneurial innovation. "Here the focus is
strongly set on the automotive industry. In this scenario a small start-up cannot create
mayor innovations."[1182] This circumstance, however, may promote the awareness that if
young entrepreneurial firms strive for innovation performance an inter-organizational approach can be considered as an obligation.

1179   Interviewee 31.
1180   Interviewee 8.
1181   See Figure 32.
1182   Interviewee 11.

This aspect is indicated by the triangular relationship of innovation, success and net-work continued by efficiency, product and development. In connection with development, there is a decisive component constituting strategic risk in terms of innovation. The rela-tionship states that the bigger the innovation project, the more intense the development efforts, the higher the financial challenges. Following this logic implies that entrepreneurial firms aim for engaging in innovation projects based on resources available rather than collaborating with external actors such as risk capital providers balancing risk and innova-tion shares. In addition, once more the term problem appears in connection with innova-tion with reference to the difficulty of young firms in identifying and employing qualified employees, on the one hand, contributing to the emergence of new ideas and business transformation processes and, on the other hand, supporting the corporation in handling the emergence of more complex market and product portfolios as well as new customers. This problem may apply to all industries but is most intensively present in such hierarchical industries where the OEM provides the most attractive working positions for highly-qualified employees. "The main issue is a lack of human resources. Identifying suitable personnel is a real problem."[1183]

These findings indicate that entrepreneurs of knowledge-intensive firms take a two-sided position toward co-innovation. On the one hand, they are well aware of the rele-vance of inter-organizational relations as source and enablers of innovation and therefore draw on substantial market knowledge and connections to potential co-innovation part-ners as well as mediating institutions brokering ties and promoting the pursuit of entre-preneurial activity.[1184] Consequently, co-innovation competence persist due to a dynamic evolvement of co-innovation resources in the form of a stock of trusted relations as well as competitive firm-specific knowledge and corresponding co-innovation capabilities creating an infrastructure of external ties to exploit external knowledge sources while performing co-innovation.[1185] On the other hand, following the entire scope of the presented con-cept,[1186] these capabilities are limited due to the prevailing concerns regarding the risk involved in engaging in innovation projects.

1183   Interviewee 20.
1184   See Simard/West 2006, p. 235; Harryson 2008, p. 297; Vanhaverbeke 2006, p. 209; .Chesbrough
        2006c, p. 152.
1185   See Lichtenthaler 2006, pp. 64-70; Lichtenthaler/Lichtenthaler 2010; Müller-Seitz 2012, pp. 90-91.
1186   See Chapter 4.1.2.2.

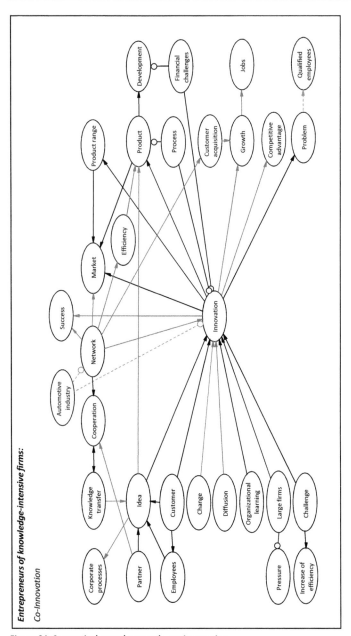

Figure 34: Semantical causal network - co-innovation

These concerns primarily relate to the apprehension of opportunistic behavior among collaboration partners,[1187] which may align to a lack of willingness and/or ability among the
firms to identify appropriate solutions to minimize strategic risk by sharing financial obligations as well as profits with complementary partners such as venture capital providers.[1188]
This problem may be of an industry-specific character constraining the range of entrepreneurial opportunities due to its hierarchical structure focusing the emergence of mayor
innovations on the OEM and its first-tier suppliers.[1189] In this regard, a more detailed analysis of the entrepreneurial climate of the area of investigation may offer insight into the
relevance of the environmental conditions to entrepreneurial performance within a co-
innovation context.

6.3 Regional Entrepreneurial Climate

This work has emphasized the relevance of the environmental context of a knowledge-
intensive entrepreneurial firm as a decisive component contributing to the emergence of
entrepreneurial opportunities and a positive future development.[1190] With reference to
the concept of the regional entrepreneurial climate specific factors were identified which
shape its characteristics.[1191] Aligned to the concept of regional innovation structures the
role of regional knowledge flows among knowledge producing, mediating, and exploiting
organizations within network structures was highlighted.[1192] Therefore, based on the presented framework of investigation this section empirically analyzes the entrepreneurial
climate of the selected are of analysis, Ingolstadt region, Germany with respect to its effects on entrepreneurial performance.[1193]

In this method the prevailing conditions are approached from a two-sided perspective.
On the one hand, quantitative results and interview data collected from entrepreneurial
firms are presented in order to assess their perception of the entrepreneurial climate
while on the other hand, in addition, an analysis of qualitative results drawing from interviews with regional innovation promotors is shown. This systematic allows for a comprehensive view from two angles widening the range perceptions of the regional context. The

---

1187   See accordingly Hoecht/Trott 1999, p. 258; Gans/Stern 2003; Keupp/Gassmann 2009, p. 338.
1188   See Shane/Locke/Collins 2003, p. 258.
1189   For an illustration of such a hierarchical industry structure see Figure 5.
1190   Also see Goetz/Freshwater 2001, pp. 64-65.
1191   See Table 6 for a systematic literature review establishing a set of critical factors characterizing the
        regional entrepreneurial climate.
1192   See Chapter 4.1.3.
1193   See RQ 2

analytical procedure is applied to the three identified conceptual columns constituting the entrepreneurial climate. Therefore, primarily the regional context as such is analyzed before attending in a second and third step characteristics of the regional innovation structure and the role of regional promotors of innovation. Since these components show intensive links among each other the following subsections may not be understood as isolated episodes rather than a subdivided discussion which as a whole contributes to an empirical analysis of the relevance of the regional context influencing entrepreneurial performance.

6.3.1 Regional Context

Social, political and economic conditions within regional structures may significantly influence the likelihood of a prosperous development of firms situated within its geographic boundaries.[1194] Such conditions can be termed a 'regional entrepreneurial climate' if they amplify the potentials for entrepreneurial firms to pursue entrepreneurial opportunities and achieve performance.[1195] In this regard, political framing conditions in the form of regulations play a critical role influencing the decision process of an entrepreneur to establish a corporation within a specific geographic setting and to engage in entrepreneurial activity.[1196] Public policy, consequently, may positively influence an entrepreneurial climate by forming the framework that facilitates and promotes entrepreneurial performance. Furthermore, 'soft-factors' such as regionally prevailing societal norms and values toward entrepreneurial behavior represent an influential factor.[1197] In accordance with the characteristics of the regional innovation structure these regional values specifically need to be determined within an economic context. Therefore, the perception of entrepreneurs regarding the willingness of established corporations to engage in inter-organizational collaboration and the corresponding accessibility of regional market structures are considered.[1198] In addition, the perceived financial infrastructure to fund entrepreneurial activity may contribute to an assessment of the prevailing conditions.[1199]

Consequently, the many components indicate that the constitution of a certain regional entrepreneurial enabling and promoting the pursuit of entrepreneurial activity may be

---

1194   See Goetz/Freshwater 2001, pp. 64-65.
1195   See Lee et al. 2000, p. 7.
1196   See Wagner/Sternberg 2004, p. 237; Bergmann/Sternberg 2007, pp. 209-210; Fritsch/Müller 2007, p. 299. Also see Porter 1998, p. 174.
1197   See Goetz/Freshwater 2001, p. 67.
1198   See Acs et al. 2009, p. 28. For a more detailed analysis of the regional innovation structure see the subsequent Section 6.3.2.
1199   See Acs/Szerb 2007, p. 116; Witte 1999, p. 15; Wagner/Sternberg 2004, p. 223.

seen as the decisive characteristic of the regional context to be termed 'entre-preneurial.'[1200] To approach the empirical investigation of the entrepreneurial climate of the selected region of analysis in a first step the discussed attributes are presented based on of statistical results before interpreting the data in more detail drawing on qualitative data from entrepreneurial firms as well as regional promotors of innovation. Table 13 illustrates the perceptions of entrepreneurs toward the regional conditions with regard to market entry, respectively innovation barriers. The table shows that most entrepreneurs (62%) do not see the political framing regarding legislation and administrative procedures nor a lack of funding as hampering factor although a considerable number (26%) perceive these conditions as highly negative. Similar impressions create the results regarding the social climate. While 30% perceive social conditions as fair, 41% consider them as medium barriers. Concerning the economic conditions however, a dominating negative perception can be identified. Specifically, 81% note a lack of willingness of established firms to collaborate and 74% name missing market accessibility as high or medium barriers.

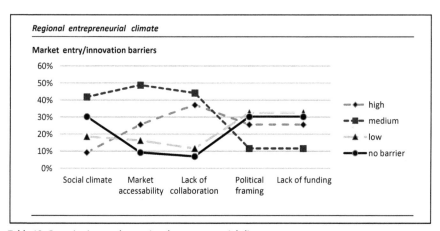

Table 13: Quantitative results - regional entrepreneurial climate

These findings indicate that the regional context cannot be considered highly entrepreneurial. In accordance with comparative national empirical studies the rather balanced perceptions regarding political framing and social conditions may not necessary refer to specific regional conditions, but rather reflect the national status of the entrepreneurial

---

1200   See Fritsch/Müller 2007, p. 309. Also see Chapter 4.1.3.1.

climate of Germany.[1201] This indicates that the region of analysis provides suitable social and political conditions to engage in entrepreneurial activity but does not exceed national characteristics. The economic conditions, however, in terms of market accessibility and the possibility to engage in collaboration projects need to be considered within a regional context and therefore require a more precise analysis. Therefore, the associations of entrepreneurs toward the entrepreneurial climate are investigated by establishing a semantical network linking corresponding terms within a cyclical network structure. Figure 35 illustrates the respective results of the qualitative data analysis including the evaluation coding of the terms enabling a more precise understanding of the relatedness of terms mentioned on a positive-negative scale.[1202]

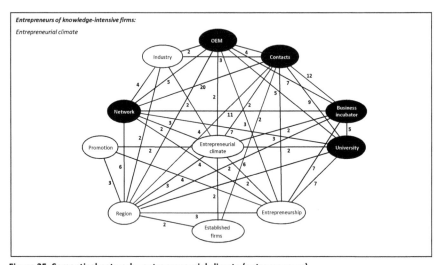

Figure 35: Semantical network - entrepreneurial climate (entrepreneurs)

Once more a two-sided perception of the entrepreneurial climate among entrepreneurs can be identified with reference to the evaluation coding which indicates three positive versus four negative perceptions. This term is predominantly surrounded by regional actors such as established firms and OEM as well as institutions in the form of business incubator, university and network influencing the entrepreneurial climate. Furthermore, the terms industry and region are displayed which may serve as decisive components for evaluating the differences in perceptions regarding the entrepreneurial climate. In this

---

1201   See Brixy/Hundt/Sternberg 2009; Brixy et al. 2011; Kelley/Bosma/Amorós 2011.
1202   See Zelger 2004a, p. 32. Also see Chapter 5.2.2.2.

regard, the statement of an entrepreneur can be identified: "Actually I am quite satisfied with the entrepreneurial climate. The only thing is that it's difficult to find qualified people, but that's in fact an issue of our industry rather than a regional matter."[1203] This implies that industrial specifics need to be considered in context of the regional entrepreneurial climate. Apparently, the OEM has a strong position within the semantical network, which indicates that a considerable number of entrepreneurs are located in the automotive industry, which has been emphasized as a rather challenging industry for entrepreneurial firms due to its hierarchical structure which leaves only limited space for entrepreneurial innovation.[1204] This leads to the conclusion that the identified problems of the regional entrepreneurial climate regarding market accessibility and cooperation may be related to industry characteristics rather than to regional conditions.[1205]

Based on these considerations it remains questionable whether regional conditions provide certain attributes to support entrepreneurial firms to overcome industry-specific entrepreneurial challenges. Subsequently if these attributes are on hand the question arises how entrepreneurs engage with the regional context to manage and approach these prevailing challenges. The figure provides insight by highlighting the relevance of networks, contacts, the business incubator and the university in the form of positively associated terms. This implies that entrepreneurs value the establishment of social relations within network structures as critical elements to approach entrepreneurial challenges. "There are several barriers. In these cases support from networks is an essential aspect."[1206] The term 'network' shows strong connections to the institutions business incubator and university, which are apparently considered as mediating organizations supporting entrepreneurial firms to establish contacts and to receive access to networks. "The business incubator represents an important connector because you automatically receive a network to engage in."[1207] "Because we are in touch with several corporations and regional universities, today we possess a broad and strongly organized network."[1208]

1203   Interviewee 33.
1204   See Figure 32; Figure 33.
1205   Interviewee 13, a former manager at an OEM provides an insight into the characteristics of the automotive industry: In these days product complexity in the automotive industry has reached a level that is creating severe challenges for everyone involved. Formerly there used to be a contract book and functional specifications to implement a new concept. Because of today's complexity this system does not apply any more. The OEM however aims for minimizing its complexity by assigning the complexity management to the first-tier suppliers. These consequently suffer severe pressure to handle the complexity and likewise to provide the requested service quality. This situation does not create much room for experimenting with young entrepreneurial firms.
1206   Interviewee 15.
1207   Interviewee 6.
1208   Interviewee 15.

To determine the attributes to support entrepreneurial firms within the region an analysis of the interview data draw from regional innovation promotors may provide additional information. Figure 36 illustrates a semantical network arranging the most frequently used terms in connection with entrepreneurial climate. In addition to the business incubator regional banks are noted as relevant institutions. Taken together, they offer financial as well as consultative support to entrepreneurial firms and contribute to the reduction of perceived risk. "The cornerstone of entrepreneurship in the region is represented by the business incubator and the local banks. This is a part of our public order and therefore we also have been involved in organizing an entrepreneurship award."[1209] The establishment of a regional entrepreneurship award may be seen as an institutionalized event to promote entrepreneurial firms in the establishment of contacts to potential customers, financiers and/or collaboration partners. These aspects indicate that the region commands a critical range of institutions supporting entrepreneurial firms to cope with industry given challenges and perceived strategic risk by providing consulting, contacts and financial resources.[1210]

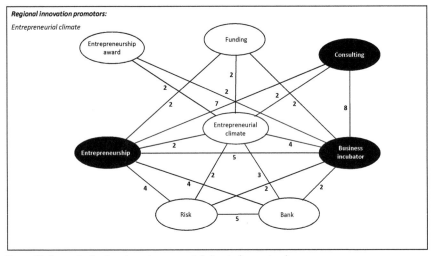

Figure 36: Semantical network - entrepreneurial climate (promotors)

1209   Interviewees 46.
1210   A more detailed analysis of the relevance of regional promotors of innovation and their range of activities contributing to entrepreneurial activity is elaborated in section 6.3.3.

These findings indicate that a regional entrepreneurial climate can be identified which accords to the national entrepreneurial climate of Germany offering suitable conditions on a political as well as social level to pursue entrepreneurial activity.[1211] With regard to the composition of the regional innovation structure industry-specific characteristics need to be considered as hampering factors for entrepreneurial firms to enter regional markets and to identify collaboration partners.[1212] In turn, regional networks and supporting institutions can be identified promoting entrepreneurial firms in their entrepreneurial pursuit to overcome prevailing challenges and handle strategic risk.[1213]

6.3.2 Regional Innovation Structure

Regional innovation structures draw on the establishment of a knowledge ecosystem in which the creation of new knowledge and its commercialization are connected to a cyclical and systemic structure.[1214] A regionally based establishment of knowledge flows can be considered an essential element of the concept that leads to an array of potentials for the emergence of entrepreneurial opportunities due to inter-organizational knowledge spillovers. In this regard, entrepreneurial firms embedded within the corresponding regional structure may be able to exploit regional knowledge sources for their entrepreneurial pursuit.[1215] Consequently, according to the concept of knowledge spillovers, the perceived relevance of entrepreneurial firms to build ties with established corporations and institutions and their ability of integration into regional resource flows can be considered decisive attribute characterizing a regional innovation structure in context of an entrepreneurial climate.[1216]

Based on the previous section, which pointed out the challenges of entrepreneurial firms to receive market access and engage in inter-organizational collaboration with established firms,[1217] this section presents a more detailed analysis of the regional innovation structure by assessing the term 'knowledge transfer' and its related components. This approach contributes to an understanding of the characteristics that shape a regional network of innovation. Furthermore, the investigation adds to the discussion of the regional context by highlighting the relations of main actors and corresponding attributes establish-

---

1211   See Bergmann/Sternberg 2007, pp. 209-210; Fritsch/Müller 2007, p. 299. Goetz/Freshwater 2001, p. 67.

1212   See Acs et al. 2009, p. 28. For a more detailed analysis of the regional innovation structure, see the subsequent section 6.3.2.

1213   See Fichter 2009; Acs/Szerb 2007, p. 116; Witte 1999, p. 15; Wagner/Sternberg 2004, p. 223.

1214   See van der Borgh/Cloodt/Romme 2012, pp. 151-152; Kirsch/Seidl/van Aaken 2010.

1215   See Acs et al. 2009, p. 28.

1216   See Franke 2002; Acs 2009; Audretsch/Aldrige 2009. Also see Chapter 4.1.3.2.

1217   See Table 13.

ing regional knowledge flows. Figure 37 illustrates the corresponding semantical network, indicating that the term knowledge transfer is strongly connected to most frequently used terms in the data sample (indicated by the dark coloring). As critical components of the semantical network the expressions university and network can be identified indicating the relevance of the university as knowledge-producing institution and network settings as platforms to gain access to knowledge flows. "Economic networks are like facebook. One exchanges knowledge and provides information and, in turn, you receive information. If you are not signed in you will not be up-to-date."[1218]

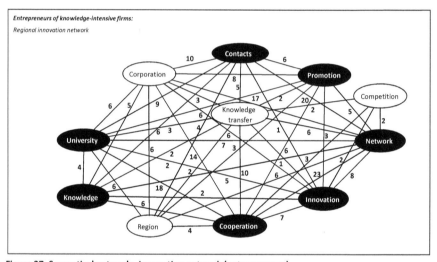

Figure 37: Semantical network - Innovation network (entrepreneurs)

The economic impact of regional networks is indicated by the strong relationship to cooperation in connection with the terms knowledge and innovation. Within these settings, consequently, knowledge transfer among corporations including competitors as well as universities may occur leading to the production of new knowledge, the establishment of inter-organizational alliances and the performance of innovation. "Our relationship to the university has helped us to reach our current market position. We collaborate closely by exchanging knowledge, supervising theses and collaboratively organizing events."[1219] In this regard, the region serves as a mediator to establish contacts and realize knowledge

---

1218   Interviewee 6.
1219   Interviewee 2.

transfer among corporations and knowledge-producing institutions. Furthermore, the relevance of regional innovation and entrepreneurship promotion is seen to support entrepreneurial firms in being locked-in to regional knowledge flows. In this regard, the perceptions of these actors may provide additional information characterizing the constitution of regional innovation networks. Therefore, a corresponding semantical network is established (see Figure 38).

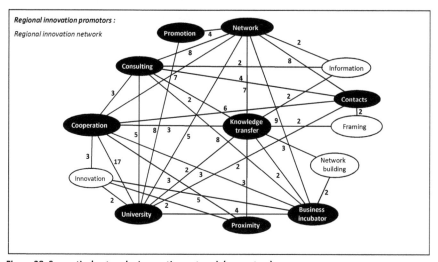

Figure 38: Semantical network - Innovation network (promotors)

Regional innovation promotors widen the frame by emphasizing the relevance of proximity as a critical factor to establishing knowledge transfer and innovation among actors.[1220] As critical institutions in this regard once more the university and the business incubator are noted offering consulting to entrepreneurial firms by providing critical information as well as access to networks, respectively support in network building. "Promoting entrepreneurial firms is our goal. So, it's not about having a business incubator but about incubating businesses. In this sense promoting entrepreneurs means promoting growth."[1221] Furthermore, as a productive outcome of promotion and a regional entrepreneurial climate, characterized by inter-organizational knowledge transfer, the emergence of spin-

---

1220   Also see Boschma 2005; Eriksson 2011; Schamp/Rentmeister/Lo 2004; Sternberg 2007; Torre/Gilly 2000.
1221   Interviewee 48.

offs needs to be considered as critical indicator.[1222] The 21% of the entrepreneurial firms participating in the quantitative analysis indicated as spin-offs provides sufficient proof of such knowledge flows and transaction processes.[1223]

The empirical results to determine regional innovation structures indicate that the importance of knowledge transfer within regional networks is emphasized by entrepreneurial firms as well as promotors as critical aspects to establishing inter-organizational collaboration and achieving innovation.[1224] As the interview statements show, the selected region of analysis is characterized by a regional innovation structure of innovation networks related to mediating institutions promoting inter-organizational knowledge flows by providing knowledge and creating contacts among young as well as established firms. Entrepreneurial firms, consequently, appear to value their environmental context and its knowledge infrastructure as decisive aspect to establish new contacts for value creation.

6.3.3 Regional Promotors of Innovation

Regional promotors of innovation in this work have been discussed as regional institutional representatives located on a 'linking level' providing expertise as well as establishing knowledge flows among regional actors and thus serving as mediators enhancing inter-organizational collaboration for innovation.[1225] These, on the one hand, may possess specific expertise offered by consultative support and, on the other hand, they may serve as 'relationship promotors' by brokering ties to potential collaboration partners and thus providing access to keepers of specific competences to pursue interactive value creation.[1226] Furthermore, in this context, actors have been identified as providing financial capital and therefore as enabling the pursuit of entrepreneurial opportunities.[1227] Promotors consequently, support corporations to achieve economic performance,[1228] by providing and/or diffusing knowledge, contacts and resources within the regional innovation structure,[1229] and therefore enhancing firm capacity to perform innovation.[1230]

As indicated in the previous sections, innovation promotors take a critical role in regional innovation structures by establishing as well as contributing to regional knowledge flows and therefore by influencing the entrepreneurial climate. In this regard, among en-

---

1222   See Etzkowitz/Klofsten 2005, p. 245; Dahlstrand 1997; Bossink 2002, p. 315.
1223   See Table 8.
1224   See Acs et al. 2009, p. 28; Franke 2002; Acs 2009; Audretsch/Aldrige 2009.
1225   See Fichter 2009, p. 360; Winch/Courtney 2007, p. 751.
1226   See Gemünden/Walter 1999, pp. 119-120.
1227   See Wagner/Sternberg 2004, p. 223. Acs/Szerb 2007, p. 116.
1228   See Witte 1999, p. 15; Hauschild/Salomo 2011, p. 125.
1229   See Doloreux 2003, p. 71.
1230   See Sternberg 2007, p. 654; 2009, p. 23. Also see Chapter 4.1.3.3.

trepreneurial firms the relevance of the business incubator and the university has received specific attention.[1231] However, as theoretical considerations originate, the field of regional innovation promotion may be exceeding these components.[1232] Therefore, this section aims for a more precise assessment of the regional infrastructure of innovation promotors aligned to the perception of entrepreneurs regarding its impact on augmenting entrepreneurial performance. In this regard, the empirical assessment of resource transfer may offer insight into the forms and practices of regional innovation promotion. Table 14 illustrates the quantitative results of entrepreneurs regarding, on the one hand, the reception of support and, on the other hand, the perception of regional financial and institutional support as sufficient to overcome market entry barriers.

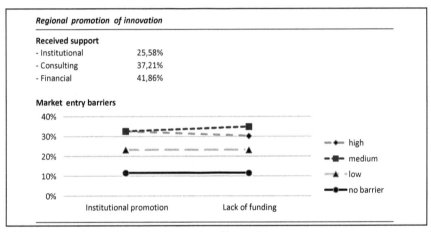

Table 14: Quantitative results - regional promotion of innovation

The illustration shows that the majority of entrepreneurial firms perceives financial (65%) as well as institutional support (64%) as insufficient to overcome entrepreneurial challenges and therefore denotes these aspects as high-level, respectively medium-level market entry barriers. Comparing these numbers to the intensity of received support, however, reveals that about 25% were embedded in a business incubator, 37% received consulting services, and 42% were funded by either formal or informal venture capital market ac-

---

1231   See Figure 33; Figure 35; Figure 37.
1232   See Fichter 2009, p. 360; Wagner/Sternberg 2004, p. 223. Acs/Szerb 2007, p. 116.

tors.[1233] These findings may indicate that, on the one hand, from an entrepreneurial perspective these efforts lack effectiveness or, on the other hand, from a promotor point of view these firms who did not receive support of any kind lack the information or the willingness to engage in collaboration with innovation promotors.[1234] A qualitative analysis in the form of a semantical network provides an opposing perspective by illustrating dominantly positively linked associations in connection with the term promotion (see Figure 39).

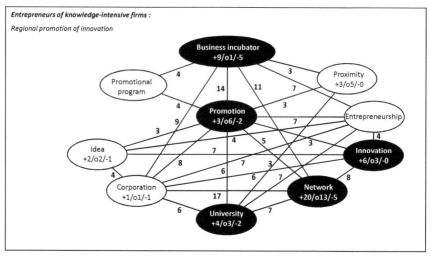

Figure 39: Semantical network - Promotion of innovation

Even though negative connotations can be identified among the critical terms promotion, business incubator, network and university, a positive view of these institutions as promotors of innovation and entrepreneurship prevails. "In the beginning the university was a strong promotor. Due to the university and the business incubator we have had great support developing our company."[1235] Furthermore, the entrepreneurs emphasize the relevance of proximity to these institutions to establishing ties with corresponding actors serving as multipliers of contacts and valuable partners to discuss current business issues. "In times of a globalized economy one thinks that geographic proximity doesn't matter, but in

---

1233   For a differenciation of formal or informal venture capital market actors see Harrison/Mason 2000, p. 224; Black/Gilson 1998
1234   Also see Rabe 2007, pp. 273-274.
1235   Interviewee 1.

fact it's very, very important!"[1236] As these findings indicate, entrepreneurs to some degree value the relevance of innovation promotors specifically in terms of providing expertise as well as brokering contacts. The differences in prevailing perceptions may either draw on the particular ability of the firm to detect and exploit the promotional infrastructure or refer to a moderate choice of available support.[1237] To gain a better understanding of the prevailing range of activities the subsequent sections analyze the interview data of regional innovation promotors based on the presented concepts of relational and expert promotors.[1238]

6.3.3.1 Relational Promotors

A critical function of promotors lies in their ability to broker ties to keepers of specific competences setting the ground for the pursuit of interactive value creation. By assigning certain attributes to innovation promotors these may be referred to as 'relational promotors' providing access to potential collaboration partners and thus may serve as mediators of co- innovation.[1239] Based on regional proximity, consequently, relational promotors leverage structural capital by establishing new ties that may be transformed into relational capital among regional actors.[1240] In this regard, managers of business incubators may serve as examples that specifically promote entrepreneurial firms by providing of an access to a network of entrepreneurial firms located within the incubator as well as to the incubator's network of collaboration partners.[1241]

The establishment of ties, however, is a challenging task since the corresponding actors need to proceed to assemble of relational capital on their own. Furthermore, drawing on the discussion of inefficient network and collaboration investments,[1242] skepticism may prevail whether the relational promotor clearly follows a value creation- and innovation performance-based perspective toward the established contacts. A semantical causal analysis may provide an insight into the mindset of regional innovation promotors regarding their ambition to establish ties (see Figure 40). The centre of the figure illustrates that promotors see proximity and contacts as critical attributes influencing the emergence of cooperations jointly leading to innovation. Proximity is consequently seen as an important

1236   Interviewee 24.
1237   See Acs et al. 2009, p. 28; Rabe 2007, pp. 273-274.
1238   See Fichter 2009, p. 360; Gemünden/Walter 1999, pp. 119-120; Witte 1999, p. 15; Hauschild/Salomo 2011, p. 125.
1239   See Gemünden/Walter 1999, pp. 119-120; Fichter 2009, p. 359.
1240   See Liao/Welch 2001, p. 167; Pena 2002, p. 181; Hayton 2005, p. 140.
1241   See Hackett/Dilts 2004, p. 57.
1242   See Witt 2004, p. 395; Woolcock/Narayan 2000, p. 231.

factor capable of increasing speed and reducing effort as well as costs in inter-organizational relations leading to knowledge transfer and sharing of experiences among close organizations. Experience and contacts show a connection to networks, which may indicate that valuable experiences and contacts result from network investments. In this regard, the term trust can be identified resulting from experience, contacts and network-ing leading to the establishment of cooperations. The aspect of value creation based on contacts is also emphasized by relating the term to the acquisition of new customers and the development of new ideas. Contacts consequently create framing conditions for inter-organizational value creation and knowledge transfer and therefore positively relate to innovation.

Interestingly, promotors emphasize the relevance of establishing trust within networks as being inclined to engage in cooperations, whereas networking as such is inversely relat-ed.[1243] This implies that networking offers an infrastructure to establish strong relations among actors, setting the basis for co-innovation. As influential components further soft-factors are named in the form of the individual willingness to cooperate and previous ex-pertise as well as reputation.[1244] Depending on the given topic and the individual capacity cooperation may lead to new orders and development projects, an increase in productivi-ty, the establishment of strong relations and the identification of qualified employees.[1245] Consequently, these findings indicate that relational promotors focus precisely on corpo-rate performance when establishing ties, being aware that they can provide only framing conditions to establish contacts, that but the emergence of cooperations depend on the individual willingness and ability of the entrepreneur to build relational capital.[1246] "The challenge is to establish trust among actors. Trust can be established by networking and dialogs and by showing the people that they cannot lose."[1247]

1243   See Mayer/Davis/Schoorman 1995, p. 712; Lin 2003, p. 147.
1244   See Lin 2001, p. 19; Nahapiet/Ghoshal, 1998, pp. 255; Burt 2005, p. 209.
1245   See Floyd/Wooldridge 1999, p. 132.
1246   See Acs et al. 2009, p. 28; Rabe 2007, pp. 273-274.
1247   Interviewee 35.

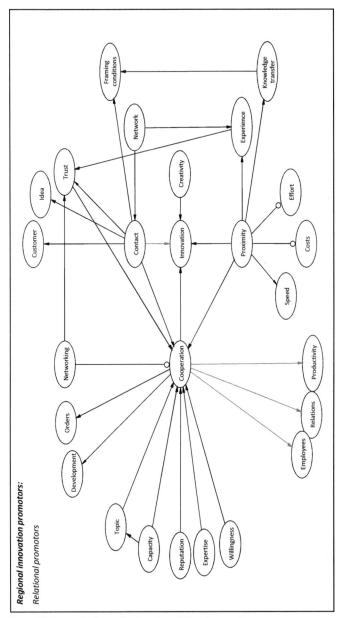

Figure 40: Semantical causal network - relational promotors

6.3.3.2 Expert Promotors

Specifically universities, respectively knowledge-producing institutions, have been empha-sized as promotors of specific expertise,[1248] by supporting corporate innovation capacity due to the provision of research results suitable for commercialization.[1249] Consequently, structuring the concept of expert promotors in accordance with knowledge spillover theo-ry, universities can be considered suppliers of knowledge creating a competitive advantage for entrepreneurial firms based on their ability to absorb and transform exogenous knowledge sources.[1250] Furthermore, apart from topic-specific knowledge, expert promo-tors may support firms in their entrepreneurial pursuit by offering coaching and consult-ing.[1251] Here, on the one hand, start-up consultants can be identified located in public in-stitutions, industry associations and public-private institutions such as business incuba-tors.[1252] On the other hand, corporate actors can be considered promotors of innovation by providing relevant knowledge-intensive services for entrepreneurial firms such as law and tax advisory as well as consulting following a professional interest.[1253] These actors, consequently, contribute to the regional range of knowledge spillovers by providing specif-ic expertise to support entrepreneurial firms which characterizes the concept of expert promotors.[1254]

Qualitative data analysis, drawing on the set of regional innovation promotors, allows for a more precise elaboration of the concept. Figure 41 illustrates a semantic network linking the term 'consulting' to surrounding associations. Here, in addition to the previous-ly dominantly mentioned institutions of university and business incubator, industry associ-ations are mentioned as important providers of expertise. Their support, respectively promotion applies in a first step in the form of consulting to the formation of a business and the elaboration and the improvement of a business plan. Furthermore, coaching is provided during the entrepreneurship process as well as additional services, respectively the establishment of contacts, to specific service providers. "Entrepreneurship promotion is an important part of our work. But I have to say that the main part is to coach and sup-

---

1248   See Witte 1973, p. 17; Witte 1999, p. 15.
1249   See Mason/Wagner 1999, pp. 97-100.
1250   See Fischer 2006, pp. 1-2; Cohen/Levintal 1990.
1251   See Hackett/Dilts 2004, p. 57; Harhoff 2000, p. 240.
1252   See Raabe 2007, pp. 273-274. Business incubators may cover the entire spectrum of public, public-private, and private organizations. In case of the region under study, one incubator was identified which is publicly organized only providing only physical infrastructure, whereas the largest regional incubator is public-privately funded, providing in addition to the physical infrastructure a manage-ment team offering business services and consulting.
1253   See Chapter 5.2.3.2. In the region of Ingolstadt these actors are organized in a network structure which is linked to the business incubator, Existenzgründerzentrum Ingolstadt (www.egz.de).
1254   See Witte, 1973, p. 17; Fichter 2009, pp. 359-360. Also see De Bondt 1997, p. 12; Harhoff 2000, p. 246; Steurs 1995, p 250.

port these firms along the way - and that's a critical issue. Entrepreneurs have to focus on their business activities. Let's take a technology entrepreneur in the automotive industry, having an order to establish a given product; he won't care about too many other things but doing his job. But when problems and critical issues occur, it's our job to provide a plausible solution."[1255]

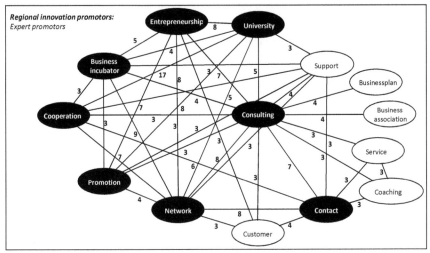

Figure 41: Semantical network - expert promotors

As the remaining terms 'network' and 'cooperation' indicate, consulting also may be of higher relevance in connection with the establishment of ties. Despite specific market expertise to establish contacts between the entrepreneurial firm and potential customers and/or collaboration partners consulting may also be of critical weight with respect to inter-organizational collaboration toward IP protection and the establishment of contracts.[1256] This concludes that the presented concepts of relational and expert promotors in connection with entrepreneurship and innovation show strong links and therefore can predominantly be understood as mutually embodied attributes of regional innovation promotors effectively supporting firms within several stages of their entrepreneurial process.

1255   Interviewee 47.
1256   See Gans/Stern 2003, pp. 338-339.

6.4 Synthesis of Main Findings

The presentation of the empirical results has contributed to a more precise understanding of entrepreneurship in regional innovation structures. This section summarizes the main findings, drawing on the formulated set of research questions.[1257] In accordance with the established framework of investigation, these are based on the assumption that the analyzed young knowledge-intensive entrepreneurial firms possess an innovation capacity characterized by a competitive resource base as well as an entrepreneurial motivation striving for the pursuit of entrepreneurial opportunities to achieve innovation. The findings illustrate that entrepreneurs emphasize motivational aspects as critical attributes to engaging in entrepreneurial activity and particularly highlight the relevance of specific knowledge, which in connection with the corporate network can be applied to achieve innovation. The prevailing selection of knowledge-intensive firms, therefore, can be characterized by a strong resource base as the essential element of their innovation capacity which in connection with personally affected motivational aspects is applied to pursue opportunities and perform innovation.[1258]

In addition to the aspect of innovation capacity the practical achievement of entrepreneurial performance was noted as the decisive component to assessing the relevance of external and internal dimensions influencing entrepreneurial activity. The results show that entrepreneurs have performed innovation and growth rates and expect a positive economic development; they consider innovation as the decisive element of entrepreneurial performance leading to future growth.[1259] Consequently, the entrepreneurial firms analyzed provide suitable characteristics to discuss the impact of co-innovation competence and the regional entrepreneurial climate on entrepreneurial performance.

The concept of co-innovation competence was introduced as a dynamic construct directed at an efficient interchange of co-innovation resources and co-innovation capabilities.[1260] Thus, as formulated in RQ 1 an assessment of the impact of co-innovation competence on entrepreneurial performance requires a twofold approach by, on the one hand, focusing on co-innovation resources and, on the other hand, by concentrating on co-innovation capabilities. Therefore, with regard to co-innovation resources the question has been posed whether entrepreneurs perceive networking and the establishment of social relations as relevant resource to identify and pursue entrepreneurial opportunities (RQ 1a). The empirical results showed that entrepreneurs value the potentials of networking and are willing to invest in the establishment and maintenance of social relations to in-

---

1257   See Chapter 4.2.2.
1258   See Chapter 6.1.1.
1259   See Chapter 6.1.2.
1260   See Chapters 3.2.2.1; 4.1.2.

crease corporate success and perform innovation in collaboration with external partners. However, this willingness is determined by the perceived necessity, respectively the demand for accessing external resources and/or collaboration partners to pursue entrepreneurial activity depending on the capacity of the entrepreneurial firm specifically in terms of available time. Due to the awareness of the likelihood of opportunistic behavior in inter-organizational collaboration entrepreneurs rather focus on the establishment of trusted relations via building a reputation based on firm performance. This attitude reflects to a transaction-based continuous development of the corporate technology base as well as its social capital constituting a dynamic perception of co-innovation resources.

To determine co-innovation capabilities the question was raised whether entrepreneurial firms approach their environmental context by a certain procedure to engage in inter-organizational collaboration and thereby overcome reciprocally perceived barriers of co-innovation (RQ 1b). The findings indicate that entrepreneurs draw on substantial market knowledge and connections to potential co-innovation partners as well as mediating institutions creating an infrastructure for co-innovation in the form of external ties to exploit exogenous knowledge sources.[1261] Consequently, co-innovation competence persist, building upon a dynamic evolvement of co-innovation resources emphasizing the relevance of trusted relationships and competitive firm-specific knowledge leading to the establishment of a reputation. However, the results also indicate that co-innovation capabilities are hampered because of prevailing concerns of innovation risk. In this context the apprehension of opportunistic behavior among collaboration partners serves as an explanatory component,[1262] which may align to a lack of willingness and/or ability among the firms to identify appropriate solutions to minimize strategic risk by sharing financial obligations as well as profits with complementary partners.[1263]

The analysis detected that hampering factors for co-innovation of entrepreneurial firms may be caused by industry specifics constraining the range of entrepreneurial opportunities. This insight indicates the relevance of analyzing co-innovation competence in relation to environmental conditions critically influencing the scope of applicability of co-innovation capabilities within a regional context. In this regard, an analysis of the corresponding entrepreneurial climate can be considered as critical aspects to gaining insight into the relevance of the environmental conditions to entrepreneurial performance (RQ 2). Based on research in economic geography critical elements constituting environmental

---

1261   See Simard/West 2006, p. 235; Harryson 2008, p. 297; Vanhaverbeke 2006, p. 209; Chesbrough 2006c, p. 152; Lichtenthaler 2006, pp. 64-70; Lichtenthaler/Lichtenthaler 2010; Müller-Seitz 2012, pp. 90-91.
1262   See accordingly Hoecht/Trott 1999, p. 258; Gans/Stern 2003; Keupp/Gassmann 2009, p. 338.
1263   See Chapter 6.2.2.

conditions in the form of an entrepreneurial climate could have been identified.[1264] Combining these aspects with prevailing concepts of the field of regional innovation network research leads to the establishment of three fundamental columns characterizing an entrepreneurial climate. These are the regional context as such representing framing and cultural aspects, the regional innovation structure and regional innovation promotors as actors supporting corporate innovation activity. These aspects are assessed individually leading to a comprehensive understanding of the environmental context and its impact on entrepreneurial performance.

To approach an analysis of the regional context the question was formulated whether specific characteristics of a regional entrepreneurial climate can be identified critically impacting entrepreneurial performance (RQ 2a). The findings indicate that the regional entrepreneurial climate analyzed accords with the national entrepreneurial climate of Germany offering suitable conditions on a political as well as social level to pursue entrepreneurial activity.[1265] However, as indicated above, industry-specific characteristics were identified as hampering factors for entrepreneurial firms to enter regional markets and to identify collaboration partners.[1266] Correspondingly, regional networks and supporting institutions may promote entrepreneurial firms in their entrepreneurial pursuit to overcome prevailing challenges.[1267] These aspects indicate that the region exhibits an entrepreneurial climate providing suitable framing conditions and innovation network structures as well as institutions supporting entrepreneurial firms to cope with industry-given challenges by providing consulting, contacts, and financial resources.[1268]

Subsequently, with reference to regional innovation structures, the recognition of regional knowledge sources to amplify the scope of entrepreneurial activity was assessed (RQ 2b). The empirical results point out that the importance of knowledge transfer within regional networks is emphasized by entrepreneurial firms as critical aspect to achieve innovation.[1269] In this regard, the selected region of analysis is characterized by a regional innovation structure constituted by innovation networks related to mediating institutions promoting inter-organizational knowledge flows by providing knowledge and creating contacts among young as well as established firms. Entrepreneurial firms, therefore, appear to value their environmental context and its knowledge infrastructure as decisive aspects for establishing new contacts for value creation.[1270]

1264   See Chapter 4.1.3.1.
1265   See Bergmann/Sternberg 2007, pp. 209-210; Fritsch/Müller 2007, p. 299. Goetz/Freshwater 2001, p. 67.
1266   See Acs et al. 2009, p. 28.
1267   See Fichter 2009; Acs/Szerb 2007, p. 116; Witte 1999, p. 15; Wagner/Sternberg 2004, p. 223.
1268   See Chapter 6.3.1.
1269   See Acs et al. 2009, p. 28; Franke 2002; Acs 2009; Audretsch/Aldrige 2009.
1270   See Chapter 6.3.2.

As the findings regarding the regional context and regional innovation structures demonstrate, institutions supporting entrepreneurial firms need to be considered as decisive components contributing to the quality of the regional entrepreneurial climate. This leads to the question whether regional promotors of innovation are perceived as collaboration partners to source-specific knowledge and critical resources to overcome entrepreneurial challenges (RQ 2c). The study results show that entrepreneurs value innovation promotors specifically in terms of providing expertise as well as brokering contacts although differentiating positions regarding their impact can be identified. The differences in prevailing perceptions may either refer to the particular ability of the firm to detect and exploit the promotional infrastructure or comprise a moderate choice of available support.[1271] To assess the prevailing range of supporting activities regional innovation promotors were analyzed with reference to their understanding of relational and expertise promotion.

Regarding relational promotion the findings indicate that relational promotors precisely focus on corporate performance within their pursuit of establishing ties, being aware that they can only provide framing conditions to establish contacts, though the emergence of cooperations depends on the individual willingness and ability to build relational capital.[1272] In terms of the promotion of expertise the university, the business incubator, and industry associations are specifically mentioned as important promotors. Their activity may, on the one hand, take place in the form of consulting concerning the formation of a business and the elaboration of a business plan. On the other hand, coaching is provided during the entrepreneurship process as well as additional services, respectively the establishment of contacts to specific service providers and knowledge keepers. Despite specific market expertise to establish contacts between the entrepreneurial firm and potential customers and/or collaboration partners, consulting also may be seen as critical aspect regarding inter-organizational collaboration with reference to IP protection and the establishment of contracts.[1273] Therefore, innovation promotors predominantly show expertise as well as relational capabilities to effectively support entrepreneurial firms during the entrepreneurial process.[1274]

These findings illustrate that young knowledge-intensive entrepreneurial firms follow the concepts of open innovation and networking, and value their potential to amplify the range of entrepreneurial activity. However, constricting aspects can be identified. Due to limited capacity in terms of time and human resources, entrepreneurs draw only on network structures if specific demand persists regarding the identification of new customers,

---

1271   See Acs et al. 2009, p. 28; Rabe 2007, pp. 273-274. Also see Chapter 6.3.3.
1272   See Chapter 6.3.3.1.
1273   See Gans/Stern 2003, pp. 338-339.
1274   See Chapter 6.3.2.

collaboration partners and knowledge sources. In this regard, entrepreneurial firms take a rather organic approach to establishing their network with reference to a set of strong inter-organizational ties with trusted organizations resulting from successful collaboration projects. This approach serves as a critical factor to preventing networking inefficiencies as well as the potential of opportunistic behavior from collaboration partners. Due to this circumstance path dependencies occur,[1275] which causes entrepreneurs to relate to a limited network suitable to explore and exploit complementary assets. Therefore, large-scale innovation projects are perceived as risky ventures because of a small scale of potential innovation partners to fairly share innovation risk and profits. If entrepreneurial firms see the necessity to reach beyond these organic network structures, they value the existence of the regional innovation structure by accessing innovation networks containing potential customers and collaboration partners as well as knowledge-producing institutions to realize knowledge spillovers. To receive access to these networks and containing institutions, if necessary, regional innovation promotors are sought out to provide structural capital as a basis to establishing relational capital as well as consulting and coaching services to support these firms in their entrepreneurial pursuit. Consequently, the awareness of the regional promotional infrastructure and the establishment of ties to these actors may be seen as a critical strategic aspect for entrepreneurial firms to expand their portfolios of trusted collaboration partners to pursue co-innovation.

1275   See Teece/Pisano/Shuen 1997, p. 522.

"It is often said that a person cannot win a game that they do not play. In the context of entrepreneurship, this statement suggests that success depends on the people's willingness to become entrepreneurs."[1276]

7. Implications and Discussion

7.1 Theoretical Implications

This work contributes to entrepreneurship research by critically discussing the applicability of the concept of open innovation and respectively, a networked approach to inter-organizational value creation processes of young knowledge-intensive entrepreneurial firms. Based on the state of discussion in the field, there is an opening of innovation processes performed by entrepreneurial firms that are increasingly becoming networked.[1277] This statement is the basis for the relevance of the prevailing investigation. Based on the circumstance that open innovation and a networked approach to entrepreneurship are aligned to the aspect of chain-linked innovation structures which build upon the interaction among specialized actors within the innovation process,[1278] the concepts strive for inter-organizational value creation based on the accessibility of complementary assets.[1279] In this regard, however, hampering factors for entrepreneurial firms to engage in such inter-active innovation processes were identified. These may be constituted by the ability of entrepreneurial firms to access and explore and exploit network structures for their entrepreneurial pursuit. In detail, a lack of trust and suspicion of opportunistic behavior among entrepreneurial firms toward potential collaboration partners is present.[1280] In turn, the liability of newness associated with uncertainty regarding the innovation capacity of the entrepreneurial firm prevails among established firms.[1281] Due to asymmetric information sharing this reciprocal uncertainty among actors may cause a lack of willingness

---

1276   Shane/Locke/Collins 2003, p. 257.
1277   Harryson 2008, p. 290.
1278   See Sternberg 2007, p. 653. Tappeiner/Hauser/Walde 2008, pp. 862-863; Chung 2002, p. 484; Schamp 2002; Schamp/Rentmeister/Lo 2004; Faltin 2001, p. 127.
1279   See Teece 1986, p.289; Harryson 2006, p. 354.
1280   See Nooteboom 2000a, p. 919; Hoecht/Trott 1999, p. 266.
1281   See e.g. Smith/Lohrke 2008, p. 315.

to build social relations apprehending networking inefficiencies which refer to an imbalance of the investment into social capital along organizational goals.[1282]

The existence of constraining factors regarding the applicability of a networked value creation approach within an open innovation format of entrepreneurial firms indicates the relevance of a strategic analysis of the topic in relation to the achievement of entrepreneurial performance. In this regard, the concept of co-innovation competence was introduced in this work. Co-innovation competence is to be understood as an efficient interplay of co-innovation resources represented by the technological base of a corporation containing core capabilities for value creation and the value of its external ties expressed by social capital and co-innovation capabilities with reference to the capability of the firm to align these resources within the corporate network for exploration of assets outside of corporate boundaries and exploitation of internal assets for cooperative value creation.[1283] The concept aims for determining the identification of precise conditions for an entrepreneurial behavior in accordance with the open innovation construct based on a competence-based approach.

Through the procedure of analysis, proximity among actors was identified as a decisive factor for establishing ties to potential collaboration partners and initiating interorganizational knowledge flows.[1284] Therefore, a regional context analysis may serve as a critical component relating open innovation and networking to entrepreneurship. In economic geography literature, compositions of regional structures are analyzed which are characterized by intense knowledge flows among regional actors leading to the conceptual approach of regional innovation structures.[1285] These may offer an entrepreneurial climate which promotes the emergence of new ideas and the pursuit of entrepreneurial opportunities based on an exploitation of regional knowledge spillovers.[1286] Therefore, the elaboration of co-innovation competence from an entrepreneurial perspective requires a consideration of attributes enabling as well as constraining the establishment of interorganizational innovation partnerships among regional actors considering regional framing conditions in the form of a regional entrepreneurial climate.

Regional specifics and especially the embeddedness of regional actors within prevailing network structures may be "crucial in explaining the differences in effectiveness of Open Innovation in different regions or nations."[1287] Consequently, regions characterized by an

---

1282   See Krackhardt/Hanson 1993, p. 110; Woolcock/Narayan 2000, p. 231; Witt 2004, p. 395.
1283   See Chapter 3.2.2.
1284   See Glaeser et al. 1992; Jacobs 1969; Storper/Veneables 2004; Boschma 2005; Eriksson 2011; Thornton/Flynn 2003, p. 426.
1285   See Asheim/Coenen 2005; Cooke 2004, p. 3; Iammarino 2005, p. 4; Asheim/Isasken 1997, p. 302.
1286   See Goetz/Freshwater 2001, pp. 64-65. Brixy et al. 2011, p. 22; Lee et al. 2000; Acs et al. 2009; Audretsch/Lehmann 2005; Audretsch/Aldridge 2009.
1287   Vanhaverbeke 2006, p. 216.

innovation structure provide certain framing conditions allowing for the pursuit of co-innovative entrepreneurial activities, though it require specific strategies and tactics from entrepreneurial firms to exploit these structures by receiving access to regional innovation networks to evolve its co-innovation resource base.[1288]

The empirical investigation performed in this work to assess a strategic approach to entrepreneurship in regional innovation structures of young knowledge-intensive entrepreneurial firms illustrates that the firms analyzed value the potentials of inter-organizational value creation and perceive networking as critical factor for entrepreneurial performance. This contributes to the relevance of analyzing these aspects in more detail from an entrepreneurial perspective to broaden the understanding of entrepreneurial specifics within the field of innovation research. In accordance with the constraining factors presented these specifics primarily relate to the limited capacity of entrepreneurial firms in terms of resources available to invest in the establishment of a large corporate network suitable for simultaneous exploration and exploitation of technologies. Therefore, entrepreneurial firms follow a specific approach toward networking minimizing the potential of opportunistic behavior and transaction costs as well as inefficient investments. This approach, on the one hand, refers to an organic emergence of trusted collaboration partners drawing on successful collaboration projects and mutual experiences.[1289] Due to this procedure to co-innovation by maximizing relational efficiency path dependencies occur[1290] which limit the range of the entrepreneurial network suitable to explore and exploit complementary assets. On the other hand, to overcome this limitation, an on demand-based perspective of networking is found which is pursued if specific demand persists regarding the identification of new customers, collaboration partners and knowledge sources to amplify entrepreneurial performance.

This finding expands the elaborations presented regarding the discussion of entrepreneurial networks interrelating the composition of the network structure to required network investments and network resources.[1291] In this context, it was acknowledged that, from a network analytical perspective, the identification of "what entrepreneurs can do to improve their chances of success"[1292] may require a case-specific approach.[1293] Consequently, one should differentiate between organically established corporate network structures with reference to strong ties and the existence of regional and/or industry-specific networks of rather loosely tied organizations aiming for knowledge exchange and

1288   See Liao/Welch 2001, p. 167. For a elaboration of co-innovation resources see Chapter 4.1.2.1.
1289   Also see Davidsson/Honig 2003, p. 325.
1290   See Teece/Pisano/Shuen 1997, p. 522.
1291   See Witt 2004, p. 395. Also see Chapter 3.1.3.
1292   Witt 2004, p. 396.
1293   See Elfring/Hulsink 2007, pp. 1853, 1866; Hoang/Antoncic 2003, pp. 181-182.

the exploration of market opportunities. If entrepreneurial firms see the necessity to access complementary assets beyond prevailing corporate network structures they draw on these regional and/or industry-specific networks containing potential customers and collaboration partners as well as knowledge-producing institutions to realize knowledge spillovers and expand their range of entrepreneurial opportunities.[1294] Based on this behavior, entrepreneurial firms overcome the potential inefficiency of strong ties hindering the emergence of new opportunities by flexibly drawing on untapped network structures.[1295]

Understanding the regional economic structure as a multi-level innovation system framed by a linking level, intermediaries and technology brokers can be identified enabling corporations to innovate by transferring knowledge and establishing social capital among regional actors.[1296] Therefore, to receive access to these networks and containing institutions, regional innovation promotors may provide structural capital as a basis for establishing relational capital as well as consulting and coaching services to support these firms in their entrepreneurial pursuit. Consequently, the awareness of the regional promotional infrastructure and the establishment of ties to these actors may be seen as critical strategic aspect for entrepreneurial firms, if capacities and demand prevail, to expand its portfolio of trusted collaboration partners to pursue co-innovation. The interplay of entrepreneurs with regional innovation promotors, therefore, may be characterized as decisive for the ability of the entrepreneur to strategically exploit regional innovation structures and to achieve entrepreneurial performance. This confirms the statement that "the facilitation and support of business networks and associations may provide the most consistent and effective support for emerging businesses,"[1297] but it should be expanded by the emphasis, that if they have the willingness, respectively the innovation capacity and co-innovation competence to achieve entrepreneurial performance.

Based on the presented outline of this work theoretical implications can be drawn regarding the conceptual elaborations as well as the methodological procedures applied. To allow for a structured overview critical components are discussed as well as implications for further research derived:

- Methodological procedures and entrepreneurship research: A triangular approach was applied in this investigation.[1298] In this procedure a multi-disciplinary analysis of prevailing literature from the fields of strategic management focusing on innovation management as well as strategic entrepreneurship and economic geography serves as the the-

---

1294   Also see Pena 2002, p. 194.
1295   Also See Uzzi 1997, p. 59; Stam/Elfring 2008, p. 109; Florida/Cushing/Gates 2002, p. 20.
1296   See Fichter 2009, p. 360; Cooke 2001, p. 949; Winch/Courtney 2007, p. 751.
1297   Davidsson/Honig 2003, p. 325.
1298   See Todd 1979.

oretical framework.[1299] The identified state of discussion is reflected upon social capital theory and the competence-based view of the firm, forming the basis for establishing of a conceptual framework applied to empirical analysis. The triangle is shaped by a mixture of a quantitative and a qualitative analytical procedure. The combination of these methodological components aims to overcome of methodological limits by elaborating a holistic view of the selected phenomenon of analysis.[1300] With regard to the quantitative approach, entrepreneurship research of young knowledge-intensive entrepreneurial firms is challenged in a two-fold manner. On the one hand; difficulties exist regarding their identifiability due to the fact that there are neither official statistics nor corporate reports available challenging the detection of a statistical population. On the other hand, entrepreneurial firms show limited motivation to participate in research surveys due to a lack of time and willingness to communicate firm-specific information.[1301] The 43 complete surveys received, therefore, can be considered a successful response rate of the total 249 young knowledge-intensive entrepreneurial firms identified in the selected region of analysis. However, the data quantity limits the range of suitable statistical analytical procedures to a descriptive presentation.[1302] In addition, a data bias cannot be obviated on the assumption that these firms, openly reacting toward university research projects share a positive perception toward networking and interorganizational collaboration. The quantitative data, therefore, serves as an indication of a defined aspect requiring a more precise analytical approach in the form of expert interviews.

With regard to the qualitative approach, the challenges presented in data collection and the bias factor may also prevail. However, the application of open-question interviews aiming for the establishment of an emergent conversation between entrepreneur and researcher allow for the assessment of context-specific knowledge and perceptions that go beyond survey results.[1303] For an analytical procedure and data coding the software application WinRelan was applied allowing for a precise qualitative data analysis and the establishment of semantical network structures.[1304] By following a systemized procedure of data generation, processing, and interpretation, the applied computer-aided analysis offers a transparent and comprehensible process for establishing qualitative research results.[1305] In this context, the qualitative results cannot be considered

1299   See Choi/Pak 2006, p. 351.
1300   See Denzin 1978, p. 291.
1301   See See Fiorito/LaForge 1986; Flatten/Greve/Brettel 2011, p. 144; Butler/Saxberg 2001, p. 420.
1302   See Chapter 5.3.2.
1303   See e.g. Bogner/Menz 2009, pp. 70-75; Reuber/Pfaffenbach 2005, p. 133.
1304   See Zelger 2004a. Also see Chapter 5.2.2.2.
1305   See Fielding, 2002, p.162. Also see Kuckartz 2005.

statistical results meeting the criteria of significance, rather they serve as points of reverence for data interpretation.[1306] Consequently, the application of the procedure mentioned contributes to a reduction of criticism toward qualitative research,[1307] nonetheless, the results presented may reflect single opinions and subjective interpretation.

In light of these methodological procedures, implications can be formulated for future entrepreneurship research projects. A triangular approach may lead to valuable results if a limited range of suitable entrepreneurial firms persist in the selected area of analysis. To determine the precise influence of the identified attributes on entrepreneurial performance large-scale quantitative datasets following a Likert-scale design may be required. [1308] Operationalization of the presented conceptual framework, in this regard, can be identified as an area of further quantitative research by aligning the components constituting the innovation capacity of the entrepreneurial firm as independent variables to entrepreneurial performance as the dependent variable. In turn, the regional entrepreneurial climate and co-innovation competence represent constructs of latent variables influencing entrepreneurial performance.[1309] The software-assisted analytical procedure of qualitative data is a valuable method for determining perceptions and implicit value patterns of interviewees which in comparison to direct questions may overcome a potential bias of social or political desired statements. Therefore, a more precise qualitative analysis of entrepreneurial motivation to engage in and interact within network structures may be seen as a field of qualitative future research utilizing semantical network analysis.

- Regional analysis and entrepreneurial climate: In the economic geography literature there is the critical statement that empirical analysis of regional innovation structures generally lacks representativeness for all regions and countries due to regional specifics limiting comparability.[1310] The findings in this work, on the one hand, support this perception elaborating the relevance of industry-specific characteristics, here in the form of the automotive industry, decisively shaping the regional economic climate.[1311] Furthermore, it is beyond doubt that regional structures may consist of an individual 'fingerprint' in connection with the characteristics of the national economic structure. On the other hand, a set of research contributions can be identified approaching regional structures and elaborating helpful results allowing for their transferability to other re-

---

1306   See e.g. Fielding 2002; Welsh 2002; Zelger/Oberprantacher 2002, p. 1.
1307   See Denzin/Lincoln 2005, p. 3.
1308   See e.g. Lichtenthaler 2006, p. 155.
1309   See Chapter 4.2.2. Also see Pinnekamp 2008, p. 149.
1310   See Sternberg 2007, p. 655.
1311   See Chapter 6.3.1.

gions and public policy.[1312] Therefore, the potential for identifying valuable insights to detect a strategic approach regarding the interplay of the entrepreneurial firm with its environmental context can be considered as given within this work. However, further research applied to similarly structured regions may broaden our understanding of the results received and determine the relevance of precise regional characteristics positively related to the emergence of entrepreneurial opportunities. In this regard, it is to be noted that the constitution of an entrepreneurial climate and its framing conditions were discussed and applied to the area of investigation.[1313] Nonetheless, research presently lacks an explanation for the precise reasons contributing to the emergence of inter-organizational knowledge flows, respectively knowledge spillovers. The emphasized relevance of regional innovation promotors and a corresponding promotional infrastructure may function as an explanatory aspect in this regard.[1314] However, a systemic analytical approach to regional innovation structures may therefore serve as a suitable field for further research aiming to assessment of critical components stimulating regional knowledge transfer.

- Open innovation, entrepreneurial networks and co-innovation competence: The conceptual analysis of the open innovation construct understood as an interactive flow of knowledge and technologies among cooperating organizations,[1315] indicates the relevance of considering inter-organizational relations in innovation management, respectively strategic entrepreneurship. In this regard, it was pointed out that analytical procedures reaching beyond dyad structures need to be recognized as a challenging task due to their more intense prevalent complexity.[1316] Research has been conducted approaching this task by conceptualizing open innovation networks and open innovation communities.[1317] However, few contributions can be identified relating these concepts to regional structure economics and linking the characteristics of a networked approach of open innovation to regional innovation structures. This work contributes to this rather untapped field of research but there is also a need for further contributions can be identified. Specifically, soft-factors such as embeddedness and social capital containing reciprocity, trust, and values as critical elements require more precise considerations in this regard. Consequently, a value-based approach toward regional open innovation structures may shed light on the relevance of the cultural dimension of open innovation

---

1312   See e.g. Asheim/Coenen 2005; Doloreux/Dionne 2008; Belussi/Sammarra/Sedita 2010; Saxenian 1990; 2000; Lee et al. 2000.
1313   See Chapter 4.1.3.1.
1314   See Fichter 2009, p. 360; Cooke 2001, p. 949; Winch/Courtney 2007, p. 751.
1315   See Chesbrough 2003a, p. 18.
1316   See Vanhaverbeke/Cloodt 2006, p. 276.
1317   See e.g. Enkel 2010; Lee et al. 2010; Cardoso et al. 2008; Fichter 2009.

as well as regional characteristics promoting the emergence of such regional open innovation structures. In this context, the role of promotors has been emphasized supporting the establishment of inter-organizational networks and knowledge transfer.[1318] This work has focused on the interplay of these promotors with young entrepreneurial firms indicating their relevance their provision of structural capital and their expertise. A widening of this aspect regarding the influence of promotors to establish regional open innovation structures may offer valuable results for public policy to shape the regional economic, respectively entrepreneurial climate. Specifically, their positioning within the regional context as a network of promotors following shared goals may be of critical value.[1319]

Especially among young knowledge-intensive entrepreneurial firms does the role of proximity have to be emphasized to contribute to a reciprocal reduction of uncertainty and thus promote the establishment of inter-organizational relations and transaction processes.[1320] The regional context of an entrepreneurial firm, therefore, is a critical component enabling the emergence and pursuit of entrepreneurial opportunities.[1321] In this regard, the establishment of entrepreneurial networks has been emphasized as "an important intangible asset that entrepreneurs must take into account during the gestation period of a firm."[1322] This work confirmed this statement but limited its range to a demand-based perspective allowing for a utility maximization of relational investments. This demand-based approach to entrepreneurial networking draws on capacity limitations entrepreneurial firms face in engaging in network activities emphasizing the establishment of ties to innovation promotors serving as hubs to establish contacts if demand and capacities prevail for expanding the organically established corporate network to trusted collaboration partners. This perspective accords to the concept of co-innovation competence introduced with the aim of a continuous evolvement of the corporate technology base and its social capital based on inter-organizational transaction respectively value creation processes. To achieve such a dynamic evolvement co-innovation capabilities are required for screening the environmental context of the firm to effectively explore and transform exogenous knowledge sources and to commercially exploit the corporate technology base. Since this competence-based approach pioneers in innovation management and strategic entrepreneurship future research may be relevant to establish the concept in these fields. In this regard, an assessment of strategies and tactics of entrepreneurial firms in evaluating its corporate environment

1318   See Fichter 2009; Winch/Courtney 2007, p. 751.
1319   See Porter/Kramer 2011; Doepfer et al. 2012. Also see Rabe 2007, pp. 69-73.
1320   See Foray 2006, p. 101; Glaeser et al. 1992; Jacobs 1969; Storper/Veneables 2004; Eriksson 2011.
1321   See Shane/Locke/Collins 2003, p. 274.
1322   Pena 2002, p. 194.

for engaging in co-innovation projects may offer a valuable insight. Specifically, with reference to I&C technologies a strategic approach to internet-based communication and the search for information may represent a relevant field for future investigation.[1323]

In light of these strategic considerations, it is to be critically noted that, in the end, the entrepreneurial motivation to strive for growth and the willingness of the entrepreneur to pursue opportunities can be considered as the most decisive enabling factors and serve as critical preconditions for achieving of entrepreneurial performance.[1324]

7.2 Derived Managerial Implications

7.2.1 Implications for Entrepreneurs of Knowledge-Intensive Firms

A review of the state of discussion in the fields of strategic entrepreneurship and innovation management has showed that the terms 'open innovation' and 'networking' have achieved a ubiquitous position and are predominantly discussed as panacea to improving corporate performance. Empirical research in the form of discussions with entrepreneurs showed that those terms are likewise being discussed among practitioners. However, skepticism persists especially among knowledge-intensive entrepreneurial firms skepticism persist as to how these concepts can be applied to daily business and working routines and effectively contribute to corporate performance. This work, therefore, has taken a critical stance toward open innovation and networking by discussing the terms from an entrepreneurial perspective and considering constraining factors involved. In this regard, a lack of trust and suspicion of opportunistic behavior among entrepreneurial firms toward potential collaboration partners was identified,[1325] as well as a lack of willingness to build social relations in apprehension of networking inefficiencies referring to an imbalance of the investment into social capital aligned to organizational goals.[1326]

Relating these aspects to specific competences to perform co-innovation allows for the establishment of a strategic approach. This approach strives for an economic exploitation of the environmental context of the firm increasing innovation performance and the achievement of a competitive advantage. The quality of prevailing corporate resources in the form of technologies and specific skills to apply them to value creation processes serve

---

1323   See Porter 2001.
1324   See Shane/Venkataraman 2000, p. 218; Shane/Locke/Collins 2003, p. 257; Littunen 2000, p. 295; Lumpkin/Dess 1996, p. 140; Stevenson/Jarillo 1990, p. 25.
1325   See Nooteboom 2000a, p. 919; Hoecht/Trott 1999, p. 266.
1326   See Krackhardt/Hanson 1993, p. 110; Woolcock/Narayan 2000, p. 231; Witt 2004, p. 395.

as fundamental component of co-innovation.[1327] This emphasizes the relevance of formulating a precise business model differentiating between core capabilities as the basis of corporate value creation competence, critical capabilities relevant to market products and services, and contextual capabilities contributing to perform market interactions and information backflows into the value-creation process. [1328] To approach an interorganizational innovation perspective, these capabilities need to be aligned to the corresponding capabilities of network partners with reference to the critical resource of corporate social capital. This resource base may result from the organic establishment of a strong-tied corporate network structure based on previous collaboration projects.

An assessment, respectively screening of capabilities accessible to the firm may result in the identification of complementary assets suitable for collaboration and achieving co-innovation.[1329] By evaluating the capabilities of potential collaboration partners specific objectives can be defined such as the spread of fixed costs and/or an extension of market access for diffusion accelerating the innovation process and reducing the risks involved.[1330] If entrepreneurial opportunities cannot be identified within these strong relations, an outreach beyond the network of trusted relations is to be carried out indicating the relevance of weak ties.[1331] The awareness of and relationship to innovation promotors may increase the effectiveness in identifying new contacts appropriate for future collaboration. These may possess the knowledge of the range of capabilities of an array of firms as well as trusted relations to these firms enabling the establishment of contacts for collaboration.[1332]

To perform co-innovation a precise structuring of the alliance is required. In this regard, an essential precondition to achieving positive results based on the realization of synergies, on the one hand, individual responsibilities and, on the other hand, interorganizational knowledge sharing routines need to be defined.[1333] This necessitates that each collaboration partner is required to continuously evolve its resource base by transferring new information and reciprocally contributing to the collective innovation competence.[1334] Furthermore, a dynamic governance structure should be applied allowing for the pursuit of emerging opportunities as well as a reaction to changing market conditions.[1335]

1327   See Sanchez/Heene/Thomas 1996, p. 7.
1328   See Chesbrough/Schwartz 2007, pp. 56-57. Also see Coombs 1996, p. 351-352; Collins 1994, p. 144; Grant 1996, pp. 377-378.
1329   See Teece 1986, p.289; Harryson 2006, p. 354.
1330   See Dyer/Singh 1998, p. 668; Chesbrough/Schwartz 2007, p. 56.
1331   See Davidsson/Honig 2003, p. 325. Also see Granovetter 1973; Burt 1992, p. 27.
1332   See Fichter 2009, p. 360; Gemünden/Walter 1999, pp. 119-120.
1333   See Chesbrough/Schwartz 2007, pp. 57-58; Dyer/Singh 1998, p. 664; Hagedoorn/Duysters 2002, p. 169.
1334   See Bossink 2002, p. 315.
1335   See Dyer/Singh 1998, p. 669.

The cornerstone of the collaboration, consequently, is the establishment of shared values, which serves as enabling factor to create inter-organizational flows of knowledge amplifying the potential co-innovation performance.[1336] Based on this procedure corporations extend their technological base as well as their range of collaboration partners serving as basis for future co-innovation projects.

This strategic approach to co-innovation contributes to a systemized management of constraining factors of open innovation and networked entrepreneurship. However, as indicated in this work, the mindset of the entrepreneur to believe in "the power of co-creation"[1337] needs to be considered as most relevant factor to engage in inter-organizational value creation processes.[1338] The application of an open entrepreneurship which builds on an open exchange of knowledge and ideas to collaboratively pursue entrepreneurial opportunities, consequently, may consequently emerge only if entrepreneurial firms are willing to invest in social relations and trust in the economic potentials of a knowledge-based economy.

7.2.2 Implications for Regional Innovation Promotors

"Firms are often not able to produce all necessary services in-house, and where these services involve transactional ambiguities (as in technology research or labour training) and asset specificity (as in acquiring and using dedicated equipment) some form of public intervention may lead to more efficient solutions for firms."[1339]

In this work has emphasized the role of regional institutional representatives acting as promotors of innovation, focusing on the interplay of these promotors with young knowledge-intensive entrepreneurial firms. Innovation promotors enable corporations to achieve economic performance, by providing and/or diffusing knowledge, contacts and resources within the regional economic structure and therefore enhancing the capacity of the firms to perform innovation.[1340] Consequently, by providing expertise as well as structural capital to establish knowledge flows among regional actors they serve as mediators and brokers enhancing inter-organizational collaboration for innovation.[1341]

The empirical investigation showed that entrepreneurial firms value the relevance of innovation promotors however, only a limited number of firms actively collaborate with

---

1336   See Porter/Kramer 2011.
1337   See Ramaswamy/Gouillart 2010.
1338   See Shane/Venkataraman 2000, p. 218; Shane/Locke/Collins 2003, p. 257; Littunen 2000, p. 295.
1339   Staber 1996, p. 4.
1340   See Witte 1999, p. 15; Hauschild/Salomo 2011, p. 125; Doloreux 2003, p. 71; Sternberg 2007, p. 654; 2009, p. 23.
1341   See Fichter 2009, p. 360; Winch/Courtney 2007, p. 751; Chesbrough 2006c, p. 152; Howells 2006a.

promotors and/or are aware of the existence of their range of promotional activities.[1342] This lack of information regarding the scope of regional promotional services and infrastructure, therefore, may serve as initial aspects for deriving practical implications to amplify the effectiveness of regional innovation promotors. A reason for this lack of information may lie in the fact that regional promotors predominantly act independently representing the individual competences and services of their corresponding institutions, such as industry associations, business incubators, universities and banks. This leads to the problem that entrepreneurs do not have a transparent overview of regional promotional services available to them to identify appropriate actors to serve their specific needs at low information costs.

An approach to overcome this problem may be seen in the establishment of inter-organizational collaboration of these actors creating a network of innovation promotors.[1343] This network may serve as the infrastructural precondition to formulate goals and determine shared values to collectively contribute to an enhancement of the regional entrepreneurial climate.[1344] The establishment of a mutual communication platform to display the prevailing range of regional services offered to support entrepreneurial firms may directly contribute to closing an information gap.[1345] By leveraging competences and assigning specific responsibilities among the actors regional innovation promotion efficiency may be amplified. Collectively, workshops and networking as well as information events can be organized to reduce the individual work load and costs while increasing the reputation of the regional entrepreneurial climate. A networked approach to regional innovation promotion, consequently, is a critical aspect for creating, or respectively, increasing regional entrepreneurship capital.[1346]

1342   This finding is also confirmed by the empirical investigation by Raabe (2007, pp. 273-274).
1343   See Rabe 2007, pp. 69-73.
1344   See Porter/Kramer 2011; Doepfer et al. 2012.
1345   The city of Münster, Germany, serves as empirical example providing an internet-based information plattform which in detail displays the range of regional services to promote entrepreneurial firms (see www.muenster-gruendet.de).
1346   See Audretsch/Keilbach 2004.

Bibliography

Abraham, S. (2005): Stretching strategic thinking. In: Strategy & Leadership, Vol. 33, No. 5, pp. 5–12.

Acs, Z./Braunerhjelm, P./Audretsch, D./Carlsson, B. (2009): The knowledge spillover theory of entrepreneurship. In: Small Business Economics, Vol. 32, No. 1, pp. 15–30.

Acs, Z./Szerb, L. (2007): Entrepreneurship, Economic Growth and Public Policy. In: Small Business Economics, Vol. 28, No. 2, pp. 109–122.

Adler, J. H. (1965): Absorptive Capacity. The Concept and Its Determinants, Washington DC.

Adler, P. S./Kwon, S.-W. (2002): Social Capital: Prospects for a New Concept. In: The Academy of Management Review, Vol. 27, No. 1, pp. 17–40.

Ahuja, G. (2000): The Duality of Collaboration: Inducements and Opportunities in the Formation of Interfirm Linkages. In: Strategic Management Journal, Vol. 21, No. 3, pp. 317–343.

Ahuja, G./Katila, R. (2001): Technological Acquisitions and the Innovation Performance of Acquiring Firms: A Longitudinal Study. In: Strategic Management Journal, Vol. 22, No. 3, pp. 197–219.

Akerlof, G. A. (1970): The Market for "Lemons": Quality Uncertainty and the Market Mechanism. In: Quarterly Journal of Economics, Vol. 84, No. 3, pp. 488–500.

Albers, S./Klapper, D./Konradt, U./Walter, A./Wolf, J. (2009): Methodik der empirischen Forschung. Gabler, Wiesbaden.

Aldrich, H.E./Zimmer, C, (1986a): Entrepreneurship through Social Networks. In: Aldrich (Ed.): Population Perspectives on Organizations.Acta Universitatis Upsaliensis, Uppsala, pp. 13–28.

Aldrich, H./Zimmer C. (1986b): Entrepreneurship through social networks. In: Sexton/Smilor (Eds.): The Art and science of entrepreneurship: Ballinger Pub. Co. Cambridge, Mass, pp. 3-23.

Almeida, P./Kogut, B. (1999):Localization of knowledge and the mobility of engineers in regional networks. In: Management Science, Vol. 45, No. 7, pp. 905-917.

Almirall, E./Casadesus-Masanell, R. (2010): Open versus closed innovation: A model of discovery and divergence. In: Academy of Management Review, Vol. 35, No. 1, pp. 27–47.

Alvarez, S. A./Barney, J. B. (2002): Resource-based theory and the entrepreneurial firm. In: Hitt/Ireland/Camp/Sexton (Eds.): Strategic entrepreneurship: Creating a new mindset. Blackwell Publishers, Oxford, pp. 89–105.

Alvesson, M. (1993): Organizations as Rhetoric: Knowledge-Intensive Firms and the Struggle With Ambiguity. In: Journal of Management Studies, Vol. 30, No. 6, pp. 997–1015.

Amabile, T. M. (1998): How to Kill Creativity. In: Harvard Business Review, Vol. 76, No. 5, pp. 77–87.

Amit, R./Schoemaker, P. J. (1993): Strategic assets and organizational rent. In: Strategic Management Journal, Vol. 14, No. 1, pp. 33–46.

Anand, B.N./Khanna, T. (2000): The structure of licensing contracts. In: Journal of Industrial Economics, Vol. 48, No. 1, pp. 103–135.

Andersson, M./Hellerstedt, K. (2009): Location Attributes and Start-ups in Knowledge-Intensive Business Services. In: Industry & Innovation, Vol. 16, No. 1, pp. 103–121.

Antonelli, C. (2008): The new economics of the university: a knowledge governance approach. In: The Journal of Technology Transfer, Vol. 33, No. 1, pp. 1–22.

Ansoff, H.I. (1984): Implementing Strategic Management. Prentice-Hall, Englewood Cliffs.

Apple Inc. (2012): Q1 2012 Unaudited Summary Data. Online: http://images.apple.com/pr/pdf/q1f y12datasum.pdf.

Armington, C./Acs, Z. J. (2002): The Determinants of Regional Variation in New Firm Formation. In: Regional Studies, Vol. 36, No. 1, pp. 33–45.

Arrow, K.J. (1962): Economic welfare and the allocation of resources for invention. In: National Bureau of Economic Research (Ed.): The Rate and Direction of Inventive Activity. Princeton University Press, Princeton, pp. 609–625.

Arthur, B. (1989): Competing technologies, increasing returns and lock-in by historical events. In: The Economic Journal, Vol. 99, No. 391, pp. 116–131.

Asheim, B. T./Coenen, L. (2005): Knowledge Bases and Regional Innovation Systems: Comparing Nordic Clusters. In: Research Policy, Vol. 34, No. 8, pp. 1173-1190.

Asheim, B. T./Cooke, P. N. (1998): Localized innovation networks in a global economy: A comparative analysis of endogenous and exogenous regional development approaches. In: Comparative Social Research, Vol. 17, pp. 199–240.

Asheim, B.T./Isaksen, A. (1997): Location, agglomeration and innovation: toward regional innovation systems in Norway? In: European Planning Studies, Vol. 5, No. 3, pp. 299-330.

Asheim, B. T./Isaksen, A./Nauwelaers, C./Tötdling, F. (2003): Regional innovation policy for smallmedium enterprises. Edward Elgar, Cheltenham.

AUDI AG (2010): Annual Report 2010. Ingolstadt.

Audretsch, D./Aldridge, T. (2009): Knowledge spillovers, entrepreneurship and regional development. In: Capello/Nijkamp (Eds.): Handbook of regional growth and development theories: Elgar. Cheltenham, pp. 201–238.

Audretsch, D./Keilbach, M. (2004): Entrepreneurship Capital and Economic Performance. In: Regional Studies, Vol. 38, No. 8, pp. 949–959.

Audretsch, D./Lehmann, E. E. (2005): Does the Knowledge Spillover Theory of Entrepreneurship hold for Regions? In: Research Policy, Vol. 34, pp. 1191–1202.

Azoulay, P./Shane, S. (2001): Entrepreneurs, Contracts, and the Failure of Young Firms. In: Management Science, Vol. 47, No. 3, pp. 337–358.

Babcock-Lumish, T. L. (2010): Trust Network Sclerosis: The Hazard of Trust in Innovation Investment Communities. In: Journal of Financial Transformation, Vol. , No. 29, pp. 163–173.

Backhaus, K./Erichson, B./Plinke, W./Weiber, R. (2003): Multivariate Analyzemethoden. Eine anwendungsorientierte Einführung. Springer, Berlin.

Baldacchino, G./Dana, L. P. (2009): The Impact of Public Policy on Entrepreneurship: A Critical Investigation of the Protestant Ethic on a Divided Island Jurisdiction. In: Journal of Small Business & Entrepreneurship, Vol. 19, No. 4, pp. 419–430.

Baldegger, R. J. (2008): Entrepreneurial strategy and innovation. Growth Publ., Fribourg.

Baloh, P./Jha, S./Awazu, Y. (2008): Building strategic partnerships for managing innovation outsourcing. In: Strategic Outsourcing: an International Journal, Vol. 1, No. 2, pp. 100–121.

Barnett, H.G. (1953): Innovation - The Basis of Cultural Change. McGraw-Hill, New York.

Barney, J. B. (1991): Firm Resources and Sustained Competitive Advantage. In: Journal of Management, Vol. 17, No. 1, pp. 99–120.

Bathelt, H./Glückler, J. (2003): Wirtschaftsgeographie. Ökonomische Beziehungen in räumlicher Perspektive. Ulmer, Stuttgart.

Battor, M./Battor, M. (2010): The impact of customer relationship management capability on innovation and performance advantages: testing a mediated model. In: Journal of Marketing Management, Vol. 26, No. 9-10, pp. 842–857.

Baum, J.A./Calabrese, T./Silverman, B.S. (2000): Dont't go it alone: Allinace network composition and startups' performance in Canadian biotechnology. In: Strategic Management Journal, Vol. 21, No. 3, pp. 267-294.

Baume, S./Ofei, A./Boateng, O. (1996): Engaging in dynamic innovation. In: Journal of Entrepreneurship and Creativity, Vol. 1, pp. 52–59.

Bavarian Ministry of Economics, Infrastructure, Traffic and Technology (2011): Konjunkturbericht Bayern, Wirtschaft und Arbeitsmarkt im 3. Vierteljahr 2011. München.

Bea, F. X./Dichtl, E./Schweitzer, M. (2000): Allgemeine betriebswirtschaftslehre. 8th Vol. Lucius & Lucius, Sututtgart.

Beaudry, C./Schiffauerova, A. (2009): Who's right, Marshall or Jacobs? The localization versus urbanization debate" In: Research Policy, Vol. 38, No. 2, pp. 318-337.

Beckman, C. M./Haunschild, P. R. (2002): Network Learning: The Effects of Partners' Heterogeneity of Experience on Corporate Acquisitions. In: Administrative Science Quarterly, Vol. 47, No. 1, pp. 92–124.

Beelaerts van Blokland, W. W./Verhagen, W. J./Santema, S. C. (2008): The Effects of Co-Innovation on the Value-time Curve: Quantitative Study on Product Level. In: Journal of business market management, Vol. 2, No. 1, pp. 5–24.

Bellu, R. (1993): Task role motivation and attributional style as predictors of entrepreneurial performance: female sample findings. In: Entrepreneurship & Regional Development, Vol. 5, No. 4, pp. 331–334.

Belussi, F./Sammarra, A./Sedita, S. R. (2010): Learning at the boundaries in an "Open Regional Innovation System": A focus on firms' innovation strategies in the Emilia Romagna life science industry. In: Research Policy, Vol. 39, No. 6, pp. 710-721.

Bengtsson, L./von Haartman, R. /Dabhilkar, M. (2009): Low-Cost versus Innovation. Contrasting Outsourcing and Integration Strategies in Manufacturing. In: Creativity & Innovation Management, Vol. 18, No. 1, pp. 35–47.

Berg, B.L. (2004): Qualitative research methods for the social sciences. Pearson, Boston.

Berger, C./Möslein, K./Piller, F./Reichwald, R. (2005): Co-designing modes of cooperation at the customer interface: learning from exploratory research. In: European Management Review, Vol. 2, No. 1, pp. 70–87.

Bergfeld, M.-M. H. (2009): Global innovation leadership. The strategic development of worldwide innovation competence. Books on Demand, Norderstedt.

Bergfeld, M.-M./Doepfer, B. C. (2009): Innovation in Outsourcing Alliances: Managing the Prisoner's Dilemma of Cooperative Competence Building. In: Proceedings of the R&D Management Conference 2009, Vienna, Austria.

Bergmann, H./Sternberg, R. (2007): The Changing Face of Entrepreneurship in Germany. In: Small Business Economics, Vol. 28, No. 2, pp. 205–221.

Bessant, J.R./Tidd, J. (2011): Innovation and entrepreneurship. Wiley, Chichester.

Bettis, R. A./Prahalad, C. K. (1995): The dominant logic: Retrospective and extension. In: Strategic Management Journal, Vol. 16, No. 1, pp. 5–14.

Birley, S. (1985): The Role of Networks in the Entrepreneurial Process. In: Journal of Business Venturing, Vol. 1, pp. 107-117.

Björk, J./Magnusson, M. (2009): Where Do Good Innovation Ideas Come From? Exploring the Influence of Network Connectivity on Innovation Idea Quality. In: Journal of Product Innovation Management, Vol. 26, No. 6, pp. 662–670.

Black, B. S./Gilson, R. J. (1998): Venture capital and the structure of capital markets: banks versus stock markets. In: Journal of Financial Economics, Vol. 47, No. 3, pp. 243–277.

Block, J./Koellinger, P. (2009): I Can't Get No Satisfaction—Necessity Entrepreneurship and Procedural Utility. In: Kyklos, Vol. 62, No. 2, pp. 191–209.

Bogner, A./Menz, W. (2009): Das theoriegeleitete Experteninterview. Erkenntnisinteresse, Wissensformen, Interaktion. In: Bogner/Littig/Menz (Eds.): Das Experteninterview. Theorie, Methode, Anwendungsfelder. VS Verlag für Sozialwissenschaften, Wiesbaden, pp. 61-98.

Bortenschlager, K./Gehre, C./Hartlieb, M./Wernicke, P. (2010): Development of Crash Test Dummies - Requirements of the Automotive Industry. FISITA-World Automotive Congress, Budapest, Hungary.

Boschma, R. (2005): Proximity and innovation: a critical assessment. In: Regional Studies, Vol. 39, No. 1, pp. 61-74.

Boschma, R./Iammarino, S. (2009): Related Variety,Trade Linkages, and Regional Growth in Italy. In: Economic Geography, Vol. 85, No. 3, pp. 289-311.

Bossink, B. A. (2002): The development of co-innovation strategies: stages and interaction patterns in interfirm innovation. In: R&D Management, Vol. 32, No. 4, pp. 311–320.

Boutellier, R./Gassmann, O./von Zedtwitz, M. (2008): Managing Global Innovation. Uncovering the secrets of future competitiveness. 3rd Vol., Springer, Berlin.

Bouwen, R./Steyaert, C. (1990): Construing Organizational Texture in Young Entrepreneurial Firms. In: Journal of Management Studies, Vol. 27, No. 6, pp. 637–649.

Boxman, E. A./de Graaf, P. M./Flap, H. D. (1991): The impact of social and human capital on the income attainment of Dutch managers. In: Social Networks, Vol. 13, No. 1, pp. 51–73.

Boyens, K. (1998): Externe Verwertung von technologischem Wissen. Gabler, Wiesbaden.

Brandt, A. (2010): Region Ingolstadt - Regional TÜV. Nord/LB Regionalwirtschaft. Hannover.

Brazeal, D. V./Herbert, T. T. (1999): The Genesis of Entrepreneurship. In: ET&P, Vol. , No. Spring, pp. 29–45.

Brenner, M. S. (1996): Technology intelligence and technology scouting. In: Competitive Intelligence Review, Vol. 7, No. 3, pp. 20–27.

Brem, A./Voigt, K.-I. (2009): Integration of market pull and technology push in the corporate front end and innovation management—Insights from the German software industry. Technology Management in the Service Economy. In: Technovation, Vol. 29, No. 5, pp. 351–367.

Breschi, S./Malerba, F. (2005): Clusters, Networks and Innovation: Research Results and New Directions. In: Breschi/Malerba (Eds.): Clusters, Networks and Innovation. Oxford University Press, Oxford, pp. 1-25.

Brixy, U./Hundt, C./Sternberg, R. (2009): Global Entrepreneurship Monitor (GEM). Länderbericht Deutschland 2009, Hannover, Nürnberg.

Brixy, U./Hundt, C./Sternberg, R./Vorderwülbecke, A. (2011): Global Entrepreneurship Monitor (GEM). Länderbericht Deutschland 2010, Hannover, Nürnberg.

Brockhoff, K. (2003): Customers' perspectives of involvement in new product development. In: International Journal of Technology Management, Vol. 26, No. 5/6, p. 464.

Brouwer, M. T. (2002): Weber, Schumpeter and Knight on entrepreneurship and economic development. In: Journal of Evolutionary Economics, Vol. 12, No. 1, pp. 83–105.

Brown, T. E./Davidsson, P./Wiklund, J. (2001): An Operationalization of Stevenson's Conceptualization of Entrepreneurship as Opportunity-Based Firm Behavior. In: Strategic Management Journal, Vol. 22, No. 10, pp. 953–968.

Brüderl, J./Preisendörfer, P. (1998): Network Support and the Success of Newly Founded Business. In: Small Business Economics, Vol. 10, No. 3, pp. 213–225.

Bruhn, M./Stauss, B. (2009): Kundenintegration. Forum Dienstleistungsmanagement.Gabler, Wiesbaden.

Bühner, M. (2003): Einführung in die Test-undFragebogenkonstruktion. Pearson, München.

Bunell, T./Coe, N. (2001): Spaces and Scales of Innovation. In: Progress in Human Geography, Vol. 25, No. 4, pp. 569–589.

Bunker Whittington, K./Owen-Smith, J./Powell, W. (2009): Networks, Propinquity and Innovation in Knowledge-intensive Industries. In: Administrative Science Quarterly, Vol. 54, March, pp. 90–122.

Burgelman, R. A. (1983): Corporate Entrepreneurship and Strategic Management: Insights from a Process Study. In: Management Science, Vol. 29, No. 12, pp. 1349–1364.

Burgers, J. H./Jansen, J./van Bosch, F. d./Volberda, H. W. (2009): Structural differtiation and corporate venturing. The moderating role of formal and informal integration mechanisms. In: Journal of Business Venturing, Vol. 24, pp. 206–220.

Burt, R.S. (1992): Structural Holes. The Social Structure of Competition. Harvard University Press, Cambridge.

Burt, R. S. (1997): The Contingent Value of Social Capital. In: Administrative Science Quarterly, Vol. 42, No. 2, pp. 339–365.

Burt, R. S. (2005): Brokerage and closure. An introduction to social capital. Oxford Univ. Press, Oxford.

Butler, P.; Saxberg, L. (2001): Entrepreneurial succession, firm growth and performance. In: Journal of Enterprising Culture, Vol.9, No.1, pp. 405–436.

Caliendo, M./Kritikos, A. S. (2010): Start-ups by the unemployed: characteristics, survival and direct employment effects. In: Small Business Economics, Vol. 35, No. 1, pp. 71–92.

Cant, M./Jeynes, L. (1998): What does outsourcing bring you that innovation cannot? How outsourcing is seen - and currently marketed - as a universal panacea. In: Total Quality Management, Vol. 9, No. 2/3, pp. 193–201.

Camagni, R. (1995): The Concept of Innovative Milieu and its Relevance for Public Policies in European Lagging Regions. In: Papers in Regional Science, Vol. 74, No. 4, pp. 317–340.

Camagni, R. (1999): Introduction: From the local milieu to innovation through cooperation networks. In: Camagni, R. (ed.): Innovation networks: spatial perspectives. Belhaven Press, London, pp. 1-12.

Cameron, K./Freeman, S. (1991): Cultural congruence, strength, and type - Relationships to effectiveness. In: Research in Organizational Change and Development, Vol. 5, pp. 23–58.

Campos, E. B./Pomeda, J. R. (2007): On knowledge, networks, social capital and trust in innovation environments. In: International Journal of Entrepreneurship and Innovation Management, Vol. 7, No. 6, p. 575.

Cardoso, M./Carvalho, J. V./Ramos, I. (2009): Open Innovation Communities...or should it be "Networks". In: Lytras/Damiani /Ordóñez de Pablos (Eds.): Web 2.0 -- The Business Model, Springer, Berlin, pp. 1–22.

Castelfranchi, C./Falcone, R. F. (2006): Being Trusted in a Social Network: Trust as Relational Capital. In: Hutchison/Kanade/Kittler/Kleinberg/Mattern/Mitchell/Naor/Nierstrasz/ Pandu-Rangan/Steffen/Sudan/Terzopoulos/Tygar/Vardi/Weikum/Stølen/Winsborough/ Martinelli/Massacci (Eds.): Lecture Notes in Computer Science: Springer, Berlin, pp. 19–32.

Chakravarthy, B. (1986): Measuring Strategic Performance. In: Strategic Management Journal, Vol.7, No.5, pp. 437–458.

Chatterji, A. K. (2009): Spawned with a silver spoon? Entrepreneurial performance and innovation in the medical device industry. In: Strategic Management Journal, Vol. 30, No. 2, pp. 185–206.

Chen, H./Gompers, P./Kovner, A./Lerner, J. (2010): Buy local? The geography of venture capital. In: Journal of Urban Economics, Vol. 67, No. 1, pp. 90–102.

Chen, M.-J./Hambrick, D. C. (1995): Speed, Stealth, and Selective Attack: How Small Firms Differ from Large Firms in Competitive Behavior. In: The Academy of Management Journal, Vol. 38, No. 2, pp. 453–482.

Chen, Y. (2005): Vertical Disintegration. In: Journal of Economics and Management Strategy, Vol. 14, No. 1, pp. 209–229.

Chesbrough, H.W. (2003a): Open innovation: The new imperative for creating and profiting from technology. Harvard Business School Press, Boston.

Chesbrough, H.W. (2003b): The Era of Open Innovation. In: MIT Sloan Management Review, 44. Vol., No. 3, pp. 35-41.

Chesbrough, H.W. (2004): Managing Open Innovation. In: Research Technology Management, Vol. 44, No. 3, p. 23-26.

Chesbrough, H. W. (2006a): Open Innovation: A new paradigm for understanding industrial innovation. In: Chesbrough/Vanhaverbeke/West (Eds.): Open innovation. Researching a new paradigm: Oxford University Press. Oxford, pp. 1–14.

Chesbrough, H. W. (2006b): Open Innovation: New Puzzles and New Findings. In: Chesbrough/Vanhaverbeke/West (Eds.): Open innovation. Researching a new paradigm: Oxford University Press. Oxford, pp. 15-34.

Chesbrough, H. W. (2006c): Open business models. How to thrive in the new innovation landscape. Harvard Business School Press, Boston, Mass.

Chesbrough, H. W./Prencipe, A. (2008): Networks of innovation and modularity: a dynamic perspective. In: International Journal of Technology Management, Vol. 42, No. 4, p. 414.

Chesbrough, H. W./Schwartz, K. (2007): Innovating Business Models with Co-Development Pertnerships. In: Research Technology Management, Vol. 50, No. 1, pp. 55–59.

Chiaroni, D./Chiesa, V./Frattini, F. (2010): Unravelling the process from Closed to Open Innovation: evidence from mature, asset-intensive industries. In: R&D Management, Vol. 40, No. 3, pp. 222–245.

Chiles, T. H./McMackin, J. F. (1996): Integrating Variable Risk Preferences, Trust, and Transaction Cost Economics. In: The Academy of Management Review, Vol. 21, No. 1, pp. 73–99.

Choi, B. C./Pak A. W. (2006): Multidisciplinarity, interdisciplinarity and transdisciplinarity in health research, services, education and policy: 1. Definitions, objectives, and evidence of effectiveness. In: Clinical and investigative medicine, Vol. 29, No. 6, pp. 351-364.

Christensen, J. F./Olesen, M. H./Kjaer, J. S. (2005): The industrial dynamics of open innovation: evidence from the transformation of consumer electronics. In: , Vol. 34, No. 10, pp. 1533–1549.

Chu, K./Chan H.C (2009): Community based innovation: its antecedents and its impact on innovation success. In: Internet Research, Vol. 19, No. 5, pp. 496–516.

Chung, S. (2002): Building a national innovation system through regional innovation systems. In: Technovation, Vol. 22, No. 8, pp. 485-491.

Ciappini, A./Corso, M./Perego, A. (2008): From ICT outsourcing to strategic sourcing. managing customer-supplier relations for continuous innovation capabilities. In: International Journal of Technology Management, Vol. 42, No. 1/2, pp. 185–203.

Coenen, L./Moodysson, J./Asheim, B. T. (2004): Nodes, networks and proximities: on the knowledge dynamics of the Medicon Valley biotech cluster. In: European Planning Studies, Vol. 12, No. 7, pp. 1003–1018.

Cohen, S./Fields, G. (2000): Social Capital and Capital Gains in Silicon Valley. In: Lesser (Ed.): Knowledge and Social Capital. Foundations and Applications. Butterworth-Heinemann, Boston, pp. 179-200.

Cohen, W.M./Levinthal, D.A. (1990): Absorptive capacity: a new perspective on learning and innovation. In: Administrative science quarterly, Vol. 35, No. 1, pp. 128-152.

Coleman, J. S. (1988): Social Capital in the Creation of Human Capital. In: American Journal of Sociology, Vol. 94, pp. 95-120.

Collis, D. J. (1994): Research Note: How Valuable are Organizational Capabilities? In: Strategic Management Journal, Vol. 15, No. S1, pp. 143–152.

Cooke, P. (2001): Regional Innovation Systems, Clusters, and the Knowledge Economy. In: Industrial and Corporate Change, Vol. 10, No. 4, pp. 945–974.

Cooke, P. (2004): Regional innovation systems: an evolutionary approach. In: Cooke, P./Heidenreich, M./Braczyk, H.-J. (Eds.): Regional Innovation Systems: The Role of Governance in a Globalized World, London, pp. 1–18.

Cooke, P. (2005): Regionally asymmetric knowledge capabilities and open innovation. Exploring 'Globalisation 2' – A new model of industry organization, In: Research policy, Vol. 34, No. 3, pp. 1128-1149.

Cooke, p. (2009): Rgionale Innovationssysteme, Cluster und die Wissensökonomie. In: Blättel-Mink/Ebner (Eds.): Innovationssysteme. Gabler, Wiesbaden, pp. 87-116.

Cooke, P./Boekholt, P./Tödtling, F. (2000): The governance of innovation in Europe. Regional perspectives on global competitiveness. Pinter, London, New York.

Cooke, P./Uranga, M. G./Etxebarria, G. (1998): Regional systems of innovation: an evolutionary perspective. In: Environment and Planning A, Vol. 30, No. 9, pp. 1563–1584.

Coombs, R. (1996): Core competencies and the strategic management of R&D. In: R&D Management, Vol. 26, No. 4, pp. 345–355.

Cordero, R. (1990): The measurement of innovation performance in the firm: an overview. In: Research Policy, Vol. 19, No. 2, pp. 185–192.

Corno, F./Reinmoeller, P./Nonaka, I. (1999): Knowledge Creation within Industrial Systems. In: Journal of Management and Governance, Vol. 3, No. 4, pp. 379–394.

Coulter, K. S./Coulter, R. A. (2003): The effects of industry knowledge on the development of trust in service relationships. In: International Journal of Research in Marketing, Vol. 20, No. 1, pp. 31–43.

Covin, J. G./Slevin, D. P. (1989): Strategic management of small firms in hostile and benign environments. In: Strategic Management Journal, Vol.10, No.1, p. 75–87.

Covin, J. G./Slevin, D. P. (2002): The entrepreneurial imperatives of strategic leadership. In: Hitt/Ireland/Camp/Sexton (Eds.): Strategic entrepreneurship: Creating a new mindset. Oxford: Blackwell Publishers, pp. 309–327.

Creswell, J.W. (1998): Qualitative inquiry and research design: choosing among five traditions. Sage, Thousand Oaks.

Cropper, S./Ebers, M./Huxham, C./Ring, P. S. (2008, Eds.): The Oxford handbook of interorganizational relations. Oxford Univ. Press, Oxford.

Crossan, M. M./Lane, H. W./White, R. E. (1999): An Organizational Learning Framework: From Intuition to Institution. In: The Academy of Management Review, Vol. 24, No. 3, pp. 522–537.

Dahlander, L./Gann, D. M. (2010): How open is innovation? In: Research Policy, Vol. 39, No. 6, pp. 699–709.

Dahlander, L./Wallin, M. W. (2006): A man on the inside: Unlocking communities as complementary assets. In: Research Policy, Vol. 35, No. 8, pp. 1243–1259.

Dahlstrand, Å. L. (1997): Growth and inventiveness in technology-based spin-off firms. In: Research Policy, Vol. 26, No. 3, pp. 331–344.

Dal Fiore, F. (2007): Communities Versus Networks: The Implications on Innovation and Social Change. In: American Behavioral Scientist, Vol. 50, No. 7, pp. 857–866.

Damanpour, F. (1991): Organizational Innovation: A Meta-Analysis of Effects of Determinants and Moderators. In: The Academy of Management Journal, Vol. 34, No. 3, pp. 555–590.

Damanpour, F./Evan, W. M. (1984): Organizational Innovation and Performance: The Problem of Organizational Lag. In: Administrative Science Quarterly, Vol. 29, No. 3, pp. 392–410.

David, P. A. (1985): Clio and the economics of QWERTY. In: American Economic Review, Vol. 75, pp. 332-337.

Davidsson, P./Honig, B. (2003): The role of social and human capital among nascent entrepreneurs. In: Journal of Business Venturing, Vol. 18, No. 3, pp. 301–331.

Debackere, K./Clarysse, B./Wijneberg, N. M./Rappa, M. A. (1994): Science and industry: a theory of networks and paradigms. In: Technology Analysis & Strategic Management, Vol. 6, No. 1, pp. 21–38.

de Bondt, R. (1997): Spillovers and innovative activities. In: International Journal of Industrial Organization, Vol. 15, No. 1, pp. 1–28.

de Jong, J./van de Vrande, V./Vanhaverbeke, W./Rochemont, M. de (2009): Open innovation in SMEs: Trends, motives and management challenges. In: Technovation, Vol. 29, No. 6-7, pp. 423–437.

Delmar, F./Davidsson, P. (2000): Where do they come from? Prevalence and characteristics of nascent entrepreneurs. In: Entrepreneurship & Regional Development, Vol. 12, No. 1, pp. 1–23.

Denti, D. (2009): R&D spillovers and regional growth. In: Capello/Nijkamp (Eds.): Handbook of regional growth and development theories: Elgar. Cheltenham, pp. 211–237.

Denzin, N. K. (1978): The Research Act. McGraw-Hill, New York.

Denzin, N.K. (2003, Ed.): The landscape of qualitative research: theories and issues. Sage, Thousand Oaks.

Denzin, N. K./Lincoln, Y. S. (2005): Introduction: The Discipline and Practice of Qualitative Research. In: Denzin/Lincoln (Eds.): The SAGE Handbook of Qualitative Research. 3rd Vol., Sage Publications, Thousand Oaks, California, pp. 1–32.

De Wet, A. G./Pothas, A.–M./De Wet, J. M. (2001). Country of origin: Does it matter? In: Total Quality Management, Vol. 12, No. 2, pp. 191–200.

Dicken, P./Malmberg, A. (2009): Firms in Territories: A Relational Perspective. In: Economic Geography, Vol. 77, No. 4, pp. 345–363.

Diez, J./Kiese, M. (2009): Regional Innovation Systems. In: Thrift/Kitchin (Eds.): International encyclopedia of human geography. Elsevier, Amsterdam, pp. 246–251.

Di Gangi, P. M./Wasko, M. (2009): Steal my idea! Organizational adoption of user innovations from a user innovation community: A case study of Dell IdeaStorm. In: Decision Support Systems, Vol. 48, No. 1, pp. 303–312.

Dittrich, K./Duysters, G. (2007): Networking as a Means to Strategy Change: The Case of Open Innovation in Mobile Telephony. In: Journal of Product Innovation Management, Vol. 24, No. 6, pp. 510–521.

Doellgast, V./Greer, I. (2007): Vertical Disintegration and the Disorganization of German Industrial Relations. In: British Journal of Industrial Relations, Vol. 45, No. 1, pp. 55–76.

Doepfer, B. C. (2008): Outsourcing von Geschäftsprozessen. Effizienz versus Innovation? Igel Verlag, Hamburg.

Doepfer, B.C./Habisch, A./Pechlaner, H./Schwarz C. (2012): Entrepreneurship, Shared Values and the Region - Assessing the Conditions for Regional Social Performance of Entrepreneurial Behavior. In: Business & Society, Special Issue: The Social Performance and Responsibilities of Entrepreneurship (under Review).

Dolan, R. J./Matthews, J. M. (1993): Maximizing the Utility of Customer Product Testing: Beta Test Design and Management. In: Journal of Product Innovation Management, Vol. 10, No. 4, pp. 318–330.

Doloreux, D. (2002): What we should know about regional systems of innovation. In: Technology in Society, Vol. 24, No. 3, pp. 243–263.

Doloreux, D. (2003): Regional Innovation Systems in the Periphery: The Case of the Beauce in Québec (Canada). In: International Journal of Innovation Management, Vol. 7, No. 1, pp. 67–94.

Doloreux, D./Dionne, S. (2008): Is regional innovation system development possible in peripheral regions? Some evidence from the case of La Pocatière, Canada. In: Entrepreneurship & Regional Development, Vol. 20, No. 3, pp. 259–283.

Doloreux, D./Parto, S. (2005): Regional innovation systems: Current discourse and unresolved issues. In: Technology in Society, Vol. 27, No. 2, pp. 133–153.

Doz, Y. L. (1996a): The evolution of cooperation in strategic alliances: Initial conditions or learning processes? In: Strategic Management Journal, Vol. 17, No. 1, pp. 55–83.

Doz, Y. L. (1996b): Managing Core Competency. In: Dosi/Malerba (Eds.): Organization and Strategy in the Evolution of the Enterprise. Macmillan, Basingstoke, pp. 155-178.

Drucker, P. F. (2002): Innovation and entrepreneurship. Practice and principles. 2. Vol., Butterworth-Heinemann, Oxford.

Duranton, G./Puga, D. (2000): Diversity and Specialisation in Cities: Why, Where and When does it matter? In: Urban Studies, Vol. 37, No. 3, pp. 533-555.

Duscheck, S. (2002): Innovationen in Netzwerken, Wiesbaden.

Dyer, J. H./Singh, H. (1998): The Realtional View: Cooperative Strategy and Sources of Interorganizational Competitve Advantage. In: Academy of Management Review, Vol. 23, No. 4, pp. 660–679.

Dzisah, J./Etzkowitz, H. (2012): The age of knowledge. The dynamics of universities, knowledge and society. Leiden; Boston.

Eckey, H.F./Kosfeld, R./Türck, M. (2008): Deskriptive Statistik. Gabler, Wiesbaden.

Edquist, C. (2005): Systzems of Innovation: Perspectives and Challenges. In: Fagerberg/Mowery/Nelson (Eds.): The Oxford Handbook of Innovation. Oxford University Press, Oxford, pp. 181-208.

Elfring, T./Hulsink, W. (2007): Networking by Entrepreneurs: Patterns of Tie Formation in Emerging Organizations. In: Organization Studies, Vol. 28, No. 12, pp. 1849–1872.

Elmquist, M./Fredberg, T./Ollila, S. (2009): Exploring the field of open innovation. In: European Journal of Innovation Management, Vol. 12, No. 3, pp. 326–345.

Enkel, E. (2009): Chancen und Risiken von Open Innovation. In: Zerfass/Möslein (Eds.): Kommunikation als Erfolgsfaktor im Innovationsmanagement. Strategien im Zeitalter der open innovation: Gabler. Wiesbaden, pp. 177–192.

Enkel, E. (2010): Attributes required for profiting from open innovation in networks. In: International Journal of Technology Management, Vol. 52, No. 3/4, pp. 344–371.

Enkel, E./Gassmann, O./Chesbrough, H. (2009): Open R&D and Open Innovation. Exploring the Phenomenon. In: R&D Management Journal, Vol. 39, No. 4, pp. 311–430.

Eriksson, R. H. (2011): Localized Spillovers and Knowledge Flows: How Does Proximity Influence the Performance of Plants? In: Economic Geography. Vol. 87, Vol. 2, pp. 127–152.

Esbensen, K. H./Guyot, D./Westad, F./Houmoller, L. P. (2006): Multivariate data analysis - in practice. An introduction to multivariate data analysis and experimental design. CAMO Software, Oslo.

Espino-Rodríguez, T. F./Padrón-Robaina, V. (2006): A Review of Outsourcing from the Resource-Based View of the Firm. In: International Journal of Management Reviews, Vol. 8, No. 1, pp. 49–70.

Ethiraj, S. K./Kale, P./Krishnan, M. S./Singh, J. V. (2004): Where do capabilities come from and how do they matter? A Study in the software services Industry. In: Strategic Managemnt Journal, Vol. 26, pp. 25–45.

Etzkowitz, H. (2002): Incubation of incubators: innovation as a triple helix of University–industry–government networks. In: Science and Public Policy, Vol. 29, No. 2, pp. 115–128.

Etzkowitz, H./Dzisah, J. (2008): Rethinking development: Circulation in the triple helix. In: Technology Analysis & Strategic Management, Vol. 20, No. 6, pp. 653-666.

Etzkowitz, H./Klofsten, M. (2005): The innovating region: toward a theory of knowledge-based regional development. In: R&D Management, Vol. 35, No. 3, pp. 243-255.

Etzkowitz, H./Leydesdorff, L. (2000): The dynamics of innovation: from National Systems and „Mode 2" to a Triple Helix of university-industry-government relations. In Research Policy, Vol. 29, No. 2, pp. 109-123.

Faltin, G. (2001): Creating a Culture of Innovative Entrepreneurship. In: Journal of International Business and Economy, Vol. 2, No. 1, pp. 123–140.

Faltin, G. (2010): Kopf schlägt Kapital. Die ganz andere Art, ein Unternehmen zu gründen ; von der Lust, ein Entrepreneur zu sein. Hanser, München.

Federal Bureau of Statistics Bavaria (2010). Statistisches Jahrbuch für Bayern 2010. Bayerisches Landesamt für Statistik und Datenverarbeitung, München.

Fichter, K. (2005): Innovation Communities. Die Rolle von Promotorennetzwerken bei Nachhaltigkeitsinnovationen. In: Pfriem/Antes/Fichter/Müller/Paech/Seuring/ Siebenhüner (Eds.): Innovationen für nachhaltige Entwicklung. Gabler, Wiesbaden, pp. 287–300.

Fichter, K. (2009): Innovation communities: the role of networks of promotors in Open Innovation. In: R&D Management Journal, Vol. 39, No. 4, pp. 357–372.

Fielding, N. G. (2002): Automating the Ineffable: Qualitative Software and the Meaning of Qualitative Research. In: May (Ed.): Qualitative Research in Action. Sage, London, pp.161-178.

Fikfak, J./Adam, F./Garz, D. (2004, Eds.): Qualitative Research. Different Perspectives – Emerging Trends. Zalozba, Lubljana.

Fine, C.H. (2010): Clockspeed: Winning Industry Control in the Age of Temporary Advantage. ReadHowYouWant.

Fiorito, S. S./Laforge, R. (1986): A Marketing Strategy Analysis of Small Retailers. In: American Journal of Small Business, Vol. 10, No. 4, pp. 7–17.

Fischer, M. M. (2006): Innovation, networks, and knowledge spillovers. Selected essays. Springer, Berlin.

Flatten, T./Greve G./Brettel M. (2011): Absorptive Capacity and Firm Performance in SMEs: The Mediating Influence of Strategic Alliances. In: European Management Review, Vol. 8, No. 3, pp. 137–152.

Fleming, L./Waguespack, D. M. (2007): Brokerage, Boundary Spanning, and Leadership in Open Innovation Communities. In: Organization Science, Vol. 18, No. 2, pp. 165–180.

Flick, U. (2000): Qualitative Forschung. Theorie, Methoden, Anwendung in Psychologie und Sozialwissenschaften. Rowohlt-Taschenbuch-Verlag, Reinbek.

Florida, R./Cushing, R./Gates, G. (2002): When social capital stifles innovation. In: Harvard Business Review, Vol. 80, No. 8, p. 20.

Floyd, S. W./Woolridge, B. (1999): Knowledge creation and social networks in corporate entre-preneurship: The renewal of organizational capability. In: Entrepreneurship: Theory and Practice, Vol. 23, No. 3, pp. 123–143.

Foray, D. (2006): Economics of knowledge. MIT Press, Cambridge, Mass.

Fosfuri, A./Giarratana, M. S. (2010): Introduction: Trading under the Buttonwood--a foreword to the markets for technology and ideas. In: Industrial and Corporate Change, Vol. 19, No. 3, pp. 767–773.

Franke, G. (2002): Regionale Wissens-Spillover und Innovationserfolg industrieller Unternehmen. Lang, Frankfurt am Main u.a.

Franke, N./Shah, S. (2003): How communities support innovative activities: an exploration of assistance and sharing among end-users. In: Research Policy, Vol. 32, No. 1, pp. 157–178.

Franke, N./ von Hippel, E. /Schreier, M. (2006): Finding Commercially Attractive User Innovations: A Test of Lead-User Theory. In: Journal of Product Innovation Management, Vol. 23, No. 4, pp. 301–315.

Freeman, C. (1987): Technology Policy and Economic Performance: Lessons from Japan. Pinter, London, New York.

Freeman, C. (1991): Networks of innovation: a synthesis of research issues. In: Research Policy, Vol. 20, No. 5, pp. 499-514.

Freiling, J. (2009): Uncertainty, innovation, and entrepreneurial functions. working out an entrepreneurial management approach. In: International Journal of Technology Intelligence and Planning, Vol. 5, No. 1, pp. 22–35.

Frenken, K./van Oort, F./Verburg, T. (2007): Related Variety, Unrelated Variety and Regional Economic Growth. In: Regional Studies, Vol. 41, No. 5, pp. 685 - 697.

Fritsch, M./Mueller, P. (2007): The persistence of regional new business formation-activity over time – assessing the potential of policy promotion programs. In: Journal of Evolutionary Economics, Vol. 17, No. 3, pp. 299–315.

Fueglistaller, U./Müller, C./Volery, T./Müller, S. (2008): Entrepreneurship. Modelle, Umsetzung, Perspektiven. 2nd Vol., Gabler, Wiesbaden.

Füller, J./Bartl, M./Ernst, H./Mühlbacher, H. (2006): Community based innovation: How to integrate members of virtual communities into new product development. In: Electronic Commerce Research, Vol. 6, No. 1, pp. 57–73.

Fukuyama, F. (1997): The End of Order. Social Market Foundation, London.

Furman, J. L./Porter, M. E./Stern, S. (2002): The determinants of national innovative capacity. In: Research Policy, Vol. 31, No. 6, pp. 899–933.

Fosfuri, A. (2006): The licensing dilemma: understanding the determinants of the rate of technology licensing. In: Strategic Management Journal, Vol. 27, No. 12, pp. 1141–1158.

Gallouj, F. (2002): Knowledge - intensive business services: processing knowledge and producing innovation. In: Gadrey/Galluj (Eds.): Productivity, Innovation and Knowledge in Services. Cheltenham u.a., pp. 256–284.

Gallouj, F./Weinstein, O. (1997): Innovation in services. In: Research Policy, Vol. 26, No. , pp. 537–556.

Gans, J./Stern, S. (2003): The product market and the market for "ideas": commercialization strategies for technology entrepreneurs. In: Research Policy, Vol. 32, pp. 333–350.

García, M. S. (2006): Social capital, networks and economic development. An analysis of regional productive systems. Edward Elgar, Cheltenham.

García-Morales, V.J./Moreno, A.R./Llorens-Montes, F.J. (2006): Strategic capabilities and their effects on performance: entrepreneurial, learning, innovator and problematic SMEs. In: International Journal of Management and Enterprise Development, Vol. 3, No. 3, pp. 191-211.

Gassmann, O. (2006): Opening up the innovation process. In: R&D Management Journal, Vol. 36, No. 3, pp. 223–228.

Gassmann, O./Enkel, E. (2006): Open Innovation: Die Öffnung des Innovationsprozesses erhöht das Innovationspotential. In: ZFO - Zeitschrift Führung und Organization, Vol. 11, No. 3, pp. 132–138.

Gassmann, O./Enkel, E./Chesbrough, H. (2010): The Future of Open Innovation. In: R&D Management Journal, Vol. 40, No. 3, pp. 213–343.

Gemünden, H.G./Walter, A. (1995): Der Beziehungspromotor - Schlüsselperson für interorganizationale Innovationsprozesse. In: Zeitschrift für Betriebswirtschaft, Vol. 65., No. 9, pp. 971-986.

Gemünden, H. G./Walter, A. (1999): Beziehungspromotoren - Schlüsselpersonen für zwischenbetriebliche Innovationsprozesse. In: Hauschildt/Gemünden (Eds.): Promotoren. Champions der Innovation. 2. Aufl.: Gabler. Wiesbaden, pp. 111–131.

Gemünden, H./Rittera, T./Heydebreck, P. (1996): Network configuration and innovation success: An empirical analysis in German high-tech industries. In: International Journal of Research in Marketing, Vol. 13, No. 5, pp. 449–462.

George, V./Farris, G. (1999): Performance of alliances: formative stages and changing organizational and environmental influences. In: R&D Management, Vol. 29, No. 4, pp. 379–390.

Gehre, C. (2010): Ergebnisse aus aktuellen PDB-Projekten. Denton Crash Meeting, Heidelberg, Germany.

Gerybadze, A. (1998): Kompetenzverteilung und Integrationskonzepte für Wissenszentren in transnationalen Unternehmen. In: Kutschker (Ed.): Integration in der internationalen Unternehmung: Gabler. Wiesbaden, pp. 239–270.

Gerybadze, A. (2007): Gruppendynamik und Verstehen in Innovation Communities. In: Herstatt/Verworn (Eds.): Management der frühen Innovationsphasen. Grundlagen - Methoden - Neue Ansätze. 2. Aufl. Wiesbaden, pp. 199–213.

Gibb, A. (2002): In pursuit of a new 'enterprise' and 'entrepreneurship' paradigm for learning. creative destruction, new values, new ways of doing things and new combinations of knowledge. In: International Journal of Management Reviews, Vol. 4, No. 3, pp. 233–269.

Giddens, A. (1979): Central problems in social theory. Action, structure and contradiction in social analysis. Macmillan, London.

Giddens, A., (1976): New Rules of Sociological Method. Hutchinson, London.

Gilsing, V./Nooteboom, B. (2005): Density and strength of ties in innovation networks: an analysis of multimedia and biotechnology. In: European Management Review, Vol. 2, No. 3, pp. 179–197.

Gittell, R./Vidal, A. (1998): Community Organizing: Building Social Capital as a Development Strategy. Sage Publications, Thousand Oaks

Glaeser, E. L/Kallal, H. D./Scheinkman, J. A./Shleifer, A. (1992): Growth in cities. In: Journal of Political Economy. Vol. 100, No. 6, pp. 1126-1152.

Glaser, B.G./Strauss, A.L. (1967): The discovery of grounded theory: Strategies for qualitative research. Aldine, Chicago.

Gläser, J./Laudel, G. (2010): Experteninterviews und qualitative Inhaltsanalyse. Als Instrumente rekonstruierender Untersuchungen. VS Verlag für Sozialwissisenschaften, Wiesbaden.

Goetz, S. J./Freshwater, D. (2001): State-Level Determinants of Entrepreneurship and a Preliminary Measure of Entrepreneurial Climate. In: Economic Development Quarterly, Vol. 15, No. 1, pp. 58–70.

Gooroochurn, N./Hanley, A. (2007): A tale of two literatures. Transaction costs and property rights in innovation outsourcing. In: Research Policy, Vol. 36, No. 10, pp. 1483–1495.

Gouldner, A. W. (1960): The Norm of Reciprocity: A Preliminary Statement. In: American Sociological Review, Vol. 25, No. 2, pp. 161–178.

Gounaris, S. P. (2005): Trust and commitment influences on customer retention: insights from business-to-business services. Business-to-business relationship architecture and networks among Australia, NZ, and Asian firms. In: Journal of Business Research, Vol. 58, No. 2, pp. 126–140.

Graf, H. (2006): Networks in the Innovation Process. Local and Regional Interactions. Edward Elgar, Cheltenham.

Grafton, R. Q. (2005): Social capital and fisheries governance. In: Ocean & Coastal Management, Vol. 48, No. 9–10, pp. 753–766.

Granovetter, M. (1973): The strength of weak ties. In: American Journal of Sociology, Vol. 78, No. 6, pp. 1360–1380.

Granovetter, M. (1985): Economic action and social structure: The problem of embeddedness. In: American Journal of Sociology. 91, 3:481-510.

Grant, R. M. (1991): The resource-based theory of competitive advantage -. implications for strategy formulation. In: California Management Review, Vol. 33, No. 3, pp. 114 – 13.

Grant, R. M. (1996a): Toward a Knowledge-Based Theory of the Firm. In: Strategic Management Journal, Vol. 17, No. Special Issue: Knowledge and the Firm, pp. 109–122.

Grant, R. M. (1996b): Prospering in Dynamically-Competitive Environments: Organizational Capability as Knowledge Integration. In: Organization Science, Vol. 7, No. 4, pp. 375–387.

Gray, C. (2006): Absorptive capacity, knowledge management and innovation in entrepreneur-ial small firms. In: International Journal of Entrepreneurial Behavior & Research, Vol. 12, No. 6, pp. 345–360.

Gronhaug, K./Reve, T. (1988): Entrepreneurship and Strategic Management: Synergy or Antag-ony? In: Kaufmann (Ed.): Innovation: a cross-disciplinary perspective: Norwegian Uni-versity Press. London, pp. 331–345.

Grossman, S. J./Hart, O. (1983): An Analysis of the Principla-Agent Problem. In: Econometrica, Vol. 51, No. 1, pp. 7–45.

Hackett, S. M./Dilts, D. (2004): Systematic Review of Business Incubation Research. In: Journal of Technology Transfer, Vol. 29, No. , pp. 55–82.

Hagedoorn, J./Duysters, G. (2002): External Sources of innovative Capabilities. The preference for strategic alliances or mergers and acquisitions. In: Journal of Management Stud-ies, Vol. 39, No. 2, pp. 167–188.

Hakansson, H./Johansson, J. (2002): Formal and informal cooperation strategies in industrial networks. In: Contractor/Lorange (Eds.): Cooperative strategies in international busi-ness. Joint ventures and technology partnerships between firms. 2. Vol. Pergamon, Amsterdam, pp. 369–379.

Hamel, G./Doz, Y. L./Prahalad, C. K. (1989): Collaborate with Your Competitors--and Win. In: Harvard Business Review, Vol. 67, No. 1, pp. 133–139.

Hamel, G./Prahald, C. K. (1994a): Competing for the Future. In: Harvard Business Review, Vol. 72, No. 4, pp. 122–128.

Hamel, G./Prahalad, C. (1994b): Competing for the future. Harvard Business School Press, Bos-ton.

Hamel, G. (1991): Competition for Competence and interpartner learning within international strategic alliances. In: Strategic Management Journal, Vol. 12, No. 1, pp. 83–103.

Hansen, E. L. (1995): Entrepreneurial Networks and New Organization Growth, In: Entrepre-neurship Theory and Practice, Vol. 19, pp. 7–19.

Hansen, H. (2009): Gründungserfolg wissensintensiver Dienstleister. Theoretische und empiri-sche Überlegungen aus Sicht der Competence-based-Theory of the Firm. Gabler, Wiesbaden.

Harhoff, D. (2000): R&D Spillovers, Technological Proximity, And Productivity Growth – Evi-dence From German Panel Data. In: Schmalenbach Business Review, Vol. 52, No. 3, pp. 238–260.

Harrison, R. T./Mason, C. M. (2000): Venture capital market complementarities: The links be-tween business angels and venture capital funds in the United Kingdom. In: Venture Capital, Vol. 2, No. 3, pp. 223–242.

Harryson, S. J. (2000): Managing know-who based companies. A multinetworked approach to knowledge and innovation management, Cheltenham.

Harryson, S. J. (2006): Know-who based entrepreneurship. From knowledge creation to busi-ness implemenation. Elgar, Cheltenham.

Harryson, S. J. (2008): Entrepreneurship through relationships – navigating from creativity to commercialisation. In: R&D Management, Vol. 38, No. 3, pp. 290-310.

Hauschildt, J./Chakrabarti, A.K. (1988): Arbeitsteilung im Innovationsmanagement– Forschungsergebnisse, Kriterien und Modelle. In: Zeitschrift Führung und Organization, Vol. 57, No. 6, pp. 378-388.

Hauschildt, J./Kirchmann, E. (1997): Arbeitsteilung im innovationsmanagement zur Existenz und Effizienz von Prozesspromotoren. In: Zeitschrift Führung und Organization, Vol. 66, pp. 68–73.

Hauschildt, J./Salomo, S. (2011): Innovationsmanagement. 5. Vol. Vahlen, München.

Hayton, J. C. (2003): Strategic human capital management in SMEs: An empirical study of entrepreneurial performance. In: Human Resource Management, Vol. 42, No. 4, pp. 375–391.

Hayton, J. C. (2005): Competing in the new economy: the effect of intellectual capital on corporate entrepreneurship in high-technology new ventures. In: R&D Management, Vol. 35, No. 2, pp. 137–155.

He, Z.-L./Wong, P.-K. (2004): Exploration vs. Exploitation: An Empirical Test of the Ambidexterity Hypothesis. In: Organization Science, Vol. 15, No. 4, pp. 481–494.

Hellström, T./Malmquist, U. (2000): Networked innovation: developing the AXE110 "miniexchange" at Ericsson. In: European Journal of Innovation Management, Vol. 3, No. 4, pp. 181-189.

Henderson, K. V./Turner A./Turner, M. (1995): Industrial Development in Cities. In: Journal of Political Economy, Vol. 103, No. 5, pp. 1067-1090.

Henry, N./Massey, D./Wield, D. (1995): Along the road: R & D, society and space. In: Research Policy, Vol. 24, No. 5, pp. 707–726.

Herzog, P. (2008): Open and closed innovation. Different cultures for different strategies. Gabler, Wiesbaden.

Hipp, C. (1999): Knowledge Intensive Business Services in the New Mode of Knowledge Production. In: AI & Society, Vol. 13, No. 1/2, pp. 88–106.

Hipp, C./Hariolf, G. (2005): Innovation in the service sector: The demand for service-specific innovation measurement concepts and typologies. In: Research Policy, Vol. 34, No. 4, pp. 517–535.

Hitt, M. A./Ireland, R. D./Camp, S. M./Sexton, D. L. (2001): Strategic entrepreneurship: entrepreneurial strategies for wealth creation. In: Strategic Management Journal, Vol. 22, No. 6-7, pp. 479–491.

Hoang, H./Antoncic, B. (2003): Network-based research in entrepreneurship: A critical review. In: Journal of Business Venturing, Vol. 18, No. 2, pp. 165–187.

Hodgson, G.M. (1988): Economics and Institutions: A Manifesto for a Modern Institutional Economics, Polity Press, Cambridge.

Hoecht, A./Trott, P. C. (1999): Trust Risk and Control in the Management of Collaborative Technology Development. In: International Journal of Innovation Management– Vol. 3, No. 3, pp. 257–271.

Hofstede, G. (1994): The business of international business is culture. In: International Business Review, Vol. 3, No. 1, pp. 1–14.

Hollekamp, M. (2005): Strategisches Outsourcing von Geschäftsprozessen: eine empirische Analyze der Wirkungszusammenhänge und der Erfolgswirkungen von Outsourcing-projekten am Beispiel von Großunternehmen in Deutschland, München u.a.

Howe, J. (2006): The Rise of Crowdsourcing. In: Wired Magazine, No. 14.06, pp. 1–5.

Howells, J. (1999): Research and technology outsourcing. In: Technology Analysis & Strategic Management, Vol. 11, No. 1, pp. 17-29.

Howells, J. (2000): Outourcing Novelty. The Externalization of Innovative Activity. In: Andersen/Howells/Hull/Miles/Roberts (Eds.): Knowledge and innovation in the new service economy. Cheltenham, pp. 196–214.

Howells, J. (2006a): Intermediation and the role of intermediaries in innovation. In: Research Policy, Vol. 35, No. 5, pp. 715–728.

Howells, J. (2006b): Outsourcing for innovation. systems of innovation and the role of knowledge intermediaries. In: Miozzo/Grimshaw (Eds.): Knowledge intensive business services. Organizational forms and national institutions: Elgar. Cheltenham, pp. 61–81.

Hsueh, J.-T./Lin, N.-P./Li, H.-C. (2010): The effects of network embeddedness on service innovation performance. In: The Service Industries Journal, Vol. 30, No. 10, pp. 1723–1736.

Hughes, B./Wareham, J. (2010): Knowledge arbitrage in global pharma: a synthetic view of absorptive capacity and open innovation. In: R&D Management Journal, Vol. 40, No. 3, pp. 324–344.

Iammarino, S. (2005): An evolutionary integrated view of regional systems of innovation: concepts, measures and historical perspectives. In: European Planning Studies, Vol. 13, No. 4, pp. 497-519.

Ili, S./Albers, A./Miller, S. (2010): Open innovation in the automotive industry. In: R&D Management, Vol. 40, No. 3, pp. 246–255.

Ireland, R. D. (2007): Strategy vs. entrepreneurship. In: Strategic Entrepreneurship Journal, Vol. 1, No. 1-2, pp. 7–10.

Ireland, R. D./Hitt, M. A./Sirmon, D. G. (2003): A Model of Strategic Entrepreneurship: The Construct and its Dimensions. In: Journal of Management, Vol. 29, No. 6, pp. 963–989.

Ireland, D./Webb, J. (2007a): Strategic entrepreneurship: Creating competitive advantage through streams of innovation. In: Business Horizons, Vol. 50, No. 1, pp. 49–59.

Ireland, D./Webb, J. (2007b): A Cross-Disciplinary Exploration of Entrepreneurship Research. In: Journal of Management, Vol. 33, No. 6, pp. 891–927.

Jack, S. L./Anderson, A. R. (2002): The effects of embeddedness on the entrepreneurial process. Qualitative methods in entrepreneurial research. In: Journal of Business Venturing, Vol. 17, No. 5, pp. 467–487.

Jacobs, J. (1969): The Economy of Cities. Random House, New York.

Janssens, W. (2008): Marketing research with SPSS. Prentice Hall/Financial Times, Harlow, UK.

Johne, A. (1999): Successful market innovation. In: European Journal of Innovation Management, Vol. 2, No. 1, pp. 6-11.

Johnson, D./Grayson, K. (2005): Cognitive and affective trust in service relationships. Special Section: Attitude and Affect. In: Journal of Business Research, Vol. 58, No. 4, pp. 500–507.

Jones, O. (2000): Innovation Management as a Post-Modern Phenomenon: The Outsourcing of Pharmaceutical R&D. In: British Journal of Management, Vol. 11, No. 4, pp. 341-356.

Kachigan, S. K. (1991): Multivariate statistical analysis. A conceptual introduction. Radius Press, New York.

Kaiser, H.F./Rice, J. (1974): Little Jiffy, Mark IV. In: Education and Psychological Measurements, Vol 34, pp. 111-117.

Kang, K. H./Kang, J. (2009): How do firms source external knowledge for innovation? Analyzing effects of different knowledge sourcing methods. In: International Journal of Innovation Management, Vol. 13, No. 1, pp. 1–17.

Kao, J. (2009): Tapping the World's Innovation Hot Spots. In: Harvard Business Review, Vol. 87, No. 3, pp. 109–114.

Kelley, D. J., Bosma, N., Amorós, J. E. (2011): Global Entrepreneurship Monitor 2010 - Global Report. Global Entrepreneurship Research Association. Online: http://www.gemconsortium.org/ docs/266/gem-2010-global-report.

Keupp, M. M./Gassmann, O. (2009): Determinants and archetype users of open innovation. In: R&D Management, Vol. 39, No. 4, pp. 331–341.

Kieser, A. (2002): Organisationstheorien. Kohlhammer, Stuttgart.

Kirsch, W. (2001): Die Führung von Unternehmen, Herrsching.

Kirsch, W./Seidl, D./van Aaken , D. (2010): Evolutionäre Organizationstheorie, Schäfer Poeschel.

Kirschbaum, R. (2005): Open Innovation in Practice. In: Research-Technology Management, Vol. 48, No. 4, pp. 24–28.

Kirzner, I. M. (1973): Competition and entrepreneurship. Univ. of Chicago Press, Chicago.

Kitchell, S. (1995): Corporate Culture, Environmental Adaptation, and Innovation Adoption: A Qualitative/Quantitative Approach. In: Journal of the Academy of Marketing Science, Vol. 23, No. 3, pp. 195–205.

Kline, S./Rosenberg, N. (1986): An Overview of Innovation. In: Landau/Rosenberg (Eds.): The Positive sum strategy: harnessing technology for economic growth: National Academy Press, pp. 275–304.

Knight, K.E. (1967): A Descriptive Model of the Intra-Firm Innovation-Process. In: The Journal of Business, Vol. 40, pp. 478-496.

Koch, A./Strahlecker, T. (2006): Regional innovation systems and the foundation of knowledge intensive business services. A comparative study in Bremen, Munich, and Stuttgart, Germany. In: European Planning Studies, Vol. 14, No. 2, pp. 123–146.

Koe Hwee Nga, J./Shamuganathan, G. (2010): The Influence of Personality Traits and Demographic Factors on Social Entrepreneurship Start Up Intentions. In: Journal of Business Ethics, Vol. 95, No. 2, pp. 259–282.

Kogut, B./Zander, U. (1992): Knowledge of the Firm, Combinative Capabilities, and the Replication of Technology. In: Organization Science, Vol. 3, No. 3, pp. 383–397.

Kolm, S.-C. (2008): Reciprocity. An economics of social relations. Cambridge University Press, New York.

Kotler, P./Armstrong, G./Wong, V./Saunders, J.(2011): Grundlagen des Marketing. Pearson, München.

Kotler, P./Singh, R. (1981): Marketing Warfare in the 1980s. In: Journal of Business Strategy, Vol. 1, Winter, pp. 20-41.

Krackhardt, D. (1995): Entrepreneurial Opportunities in an Entrepreneurial Firm: A Structural Approach. In: Entrepreneurship: Theory and Practice, Vol. 19, No. 3, pp. 53–69.

Krackhardt, D./ Hanson J.R. (1993): Informal networks: The company behind the chart. In: Harvard Business Review, Vol. 71, No. 4, pp. 104–111.

Kreiner, K./Schultz, M. (1993): Informal Collaboration in R&D. The formation of Networks Across Organizations. In: Organization Studies, Vol. 14, No. 2, pp. 189–209.

Kreps, D./Milgrom, P./Roberts, J./Wilson, R. (1982): Rational cooperation in the finitely repeated prisoners' dilemma. In: Journal of Economic Theory, Vol. 27, No. 2, pp. 245–252.

Kroll, M./Walters, B. A. (2007): The Impact of Board Composition and Top Management Team Ownership Structure on Post-IPO Performance in Young Entrepreneurial Firms. In: The Academy of Management Journal, Vol. 50, No. 5, pp. 1198–1216.

Kromrey, H. (2002): Empirische Sozialforschung. Modelle und Methoden der Datenerhebung und Datenauswertung. UTB, Opladen.

Krugman, P. (2000): Where in the world is the "new economic geography"? In: Clark/Feldman/Gertler (Eds.): The Oxford handbook of economic geography: Oxford Univ. Press. Oxford, pp. 49–60.

Kuckartz, U. (2005): Einführung in die computergestütze Analyze qualitativer Daten. Wiesbaden, VS-Verlag.

Kutschker, M. (1994): Strategische Kooperationen als Mittel der Internationalisierung. In: Schuster (Ed.): Die Unternehmung im internationalen Wettbewerb. ESV, Berlin, pp. 121-157.

Kutschker, M. (2005): Prozessuale Aspekte der Kooperation. In: Zentes/Swoboda/Morschett (Eds.): Kooperationen, Allianzen und Netzwerke. Grundlagen - Ansätze - Perspektiven. 2. Aufl.: Gabler. Wiesbaden, pp. 1125–1154.

Kutschker, M./Schmid, S. (2008): Internationales Management. 6th Vol., Oldenbourg, München.

Kuß, A./Eisend, M. (2010): Marktforschung. Gabler, Wiesbaden.

Lamnek, S. (1995): Qualitative Sozialforschung. Vol. 1: Methodologie. Beltz, Weinheim.

Lane, P.J./Koka, B.R./Pathak, S. (2006): The reification of absorptive capacity: a critical review and rejuvenation of the construct. In: Academy of Management Review, Vol. 31, No. 4, pp. 833–863.

Lane, P./Lubatkin, M. (1998): Relative Absortive Capacity and Interorganizational Learning. In: Strategic Management Journal, Vol. 19, No. 5, pp. 461–477.

Lant, T.K./Mezias, S. J. (1990): Managing Discontinuous Change: A Simulation Study of Organizational Learning and Entrepreneurship. In: Strategic Management Journal, Vol. 11, No. Special Issue: Corporate Entrepreneurship, pp. 147–179.

Larson, A. (1991): Partner networks: Leveraging external ties to improve entrepreneurial performance. In: Journal of Business Venturing, Vol. 6, No. 3, pp. 173–188.

Larson, A. (1992): Network Dyads in Entrepreneurial Settings: A Study of the Governance of Exchange Relationships. In: Administrative Science Quarterly, Vol. 37, No. 1, pp. 76–104.

Laursen, K./Masciarelli, F./Prencipe, A. (2012): Regions Matter: How Localized Social Capital Affects Innovation and External Knowledge Acquisition. In: Organization Science, Vol. 23, No. 1, pp. 177–193.

Leana, C. (1999): Organizational Social Capital and Employment Practices. In: The Academy of Management Review, Vol. 24, No. 3, pp. 538–555.

Leana, C./van Buren, H. J. (1999): Organizational social capital and employment practices. In: Academy of Management Review, Vol. 24, pp. 538–555.

Lee, C.-M./Miller, W.F./Gong Hancock, M./Rowen, H.S. (2000): The Silicon Valley Habitat. In: Lee/Miller/Gong Hancock/Rowen (Eds.): The Silicon Valley edge. A habitat for innovation and entrepreneurship. Stanford University Press, Stanford, pp. 1-15.

Lee, R. (2009): Social capital and business and management: Setting a research agenda. In: International Journal of Management Reviews, Vol. 11, No. 3, pp. 247–273.

Lee, S./Park, G./Yoon, B./Park, J. (2010): Open innovation in SMEs — An intermediated network model. In: Research Policy, Vol. 39, No. 2, pp. 290-300.

Legler, H./Frietsch, R. (2006): Neuabgrenzung der Wissenswirtschaft – Forschungsintensive Industrien und wissensintensive Dienstleistungen (NIW/ISI-Listen 2006). Studien zum deutschen Innovationssystem. Karlsruhe.

Leimeister, J.M./Huber, M./Bretschneider, U./Krcmar, H. (2009): Leveraging Crowdsourcing: Activation-Supporting Components for IT-Based Ideas Competition. In: Journal of Management Information Systems, Vol. 26, No. 1, pp. 197–224.

Lerner, J./Merges, R.P. (1998): The control of technology alliances: an empirical analysis of the biotechnology industry. In: Journal of Industrial Economics, Vol. 46, No. 2, pp. 125–150.

Lerner, M./Haber, S. (2000): Performance Factors of Small Tourism Ventures. The Interface of Tourism, Entrepreneurship and the Environment. In: Journal of Business Venturing, Vol. 16, No. , pp. 77–100.

Leydesdorff, L./Fritsch, M. (2006): Measuring the knowledge base of regional innovation systems in Germany in terms of a Triple Helix dynamics. Triple helix Indicators of

Knowledge-Based Innovation Systems. In: Research Policy, Vol. 35, No. 10, pp. 1538–1553.

Liao, J./Welsch, H. (2003): Social Capital and Entrepreneurial Growth Aspiration: A Comparison of technology- and non-technology-based nascent Entrepreneurs. In: Journal of High Technology Management Research, Vol. 14, pp. 149-170.

Lichenthaler, U. (2006): Leveraging Knowledge Assets – Success Factors of External Technology Commercialization, Wiesbaden.

Lichtenthaler, U. (2009): Absorptive Capacity, Environmental Turbulence, and the Complementarity of Organizational Learning Processes. In: Academy of Management Journal, Vol. 52, No. 4, pp. 822–846.

Lichtenthaler, U. (2009): Outbound open innovation and its effect on firm performance: examining environmental influences. In: R&D Management Journal, Vol. 39, No. 4, pp. 317–330.

Lichtenthaler, U./Ernst, H. (2006): Attitudes to externally organising knowledge management tasks: a review, reconsideration and extension of the NIH syndrome. In: R and D Management, Vol. 36, No. 4, pp. 367–386.

Lichtenthaler, U./Lichtenthaler, E. (2009): A Capability-Based Framework for Open Innovation: Complementing Absorptive Capacity. In: Journal of Management Studies, Vol. 46, No. 8, pp. 1315–1338.

Löfsten, H./Lindelöf, P. (2003): Determinants for an entrepreneurial milieu: Science parks and business policy in growing firms. In: Technovation, Vol. 23, pp. 51-61.

López-Nicolás, C./Meroño-Cerdán, Á. L. (2011): Strategic knowledge management, innovation and performance. In: International Journal of Information Management, Vol. 31, No. 6, pp. 502–509.

Lin, N. (2001): Building a Network Theory of Social Capital. In: Lin/Cook/Burt (Eds.): Social Capital. Theory and Research, Aldine de Gruyter, New York, pp. 3-30.

Lin, N. (2003): Social capital. A theory of social structure and action. Cambridge Univ. Press, Cambridge.

Linder, J.C./Jarvenpaa, S./Davenport, T.H. (2003): Toward an Innovation Sourcing Strategy. In: MIT Sloan Management Review, Vol. 44, No. 4, pp. 43–49.

Littunen, H. (2000): Entrepreneurship and the characteristics of the entrepreneurial personality. In: International Journal of Entrepreneurial Behavior & Research, Vol. 6, No. 6, pp. 295–309.

Love, J.H./Roper, S. (2001): Outsourcing in the innovation process: Locational and strategic determinants. In: Papers in Regional Science, Vol. 80, No. 3, pp. 317–336.

Loebecke, C./van Fenema, P. C./Powell, P. (1999): Co-opetition and knowledge transfer. In: ACM SIGMIS Database, Vol. 30, No. 2, pp. 14–25.

Löfsten, H./Lindelöf, P. (2003): Determinants for an entrepreneurial milieu: Science Parks and business policy in growing firms. In: Technovation, Vol. 23, No. 1, pp. 51–64.

Lumpkin, G. T./Dess, G. G. (1996): Clarifying the entrepreneurial orientation construct and linking it to performance. In: Academy of Management Review, Vol. 21, No. 1, pp. 135–172.

Lundvall, B.-Å. (1992): National systems of innovation. Toward a theory of innovation and interactive learning. Pinter, London.

Lüthje, C. (2007): Methoden zur Sicherstellung von Kundenintegration in den frühen Phasen des innovationsprozesses. In: Herstatt/Verworn (Eds.): Management der frühen Innovationsphasen. Grundlagen - Methoden - Neue Ansätze. Wiesbaden, pp. 36–56.

Lynn, L.H./Mohan, R.N./Aram, J.D. (1996): Linking technology and institutions: the innovation community framework. In: Research Policy, Vol. 25, No. 1, pp. 91-106.

MacPherson, A. (1997): The Role of Producer Service Outsourcing in the Innovation Performance of New York State Manufacturing Firms. In: Annals of the Association of American Geographers, Vol. 87, No. 1, pp. 52–71.

Mahnke, V./Özcan, S. (2006): Outsourcing Innovation and Relational Governance. In: Industry & Innovation, Vol. 13, No. 2, pp. 121–125.

Maillat, D. (1995): Territorial dynamic, innovative milieus and regional policy. In: Entrepreneurship & Regional Development, Vol. 7, No. 2, pp. 157–165.

Malerba, F. (2002): Sectoral Systems of Innovation and Production. In: Research Policy, Vol. 31, No. 2, pp. 247-246.

Malerba, F. (2005): Sectoral systems of innovation – A framework for linking innovation to the knowledge base, structure and dynamics of sectors. In: Economics of Innovation & New Technology, Vol. 14, No. 1-2, pp. 63–82.

Malmberg, A./Maskell, P. (2002): The elusive concept of localization economies: toward a knowledge-based theory of spatial clustering. In: Environmen and Planning A, Vol. 34, pp. 429-449.

Man, T./Lau, T./Chan, K. F. (2002): The competitiveness of small and medium enterprises. A conceptualization with focus on entrepreneurial competencies. In: Journal of Business Venturing, Vol. 17, No. 2, pp. 123–142.

Mandell, M.P./Keast, R. (2008): Introduction. In: Public Management Review, Vol. 10, No. 6, pp. 687-698.

March, J. (1991): Exploration and Exploitation in Organizational Learning. In: Organization Science, Vol. 2, No. 1, pp. 71–87.

Marshall, A. (1920): The Principles of Economics. MacMillan, London.

Martin, R./Sunley, P. (2003): Deconstructing Clusters. Chaotic concept or policy panacea. In: Journal of Economic Geography, Vol. 3, No. 1, pp. 5-35.

Martin, R./Sunley, P. (2006): Path dependence and regional economic evolution. In: Journal of Economic Geography, Vol. 6, No. 4, pp. 395-437.

Martínez-Cañas, R./Saez-Martinez, F./Ruiz-Palomino, P. (2012): Knowledge acquisition's mediation of social capital–firm innovation. In: Journal of Knowledge Management, Vol. 16, No. 1, pp. 61-76.

Maurer, I./Ebers, M. (2006): Dynamics of Social Capital and Their Performance Implications: Lessons from Biotechnology Start-Ups. In: Administrative Science Quarterly, Vol. 51, No. 2, pp. 262–292.

Mason, G./Wagner, K. (1999): Knowledge Transfer and Innovation in Germany and Britain: 'Intermediate Institution' Models of Knowledge Transfer under Strain? In: Industry and Innowatton, Vol. 6, No. 1, pp. 85–109.

Mayer, R. C./Davis, J. H./Schoorman, F. D. (1995): An Integrative Model of Organizational Trust. In: The Academy of Management Review, Vol. 20, No. 3, pp. 709–734.

Mayring, P. (2002): Einführung in die qualitative Sozialforschung. Eine Anleitung zu qualitativem Denken. Beltz, Weinheim.

McAllister, D. J. (1995): Affect- and Cognition-Based Trust as Foundations for Interpersonal Cooperation in Organizations. In: The Academy of Management Journal, Vol. 38, No. 1, pp. 24–59.

McDermott, C./Handfield, R. (2000): Concurrent development and strategic outsourcing. do the rules change in breakthrough innovation? In: Journal of High Technology Management Research, Vol. 11, No. 1, pp. 35–57.

McGrath, R. G. (1999): Falling Forward: Real Options Reasoning and Entrepreneurial Failure. In: The Academy of Management Review, Vol. 24, No. 1, pp. 13–30.

McKnight, D.H./Chervany, N.L. (2006): Reflections on an Initial Trust-building Model. In: Bachmann/Zaheer (Eds.): Handbook of Trust Research. Edward Elgar, Cheltenham, pp. 29-51.

Meier Kruker, V./Rauh, J. (2005): Arbeitsmethoden der Humangeographie. Wissenschaftliche Buchgesellschaft, Darmstadt.

Melese, T./Lin, S. M./Chang, J. L./Cohen, N. H. (2009): Open innovation networks between academia and industry: an imperative for breakthrough therapies. In: Nature Medicine, Vol. 15, No. 5, pp. 502–507.

Metcalfe, J.S. (1995): The economic foundations of technology policy: Equilibrium and Evolutionary Perspectives. In: Stoneman, P. (eds.): Handbook of the Economics of Innovation and Technical Change. Blackwell, Oxford.

Metcalfe, J.S. (2006): Entrepreneurship. An Evolutionary Perspective. In: Casson/Yeung/Basu/Wadeson (Eds.): The Oxford handbook of entrepreneurship: Oxford University Press. Oxford ;, New York, pp. 59–90.

Meuser, M./Nagel, U. (2005): ExpertenInneninterviews. Vielfach erprobt, wenig bedacht. Ein Beitrag zu qualitativen Methodendiskussion. In: Bogner/Littig/Menz (Eds.): Das Experteninterview. Theorie, Methode, Anwendung. VS Verlag für Sozialwissenschaften, Wiesbaden, pp. 71-94.

Millar J./Demaid A./Quintas P. (1997): Trans-organizational innovation: a framework for research. In: Technology Analysis & Strategic Management, Vol. 9, No. 4, pp. 383–402.

Miller, D. (1983): The correlates of entrepreneurship in three types of firms. In: Management Science, Vol. 29, No. 7, pp. 770-791.

Miller, K. D. (2007): Risk and rationality in entrepreneurial processes. In: Strategic Entrepreneurship Journal, Vol. 1, No. 1-2, pp. 57–74.

Miles, G./Heppard, K. A./Miles, R. E./Snow, C. C. (2000): Entrepreneurial strategies: The critical role of top management. In: Meyer/Heppard (Eds.): Entrepreneurship as strategy: Competing on the entrepreneurial edge: Sage Publications, Thousand Oaks, pp. 101–114.

Mizruchi, M. S./Schwartz, M. (1992, Eds.): Intercorporate Relations. The structural analysis of business. Univ. Press, Cambridge.

Mokre, M. (2006): Deregulation and Democracy: The Australian Case. In: Jounal of Arts Management, Law and Society, Vol. 35, No. 4, pp. 305-316.

Moore, W.L./Tushman, M.L. (1982): Managing Innovation over the Product Life Cycle. In: Tushman/Moore (Eds.): Readings in the Management of Innovation. Ballinger, Boston, pp. 131-150.

Morecroft, J./Sanchez, R./Hene, A. (2002): Integrating systems thinking and competence concepts in a new view of resources, capabilities, and management processes. In: Morecroft/Sanchez/Heene (Eds.): Systems perspectives on resources, capabilities, management processes. Elsevier, Oxford, pp. 3-16.

Mortara, L./Napp, J. J./Slacik, I./Minshall, T. (2009): How to implement open innovation. Lessons from studying large multinational companies. IFM, Cambridge.

Mosey, S./Wright, M. (2007): From Human Capital to Social Capital: A Longitudinal Study of Technology-Based Academic Entrepreneurs. In: Entrepreneurship Theory and Practice, Vol. 31, No. 6, pp. 909–935.

Möslein, K./Bansemir, B. (2011): Strategic Open Innovation: Basics, Actors, Tools and Tensions. In: Hülsmann, M./Pfeffermann, N. (Eds.): Strategies and Communications for Innovations: An Integrative Management View for Companies and Networks, Heidelberg, pp. 11-24.

Mueller, P. (2006): Exploring the knowledge filter: How entrepreneurship and university–industry relationships drive economic growth. Triple helix Indicators of Knowledge-Based Innovation Systems. In: Research Policy, Vol. 35, No. 10, pp. 1499–1508.

Müller-Seitz, G. (2012): Absorptive and desorptive capacity-related practices at the network level - the case of SEMATECH. In: R&D Management, Vol. 42, No. 1, pp. 90–99.

Murphy, S./Kumar, V. (1997): The front end of new product development: a Canadian survey. In: R and D Management, Vol. 27, No. 1, pp. 5–15.

Murphy, G. B./Trailer, J. W./Hill, R. C. (1996): Measuring performance in entrepreneurship research. Entrepreneurship and New Firm Development. In: Journal of Business Research, Vol. 36, No. 1, pp. 15–23.

Nalebuff, B. J./Brandenburger, A. M. (1997): Co-opetition: Competitive and cooperative business strategies for the digital economy. In: Strategy & Leadership, Vol. 25, No. 6, pp. 28–35.

Nahapiet, J. (2008): Social capital and interorganizational relations. In: Cropper/Ebers/Huxham/Ring (Eds.): The Oxford handbook of inter-organizational relations. Oxford University Press, Oxford, pp. 580–605.

Nahapiet, J./S. Ghoshal (1998): Social Capital, Intellectual Capital, and the Organizational Advantage. In: Academy of Management Review, Vol. 23, No. 2, pp. 242–266.

Neffke, F./Henning, M./Boschma, R. (2011) How Do Regions Diversify over Time? Industry Relatedness and the Development of New Growth Paths in Regions. In: Economic Geography, Vol. 87, No. 3, pp. 237-265.

Nelson, R. (1993, Ed.): National Systems of Innovation: A Comparative Study. Oxford University Press, Oxford.

Nelson, R. R./Winter, S. G. (1982): An evolutionary theory of economic change. Belknap Press of Harvard University Press, Cambridge, Mass.

Neyman, A. (1985): Bounded complexity justifies cooperation in the finitely repeated prisoners' dilemma. In: Economics Letters, Vol. 19, No. 3, pp. 227–229.

Ndonzuau, F. N./Pirnay, F./Surlemont, B. (2002): A stage model of academic spin-off creation. In: Technovation, Vol. 22, No. 5, pp. 281–289.

Nonaka, I. (1994): A Dynamic Theory of Organizational Knowledge Creation. In: Organization Science, Vol. 5, No. 1, pp. 14–37.

Nonaka, I./Konno, N. (1998): The Concept of Ba. Building a Foundation for Knowledge Creation. In: Californian Management Review, Vol. 40, No. 3, pp. 41-54.

Nooteboom, B. (1996): Trust, Opportunism and Governance: A Process and Control Model. In: Organization Studies, Vol. 17, No. 6, pp. 985–1010.

Nooteboom, B. (1999): Innovation and inter-firm linkages: new implications for policy. In: Research Policy, Vol. 28, No. 8, pp. 793–805.

Nooteboom, B. (2000a): Institutions and Forms of Co-ordination in Innovation Systems. In: Organization Studies, Vol. 21, No. 5, pp. 915–939.

Nooteboom, B. (2000b): Learning by Interaction: Absorptive Capacity, Cognitive Distance and Governance. In: Journal of Management and Governance. Vol. 4, No. 1-2, pp. 69-92.

Nooteboom, B. (2002): Trust. Forms, foundations, functions, failures and figures. Edward Elgar, Cheltenham.

Nooteboom, B. (2006): Principles of inter-organizational relationships: an integrated survey. In: Miozzo, M./Grimshaw, D. (Eds.): Knowledge intensive business services Organizational forms and national institutions. Elgar, Cheltenham, pp. 29–60.

Nooteboom, B. (2007): Social Capital, Institutions and Trust. In: Review of Social Economy, Vol. 65, No. 1, pp. 29–64.

Nooteboom, B./Berger, H./Noorderhaven, N. G. (1997): Effects of trust and governance on relational risk. In: Academy of Management Journal, Vol. 40, No. 2, pp. 308–338.

North, D. (1990) Institutions, Institutional Change, and Economic Performance. Cambridge University Press, New York.

Nowotny, H. (2003): The Potential of Transdisciplinarity. In: Rethinking Interdisciplinarity, online: http://www.interdisciplines.org/medias/confs/archives/archive_3.pdf

Nyström, H. (1990): Technological and market innovation: Strategies for product and company development, Chichester.

O'Donnell, A./Gilmore, A./Cummins, D./Carson, D. (2001): The Network Construct in Entrepreneurship Research: A Review and Critique. In: Management Decision, Vol. 39, No. 9, pp.749-760.

O'Farrell, P. N./Moffat, L. A./Hitchens, D. M. (1993): Manufacturing Demand for Business Services in a Core and Peripheral Region: Does Flexible Production Imply Vertical Disintegration of Business Services? In: Regional Studies, Vol. 27, No. 5, pp. 385–400.

Ohly, S./Kase, R./Skerlavaj, M. (2010): Networks for Generating and for Validating Ideas: The Social Side of Creativity. In: Innovation: Management Policy and Practice, Vol. 12, No. 1, pp. 41–52.

Organ, D. C. (1981): The effects of formalization on professional involvement: A compensatory process approach. In: Administrative Science Quarterly, Vol. 26, pp. 237–252.

Østergaard, S. D. (2008): IBM Innovation Jam – Experiences & Techniques. IBM Corporate presentation. URL: http://www.epractice.eu/files/Soren%20Duus%20-%20IBM%20 Innovation%20Jam.pdf.

Osterloh, M./Frost, J. (2000): Prozessmanagement als Kernkompetenz. Wie Sie business reengineering strategisch nutzen können. Gabler, Wiesbaden.

Ozcan, Pinar/Eisenhardt, Katleen (2009): Origin of alliance portfolios: Entrepreneurs, network strategies, and firm performance. In: Academy of Management Journal, Vol. 52, No. 2, pp. 246–279.

Paladino, A. (2007): Investigating the Driver of Innovation and New Product Success: A Comparison of Strategic Orientations. In: Journal of Product Innovation Management, Vol. 24, pp. 534-553.

Pechlaner, H./Bachinger, M. (2010): Knowledge networks of innovative businesses: an explorative study in the region of Ingolstadt. In: The Service Industries Journal, Vol. 30, No. 10, pp. 1737–1756.

Pechlaner, H./Doepfer, B.C. (2010): Entrepreneurial Services Management. Ein Ansatz zur Integration des Entrepreneurial Managements in das Dienstleistungsmanagement. In: Bruhn/Stauss (Eds.): Service Orientierung im Unternehmen. Forum Dienstleistungsmanagement. Gabler, Wiesbaden, pp. 81-102.

Pechlaner, H./Stechhammer, B./Hinterhuber, H. H. (2010, Eds.): Scheitern: Die Schattenseite unternehmerischen Handelns. Die Chance zur Selbsterneuerung. ESV, Berlin.

Pelham, A. (1999): Influence of Environment, Strategy, and Market Orientation on Performance in Small Manufacturing Firms. In: Journal of Business Research, Vol.45, No.1, pp. 33–46.

Peña, I. (2002): IC and business start-up success. In: Journal of Intellectual Capital, Vol. 3, No. 2, pp. 180–198.

Perrons, R. K./Platts, K. W. (2004): The role of clockspeed in outsourcing decisions for new technologies. insights from the prisoner's dilemma. In: Industrial Management and Data Systems, Vol. 104, No. 7, pp. 624–632.

Perry-Smith, J. (2006): Social Yet Creative: The Role of Social Relationships in Facilitating Individual Creativity. In: The Academy of Management Journal, Vol. 49, No. 1, pp. 85–101.

Perry-Smith, J. E./Shalley, C. E. (2003): The social side of creativity: A static and dynamic social network perspective. In: Academy of Management Review, Vol. 28, pp. 89–106.

Picot, A./Hardt, P. (1998): Make-or-Buy-Entscheidungen. In: Meyer (Ed.): Handbuch Dienstleistungsmarketing. Schäfer-Poeschel, Stuttgart, pp. 625–646.

Piller, F./Walcher, D. (2006): Toolkits for Idea Competitions: A Novel Method to Integrate Users in New Product Development. In: R&D Management, Vol. 36, No. 3, pp. 307–318.

Pinchot, G./Pellman, R. (1999): Intrapreneuring in action. A handbook for business innovation. Berrett-Koehler Publishers, San Francisco.

Pinchot, G. (1985): Intrapreneuring. Why you don't have to leave the corporation to become an entrepreneur. Harper & Row, New York.

Pindyck, R. S./Rubinfeld, D. L. (2009): Microeconomics. Pearson/Prentice Hall, Upper Saddle River, NJ.

Pinnekamp, H.J./Siegmann, F. (2008): Deskriptive Statistik. Oldenbourg, München.

Pirnay, F./Surlemont, B./Nlemvo, F. (2003): Toward a Typology of University Spin-offs. In: Small Business Economics, Vol. 21, No. 4, pp. 355–369.

Pisano, G.P./Verganti, R. (2008): Which Kind of Collaboration Is Right for You? In: Harvard Business Review, Vol. 86, No. 12, S. 78-86.

Pisano, G.P. (1990): The R&D boundaries of the firm: an empirical analysis. In: Administrative Science Quarterly, Vol. 35, No. 1, S. 153-176.o

Pisano, G.P. (1991): The governance of innovation: Vertical integration and collaborative arrangements in the biotechnology industry. In: Research Policy, Vol. 20, No. 3, S. 237-249.

Pittaway, L./Robertson, M./Munir, K./Denyer, D./Neely, A. (2004): Networking and innovation: a systematic review of the evidence, In: International Journal of Management Reviews, Vol. 5, No. 3-4, pp. 137-168.

Podsakoff, P./MacKenzie S./Lee J./Podskoff N. (2003): Common method biases in behavioral research: A critical review of the literature and recommended remedies. In: Journal of Applied Psychology, Vol. 88, No. , pp. 879–903.

Popper, K.R. (2005): Alles Leben ist Problemlösen. Über Erkenntnis, Geschichte und Politik, München.

Porter, M. E. (1996): What is Strategy? In: Harvard Business Review, Vol. 74, No. 6, pp. 61–78.

Porter, M.E. (1998a): Clusters and the new economics of competition. In: Harvard Business Review, Vol. 76, No. 6, pp. 77-90.

Porter, M. E. (1998b): The competitive advantage of nations. Free Press, New York.

Porter, M. E. (1998c): On competition. Harvard Business School Pub., Boston, MA.

Porter, M.E. (2000a): Location, Competition, and Economic Development: Local clusters in a Global Economy. Economic Development Quarterly, 14 (1), 15–34.

Porter, M.E. (2000b): Location, Clusters, and Company Strategy. In: Clark, G. L./Feldman, M. P./Gertler, M. S. (Eds.): The Oxford handbook of economic geography. Oxford Univ. Press, Oxford, pp. 253–274.

Porter, M. E. (2001): Strategy and the Internet. In: Harvard Business Review, Vol. 79, No. 3, pp. 62–78.

Porter, M. E. (2004): Competitive advantage: Creating and Sustaining Superior Performance. Free Press, New York, London.

Porter, M. E./Kramer, M. R. (2011): Creating Shared Value. In: Harvard Business Review, Vol. 89, No. 1/2, pp. 62–77.

Porter, M.E./Stern, S. (2001): Innovation: Location matters. In: Sloan Management Review, Vol. 42, No. 4, pp. 28–43.

Portes, A. (2000): Social Capital. Its Origins and Applications in Modern Sociology. In: Lesser (Ed.): Knowledge and Social Capital. Foundations and Applications. Butterworth-Heinemann, Boston, pp. 43-69.

Pothas, A.–M., De Wet, A. G., & De Wet, J. M. (2001). Customer satisfaction: Keeping tabs on the issues that matter. In: Total Quality Management, Vol. 12, No. 1, pp. 83–94.

Powell, W.W./Koput, K.W./Smith-Doerr, L. (1996): Interorganizational collaboration and the locus of innovation: Networks of learning in biotechnology. In: Administrative science quarterly, Vol. 41, No. 1, pp. 116-145.

Powell, W.W./Smith-Doerr, L. (1994): Networks and economic life. In: Smelser/Swedberg (Eds.): The handbook of economic sociology. Princeton University Press, Princeton, pp. 368-402.

Prahalad, C. K./Bettis, R. A. (1986): The dominant logic: A new linkage between diversity and performance. In: Strategic Management Journal, Vol. 7, No. 6, pp. 485–501.

Prahalad, C. K./Hamel, G. (1990): The Core Competence of the Corporation. In: Harvard Business Review, Vol. 68, No. 3, pp. 79–91.

Prahalad, C. K./Ramaswamy, V. (2004a): The future of competition. Co-creating unique value with customers. Harvard Business School Pub., Boston, Mass.

Prahalad, C./Ramaswamy, V. (2004b): Co-creation experiences: The next practice in value creation. In: Journal of Interactive Marketing, Vol. 18, No. 3, pp. 5–14.

Prognos (2010a): Prognos Zukunftsatlas 2010 - Deutschlands Regionen im Zukunftswettbewerb. Berlin u.a.

Prognos (2010b). Impact-Analyze des Wissenschaftsstandortes Europäische Metropolregion München (EMM). Prognos: Basel.

Putnam, R. D. (1993): The Prosperous Community - Social Capital and Public Life. In: The American Prospect, Vol. 4, No. 13, pp. 35-42.

Putnam, R.D. (1993): Making Democracy Work. Civic Traditions in Modern Italy, Prenceton, N.J.

Putnam, R. D. (2000): Bowling alone. The collapse and revival of American community. Simon & Schuster, New York, NY.

Putnam, R.D./Goss, K.S. (2002): Introduction. In: Putnam, R.D. (Ed.): Democracies in Flux. The Evolution of Social Capital in Contemporary Society. Oxford University Press, Oxford, pp. 3-19.

Quélin, B./Duhamel, F. (2003): Bringing together strategic sourcing and corporate strategy: Outsourcing motives and risks. In: European Management Journal, Vol. 21, No. 5, pp. 647–661.

Quinn, J. B./Anderson, P./Finkelstein, S. (1996): Leveraging intellect. In: Academy of Management Executive, Vol. 10, No. 3, pp. 7 - 27.

Quinn, J. B. (1999): Strategic outsourcing: leveraging knowledge capabilities. In: Sloan Management Review, Vol. 40, No. 4, pp. 9–21.

Quinn, J.B. (2000): Outsourcing innovation: the new engine of growth. In: Sloan management review, Vol. 41, No. 4, pp. 13-28.

Quinn, J. B. (2002): Core-Competencie-with-Outsourcing Strategies in Innovative Companies. In: Hahn/Kaufmann (Eds.): Handbuch industrielles Beschaffungsmanagement. Internationale Konzepte - innovative Instrumente - aktuelle Praxisbeispiele, Gabler, Wiesbaden, pp. 35–54.

Rabe, C. (2007): Unterstützungsnetzwerke von Gründern wissensintensiver Unternehmen. Zur Bedeutung der regionalen gründungsunterstützenden Infrastruktur. Selbstverlag, Universität Heidelberg, Heidelberg.

Rae, D. (2007): Achieving Business Focus: Promoting the Entrepreneurial Management Capabilities of Owner-Managers. In: Industry and Higher Education, Vol. 21, No. 6, pp. 415–426.

Raich, M. (2008). Basic values and objectives regarding money. Implications for the management of customer relationships. In: International Journal of Bank Marketing, Vol. 26, No. 1, pp. 25–41.

Ramaswamy, V./Gouillart, F. J. (2010): The power of co- creation. Build it with them to boost growth, productivity, and profits. Free Press, New York.

Rampersad, G./Quester, P./Troshani, I. (2010): Examining network factors: commitment, trust, coordination and harmony. In: Journal of Business & Industrial Marketing, Vol. 25, No. 7, pp. 487–500.

Reichelt, S./Schmidt, K./Gesele, F./Seidler, N./Hardt, W. (2008): Nutzung von FlexRay als zeitgesteuertes automobiles Bussystem im AUTOSAR-Umfeld. In: Brauer/Holleczek/Vogel-Heuser (Eds.): Informatik aktuell: Springer Berlin, pp. 79–87.

Reichwald, R./Piller, F. (2006): Interaktive Wertschöpfung. Open Innovation, Individualisierung und neue Formen der Arbeitsteilung, Wiesbaden.

Reuber, P./Pfaffenbach, C. (2005): Methoden der empirischen Humangeographie. Beobachtung und Befragung. Westermann, Braunschweig.

Rickards, T. (1985): Stimulating innovation. A system approach. Pinter, London.

Ricketts, M. (2006): Theories of Entrepreneurship. Historical Development and Critical Assessment. In: Casson/Yeung/Basu/Wadeson (Eds.): The Oxford handbook of entrepreneurship: Oxford University Press. Oxford ;, New York, pp. 33–58.

Rigby, D./Zook, C. (2002): Open-market innovation: A systems approach. In: Harvard Business Review, Vol. 80, No. 10, pp. 80–93.

Roberts, E.B. (1987): Introduction: Managing Technological Innovation. In: Roberts, E.B. (Eds.): Generating Technological Innovation. Oxford University Press, New York, pp. 3-21.

Rocha, H. O./Sternberg, R. (2005): Entrepreneurship: The Role of Clusters Theoretical Perspectives and Empirical Evidence from Germany. In: Small Business Economics, Vol. 24, No. 3, pp. 267–292.

Rogers, E.M. (1983): Diffusion of Innovations. Free Press, New York.

Rogers, E.M. (2003): Diffusion of innovations. 5th Vol. Free Press, New York.

Rohrbeck, R. (2010): Harnessing a network of experts for competitive advantage: technology scouting in the ICT industry. In: R&D Management, Vol. 40, No. 2, pp. 169–180.

Romer, P. M. (1986): Increasing Returns and Long-Run Growth. In: Journal of Political Economy, Vol. 94, No. 5, pp. 1002–1037.

Romer, P. M. (1991): Economic Integration and Endogenous Growth. In: Quarterly Journal of Economics, Vol. CVI, No. 425, pp. 531–555.

Romer, P. (1996): Why, indeed, in America? Theory, history, and the origins of modern economic growth. In: American Economic Review, Vol. 86, No. 2, pp. 202–206.

Rothwell, R./Bessant, J. (1987, Eds.): Innovation: Adaptation and Growth. Elsevier, Amsterdam.

Rowley, T./Behrens, D./Krackhardt, D. (2000): Redundant governance structures: an analysis of structural and relational embeddedness in the steel and semiconductor industries. In: Strategic Management Journal, Vol. 21, No. 3, pp. 369–386.

Rugman, A. M./Brain, C. (2004): Regional Strategies of Multinational Pharmaceutical Firms. In: Management International Review, Vol. 44, No. 3, pp. 7–25.

Sanchez, R./Heene, A./Thomas, H. (1996): Introduction: Toward the theory and practice of competence-based competition. In: Sanchez/Heene/Thomas (Eds.): Dynamics of competence based competition. Theory and Practice in the New Strategic Management. Elsevier, Oxford, pp. 1–35.

Sanchez, R./Heene, A. (1996): A Systems View of the Firm in Competence-based Competition. In: Sanchez/Heene/Thomas (Eds.): Dynamics of competence based competition. Theory and Practice in the New Strategic Management. Elsevier, Oxford, pp. 39–62.

Sanchez, R./Heene, A. (1997): Managing for uncertain Future. A Systems View of Strategic Organizational Change. In: International Studies of Management & Organization, Vol. 27, No. 2, pp. 21–42.

Sanchez, R./Heene, A. (2002): Managing strategic change: A systems view of strategic organizational change and strategic flexibility. In: Morecroft/Sanchez/Heene (Eds.): Systems perspectives on resources, capabilities, management processes. Elsevier, Oxford, pp. 71-91.

Sanchez, R./Heene, A. (2004): The new strategic management. Organization, competition, and competence. Wiley, New York.

Sanchez, R. (2004): Understanding competence-based management: Identifying and managing five modes of competence. Success factors, competitive advantage and competence development. In: Journal of Business Research, Vol. 57, No. 5, pp. 518–532.

Sandefur, R. L./Laumann, E. O. (1998): A Paradigm for Social Capital. In: Rationality and Society, Vol. 10, No. 4, pp. 481–501.

Sapienza, H. J./ de Clercq, D. (2000): Venture Capitalist-Entrepreneur Relationships in Technology-Based Ventures. In: Enterprise and Innovation Management Studies, Vol. 1, No. 1, pp. 57–71.

Saracho, A.I. (2002): Patent licensing under strategic delegation. In: Journal of Economics and Management Strategy, Vol. 11, No. 2, pp. 225–251.

Sarason, Y./Dean, T./Dillard, J. F. (2006): Entrepreneurship as the nexus of individual and opportunity: A structuration view. In: Journal of Business Venturing, Vol. 21, No. 3, pp. 286–305.

Saravasvathy, S. (2004): Constructing corridors to economic primitives: entrepreneurial opportunities as demand-side artifacts. In: Butler (Ed.): Opportunity identification and entrepreneurial behavior: Information Age Pub. Greenwich, pp. 291–312.

Saravasvathy, S./Dew, N./Ramakrishna Velamuri, S./Venkataraman, S. (2005): Three views of entrepreneurial opportunity. In: Acs/Audretsch (Eds.): Handbook of Entrepreneurship Research. An Interdisciplinary Survey and Introduction: Springer Science+Business Media Inc. Boston, MA, pp. 141–160.

Sawhney, M./Prandelli, E. (2000): Communities of Creation: Managing Distributed Innovation in Turbulent Markets. In: California Management Review, Vol. 42, No. 4, pp. 24–54.

Saxenian, A. (1990): Regional networks and the resurgence of Silicon Valley. In California Management Review, Vol 33, No. 1, pp. 89-112.

Saxenian, A. (2000): Regional advantage. Culture and competition in Silicon Valley and Route 128. Harvard University, Cambridge, Mass.

Schamp, E. W. (2002): Evolution und Institution als Grundlagen einer dynamischen Wirtschaftsgeographie: Die Bedeutung von externen Skalenerträgen für geographische Konzentration. In: Geographische Zeitschrift. Vol. 90, No. 1, pp. 40-51.

Schamp, E.W. (2005): Cluster und Wetterbersfähigkeit von Regionan. Erfolgsfaktoren regionaler Wirtschaftsentwicklung. In: Cernavin/Führ/Kaltenbach/Thießen (Eds.): Volkswirtschaftliche Schriften. Duncker und Humboldt, Berlin, pp. 91-110.

Schamp, E. W./Rentmeister, B./Lo, V. (2004): Dimensions of Proximity in Knowledge-based Networks: The Cases of Investment Banking and Automobile Design. In: European Planning Studies. Vol. 12, No. 5, pp. 607-624.

Schartinger, D./Schibany, A./Gassler, H. (2001): Interactive Relations Between Universities and Firms: Empirical Evidence for Austria. In: The Journal of Technology Transfer, Vol. 26, No. 3, pp. 255–268.

Scherer, R./ Bortenschlager, K./ Akiyama, A./ Tylko, S./ Hartlieb, M./Harigae, T. (2009): WorldSID Production Dummy Biomechanical Responses. WorldSID Tri-Chair Committee 21st ESV, Stuttgart, Germany.

Scheuing, E.E./Johnson, E. M. (1989): A Proposed Model for New Service Development. In: Journal of Services Marketing, Vol. 3, No. 2, pp. 25–34.

Schnell, R./Hill, P.B./Esser, E. (2005): Methoden der empirischen Sozialforschung. Oldenbourg, München.

Schumpeter, J. A. (1996): Capitalism, socialism and democracy. 7. Vol., Routledge, London.

Schumpeter, J. A. (1978): The theory of economic development: an inquiry into profits, capital, credit, interest and the business cycle, New York, London, Oxford University Press.

Schutjens, V./Stam, E. (2003): The Evolution and Nature of Young Firm Networks: a longitudinal Perspective. In: Small Business Economics, Vol. 21, No. 2, pp. 115–134.

Scott, A. J. (2006): Entrepreneurship, innovation and industrial development: Geography and the creative field revisited. In: Small Business Economics, Vol. 26, No. 1, pp. 1–24.

Scott, J. (1991): Networks of Corporate Power: A Comparative Assessment. In: Annual Review of Sociology, Vol. 17, No. , pp. 181–203.

Segal, I. R./Whinston, M. D. (2000): Exclusive Contracts and Protection of Investments. In: The RAND Journal of Economics, Vol. 31, No. 4, pp. 603–633.

Sen, A./MacPherson, A. (2009): Outsourcing, external collaboration, and innovation among u.s. firms in the biopharmaceutical industry. In: Industrial Geographer, Vol. 6, No. 1, pp. 20–37.

Setterfield, M. (1993): A Model of Institutional Hysteresis. In: Journal of Economic Issues, Vol. 27, No. 3, pp. 755-75.

Shan, W./Walker, G./Kogut, B. (1994): Interfirm cooperation and startup innovation in the biotechnology industry. In: Strategic Management Journal, Vol. 15, No. 5, pp. 387–394.

Shane, S./Locke, E. A./Collins, C. J. (2003): Entrepreneurial motivation. In: Human Resource Management Review, Vol. 13, No. 2, pp. 257–279.

Shane, S./Venkataraman, S. (2000): The Promise of Entrepreneurship as a Field of Research. In: Academy of Management Review, Vol. 25, No. 1, pp. 217–226.

Shepherd, D. A. (2004): Educating Entrepreneurship Students about Emotion and Learning from Failure. In: Academy of Management Learning & Education, Vol. 3, No. 3, pp. 274–287.

Shepherd, D. A./McMullen, J. S./Jennings, P. D. (2007): The formation of opportunity beliefs: overcoming ignorance and reducing doubt. In: Strategic Entrepreneurship Journal, Vol. 1, No. 1-2, pp. 75–95.

Simard, C./West, J. (2008): Knowledge Networks and the Geographic Locus of Innovation. In: Chesbrough/Vanhaverbeke/West (Eds.): Open innovation. Researching a new paradigm: Oxford Univ. Press. Oxford, pp. 220–240.

Simmie, J. (2005): Innovation and space. A critical review of the literature. In: Regional Studies, Vol. 39, No. 6, pp. 789-804.

Sirmon, D. G./Hitt, M. A./Ireland, R. D. (2007): Managing Firm Resources in Dynamic Environments to Create Value: Looking Inside the black Box. In: Academy of Management Review, Vol. 32, No. 1, pp. 273–292.

Skocpol, T./Ganz, M./Munson, Z. (2000): A Nation of Organizers: The Institutional Origins of Civic Voluntarism in the United States. In: The American Political Science Review, Vol. 94, No. 3, pp. 527–546.

Smith, B. (1988) Gestalt Theory: An Essay in Philosophy.In: Smith (Ed.): Foundations of Gestalt Theory. Philosophia, Munich, pp. 11–81.

Smith, D. A./Lohrke, F. T. (2008): Entrepreneurial network development: Trusting in the process. In: Journal of Business Research, Vol. 61, No. , pp. 315–322.

Srnka, K.J (2007): Integration qualitativer und quantitativer Forschungsmethoden. Der Einsatz kombinierter Forschungsdesigns als Möglichkeit zur Förderung der Theorieentwicklung in der Marketingforschung als betriebswirtschaftliche Disziplin. In: Marketing ZFP, Vol. 29, No. 4, pp. 247-260.

Staber, U. (1996): Networks and regional development. Perspectives and Unresolved Issues. In: Staber/Schaefer/Sharma (Eds.): Business networks. Prospects for regional development: W. de Gruyter. Berlin, pp. 1–23.

Stam, W./Elfering, T. (2008): Entrepreneurial Orientation and New Venture Performance: The Moderating Role of Intra- and Extraindustry Social Capital. In: The Academy of Management Journal, Vol. 51, No. 1, pp. 97–111.

Starr, J.A./Macmillan, I.C. (1990). Resource cooptation via social contracting: Resource acquisition strategies for new ventures. In: Strategic Management Journal, Vol. 11, pp. 79-92.

Steier, L. P./Chrisman, J. J./Chua, J. H. (2004): Entrepreneurial Management and Governance in Family Firms: An Introduction. In: Entrepreneurship: Theory and Practice, Vol. 28, No. 4, pp. 295–303.

Stephan, P. E. (1996): The Economics of Science. In: Journal of Economic Literature, Vol. 34, No. 3, pp. 1199–1235.

Stephan, P. E. (2001): Educational Implications of University–Industry Technology Transfer. In: The Journal of Technology Transfer, Vol. 26, No. 3, pp. 199–205.

Sternberg, R. (2000): Innovation networks and regional development – evidence from the European Regional Innovation Survey (ERIS). European Planning Studies, Vol. 8, No. 4, pp. 389-407.

Sternberg, R. (2007): Entrepreneurship, proximity and regional innovation systems. In: Tijdschrift voor Economische en Sociale Geografie, Vol. 98, No. 5, pp. 652–666.

Sternberg, R. (2009): Regional Dimensions of Entrepreneurship. In: Foundations and Trends in Entrepreneurship, Vol. 5, No. 4, pp. 211-340.

Sternberg, R./Pretz, J./Kaufman, J. (2003): Types of Innovations. In: Shavinina (Ed.): The International Handbook on Innovation. Elsevier. Oxford, pp. 158–169.

Steurs, G. (1995): Inter-industry R&D spillovers: What difference do they make? In: International Journal of Industrial Organization, Vol. 13, No. 2, pp. 249–276.

Stevenson, H.H. (1983): A Perspective on Entrepreneurship. Harvard Business School Working Paper 9-384-131, Boston.

Stevenson, H.H./Gumpert, D. E. (1985): The Heart of Entrepreneurship. In: Harvard Business Review, Vol. 63, No. , pp. 85–94.

Stevenson, H.H./Jarillo, J. C. (1986): Perserving Entrepreneurship as Companies Grow. In: Journal of Business Strategy, Vol. 7, No. 1, pp. 10–23.

Stevenson, H.H./Jarillo, J. C. (1990): A paradigm of entrepreneurship: Entrepreneurial management. In: Strategic Management Journal, Vol. 11, No. Special Issue: Corporate Entrepreneurship, pp. 17–27.

Stewart, T. A. (1998): Intellectual capital. The new wealth of organizations. Currency; Doubleday, New York.

Stuart, T. (2000): Interorganizational Alliances and the Performance of Firms: A Study of Growth and Innovation Rates in a Hightechnology Industry. In: Strategic Management Journal, Vol. 21, No. 8, pp. 791–811.

Storper, M./Scott, A. J. (1995): The wealth of regions: Market forces and policy imperatives in local and global context. In: Futures, Vol. 27, No. 5, pp. 505–526.

Storper, M./Veneables, A.J. (2004): Buzz: Face-to-Face contact and the Urban Economy. In: Journal of Economic Geography, Vol. 4, No. 4, pp. 351-370.

Stuart, T. (2000): Interorganizational Alliances and the Performance of Firms: A Study of Growth and Innovation Rates in a Hightechnology Industry. In: Strategic Management Journal, Vol. 21, No. 8, pp. 791–811.

Sundbo, J. (1997): Management of Innovation in Services. In: The Service Industry Journal, Vol. 17, No. 3, pp. 432–455.

Surowiecki, J. (2005): The wisdom of crowds. Anchor Books, New York.

Sydow, J. (1992): Strategische Netzwerke. Wiesbaden, Gabler.

Sydow, J. (2000): Understnding the conditions of interorganizational trust. In: Lane/Bachmann (Eds.): Trust within and between organizations. Conceptual issues and empirical applications: Oxford Univ. Press. Oxford, pp. 31–63.

Tappeiner, G./Hauser, C./Walde, J. (2008): Regional knowledge spillovers: Fact or artifact? In: Research Policy, Vol. 37, No. 5, pp. 861–874.

Teece, D. J. (1986): Profiting from technological innovation: Implications for integration, collaboration, licensing and public policy. In: Research Policy, Vol. 15, No. 6, pp. 285–305.

Teece, D. J. (2007): Explicating dynamic capabilities: the nature and microfoundations of (sustainable) enterprise performance. In: Strategic Management Journal, Vol. 28, No. 13, pp. 1319–1350.

Teece, D. J. (2009): Dynamic capabilities and strategic management. Organizing for innovation and growth. Oxford Univ. Pr., Oxford.

Teece, D./Pisano, G. (1994): The Dynamic Capabilities of Firms: an Introduction. In: Industrial and Corporate Change, Vol. 3, No. 3, pp. 537–556.

Teece, D. J./Pisano, G./Shuen, A. (1997): Dynamic Capabilities and Strategic Management. In: Strategic Management Journal, Vol. 18, No. 7, pp. 209–533.

Terwiesch, C./Ulrich, K. T. (2009): Innovation tournaments. Creating and selecting exceptional opportunities. Harvard Business Press, Boston, Mass.

Tether, B./Hipp, C. (2002): Knowledge intensive, technical and other services. In: Technology Analysis and Strategic Management, Vol. 14, No. 2, pp. 163–182.

Tether, B./Tajar, A. (2008): Beyond industry–university links: Sourcing knowledge for innovation from consultants, private research organizations and the public science-base. In: Research Policy, Vol. 37, No. 6/7, pp. 1079–1095.

Thierstein, A./Bentlage, M./Pechlaner, H./Doepfer, B.C./Brandt, A./Drangmeister, C./ Schrödl, D./Floeting, H./Buser, B.(2011): Wertschöpfungskompetenz der Region Ingolstadt, München. Online: www.wertschoepfungplus.de.

Thompson, C. (1989): The geography of venture capital. In: Progress in Human Geography, Vol. 13, No. 1, pp. 62–98.

Thornton, P. H./Flynn, K. H. (2003): Entrepreneurship, Networks, and Geographics. In: Acs/Audretsch (Eds.): Handbook of Entrepreneurship Research. An Interdisciplinary Survey and Introduction: Springer, Boston, pp. 401–433.

Tidd, J./Bessant, J. R. (2009): Managing innovation. Integrating technological, market and organizational change. 4.th Vol. Wiley, Chichester.

Todd, D. J. (1979): Mixing Qualitative and Quantitative Methods: Triangulation in Action. In: Administrative Science Quarterly, Vol. 24, No. , pp. 602–611.

Torre, A./Gilly, J.-P. (2000): On the analytical dimensions of proximity dynamics. In: Regional Studies, Vol. 34, No. 3, pp. 169-180.

Trompenaars, F./Prud'homme, P. (2004): Managing change. Across corporate cultures. Capstone, Chichester.

Trott, P. (2008): Innovation management and new product development. 4th Vol., Prentice Hall, Harlow.

Türck, R. (1998): Organisatorische Integration des Innovationsmanagements internationaler Unternehmen. In: Kutschker (Ed.): Integration in der internationalen Unternehmung: Gabler. Wiesbaden, pp. 207–238.

Tsai, W. (2000): Social Capital, Strategic Relatedness and the Formation of Intraorganizational linkages. In: Strategic Management Journal, Vol. 21, No. 9, pp. 925–939.

Tsai, W./Ghoshal, S. (1998): Social Capital and Value Creation: The Role of Intrafirm Networks. In: The Academy of Management Journal, Vol. 41, No. 4, pp. 464–476.

Tsai, W./Kuo, H.-C. (2011): Entrepreneurship policy evaluation and decision analysis for SMEs. In: Expert Systems with Applications, Vol. 38, No. 7, pp. 8343–8351.

Tsai, K.-H./Wang, J.-C. (2009): External technology sourcing and innovation performance in LMT sectors: An analysis based on the Taiwanese Technological Innovation Survey. In: Research Policy, Vol. 38, No. 3, pp. 518–526.

Tuominen, P./Jussila, I./Saksa, J.-M. (2006): Locality and Regionality in Management of Finnish Customer Owned Co-operatives. In: International Journal of Co-operative Management, Vol. 3, No. 1, pp. 9–19.

Tushman, M. L. (1982): Readings in the management of innovation. Ballinger, Cambridge.

Ulwick, A. (2002): Turn Customer Input into Innovation. In: Harvard Business Review, Vol. 80, No. 1, pp. 91–97.

Utterback, J. M. (1996): Mastering the dynamics of innovation. Harvard Business School Press, Boston, Mass.

Uzzi, B. (1996): The Sources and Consequences of Embeddedness for the Economic Performance of Organizations: The Network Effect. In: American Sociological Review, Vol. 61, No. 4, pp. 674–698.

Uzzi, B. (1997): Social Structure and Competition in Interfirm Networks: The Paradox of Embeddedness. In: Administrative Science Quarterly, Vol. 42, No. 1, pp. 35–67.

Vahs, D./Schäfer-Kunz, J. (2007): Einführung in die Betriebswirtschaftslehre. Lehrbuch mit Beispielen und Kontrollfragen. 5th Vol. Schäffer-Poeschel, Stuttgart.

van der Borgh, M./Cloodt, M./Romme, A. G. (2012): Value creation by knowledge-based ecosystems: evidence from a field study. In: R&D Management, Vol. 42, No. 2, pp. 150–169.

van den Bosch, F. A./Volberda, H. W./ de Boer, M. (1999): Coevolution of Firm Absorptive Capacity and Knowledge Environment: Organizational Forms and Combinative Capabilities. In: Organization Science, Vol. 10, No. 5, pp. 551–568.

van de Vrande, V./Vanhaverbeke, W./Duysters, G. (2009): External technology sourcing. The effect of uncertainty on governance mode choice. In: Journal of Business Venturing, Vol. 24, No. 1, pp. 62–80.

Vanhaverbeke, W. (2006): The interorganizational context of open innovation. In: Chesbrough/Vanhaverbeke/West (Eds.): Open innovation. Researching a new paradigm: Oxford University Press. Oxford, pp. 205–219.

Vanhaverbeke, W./Cloodt, M. (2006): Open Innovation in value networks. In: Chesbrough/Vanhaverbeke/West (Eds.): Open innovation. Researching a new paradigm: Oxford Univ. Press. Oxford, pp. 258–284.

van Johnston, R. (2000, Ed.): Entrepreneurial management and public policy. Nova Science Publ., Huntington, NY.

Varga, A. (2000): Local Academic Knowledge Transfers and the Concentration of Economic Activity. In: Journal of Regional Science, Vol. 40, No. 2, pp. 289–309.

von Hippel, E. (1986): Lead users: A source of novel product concepts, in Management science, Vol. 32, No. 7, pp. 791-805.

von Hippel, E. (1987): Cooperation between rivals: Informal know-how trading. In: Research Policy, Vol. 16, No. 6, pp. 291–302.

von Hippel, E. (1988): The sources of innovation, New York.

von Hippel, E. (2005): Democratizing Innovation. MIT Press, Cambridge, Mass.

von Nell, P. S /Lichtenthaler, U. (2011): The role of innovation intermediaries in the markets for technology. In: International Journal of Technology Intelligence and Planning, Vol. 7, No. 2, p. 128.

von Oetinger, B. (2001): Clausewitz. Strategie denken. Hanser, München.

Wagner, J./Sternberg, R. (2004): Start-up activities, individual characteristics, and the regional milieu: Lessons for entrepreneurship support policies from German micro data. In: The Annals of Regional Science, Vol. 38, No. 2, pp. 219–240.

Wallenburg, C. M. (2009): Innovation in logistics outsourcing relationships: proactive improvement by logistics service providers as a driver of customer loyalty. In: Journal of Supply Chain Management: A Global Review of Purchasing & Supply, Vol. 45, No. 2, pp. 75–94.

Walter, A./Auer, M./Ritter, T. (2006): The impact of network capabilities and entrepreneurial orientation on university spin-off performance. Entrepreneurship and Strategic Alliances. In: Journal of Business Venturing, Vol. 21, No. 4, pp. 541–567.

Wang, P./Ramiller, N. C. (2009): Community learning in information technology innovation. In: MIS Quarterly, Vol. 33, No. 4, pp. 709–734.

Wassmer, U./Dussauge, P. (2011): Value Creation in Alliance Portfolios: The Benefits and Costs of Network Ressource Interdependencies. In: European Management Review, Vol. 8, No. 1, pp. 47–64.

Weeks, M. R./Davis, K. J. (2007): Technology and Knowledge Transfer within Outsourcing Relationships. The Development of a Model of Interorganizational Innovation. In: Comparative Technology Transfer and Society, Vol. 5, No. 1, pp. 66–96.

Weeks, M. R./Feeny, D. (2008): Outsourcing. From cost management to innovation and business value. In: California Management Review, Vol. 50, No. 4, pp. 127–146.

Welsh, E. (2002): Dealing with Data: Using NVivo in the Qualitative Data Analysis Process. In: Forum Qualitative Social Research, Vol. 3, No. 2, Art. 26.

West, J./Gallagher, S. (2006): Patterns of Open innovation in Open Source Software. In: Chesbrough/Vanhaverbeke/West (Eds.): Open innovation. Researching a new paradigm: Oxford University Press. Oxford, pp. 82–106.

West, J./Lakhani, K. R. (2008): Getting Clear About Communities in Open Innovation. In: Industry & Innovation, Vol. 15, No. 2, pp. 223–231.

Westerlund, M./Svahn, S. (2008): A relationship value perspective of social capital in networks of software SMEs. In: Industrial Marketing Management, Vol. 37, No. 5, pp. 492–501.

Williamson, O.E. (1975):Markets and hierarchies: Analysis and antitrust implications. Free Press, New York.

Williamson, O. (1979): Transaction cost economics The Transaction Cost Approach. In: American Journal of Sociology, Vol. 87, November, pp. 233-261.

Williamson, O. E. (1985): The Economic Institutions of Capitalism. Free Press, New York.

Williamson, O. E. (1987): Transaction cost economics The comparative contracting perspective. In: Journal of Economic Behavior & Organization, Vol. 8, No. 4, pp. 617–625.

Williamson, O. E. (1999): Strategy Research: Governance and Competence Perspectives. In: Strategic Management Journal, Vol. 20, No. 12, pp. 1087–1108.

Wincent, J./Anokhin, S./Boter, H. (2009): Network board continuity and effectiveness of open innovation in Swedish strategic small-firm networks, in: R&D Management, Vol. 39, No. 1, pp. 55-67.

Winch, G. M./Courtney, R. (2007): The Organization of Innovation Brokers: An International Review. In: Technology Analysis & Strategic Management, Vol. 19, No. 6, pp. 747–763.

Witt, P. (2004): Entrepreneurs' Networks and the Success of Start-Ups, in: Entrepreneurship & Regional Development, Vol. 16, S. 391-412.

Witte, E. (1973): Organization für Innovationsentscheidungen: Das Promotoren-Modell. Schwartz, Göttingen.

Witte, E. (1999): Das Promotoren-Modell. In: Hauschildt/Gemünden (Eds.): Promotoren. Champions der Innovation. 2. Vol., Gabler, Wiesbaden, pp. 9–42.

Woolcock, M./Narayan, D. (2000): Social Capital: Implications for Development Theory, Research, and Policy. In: World Bank Research Observer, Vol. 15, No. 2, pp. 225–249.

Yli-Renko, H./Autio, E./Sapienza, H. (2001): Social capital, knowledge acquisition, and knowledge exploitation in young technology-based firms. In: Strategic Maangement Journal, Vol. 22, pp. 587-613.

Zaheer, A./Ventraman, N. (1995): Relational Governance as an Interorganizational Strategy. An empirical test on the role of trust in economic exchange. In: Strategic Management Journal, Vol. 16, No. 5, pp. 373–392.

Zahra, S. A./Nielsen, A. P./Bogner, W. C. (1999): Corporate Entrepreneurship, Knowledge, and Competence Development. In: ET&P, Vol. , No. Spring, pp. 169–189.

Zahra, S. A./George, G. (2002): Absorptive Capacity: A Review, Reconceptualization, and Extension. In: Absorptive Capacity: A Review, Reconceptualization, and Extension, Vol. 27, No. 2, pp. 185–203.

Zahra, S. A./Sapienza, H. J./Davidsson, P. (2006): Entrepreneurship and Dynamic Capabilities: A Review, Model and Research Agenda. In: Journal of Management Studies, Vol. 43, No. 4, pp. 917–955.

Zaltman, G./Duncan, R./Holbeck, J. (1984): Innovations and organizations. Krieger, Malabar.

Zelger, J. (2000): Twelve steps of GABEKWinRelan. A Procedure for Qualitative Opinion Research, Knowledge Organization and Systems Development. In: Buber/Zelger (Eds.): GABEK II. Zur Qualitativen Forschung. On Qualitative Research. Studienverlag, Wien, pp. 205-220.

Zelger, J. (2002): GABEK. Handbook for the Method GABEK-WinRelan 5.2., Vol. 1, Innsbruck.

Zelger, J. (2004a):WinRelan Windows Relation Analysis, Short Manual. Innsbruck.

Zelger, J. (2004b): Qualitative Research by the ‚GABEK® Method. In: Fikfak/Adam/Garz (Eds.): Qualitative Research. Different Perspectives – Emerging Trends. Zalozba, Lubljana, pp. 231–261.

Zelger, J./Oberprantacher, A. (2002). Processing of verbal data and knowledge representation by GABEK-WinRelan. In: Forum: Qualitative Social Research, Vol. 3, No. 2, Art. 27.

Zentes, J./Swoboda, B./Morschett, D. (2005, Eds.): Kooperationen, Allianzen und Netzwerke. Grundlagen - Ansätze - Perspektiven. Gabler, Wiesbaden.

Zheng, W. (2010): A social capital perspective of innovation from individuals to nations: where is empirical literature directing us? In: International Journal of Management Reviews, Vol. 12, No. 2, pp. 151-83.

Zook, M. A. (2002): Grounded capital: venture financing and the geography of the Internet industry, 1994–2000. In: Journal of Economic Geography, Vol. 2, No. 2, pp. 151–177.

Zou, G./Yilmaz, L. (2011): Dynamics of knowledge creation in global participatory science communities: open innovation communities from a network perspective. In: Computational and Mathematical Organization Theory, Vol. 17, No. 1, pp. 35–58.

Appendix 1: Area of Research –Ingolstadt Region, Germany

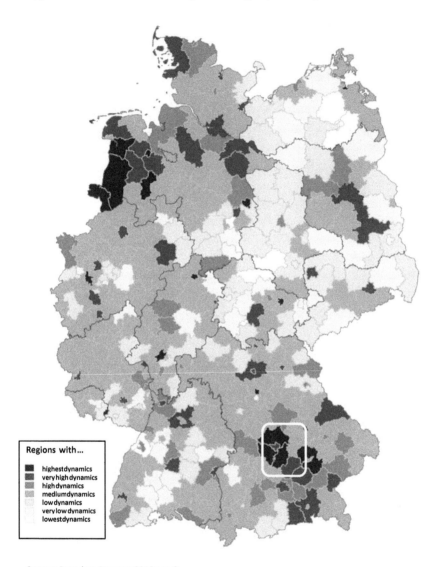

Regions with...

- highest dynamics
- very high dynamics
- high dynamics
- medium dynamics
- low dynamics
- very low dynamics
- lowest dynamics

Source: Based on Prognos 2010a, p. 9.